# Principles of Minnesota Insurance

License Exam Manual

1st Edition, Revised

PRINCIPLES OF MINNESOTA INSURANCE LICENSE EXAM MANUAL, 1ST EDITION, REVISED
©2008 DF Institute, Inc. All rights reserved.

Published by DF Institute, Inc.

Printed in the United States of America.

ISBN: 1-4277-7991-0

PPN: 5308-401A

**08** 09  10  9  8  7  6  5  4  3  2  1
J  **F**  M  A  M  J  J  A  S  O  N  D

# Contents

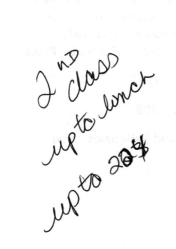

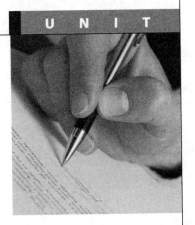

# 1

# An Introduction to Insurance Principles

## KEY CONCEPTS

- ■ Insurance and the pooling of risk
- ■ Risk management techniques
- ■ Insurable interest, insurable risks, and indemnity
- ■ Insurance contracts and contract law
- ■ The concept of agency

Insurance plays an important role in helping people manage risk and attain financial security. The insurance industry provides a wide range of products and services to individual consumers and businesses. As you begin your study of the industry, and prepare for your license exam, there are some terms and concepts you must understand. This unit will introduce you to concepts and terms that will be used throughout this textbook.

## OBJECTIVE

When you complete this unit, you should be able to:

- explain the principles of risk pooling and the law of large numbers;

- explain the different types of risk and how risk can be managed;

- distinguish elements common to all legal contracts from those unique to insurance contracts; and

- explain the concept of agency and the agency/principal relationship.

# HISTORY OF INSURANCE

The insurance industry enjoys a long history dating back many centuries. In fact, the earliest form of insurance occurred when wealthy Chinese merchants along the Yangtze River decided that it was too risky to place all their merchandise on a single vessel and sail it down the river. Instead, they split the shipment into smaller portions and placed them on several boats. They knew that it was unlikely all the vessels would sink or suffer damage, and if one did sink, the majority of the cargo would reach its destination safely. Although this arrangement was not formally called insurance, it was the forerunner of the modern insurance company, which also recognizes the importance of spreading risk.

# THE ROLE OF INSURANCE: COSTS AND BENEFITS

The products and services the insurance industry provides offer many positive aspects. Insurance helps individuals and business owners resume their normal standard of living and operations, which actually benefits society as a whole. For instance, if your home burns down and you have no means to pay for the repairs, it is unlikely you would have the funds to make other purchases. In addition to the impact on your life, others from whom you ordinarily buy things would also be affected. A negative ripple effect on the economy occurs. The proceeds of an insurance policy benefit everyone by restoring the insured person or organization to the same financial condition as before the loss.

Another way insurance benefits society is by encouraging activities and devices that reduce the amount of losses and their economic impact.

**EXAMPLE**    It has been proven that seat belts and other passive restraints in automobiles significantly reduce the extent of injuries suffered by vehicle occupants involved in auto accidents. Insurance companies were a major force behind requiring seat belts as standard equipment in all vehicles. Or you may have noticed the "UL Approved" label on an appliance you own. UL stands for Underwriters Laboratories, an insurance industry think tank that develops safety standards for items used in residences and businesses.

Although these examples represent more recent efforts of insurers to eliminate or reduce the amount of loss and human suffering, such efforts long have been a part of the insurance industry.

# BASIC INSURANCE PRINCIPLES

Insurance is based on two fundamental principles: the spreading or pooling of risks (also known as loss sharing) and the law of large numbers. To understand these principles, consider the following examples.

## RISK POOLING

Assume that 1,000 individuals in the same social club agree that if any member of their group dies, all of the members will pitch in to provide the deceased's family with $10,000. This $10,000, it was determined, would provide the family with enough funds to cover the immediate costs associated with death and to provide a cushion for at least a few months. Because it is not known when any one individual within the group will die, the decision is made to pre-fund the benefit by assessing each member $10, thus creating the $10,000 fund. Without the agreement to help provide for each other's potential loss, each group member (and his family) would have to face the economic cost of death alone. But by sharing the burden and spreading the risk of death over all 1,000 group members, the most any one member pays is $10.

This is, of course, a simplified example, but it explains the basic concept of loss sharing. By spreading a risk, or by sharing the possibility of a loss, a large group of people can substitute a small certain cost ($10 in our example) for a large unknown risk (the economic risk of dying). In other words, the risk is transferred from an individual to a group, each member of which shares the losses and has the promise of a future benefit. Insurance companies pool risks among thousands and thousands of insureds and apply certain mathematical principles to guarantee policy owners that the money will be there to pay a claim when it arises.

## LAW OF LARGE NUMBERS

In addition to spreading risks, insurance relies on the principle that the larger the number of individual risks (or exposures) in a group, the more certainty there is as to the amount of loss incurred in any given period. In other words, given a large enough pool of risks, an insurer can predict with reasonable accuracy the number of claims it will face during any given time. No one can predict when any one person will die or if any one person will lose their home to a fire. However, it is possible to predict the approximate number of deaths or the likelihood that a house fire will occur among a certain group during a certain period. This principle, known as the law of large numbers, is based on the science of probability and statistics. The larger and more homogeneous the group, the more certain the predictions.

**E X A M P L E**
Statistics may show that among a group of 100,000 40-year-old males, 300 will die within one year. While it is not possible to predict who the 300 will be, the number will prove quite accurate. Conversely, with a small group, an accurate prediction is not possible. Among a group of 100 40-year-old males, it is not statistically feasible to predict if any in the group will die within one year. Because insurers cover thousands and thousands of lives, it is possible to predict when and to what extent losses will occur and, consequently, when claims will arise.

All forms of insurance—life, health, accident, property, and casualty—rely on risk pooling and the law of large numbers. These principles form the foundation on which insurance is based and allow for its successful operation.

## THE CONCEPT OF RISK

As we have learned so far, insurance replaces the uncertainty of risk with guarantees. But what exactly does the word risk mean? And how does insurance remove the uncertainty and minimize the adverse effects of risk?

*Risk* is defined as the uncertainty regarding loss. Property loss, such as the destruction of a home due to fire, is an example of risk. The inability to work and earn a living due to a disability is another example of risk, as is loss of a family's income due to the death of the breadwinner. The loss inherent in all of these risks is characterized by a lessening (or disappearance) of value. Risks can be divided into two classes: speculative and pure.

*Speculative risks.* Speculative risks involve the chance of both loss and gain. Betting at the race track and investing in the stock market are examples of speculative risks.

*Pure risks.* Pure risks involve only the chance of loss; there is never a possibility of gain or profit. The risk associated with the chance of injury from an accident is an example of pure risk. There is no opportunity for gain if the event does not occur, only the opportunity for loss if it does occur. Only pure risks are insurable.

*Exposures.* Exposure means the potential for loss to an item of property, or to the assets of an individual, family, firm, or organization; the measure of risk to an insurer.

## PERILS AND HAZARDS

A *peril* is the immediate specific event causing loss and giving rise to risk. It is the cause of a loss.

**E X A M P L E**
When a building burns, fire is the peril. When a person dies, death is the peril. When an individual is injured in an accident, the accident is the peril. When a person becomes ill from a disease, the disease is the peril.

---

### TAKE NOTE

The distinction between speculative and pure risks is an important one. Insurance does not protect individuals against losses arising out of speculative risks because these risks are undertaken voluntarily.

---

A *hazard* is any factor that gives rise to a peril. There are three basic types of hazards: physical, moral, and morale.

■ *Physical hazards.* Physical hazards are visible conditions such as defective wiring in an older home. This condition increases the likelihood of a house fire.

■ *Moral hazards.* Moral hazards are character defects that people may have that increase risk and the chance of loss. An individual may stage an auto accident or set fire to their business for the purposes of collecting an insurance claim settlement.

■ *Morale hazards.* Morale hazards are tendencies that arise from an indifferent or careless attitude because insurance protection exists. Some people are more inclined to engage in dangerous activities because they have life and health insurance.

## TREATMENT OF RISK

How risks are treated varies greatly, depending on the situation, the degree of potential loss, and the individual. Generally, there are four options: avoid, reduce, retain, or transfer the risk.

**Risk Avoidance**   One method of dealing with risk is avoidance—simply avoiding as many risks as possible. By choosing not to drive or own an automobile, one could avoid the risks associated with driving. By never flying, one could eliminate the risk of being in an airplane crash. By never investing in stocks, one could avoid the risk of a market crash.

**Risk Reduction**   Risk reduction is another means of dealing with risk. Because we cannot avoid risk entirely, we often attempt to lessen the possibility of loss by taking action to reduce the risk. Installing a smoke alarm in a home will not lessen the possibility of fire, but it may reduce the risk of loss from fire.

**Risk Retention**   Risk retention is another method of coping with risk. This means accepting the risk and confronting it if and when it occurs. One way to handle a retained risk is self-insurance, for instance, setting up a fund to offset the costs of a potential loss.

**Risk Transference**   The most effective way to handle risk is to transfer it so that the loss is assumed by another party. Insurance is the most common method of transferring risk—from an individual or group to an insurance company. Though purchasing insurance will not eliminate the risk of death or illness, it relieves the insured individual or group of the losses these risks bring. Insurance satisfies both economic and emotional needs; it replaces the uncertainty surrounding risk with the assurance of guarantees, and it transfers the financial consequences of a loss to the insurer.

## INSURABLE INTEREST

As we have seen, insurance protects us against loss. We purchase insurance to protect ourselves and our property, and to provide benefits to those dependent upon us—in all of these instances an insurable interest exists. An insurable interest exists when individuals can demonstrate that they will be or have been harmed (financially/emotionally) by a loss.

In property insurance, such an interest comes about through owning property or having an ownership interest in the property, such as a mortgage holder's interest in a home. In life/health insurance, relationships provide the basis for insurable interest. Examples include the insurable interest that an individual has in the life of his spouse, or the interest between business partners.

Generally, state law requires that the buyer of insurance have an insurable interest at the time of application for the insurance policy and at the time of a loss (claim). However, insurable interest need not be maintained throughout the life of the contract.

---

**EXAMPLE**    A loan can be paid off, extinguishing the lender's interest. The policy does not have to be canceled nor the name of the lender removed, but it will not receive any benefits under the policy because its insurable interest has ended.

For test-taking purposes, an insurable interest must exist at the time of application for life/health contracts and at the time of loss for property/casualty contracts.

## REQUIREMENTS OF AN INSURABLE RISK

Not all pure risks are insurable. Insurance companies generally are unwilling to insure unusual risks or those that represent a potential for catastrophic loss. Certain requirements must be met for a risk to be insurable from a company's viewpoint. The mnemonic device CANHAM will help you remember them:

- **C**  Chance of loss must be calculable by the insurer;
- **A**  Premiums must be affordable;
- **N**  Loss must be noncatastrophic;
- **H**  Large number of homogeneous (similar) exposures must exist;
- **A**  Loss must be accidental from the insured's standpoint; and
- **M**  Loss must be measurable (number and amount).

Of course, a few exceptions to these requirements apply. Certain natural disasters that may cause widespread damage, such as floods, brush fires, hail, and earthquakes, may appear to be uninsurable. However, coverage can be purchased through certain specialty insurers or particular government programs.

## THE PRINCIPLE OF INDEMNITY

The principle of indemnity is one of the foundations upon which the insurance industry is built. This is similar to insurable interest, but rather than defining under what circumstances a policyholder can collect on an insurance policy, the principle of indemnity determines how much he can collect. Under this rule, insurance policies are considered to be contracts of indemnity, meaning they are designed to put someone back in the same general financial condition he was in before the loss. In other words, a person shouldn't be able to profit by collecting on insurance. The elimination of gain also supports the idea that insurance is designed to insure only pure risk situations.

# GENERAL LAW OF CONTRACTS

A contract is an agreement enforceable by law. It is the means by which one or more parties bind themselves to certain promises. With a life insurance contract, the insurer binds itself to pay a certain sum on the death of the insured. In exchange, the policyowner pays premiums.

For a contract to be legally valid and binding, it must contain certain elements—an offer and acceptance, consideration, legal purpose, and competent parties. Let's consider each.

## OFFER AND ACCEPTANCE

To be legally enforceable, a contract must be made with a definite, unqualified offer by one party and the acceptance of its exact terms by the other party. In many cases, the offer of an insurance contract is made by the applicant when he submits the application with the initial premium. The insurance company accepts the offer when it issues the policy as applied for. In other cases, the insurance company will not issue the policy as applied for; instead, it may counteroffer with the issuance of another policy at different premium rates or with different terms. In these situations, the applicant has the right to accept or reject the counteroffer.

If an applicant does not submit an initial premium with the application, he simply is inviting the insurance company to make the contract offer. The insurer can respond by issuing a policy (the offer) that the applicant can accept by paying the premium when the policy is delivered. Until an offer has been accepted, the person making the offer has the right to rescind it. Thus, if an applicant wishes to withdraw his application before the insurer accepts it, the offer is terminated, even if the initial premium has been submitted. The insurer must return the premium.

## CONSIDERATION

For a contract to be enforceable, the promise or promises it contains must be supported by consideration. Consideration is something of value given in exchange for the promises sought. In an insurance contract, consideration is given by the applicant in exchange for the insurer's promise to pay benefits; this consideration consists of the application and the initial premium. This is why the offer and acceptance of an insurance contract are not completed until the insurer receives the application and the first premium.

## LEGAL PURPOSE

To be legally enforceable, a contract must have a legal purpose. This means that the goal of the contract and the reason the parties enter into the agreement must be legal. A contract in which one party agrees to commit murder for money would be unenforceable in court because the goal or purpose of the contract is not legal.

T A K E   N O T E

In many states, a minor is considered to be any person under age 21. However, in recent years, a majority of states have lowered this age to 18. With respect to insurance contracts, several states have enacted statutes that give minors of a certain age (varying from 14 to 18) the capacity to enter into valid and enforceable life insurance contracts. In the absence of such a statute, however, insurance contracts with minors are voidable at the minor's option.

## COMPETENT PARTIES

To be enforceable, a contract must be entered into by competent parties. With a contract of insurance, the parties to the contract are the applicant and the insurer. The insurer is considered competent if it has been licensed or authorized by the state (or states) in which it conducts business. The applicant, unless proven otherwise, is presumed to be competent, with three possible exceptions:

- minors;
- the mentally infirm; and
- those under the influence of alcohol or narcotics.

Each state has its own laws governing the legality of minors and the mentally infirm entering into contracts of insurance. These laws are based on the principle that some parties are not capable of understanding the contract they agree to.

It should be noted that beneficiaries and insureds (if different from the applicant) are not parties to an insurance contract. As such, they need not have contractual capability. Other competent parties that may enter into contracts of insurance with an insurance company include business entities, trusts, and estates.

Use this mnemonic device to recall the four elements of a legal contract: CLOC (competent parties, legal purpose, offer and acceptance, and consideration).

# SPECIAL LEGAL CHARACTERISTICS OF INSURANCE POLICIES AS CONTRACTS

All legal contracts share certain characteristics. As legal contracts, insurance policies are characterized by the following legal doctrines.

## CONTRACT OF ADHESION

An insurance contract is drawn up by the insurer and is either accepted or rejected by the applicant. The applicant cannot modify or alter the contract. This type of contract is referred to as a contract of adhesion. Because the insurer alone draws up the contract, courts generally have held that any ambiguity in the contract should be interpreted in favor of the insured. An ambiguity exists whenever a term in the policy could be interpreted in two different ways.

## UNILATERAL CONTRACT

An insurance contract is also a unilateral contract, which means only one party (the insurer) makes a legally enforceable promise (to pay a claim). The insured can stop paying the premium at any time.

## ALEATORY CONTRACT

Aleatory means that the outcome of the contract is affected by chance and that the consideration given up is unequal. The insured pays a relatively small premium and receives no dollars back if no loss occurs. If a loss does occur, however, the insurer may pay a claim that exceeds the premium dollars received.

## PERSONAL CONTRACT

In most cases, insurance is a personal contract between the insured and insurer. It may not be transferred (assigned) to another person or organization without the insurer's written consent.

Life Insurance is *not* considered a personal contract. The policyowner has the rights of ownership and may transfer the contract to someone else. When this has happened, the policyowner need only provide notice to the insurer.

## CONDITIONAL

An insurance contract is conditional because the insurer's promise to pay is conditioned upon several things: the occurrence of an insured event, the insured's fulfillment of the policy terms, and the existence of insurable interest.

**FIGURE 1.1   Elements and Characteristics of a Property and Casualty Insurance Contract**

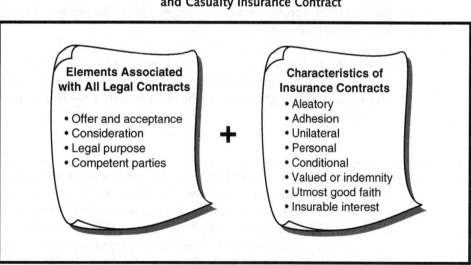

**Elements Associated with All Legal Contracts**

- Offer and acceptance
- Consideration
- Legal purpose
- Competent parties

**+**

**Characteristics of Insurance Contracts**

- Aleatory
- Adhesion
- Unilateral
- Personal
- Conditional
- Valued or indemnity
- Utmost good faith
- Insurable interest

# THE INSURANCE APPLICATION

## UTMOST GOOD FAITH

Insurance is a contract of utmost good faith. Both the policyowner and the insurer must know all material facts and relevant information. There can be no attempt by either party to conceal, disguise, or deceive. A consumer purchases a policy based largely on what the insurer and its agent claim are its features, benefits, and advantages; an insurer issues a policy based primarily on what the applicant reveals in the application.

The concepts of warranties, representations, and concealment are associated with this idea of utmost good faith. These represent grounds through which an insurer might seek to avoid payment under a contract.

## WARRANTY

A warranty in insurance is a statement made by the applicant that is guaranteed to be true. It becomes part of the contract and, if found to be untrue, can be grounds for revoking the contract. Warranties are presumed to be material because they affect the insurer's decision to accept or reject an applicant.

## REPRESENTATION

A representation is a statement made by the applicant that he believes to be true. It is used by the insurer to evaluate whether or not to issue a policy. Unlike warranties, representations are not part of the contract and need be true only to the extent that they are material and related to the risk. Most states require that life insurance policies contain a provision that all statements made in the application be deemed representations, not warranties. If an insurance company rejects a claim on the basis of a representation, the company bears the burden of proving that the representation was material and related to risk.

The practical distinction between a warranty and a representation is this—if a warranty is untrue, the insurer has the right to cancel the contract; if a representation is untrue (a misrepresentation), the insurer has the right to cancel the contract only if the representation was material to the creation of the contract.

---

EXAMPLE        If an insured falsely stated in a life insurance application that his cancer was in remission when the insured was, in fact, terminally ill, this statement would be a misrepresentation. If the insurance company had known this information, it would either have rejected the application or issued the policy on substantially different terms. As a result, this *material* misrepresentation may provide grounds for the insurer to cancel the contract. However, if an insured misstated the age at which a grandparent died, the insurer probably would not be able to rescind the contract because such misrepresentation would have had no influence on the terms of the contract.

## CONCEALMENT

The issue of concealment also is important to insurance contracts. Concealment is defined as the applicant's failure to disclose a known material fact when applying for insurance. If the purpose for concealing information is to defraud the insurer (that is, to obtain a policy that might not be issued otherwise if the information were revealed), the insurer may have grounds for voiding the policy. Again, the insurer must prove concealment and materiality.

**EXAMPLE**   An applicant for homeowner's insurance does not disclose that he manufactures firecrackers in the basement as a hobby. Although the insurance company did not specifically ask about this hobby, the applicant has an obligation to disclose extraordinary facts such as these that are within his scope of knowledge. Not disclosing this fact would be considered concealment.

## FRAUD

Fraud is an intentional misrepresentation of the facts. Insurance fraud has become a serious problem in recent years. An insurance contract requires that an applicant deal in good faith with the insurance company in providing necessary underwriting information. In many cases, neither the company nor the agent actually has seen or inspected the property to be insured. The issuance of a policy presumes that any losses will be accidental, not within the policyholder's control. When a policy has been issued with the intent to commit insurance fraud, the insurer may rescind the contract, effectively saying that it never was recognized as valid. Insurance fraud is a felony in most states, and insurance companies have been much more aggressive in pursuing legal action against people who commit this crime.

## WAIVER AND ESTOPPEL

Waiver is the voluntary relinquishment of a known right. A waiver may be intentional or unintentional. For example, if an insurance company sends out a renewal policy, it has waived its right to refuse renewal coverage. Estoppel means that when something is allowed to occur repeatedly, the defenses to it are waived. Estoppel prevents an insurance company from reasserting a right it has waived previously. Thus, an insurance company that continually accepts late payments from the insured is estopped from denying coverage when a policy is in a state of cancellation because of nonpayment.

# BASIC PARTS OF AN INSURANCE POLICY

The four basic parts of a policy are: declarations, insuring agreement, conditions, and exclusions. They can be remembered by the acronym DICE:

- **D**  Declarations (or simply dec page);
- **I**  Insuring agreement;
- **C**  Conditions; and
- **E**  Exclusions.

Not all policies are arranged the same way, but all contain the four basic policy parts. In addition, most policies include a section containing important definitions and endorsements or amendments to the basic policy.

## DECLARATIONS, DECLARATIONS PAGE

While any two policies issued by a company may look very similar, the declarations page is the "cover page" providing information specific to the person or property insured. The declarations page provides personal information about the policyholder/policyowner, policy limits, deductibles, and the policy's effective date. Property and casualty policies will provide additional information such as the year, make and model of the vehicle or the street address of the building insured by the policy. A life insurance policy will state the death benefit and the age of the insured when the contract was issued.

## INSURING AGREEMENT

The insuring agreement outlines the insurer's promise to pay for losses covered by the policy in exchange for the customer's premium dollars. This section of the policy lists the benefits and coverage provided by the policy.

## CONDITIONS

The conditions section of the policy explains the duties of the customer and the company. The provisions that will be discussed throughout this textbook are most often built into the conditions section of a policy. Duties of a customer may include prompt reporting of claims or protecting property from further damage; duties of the company may include providing advance notice of policy cancellation or defending the insured against liability claims.

## EXCLUSIONS

The exclusions section of the policy outlines the perils not covered by the policy. While the list of exclusions may be very small in a life insurance policy, other policies will often provide a detailed list. Excluded losses in life insurance may include death resulting from military service; property policies often exclude damage resulting from floods. Generally, excluded perils may be covered through a separate contract. By encouraging individuals to purchase separate policies to cover their unique individual needs, the insurer can provide a less expensive policy to the majority of their customers.

## RIDERS AND ENDORSEMENTS

While the four main parts already discussed are common to most insurance policies, a policy will often include riders and endorsements. These are optional coverages added to the policy by the client. Generally, they represent and upgrade or improvement in policy benefits and, consequently, they usually increase the overall cost of the insurance.

*Riders* are used to modify a life and health policy. For example, long-term care insurance (associated with nursing home care) may include an inflation rider that will adjust benefits each year to accommodate for the increasing costs of care. *Endorsements* are used to modify property/casualty policies. Replacement cost coverage may be added to a homeowners policy by endorsement so that depreciation will not be subtracted from personal property claims.

# THE AGENT AND INSURER RELATIONSHIP

## AGENTS AND BROKERS

Because insurance contracts are binding and enforceable, certain legal concepts extend to those who bring together the contract parties—the applicant and the insurer. In most cases, bringing the parties together is done by an agent or a broker.

## THE CONCEPT OF AGENCY

An agent is an individual who has been authorized by an insurer to be its representative to the public and to offer its goods and services for sale. Specifically, this role entails:

- describing the company's insurance policies to prospective buyers;

- explaining the conditions under which the policies may be obtained;

- soliciting applications for insurance;

- in some cases, collecting premiums from policyowners; and

- rendering service to prospects and to those who have purchased policies from the company.

An agent's authority to undertake these functions is defined clearly in a contract of agency (or agency agreement) between the agent and the company. Within the authority granted, the agent is considered identical with the company. The relationship between an agent and the company he represents is governed by agency law.

## PRINCIPLES OF AGENCY LAW

By legal definition, an agent is a person who acts for another person or entity (known as the principal) with regard to contractual arrangements with third parties. The concept of power is implicit in this definition—an authorized agent has the power to bind the principal to contracts (and to the rights and responsibilities of those contracts). With this in mind, we can review the following main principles of agency law:

- The acts of the agent (within the scope of his authority) are the acts of the principal.

- A contract completed by an agent on behalf of the principal is a contract of the principal.

- Payments made to an agent on behalf of the principal are payments made to the principal.

- The agent's knowledge regarding the principal's business is presumed to be the principal's knowledge.

## AGENT AUTHORITY

Note the above parenthetical explanation "within the scope of his authority." Authority—that which an agent is authorized to do on behalf of his company—is another important concept in agency law. Technically, only those actions for which an agent is authorized can bind a principal. In reality, however, an agent's authority can be quite broad. There are three types of agent authority: express, implied, and apparent. Let's take a look at each.

**Express Authority** Express authority is the authority a principal intends to—and actually does—give to its agent. Express authority is granted by means of the agent's contract, which is the principal's appointment of the agent to act on its behalf.

---

E X A M P L E    The agency contract generally contains clauses dealing with the specific and general powers of the agent, the scale of commissions, and the ownership of contracts sold.

---

**Implied Authority** Implied authority is authority that is not expressly granted but which the agent is assumed to have to transact the principal's business. Implied authority is incidental to express authority, because not every single detail of an agent's authority can be spelled out.

---

E X A M P L E    An agent's contract may not specifically state that he can print business cards that contain the company's name, but the authority to do so is implied.

---

**Apparent Authority** Apparent authority is the appearance or assumption of authority based on the actions, words, or deeds of the principal or because of circumstances the principal created.

---

E X A M P L E    By providing an individual with a rate book, application forms, and sales literature, an insurance company creates the impression that an agency relationship exists between itself and the individual. The company will not later be allowed to deny that such a relationship existed.

---

The significance of authority—whether express, implied, or apparent—is that it ties the company to the acts and deeds of its agent. The law will view the agent and the company as the same entity when the agent acts within the scope of his authority.

## AGENT AS FIDUCIARY

Another legal concept that governs the activity of an agent is that of fiduciary. A fiduciary is a person who holds a position of special trust and confidence. Agents act in a fiduciary capacity when they accept premiums on behalf of the insurer or offer advice that affects people's financial security. Agents have fiduciary responsibilities to both their clients and the insurance companies they represent. Acting as a fiduciary requires that an agent:

- be fit and proper;

- be honest and trustworthy;

- have a good business reputation;

- be qualified to perform insurance functions;

- have knowledge of, and abide by, state laws and regulations; and

- act in good faith.

## BROKERS VERSUS AGENTS

Unlike agents, brokers legally represent the insureds and do not have the legal authority to bind the insurer. Brokers solicit and accept applications for insurance and then place the coverage with an insurer. The business is not in force and the insurance company is not bound until it accepts the application. Technically, brokers represent themselves in the solicitation of insurance policies; once prospects or clients request coverage, brokers represent their buyers.

In practice, the legal distinction between brokers and agents is insignificant. Both brokers and agents are licensed as insurance producers and both are subject to insurance laws and regulations. In fact, in some states, including Minnesota, any individual who solicits insurance and places a policy will be considered an agent of the insurer with regard to that policy.

# SUMMARY

Insurance involves the transfer of risk from one to many. Insurers *pool* the premiums paid by consumers and establish a large reserve of money from which claims are paid. To establish an adequate reserve, insurers must predict how many losses are likely to occur and estimate the cost of an average claim. The *law of large numbers* states that actual results become closer to predicted results as the number of insured exposures (cars, people, homes) increases. Risk can be managed in several ways; if insurance will be used, an *insurable interest* must exist. The principle of *indemnity* states that insurers should return claimants to their pre-loss condition.

For contracts to be deemed legal there must be offer and acceptance, consideration, competent parties, and a legal purpose. Insurance contracts have features that make them unique from other legal contracts. As a contact is established between an insurance company and customer, both parties are expected to act in utmost good faith. Insurance agents are authorized to act of behalf of the insurer they represent (principal). In their actions and statements, agents are acting on behalf of the insurer and are granted different kinds of authority through that relationship.

# U N I T   Q U I Z

1. The purpose of insurance is to
   A. eliminate risk
   B. transfer risk
   C. increase hazards
   D. reduce hazards

2. Which of the following is an example of a pure risk?
   A. Deciding to manufacture a new drug
   B. Purchasing a piece of real estate
   C. Threat of fire damage to property
   D. Playing the lottery

3. Insurance has which one of the following purposes?
   A. It eliminates risk by accumulating funds.
   B. It makes risk predictable by transferring funds.
   C. It eliminates risk by transferring funds.
   D. It transfers risk by accumulating funds.

4. An insured's acceptance of a large deductible is an example of which method of handling risk?
   A. Loss control
   B. Retention
   C. Insurance
   D. Avoidance

5. Which of the following is NOT an example of a hazard?
   A. Oily rags stacked in a corner of a building
   B. Homeowner's carelessness because he has insurance
   C. Fire that destroys personal property in a building
   D. Insured who sets fire to his own building

6. To have an insurable interest in property, the insured must
   A. have some current relationship to the property
   B. have had a past financial relationship to the property
   C. be the sole owner of the property
   D. be the person who purchases insurance on the property

7. Under the law of large numbers, what happens to estimated losses when the number of observations increases?
   A. Increase
   B. Decrease
   C. Stay the same
   D. More predictable

8. Which of the following is an example of a direct loss?
   A. Loss of rental income after a building is destroyed
   B. Loss of income when a store must shut down following a theft
   C. Loss due to fire damage to a building
   D. Loss due to amounts spent on hotels following fire damage to a home

9. Which of the following statements is CORRECT?
   A. Only speculative risks are insurable.
   B. Only pure risks are insurable.
   C. Both pure risks and speculative risks are insurable.
   D. Neither pure risks nor speculative risks are insurable.

10. Which of the following statements does NOT describe an element of an insurable risk?
    A. The loss must not be due to chance.
    B. The loss must be definite and measurable.
    C. The loss cannot be catastrophic.
    D. The loss exposures to be insured must be large.

11. In an insurance transaction, licensed agents legally represent which of the following?
    A. The insurer
    B. The applicant and insured
    C. The state insurance department
    D. Themselves

12. The three types of authority given to agents are
    A. express, implied, and appealing
    B. express, compliance, and apparent
    C. implied, apparent, and agreed
    D. express, implied, and apparent

13. An insurance contract is prepared by one party, the insurer, rather than by negotiation between the contracting parties. This feature means that the insurance contract
    A. is an aleatory contract
    B. is a contract of acceptance
    C. is a contract of adhesion
    D. names only the insurer as the competent party

14. Which of the following statements regarding utmost good faith in insurance contracts is CORRECT?
    A. The concept of utmost good faith—that there is no attempt to conceal, disguise, or deceive—applies only to the insurer.
    B. Although a warranty is a statement, it technically is not part of the contract.
    C. A representation is a statement that the applicant guarantees to be true.
    D. Most state insurance laws consider statements made in an application for an insurance policy to be representations, not warranties.

15. With life and health contracts, when must an insurable interest exist?
    A. After the policy is issued
    B. Before the beneficiary is named
    C. While the policy is in force
    D. At the inception of the policy

16. Which of the following describes the voluntary giving up of known right?
    A. Estoppel
    B. Adhesion
    C. Waiver
    D. Unilateral

17. Statements a person makes in an application for insurance that he claims are true to the best of his knowledge are
    A. warranties
    B. concealments
    C. representations
    D. misrepresentations

18. Deliberate failure to reveal material facts that would affect the validity of a policy of insurance is known as
    A. inducement
    B. concealment
    C. collusion
    D. rebating

19. To have a legally valid contract, each of the following must be present EXCEPT
    A. consideration
    B. competent parties
    C. notarization
    D. acceptance of an offer

20. The legal doctrine that holds that the parties to a contract may give up unequal consideration is called
    A. adhesion
    B. aleatory
    C. alienation
    D. ad hoc

# ANSWERS AND RATIONALES TO UNIT QUIZ

1. **B.** Insurance in and of itself does not eliminate risk, but transfers it to insurers. While it also attempts to reduce hazards, that is not the primary purpose of insurance.

2. **C.** A pure risk is one in which there is no potential for gain, only loss or no loss.

3. **D.** Insurance does not eliminate risk; it allows an insured to transfer his risk to an insurance company, which accumulates funds to pay losses when they occur.

4. **B.** When an insured agrees to pay all or any part of losses that take place, he uses the risk management technique of retention. A deductible is partial retention.

5. **C.** Fire is a cause of loss or peril, not a hazard.

6. **A.** Property and casualty insurance requires that an insurable interest be present at the time of loss.

7. **D.** The law of large numbers states that as the number of observations increases, the ability to predict the outcome is more precise.

8. **C.** Fire damage is a direct loss, while loss of rents, income, or additional expenses is indirect or consequential.

9. **B.** Unlike speculative risk, pure risk involves only the chance of loss and never a possibility of gain or profit. Only this type of risk is insurable.

10. **A.** To be an insurable risk, the loss must be due to chance. A risk must involve the chance of loss that is fortuitous and outside the insured's control.

11. **A.** A licensed insurance agent legally represents the insurer in a sales transaction and in any disputes between the insured or beneficiary and the insurer.

12. **D.** The authority an agent possesses is either expressed in a contract, called the *agency agreement*, implied by necessity to carry out duties expressly authorized, or apparent to the buying public by virtue of the agent's conduct.

13. **C.** Insurance contracts are contracts of adhesion. This means that the contract has been prepared by one party (the insurer) rather than as the result of negotiation between the parties.

14. **D.** According to most states, insurance policies must contain a provision that all statements made in the application are deemed representations, not warranties. If a warranty or representation is untrue, the insurer may cancel the contract; however, the insurer may cancel the contract only if the representation was material to the creation of the contract.

15. **D.** In life and health insurance, an insurable interest must exist between the policyowner and insured at the time of application.

16. **C.** A person who voluntarily gives up a legal, given right is deemed to have waived that right.

17. **C.** Warranties are statements that are absolutely true and must continue to be so during a contract. Representations are statements that are true to the best of someone's knowledge. State law generally makes the statements made in the process of obtaining insurance representations rather than warranties.

18. **B.** Failure to reveal facts an applicant knows and should disclose is considered concealment.

19. **C.** A legal contract's requirements are offer and acceptance (agreement), consideration, competent parties, and legal purpose.

20. **B.** *Aleatory* is a term used to define an unequal exchange between two parties to a contract. In insurance, the insured must pay a certain sum, called the *premium*, that is potentially much smaller than the amount he might collect from the insurer in the event of a loss.

# 2

# Insurance Regulation and Industry Overview

## KEY CONCEPTS

- Methods of insurance regulation
- Licensing of insurers
- Licensing and conduct requirements for insurance producers
- Organizational structures in the industry
- Insurance company operations

The insurance industry is one of the most highly regulated in the United States. This is because insurance is considered to be affected with the public interest, meaning that insurance companies and their representatives are charged with the responsibility of protecting consumers. To ensure that no abuses occur, the insurance departments in the various states oversee the market conduct of insurance companies and their agents in terms of the sale of insurance, the claims process, and a number of other areas. In addition, the misdeeds of companies and agents are subject to legal action. Any conduct or practice may result in a court review to determine its appropriateness. When lawmakers believe that insurance professionals have not behaved in the public's best interest, they may pass laws that dictate the proper method for dealing with consumers.

## OBJECTIVE

When you complete this unit, you should be able to:

- describe the primary ways that insurance is regulated at the state and federal level;

- explain the required and prohibited practices that govern the conduct of producers;

- distinguish between domestic, foreign, and alien insurance companies and the legal forms of organization within the industry;

- explain insurance company operations related to underwriting and rate making;

- explain how loss, expense, and combined ratios are calculated; and

- describe the importance of loss reserves, solvency, and the role of reinsurance.

# REGULATION OF THE INSURANCE INDUSTRY

The insurance industry in the United States has been regulated primarily by the states rather than the federal government. Insurance regulation began when state legislatures granted charters to new insurers, which authorized their formation and operation.

Congress passed the McCarran-Ferguson Act (Public Law 15) in 1945. This law recognized that state regulation of insurance was in the public's best interest and thus exempted the insurance industry from the federal regulation required for most interstate commerce industries. However, the act did give the federal government the right to apply antitrust laws to the extent that such business (insurance) is not regulated by the state level (federal flood insurance programs, for example). To avoid federal intervention, each state has revised its insurance laws to conform with these requirements.

## METHODS FOR REGULATING INSURERS

Three principal methods are used to regulate insurance companies: legislation, courts, and state insurance departments. Let's briefly look at each of these methods.

**Legislation**  Each state has developed laws that regulate the formation and operation of insurance companies. These laws determine how insurance professionals are licensed, what financial requirements an insurer must meet to maintain solvency, how rates are determined, how sales and claims are handled, and how consumers are protected.

In addition to state laws, insurers are also subject to regulation by some federal laws and agencies. For example, the Securities and Exchange Commission (SEC) regulates the sale of insurance company securities to the general public. The Federal Trade Commission (FTC) regulates mail-order insurers in those states where they are not licensed to do business.

Laws also may be made by public referendum or popular vote. These laws hold the same authority as those developed through the legislative process. California's Proposition 103, for example, which mandated a rate reduction for good drivers who purchased personal automobile policies, was enacted through the state's voter initiative process rather than through the state legislature.

**Courts**   State and federal courts may hand down decisions regarding the constitutionality of state insurance laws, an insurer's interpretation of policy clauses and provisions, and decisions about the legality of a state insurance department's administrative actions. Various court decisions can affect the ways in which an insurance company handles its operations and markets its insurance products. Judicial review of voter-approved laws dealing with insurance also has become more common.

**State Insurance Departments (Regulation)**   Each state has an insurance department, division, or bureau that (in most states) is headed by an insurance commissioner or superintendent or a director of insurance. Depending on the state, the head of this department either is appointed by and at the will of the governor or is an elected official. The commissioner administers state insurance laws and wields considerable power over companies doing business in that state. The commissioner's duties include investigating the practices of anyone engaged in the business of insurance, holding hearings, issuing cease-and-desist orders, approving policies and rates, investigating policyholder complaints, and revoking or suspending an insurer's license to do business. However, the extent of these duties varies between states.

## LICENSING OF INSURERS

To transact insurance, an insurer must comply with certain state regulations. An insurer is any person or company engaged as the principal party in the business of entering into insurance contracts. This includes stock and mutual insurance companies, fraternal benefit societies, health maintenance organizations, and nonprofit corporations offering dental, hospital, and medical services.

Each state has requirements for the formation and licensing of insurance companies. Such a company receives a charter or certificate of authority from the state that authorizes the insurer's formation and legal existence. No individual, association, or corporation may engage in the business of insurance unless it is issued a *certificate of authority*. If the state insurance department is satisfied that an insurer applying to do business in the state has complied with the law fully, it issues a certificate to transact insurance business. Each certificate of authority remains in effect until revoked, canceled, or suspended according to law.

When an insurer has received a charter or certificate from its state, the company is referred to as an *admitted insurer*. An insurer, for a variety of reasons, may wish to do business in a state as a nonadmitted insurer, which generally falls into one of two categories: authorized and unauthorized. An authorized nonadmitted insurer has been approved to transact insurance in a state, but must do so only through a licensed surplus lines broker. An unauthorized nonadmitted insurer may not transact insurance in a state.

**Surplus Lines**   In most cases, insurance business is placed with an admitted insurer, that is, a company licensed to do business in the state. However, it is possible that insurance is unavailable in the standard market or from admitted companies. This can occur when an applicant possesses such unusual risk characteristics that standard insurers are unwilling or unable to accommodate the placement of the insurance. This business also is referred to as excess insurance because it is often beyond the capacity of standard insurers.

Some lines of business are placed routinely in the surplus lines market. Aviation liability, products liability, and professional liability are examples of surplus lines risks. Each state insurance department determines which types of risks may be "exported" to the excess and surplus lines market. With this accomplished, business is arranged using a licensed surplus lines agent or broker. The surplus lines broker can be thought of as a wholesaler because he passes products from the company to the retail agent. In this sense, the lines broker is an agent's agent.

If surplus lines business ultimately is placed with a nonadmitted insurer, a disclosure usually must be provided to the policyholder. This is because a state's insurance guarantee association, which provides insolvency protection to policyholders, is not available for nonadmitted insurers.

# INSURANCE PRODUCERS

Every state requires that people who sell insurance have a license from the state. However, before an insurance department will issue such a license—whether it's to a prospective agent or broker—the candidate must pass a producer licensing exam administered by the department. In some states, the agent's or broker's license is perpetual unless revoked; in other states, it must be renewed at stipulated intervals.

Individuals who sell variable contracts—variable annuities, variable life, and variable universal health—also must be licensed by the NASD. This requires passing the Series 6 (Investment Company/Variable Contracts Limited Representative) or the Series 7 (General Securities Representative) exam. Variable products are considered both securities and life insurance.

## AGENT MARKETING AND SALES PRACTICES

Marketing and selling financial products such as life insurance and annuities require a high level of professionalism and ethics. Every state requires its licensed producers to adhere to certain standards designed to protect consumers and promote suitable sales and application of insurance products. Among these standards are:

- *Selling to needs.* The ethical agent determines what needs the client has and then determines the product best suited to address those needs. Two principles of needs-based selling are:
    - fact-find (learn the client's situation and understand his goals, needs, and concerns; and
    - educate (teach the client about insurance as a financial tool).

■ *Suitability of recommended products.* The ethical agent assesses the correlation between a recommended product and the client's needs and capabilities by asking and answering the following questions:

— What are the client's needs?

— What product can help meet those needs?

— Does the client understand the product and its provisions?

— Does the client have the capability—financially and otherwise—to manage   the product?

— Is this product in the client's best interest?

■ *Full and accurate disclosure.* The ethical agent makes it a practice to inform clients fully about all aspects of the products he recommends, their limitations as well as their benefits. There never is any attempt to hide or disguise the nature or purpose of the product, nor the company that is being represented. Insurance products are highly effective financial planning tools; they should be presented clearly, completely, and accurately.

■ *Documentation.* The ethical agent documents each client meeting and transaction. He uses fact-finding forms and obtains the client's written agreement as to the needs determined, the products recommended, and the decisions made. Some documentation is required by state law. Ethical agents know these laws and follow them precisely.

■ *Client service.* The ethical agent knows that a sale does not mark the end of a relationship with a client but the beginning. Routine follow-up calls are recommended to ensure that the client's needs always are covered and the products in place still suitable. When clients contact their agents for service or information, these requests are given top priority. Complaints are handled promptly and fully.

**Prohibited Practices** Just as there are standards governing appropriate and ethical sales and marketing practices, certain practices long have been viewed as inappropriate to the business of insurance and are prohibited in virtually all jurisdictions. Practically every state bans twisting, misrepresentation, misuse of premiums, and rebating. These are known as prohibited practices.

■ *Twisting.* Twisting is the act of persuading a policyowner to drop and replace an existing policy by misrepresenting the terms or conditions of another. Typically, the motivation for twisting simply is to induce the sale of a policy without any regard to the potential disadvantages to the policyowner. Not only is twisting illegal, it is highly unethical.

■ *Misrepresentation.* Misrepresentation is a false or misleading statement or representation made by a producer regarding his own policies or those of a competitor. Agents are not allowed to misrepresent a policy's terms, benefits, or the nature of the coverage it provides. If policy dividends are payable, they cannot be represented as guaranteed.

■ *Misuse of premiums.* Misuse of premiums includes diverting premium funds for personal use. Some states require that an agent establish a separate premium account if he holds the money for any time before turning it over to the insurer. Commingling premium funds with personal funds is prohibited.

■ *Rebating.* Rebating occurs if the buyer of an insurance policy receives any part of the agent's commission or if the agent gives the buyer anything of significant value in exchange for purchasing a policy. For instance, a $25 gift certificate given in exchange for the purchase of a policy would be rebating in some jurisdictions. Most states prohibit the practice of rebating, terming it an *illegal inducement.* Where rebating is allowed, strict guidelines have been imposed to control and monitor its practice.

**Replacement**  The practice of replacement, which involves convincing a policyowner to lapse or terminate an existing policy and replace it with another, requires special attention. While replacement is not illegal, it rarely is in the best interests of the policyowner. As we will discuss in Lessons 4 and 10, permanent life insurance and annuities build cash value over time. To interrupt one cash value plan and begin another could pose serious financial consequences for the policyowner. On the other hand, if a replacement would result in a significant economic benefit for the policyowner, it might be appropriate. If and when a replacement is appropriate, the agent must provide:

■ full and fair disclosure to the policyowner of all facts regarding both the new coverage and the existing policy;

■ a document signed by the policyowner indicating that he has full understanding of the replacement transaction and its implications; and

■ notice to the existing insurer and the replacing insurer of the intended replacement.

Generally, most state insurance laws now require all life insurance and annuity sales transactions to include questions about replacement. Product application forms routinely ask if a replacement is involved; if so, additional information is necessary. For example, the agent must provide reason for the replacement and an explanation of why the existing policy cannot meet the client's needs. The additional information gives underwriters and regulators a means of assessing a replacement's suitability and requires consumers to consider the pros and cons of such transactions.

The following questions will guide agents when determining the suitability of policy replacement:

■ How does the new insurance need compare with the past need?

■ Is the client drawn to contract features in the replacement policy that the existing policy lacks?

■ What effect will the replacement policy have on future premiums, cash value accumulations, and insurance charges?

■ What guarantees are being lost or gained?

■ Will the policyowner incur surrender charges if the existing policy is cashed in?

■ Is the policyowner's instability or underwriting status different?

While no state has moved to make replacement illegal, most have initiated tracking systems that attempt to identify licensed producers who generate high levels of replacement activity. The burden of proof lies with the agent to demonstrate that a replacement is a suitable recommendation.

**Buyer's Guides and Policy Summaries**  To help insure that prospective insurance buyers select the most appropriate plan or plans for their needs and to improve their understanding of basic product features, most states require agents to deliver a buyer's guide to the consumer whenever they solicit insurance sales. These guides explain the various types of life insurance products in a way that the average consumer can understand. In addition, a policy summary, containing information about the specific policy being recommended, must be given to a potential buyer. Most states require this be done before the applicant's initial premium is accepted.

The policy summary also contains cost indexes that help the consumer evaluate the suitability of the recommended product. The *net payment cost comparison index* gives the buyer an idea of the cost of the policy at some future point in time, compared to the death benefit. The *surrender cost comparison index* compares the cost of surrendering the policy and withdrawing the cash values at some future time.

## NATIONAL ASSOCIATION OF INSURANCE COMMISSIONERS

All state insurance commissioners or directors are members of the National Association of Insurance Commissioners (NAIC). This organization has standing committees that work regularly to examine various aspects of the insurance industry and to recommend appropriate insurance laws and regulations. Basically, the NAIC has four broad objectives:

- to encourage uniformity in state insurance laws and regulations;

- to assist in the administration of those laws and regulations by promoting efficiency;

- to protect the interests of policyowners and consumers; and

- to preserve state regulation of the insurance business.

The NAIC has been instrumental in developing guidelines and model legislation that help ensure that the insurance industry maintains a high level of public trust by conducting its business competently and fairly. This group also develops standards for policy provisions, helping ensure that policies are more uniform than disparate across the country. Notable among the NAIC's accomplishments was the creation of the Advertising Code and the Unfair Trade Practices Act, which have been adopted by virtually every state.

**Advertising Code**  A principal problem of states in the past was regulating misleading insurance advertising and direct mail solicitations. Many states now subscribe to the Advertising Code developed by the NAIC. The code specifies certain words and phrases that are considered misleading and are not to be used in advertising of any kind and also requires full disclosure of policy renewal, cancellation, and termination provisions. Other rules pertain to the use of testimonials, statistics, special offers, and the like.

**Unfair Trade Practices Act**  Most jurisdictions also have adopted the NAIC's Unfair Trade Practices Act. This act, as amended in 1972, gives insurance commissioners the power to investigate insurance companies and producers, to issue cease and desist orders, and to impose penalties on violators. The act also gives commissioners the authority to seek a court injunction to restrain insurers from using any methods believed to be unfair or deceptive. Included as unfair trade practices are misrepresentation and false advertising, coercion and intimidation, unfair discrimination, and inequitable administration or claims settlements.

# ORGANIZATION OF THE INSURANCE INDUSTRY

## STATE OF DOMICILE

In the United States, insurers are classified by their states of domicile (the states where the insurers are chartered or incorporated) and are considered domestic, foreign, or alien companies or insurers.

**Domestic Insurance Company**  A domestic insurer is an insurance company incorporated and formed under the laws of the state in which it is domiciled. For example, an insurer formed under Connecticut laws is said to be a domestic insurer when conducting business in Connecticut.

**Foreign Insurance Company** A foreign insurer is one domiciled and organized under the laws of one state, but licensed to do business in another state. For example, an insurer formed under Michigan laws but licensed to do business in Illinois is said to be a foreign insurer when conducting business in Illinois.

**Alien Insurance Company** An alien insurer is an insurance company formed under the laws of a country other than the United States. An example would be a company domiciled in Toronto, Canada, doing business in Colorado.

## LEGAL FORM OF ORGANIZATION

**Stock Companies** Most insurance companies are organized as stock companies. Similar to shareholders in other businesses, insurance company shareholders appoint directors, officers, and others to manage the day-to-day operations of the companies they own.

**Mutual Companies** Under the other major form of legal ownership—the mutual company—the people or businesses the company insures are also the owners. Unlike a stock company, the mutual company has no shareholders, and the policyholders themselves bear any profit or loss the company experiences. Mutual company directors and officers are chosen by the policyholders.

**Lloyd's of London** Another type of insurer is Lloyd's of London. Although it is not really an insurance company, Lloyd's attempts to make a profit for its members, who are called "names." The names are organized into syndicates, or groups to underwrite risks. Lloyd's operates on many of the same principles as a stock exchange in that it matches buyers wishing to secure insurance with sellers who wish to underwrite the risks.

**Other Private Insurers** A reciprocal insurer is an unincorporated group of people who provide insurance to each other. They are not referred to as policyholders, but as members or subscribers. To purchase the insurance products reciprocals offer, individuals or organizations first must demonstrate that they are members of the group.

---

 EXAMPLE    Many states allow the purchase of personal lines insurance through automobile associations or auto clubs. To purchase their insurance, a person first must become a member of a club. Then, he agrees to exchange promises to insure with the other members of the club. A reciprocal also is called an interinsurance exchange.

A health association or health service plan focuses on delivering hospital, medical, or dental benefits to its members. Rather than paying the bills for services obtained from others, the association actually provides the services using prepaid plans. The best known of these types of insurers are the Blues—Blue Cross and Blue Shield.

Fraternal benefit societies provide limited insurance benefits to their members, usually restricted to life and health insurance.

**Government Insurers** At times, the private insurance marketplace leaves policyholder needs unmet. Particularly when coverage is mandated by law, such as workers' compensation or personal automobile insurance, the government becomes the insurer of last resort. In other cases, such as flood insurance, nuclear energy liability insurance, crop insurance, or unemployment compensation, the only insurer interested in underwriting these risks is the government. Thus, governmental insurance is an important and necessary complement to the private insurance market.

**Risk Retention Groups and Risk Purchasing Groups** Widespread unavailability of insurance in the 1980s led Congress to pass legislation creating two new avenues for businesses and individuals to secure much needed insurance coverage. A risk retention group (RRG) is a liability insurance company owned by its policyholders. The policyholders must possess similar liability risks, and the RRG must be licensed as an insurer under the laws of at least one state. A risk purchasing group (RPG) is formed to purchase liability insurance on behalf of its members. Unlike a risk retention group, the RPG merely buys insurance, and need not be licensed as an insurer.

# MARKETING AND DISTRIBUTION

In addition to being categorized based on form of organization and legal status, insurance companies also can be classified based on how their products are sold or distributed and by whom. Some companies use the independent agency model for selling their products. Under this system, a company finds agents in various geographic areas who agree to sell the insurer's policies in exchange for a percentage of each premium, called a commission. Most commercial insurance policies are distributed by independent insurance agencies. Rather than represent a single insurance company, independent agents work on behalf of many companies and select the company that best suits a customer's needs.

Other companies have a dedicated agency force that does not represent any other insurers. In other words, these exclusive agents have a contract with a single insurance company, and they can offer only that company's products.

Another type of insurance company, a direct writer or direct response company, may not have any local agents. All its products and services are offered from the company's home office, and the company takes care of all service. The individuals who sell and service the policies are employees of that company and typically are paid salaries rather than commissions.

# INSURANCE COMPANY OPERATIONS

## UNDERWRITING

Underwriting usually is defined as the selection, classification, and acceptance or rejection of a proposed insured according to the insurer's underwriting standards. The underwriter is the person who actually selects the applicants, prices coverage, and determines policy terms. In many instances, the agent is the first underwriter for new business. In essence, the agent is a field underwriter for the insurance company, determining whether business will be acceptable to the insurance company. It is usually the agent who selects the insured and, in many cases, quotes the premium the insured will pay. After the agent submits an application to the company, the line underwriter (usually located in the home office) makes the final determination about whether the risk can be written and at what premium. Staff underwriters are employed in the company's home office to help line underwriters implement the company's underwriting guidelines.

The underwriting process consists of four basic steps:

- ■ gathering necessary underwriting information;
- ■ making the underwriting decision;
- ■ implementing the decision; and
- ■ monitoring the decision.

## RATE MAKING

One of the most important parts of an underwriter's job is to determine the proper pricing for insurance products. Insurance rates are regulated by state insurance departments to make sure the rates are adequate to pay losses and cover expenses. In addition, the departments check to make sure the rates are not excessive (rates must be reasonable) or unfairly discriminatory (not significantly different for two insureds with essentially the same degree of risk). However, because a company does not know in advance how many claims and expenses it will incur for a certain period, it is difficult to determine how much a particular insurance product should cost.

**Rate Regulation** In addition to requirements mandating that insurance rates be adequate, not excessive, and not unfairly discriminatory, rates are subject to additional regulation. States vary in the degree of regulation they apply to the rating of different lines of insurance. The types of rate laws in effect follow:

**Prior Approval.** Under this system, all rates must be filed with an insurance department and are subject to approval before their use. This is the most restrictive form of regulation.

**File and Use.** This type of rating law requires an insurance company to file its rates, but the company is permitted to use them before their approval. If the rate filing is subsequently disapproved, the company must adjust any policies that have been issued with the new rate.

**Open Competition.** Some states have adopted a competitive rating systems, which means they encourage competition and rely on it to lead to fair and adequate rates for insurance coverages. Although such a system does not require rate filings, an insurance department monitors rates to see that they continue to be adequate and not excessive.

**Mandatory Rates.** In a limited number of states, rates for some types of insurance are mandated by law. A rating bureau develops the rates, and insurers must use these rates in pricing policies.

**Rate** The rate is the amount of dollars and cents charged for a particular amount of insurance.

---

EXAMPLE

The rate charged for a property policy might be $.50 per $100 of value. If the insured wishes to cover property valued at $50,000, the annual premium would be $250 ($.50 × 500 hundreds = $250).

The rate charged for life insurance might be $2.00 for every $1000 of 20-year term coverage purchased by 35-year-old males in average health. If the policyowner wishes to purchase a $100,000 policy, the annual premium would be $200 ($2.00 × 100 thousands = $200)

---

### TAKE NOTE

In addition to an underwriting profit, an insurance company earns a return on its investments. An underwriting loss may be offset by an investment profit, meaning the insurance company may lose money on underwriting insurance, but remain profitable overall. Investment profits normally are not contemplated in determining adequacy of insurance rates.

---

Rates for different coverages are based on different factors. In property insurance, for example, rates are based on such factors as construction, property location, and local fire protection classifications. In life insurance, rates are based on age, sex, and health factors. In automobile insurance, rates are based on the driver's age, use of car, and type of car. In workers' compensation, rates are based on the employee's job duties.

**Premium**   The premium, which is calculated from the rate, is the total cost for the amount of insurance coverage (or limit of liability) purchased.

---

**EXAMPLE**

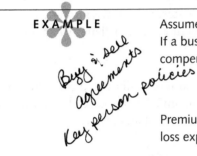

Assume the workers' compensation rate for clerical workers is $.60 per $100 of payroll. If a business has a total annual payroll of $100,000 for its clerical workers, its workers' compensation premium would be calculated as follows:

$100,000 ÷ $100 = $1,000
$1,000 × .60 = $600

Premiums can be further modified by applying credits or debits based on a policyholder's loss experience, safety efforts, or unique risk characteristics.

## LOSS RATIOS/EXPENSE RATIOS

The quality of a company's underwriting is determined in part by its *loss ratios* and *expense ratios*. A loss ratio is determined by dividing total losses by total premiums received. The resulting information may be used to make decisions about whether to continue an agent's (or agency's) contract, whether to revise underwriting guidelines, or whether to discontinue writing a certain line of business.

An *expense ratio* is determined by dividing an insurer's total operating expenses by total premiums. By adding the company's loss ratio to its expense ratio, an additional ratio, the combined ratio, is determined. The insurer breaks even if the *combined ratio* is 100%. If the combined ratio is less than 100%, an underwriting profit has occurred. If the combined ratio is more than 100%, an underwriting loss has occurred.

## LOSS RESERVES

Insurers must maintain certain funds or loss reserves for the estimated cost of settling claims that already have occurred but that have not yet been paid as of a certain date. The size of the loss reserve may be determined in one of four ways:

■ *Case reserve*—A loss reserve is established for each claim when it is reported;

■ *Average value method*—A loss reserve is established based on the average settlement for a particular type of claim;

- *Loss ratio method*—A loss reserve is established by formula based on the expected loss ratio for a particular line of business or class of insureds; and

- *Tabular method*—A loss reserve is established based on the estimated length of an insured's or a claimant's life, the estimated length of disability, and the like.

Companies are required by law to maintain minimum reserves on their balance sheets. These reserves ensure that the premiums collected in the present will be available to pay losses in the future.

## SOLVENCY AND CAPACITY

Insurers receive premiums in return for the promise to pay for losses in the future. Because the money received from the public is received in a fiduciary capacity, it must be held in trust to meet these future obligations. Therefore, it is vital that insurers guard against insolvency.

State laws impose capital and surplus requirements on insurers, require the preparation of annual financial statements, and mandate periodic examinations of the insurers' operations. State insurance departments attempt to rehabilitate companies whose financial situations falter and attempt to liquidate the companies if the insurers become insolvent. Most states also have insurance guaranty associations, which provide insolvency funds for partial repayment of unpaid claims when an admitted insurer is declared insolvent.

To further ensure company solvency, a limit is placed on the amount of business an insurer may write. This limit, called an insurer's capacity, is determined by the company's level of capital and surplus. In this case, surplus refers to assets exceeding liabilities on the insurer's balance sheet.

**Rating Services** The financial strength and stability of an insurance company are two vitally important factors to potential insurance buyers and to insurance companies themselves. Guides to insurance companies' financial integrity and claims paying ability are published regularly by various rating services, such as A.M. Best, Standard & Poor's, Moody's, and Fitch's.

## REINSURANCE

Reinsurance provides insurance protection to an insurance company should a loss occur. In this way, it serves as the insurance company's insurer. Here's how reinsurance works.

Insurance companies (or primary insurers) write insurance policies to protect insureds should a loss occur. Under state law and for sound business operations, insurance companies cannot carry on their books larger amounts at risk than they can expect to cover with their surpluses. Therefore, insurers turn over specified proportions of the risks they accept from policyholders to reinsurance companies. This is called *ceding* risk. The methods used to determine what part of the risk goes to a reinsurer vary based on the contract between the primary insurance company and the reinsurer. This contract is called the treaty.

Two types of reinsurance treaties follow:

- *Facultative*—The primary insurer makes reinsurance arrangements on a case-by-case basis; and

- *Automatic*—A portion of every risk the primary insurer accepts is ceded to the reinsurer, subject to the specific terms in the contract or treaty.

## FIGURE 2.1  Insurance Company Rating System

**A.M. Best Company**

| | |
|---|---|
| A++, A+ | Superior; very strong ability to meet obligations |
| A, A– | Excellent; strong ability to meet obligations |
| B++, B+ | Very good; strong ability to meet obligations |
| B, B– | Good; adequate ability to meet obligations |
| C++, C+ | Fair; reasonable ability to meet obligations |
| C, C– | Marginal; currently has ability to meet obligations |
| D | Below minimum standards |
| E | Under state supervision |
| F | In liquidation |
| S | Suspended |

**S&P**

| | |
|---|---|
| AAA | Superior; highest safety |
| AA | Excellent financial security |
| A | Good financial security |
| BBB | Adequate financial security |
| BB | Adequate financial security; ability to meet obligations, may not be adequate for long-term policies |
| B | Currently able to meet obligations but highly vulnerable to adverse conditions |
| CCC | Questionable ability to meet obligations |
| CC, C | May not be meeting obligations; vulnerable to liquidation |
| R | Under a court order of liquidation; in receivership |

**Moody's**

| | |
|---|---|
| Aaa | Exceptional security |
| Aa | Excellent security |
| A | Good security |
| Baa | Adequate security |
| Ba | Questionable security; moderate ability to meet obligations |
| B | Poor security |
| Caa | Very poor security; elements of danger regarding payment of obligations |
| Ca | Extremely poor security; may be in default |
| C | Lowest security |

**Fitch**

| | |
|---|---|
| AAA | Highest claims-paying ability; negligible risk |
| AA+, AA, AA– | Very high claims-paying ability; moderate risk |
| A+, A, A– | High claims-paying ability; variable risk over time |
| BBB+, BBB, BBB– | Below average claims-paying ability; considerable variability in risk over time |
| BB+, BB, BB– | Uncertain claims-paying ability |
| CCC | Substantial claims-paying ability risk; likely to be placed under state supervision |

Reinsurance treaties can be arranged in a variety of ways, depending on the primary insurer's needs. Sometimes the insurer needs surplus relief, which is required when the insurer wishes to expand its writing of primary insurance. Other times the need is to protect against catastrophic losses, such as earthquakes or hurricanes. Some additional terms concerning reinsurance follow.

- *Quota share*—The primary insurer and reinsurer agree to share the amount of insurance, premium, and loss on *some percentage basis*.

- *Surplus treaty*—The reinsurer agrees to accept some amount of insurance on each risk exceeding a designated amount, up to some specified limit, retained by the primary insurer.

- *Excess loss treaty*—The reinsurer pays only when a loss exceeds a certain amount, for any one piece of property or in any one occurrence.

- *Pooling*—Each member of a group assumes a percentage of every risk written by a member of the pool.

# SUMMARY

The insurance industry is regulated at many levels. In addition to federal and state legislation, each state has an insurance commissioner; these commissioners are members of the National Association of Insurance Commissioners (NAIC), an organization that drafts model laws adopted by many state legislatures. Insurance companies doing business within a state must be licensed to do so. These admitted carriers have been issued a certificate of authority; in unique situations, surplus lines carriers may provide insurance without a certificate of authority. The companies licensed to do business in a state may be domiciled within that state, in another state or another country; there are several legal forms of organization that insurers operate under.

Insurance producers (sales representatives) must be licensed and must abide by many regulations designed to protect consumers, which includes selling suitable products appropriate to customer needs. Insurance company operations include underwriting and rate making. Reinsurance plays an important role in the industry allowing insurers to cede a portion of the risk through reinsurance treaties.

We have completed our introduction to the insurance industry and the regulations that govern it. Through the remainder of this text, we will examine individual products and services in greater detail.

# UNIT QUIZ

1. In some states, an insurance salesperson who offers a $100 gourmet dinner in exchange for the purchase of a life insurance policy would be considered to have committed which of the following prohibited sales practices?
   A. Twisting
   B. Replacement
   C. Rebating
   D. Churning

2. Which of the following statements regarding the National Association of Insurance Commissioners (NAIC) is NOT correct?
   A. It is empowered to prosecute and punish criminal violators in the insurance industry.
   B. It seeks to preserve state rather than federal regulation of the insurance industry.
   C. It promotes uniformity in state insurance laws and regulations.
   D. It seeks to promote efficient administration of insurance laws and regulations.

3. A life insurance company organized in Illinois, with its home office in Philadelphia, is licensed to conduct business in Wisconsin. In Wisconsin, this company would be considered which of the following types of insurers?
   A. Domestic
   B. Alien
   C. Foreign
   D. Regional

4. A reinsurer is a company that
   A. accepts all the risk from another insurer
   B. assumes a portion of the risk from another insurer
   C. cedes the risk from another insurer
   D. does not take any risk

5. The head of a state insurance department generally is responsible for all of the following EXCEPT
   A. licensing and supervising agents and brokers
   B. overseeing insurance companies' marketing practices
   C. issuing rules and regulations
   D. making insurance laws

6. Each of the following is a method used to regulate insurance companies EXCEPT
   A. legislation
   B. courts
   C. NAIC
   D. state insurance departments

7. When an insurance company becomes authorized to do business in a particular state, it receives a(n)
   A. appointment
   B. certificate of authority or charter
   C. article of incorporation
   D. authorization

8. Which of the following statements about nonadmitted insurers is TRUE?
   A. They may not do business in the United States.
   B. They may place business only through other insurance companies.
   C. They may operate only as reinsurers.
   D. They may be authorized or unauthorized.

9. An agent who represents a single insurance company under contract is referred to as what type of agent?
   A. Captive
   B. Exclusive
   C. Independent
   D. Restricted

10. An insurance company underwriter may take one of several actions when reviewing applications for insurance. Which of the following is NOT an example of an appropriate underwriting action?

    A. Deciding which applicants to insure
    B. Determining the proper classification for a risk
    C. Deciding how much to charge applicants based on their income
    D. Determining which applicants do not qualify for the company's products

11. States use various types of approval systems when evaluating an insurance company's rates. Which of the following is an example of a state rate law?

    A. Prior approval
    B. File and use
    C. Open competition
    D. All of the above

12. Assuming a rate of $1 per $1,000 of insurance, a policy covering a building valued at $250,000 would produce a premium of

    A. $25
    B. $250
    C. $2,500
    D. $25,000

13. The amount of insurance a company can write based on its financial status is referred to as

    A. solvency
    B. adequacy
    C. capacity
    D. fiduciary

# ANSWERS AND RATIONALES TO UNIT QUIZ

1. **C.** Rebating occurs if an agent gives the buyer anything of significant value in exchange for purchasing a policy. A $100 gourmet dinner offered in exchange for purchasing an insurance policy, therefore, would be considered rebating.

2. **A.** Although the NAIC assists in administering state insurance laws and seeks to protect policyowners' interests, it does not have any legal authority to prosecute and punish criminal violators in the insurance industry.

3. **C.** To be considered a domestic company in Wisconsin, the insurance company must be incorporated there. However, because it was incorporated in Illinois and merely is authorized to transact business in Wisconsin, it is considered a foreign company in Wisconsin.

4. **B.** A reinsurer assumes part, but not all, of the risk from another insurer to help limit the loss the insurer would face if a large claim became payable.

5. **D.** The head of a state insurance department generally is responsible for licensing and supervising agents and brokers, overseeing insurance companies' marketing practices, and issuing rules and regulations. However, it is the state legislature rather than the head of the state insurance department that is responsible for making insurance laws.

6. **C.** Insurance is regulated by legislation, courts, and state insurance departments. The NAIC, while influential, has no authority to regulate insurers.

7. **B.** The document given to an insurer authorizing it to transact insurance in a state is known as a *certificate of authority* or *charter*.

8. **D.** Either nonadmitted insurers are authorized to do business in a state using licensed surplus lines brokers or they are unauthorized and may not transact business at all in that state.

9. **B.** An agent who represents only one company under contract is an exclusive agent.

10. **C.** Determining prices based on an applicant's income is considered unfair discrimination and is not an appropriate (or legal) underwriting action.

11. **D.** The types of rating laws in effect are prior approval, file and use, open competition, and mandatory rates.

12. **B.** 250,000 divided by 1,000 is 250. 250 times a rate of $1 equals $250.

13. **C.** Insurers may expand premiums based on the amount of policyholder surplus, or assets exceeding liabilities, that they possess.

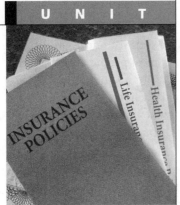

# UNIT

# 3

# Life Insurance Policies

## KEY CONCEPTS

■ The role of life insurance

■ Forms of term and permanent life insurance

■ Modified endowment contracts

■ Special use policies

Life insurance plays an important role in helping people attain financial security, and is an integral part of any comprehensive financial plan. While no one will live forever, most people anticipate living a long, productive life. Should a person die sooner than expected, they often leave behind dependents who were reliant upon the earnings of the deceased. The costs of daily living and the debts we leave behind can be overwhelming to dependents and family members who continue living beyond our death. The financial risks associated with dying early are managed through life insurance.

Insurers offer several different types of life insurance policies designed to serve different needs. In this unit, we will examine the traditional forms of life insurance that have existed for many years. In addition to these standard policies, a number of specialized insurance products have evolved to serve a variety of needs.

## OBJECTIVE

When you complete this unit you should be able to

- list and identify the basic forms and features of term life insurance;

- describe the features of whole life insurance that distinguish it from term life insurance and identify the basic types of whole life insurance;

- explain how modified endowment contracts are taxed;

- describe family plan policies, multiple protection policies, joint life policies, juvenile insurance, and credit life insurance; and

- list and explain the different features of nontraditional life policies, including, adjustable life, universal life, variable life, and variable universal life insurance.

# TERM LIFE INSURANCE

Term life insurance is the simplest type of life insurance plan. It provides insurance protection for a specified period (or term) and pays a benefit only if the insured dies during that period.

---

**EXAMPLE**     An insured has a five-year $50,000 level term life insurance policy that names a sibling as beneficiary. If the insured dies at any time within the policy's five-year period, the sibling will receive the $50,000 death benefit. If the insured lives beyond that period, nothing is payable because the policy's term has expired. If the insured cancels or lapses the policy during the five-year term, nothing is payable because there are no cash values in term policies.

---

Term life also is called temporary life insurance since it provides protection for a temporary period of time.

The period for which these policies are issued can be defined in terms of years (1-year term, 5-year term, or 20-year term, for example) or in terms of age (term to age 45, term to age 55, term to age 70, for example). Term policies issued for a specified number of years provide coverage from their issue date until the end of the years so specified. Term policies issued until a certain age provide coverage from their date of issue until the insured reaches the specified age.

## BASIC FORMS OF TERM LIFE

Insurers offer a number of forms of term life insurance. These forms, distinguished primarily by the amount of benefit payable, are known generally as *level term*, *decreasing term*, and *increasing term*.

**Level Term Insurance**   Level term insurance provides a level amount of protection for a specified period, after which the policy expires.

---

EXAMPLE        A $100,000 10-year level term policy provides a straight, level $100,000 of coverage for a period of 10 years. A $250,000 term to age 65 policy provides a straight $250,000 of coverage until the insured reaches age 65. If the insured under the $100,000 policy dies at any time within those 10 years, or if the insured under the $250,000 policy dies before age 65, their beneficiaries will receive the policies' face amount benefits.

### FIGURE 3.1   Level Term Insurance

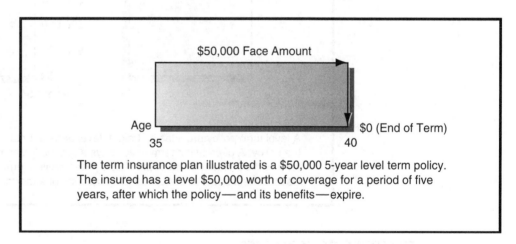

The term insurance plan illustrated is a $50,000 5-year level term policy. The insured has a level $50,000 worth of coverage for a period of five years, after which the policy—and its benefits—expire.

---

If the insureds live beyond the 10-year period or past age 65, the policies expire and no benefits are payable.

**Decreasing Term Insurance**   Decreasing term policies are characterized by benefit amounts that decrease gradually over the term of protection. A 20-year $50,000 decreasing term policy, for example, will pay a death benefit of $50,000 at the beginning of the policy term; that amount gradually declines over the 20-year term and reaches $0 at the end of the term.

Decreasing term insurance is best used when the need for protection declines from year to year. Most decreasing term insurance is sold as mortgage protection insurance.

**EXAMPLE**   A family breadwinner who has a $100,000 30-year mortgage could purchase decreasing term mortgage insurance that would retire the mortgage balance should he or she die during the 30-year mortgage paying period. Credit life insurance, sold to cover the outstanding balance on a loan, also is based on decreasing term.

FIGURE 3.2   Level Term versus Decreasing Term

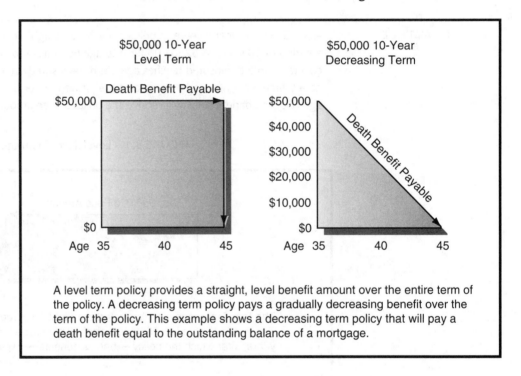

A level term policy provides a straight, level benefit amount over the entire term of the policy. A decreasing term policy pays a gradually decreasing benefit over the term of the policy. This example shows a decreasing term policy that will pay a death benefit equal to the outstanding balance of a mortgage.

## FEATURES OF TERM LIFE

Though term policies are issued for a specified period, defined in terms of years or age, most contain two options that can extend the coverage period, if the policyowner desires. These are the *option to renew* and the *option to convert* the policy.

**Option to Renew**   The option to renew allows the policyowner to renew the term policy before its termination date without having to provide evidence of insurability (that is, without having to prove good health).

**EXAMPLE**  A five-year renewable term policy permits the policyowner to renew the same coverage for another five years at the end of the first five-year term.

The premiums for the renewal period will be higher than the initial period, reflecting the insurer's increased risk (see *Term Life Premiums* later in this unit). Renewal options with most term policies typically provide for several renewal periods or for renewals until a specified age. The advantage of the renewal option is that it allows the insured to continue insurance protection, even if he has become uninsurable.

A common type of renewable term insurance is *annually renewable term* (ART)—also called *yearly renewable term* (YRT). Essentially, this type of policy represents the most basic form of life insurance. It provides coverage for one year and allows the policyowner to renew his coverage each year, without evidence of insurability. Again, most insurers limit the number of times such a policy can be renewed or specify an age limit. However, it is common for ART policies to be renewable to age 65, 70, 75 or beyond.

**Option to Convert**  The second option common to most term plans is the option to convert. The option to convert gives the insured the right to convert or exchange the term policy for a whole life (or permanent) plan without evidence of insurability. This exchange involves the issuance of a whole life policy at a premium rate reflecting the insured's age at either the time of the exchange (the attained age method) or the time when the original term policy was taken out (the original age method).

The option to convert and the option to renew can be (and typically are) combined into a single term policy. For instance, a 10-year convertible renewable policy could provide for renewals until age 65 and be convertible any time before age 55.

## TERM LIFE PREMIUMS

Though a detailed discussion of premiums will be provided later in the book, a simplified introduction is appropriate here. To begin, understand that the amount of premium any insurance plan entails reflects the degree of risk the insurer accepts when it issues a policy. With life insurance, age is a significant risk factor: the higher the age, the more likely is death.

**EXAMPLE**  Consider two males, one age 25, the other age 55. Both make an application to purchase a 10-year $50,000 term policy. Statistically, it's more likely that the 55-year-old man will die within the 10-year period than the 25-year-old; consequently, it's more likely that the insurance company will pay benefits on the older man's policy than the younger man's. Due to this increased risk (and assuming all other factors are equal), the 55-year-old will pay a higher premium for his protection than will the 25-year-old.

Because the probability of death increases with age, premiums also increase gradually with age. At older ages, this increase becomes quite sharp, reflecting the corresponding higher death rates. Few people could afford the premium rates that would be charged at higher ages; therefore, insurance companies offer term insurance plans on a *level-premium basis*—premiums are calculated and charged so that they remain level throughout the policy's term period. If the policy is renewed, the premium is adjusted upward, reflecting a higher rate for the increased age, and will remain level at that amount for the duration of the renewed term.

**FIGURE 3.3   Level Term Premium versus Renewable Term Premium**

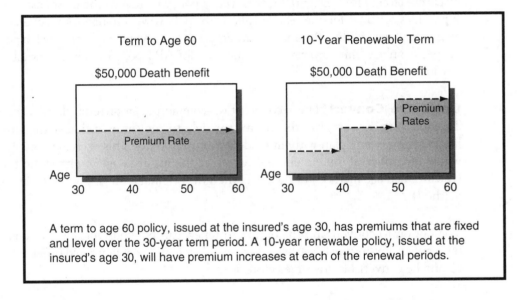

A term to age 60 policy, issued at the insured's age 30, has premiums that are fixed and level over the 30-year term period. A 10-year renewable policy, issued at the insured's age 30, will have premium increases at each of the renewal periods.

# WHOLE LIFE INSURANCE

A second type of life insurance plan is whole life insurance (also known as permanent or cash value insurance). Whole life insurance is so called because it provides permanent protection for the whole of life—from the date of issue to the date of the insured's death—provided premiums are paid. The benefit payable is the face amount of the policy, which remains constant throughout the policy's life. Premiums are set at the time of policy issue and also remain level for the policy's life.

## FEATURES OF WHOLE LIFE

In addition to its permanence, there are certain other features of whole life insurance that distinguish it from term insurance: cash values and maturity at age 100. These two features combine to produce living benefits to the policyowner.

**Cash Value**  Unlike term insurance, which provides only death protection, whole life insurance combines insurance protection with a savings or accumulation element. This accumulation, commonly referred to as the policy's cash value, builds over the life of the policy. This is because whole life insurance plans are credited with a certain guaranteed rate of interest; this interest is credited to the policy regularly and grows over time.

Though it is an important part of funding the policy, the cash value often is regarded as a savings element because it represents the amount of money the policyowner will receive if the policy ever is canceled. It often is called the cash surrender value. This value is a result of the way premiums are calculated and interest is paid, as well as of the policy reserves that build under this system.

The amount of a policy's cash value depends on a variety of factors, including:

■  the face amount of the policy;

■  the duration and amount of the premium payments; and

■  how long the policy has been in force.

Generally, the larger the face amount of the policy, the larger the cash values; the shorter the premium-payment period, the quicker the cash values grow; and the longer the policy has been in force, the greater the build-up in cash values. The reason for these things can be clarified with an understanding of a whole life policy's maturity.

**Maturity at Age 100**  Whole life insurance is designed to mature at age 100. The significance of age 100 is that, as an actuarial assumption, every insured is presumed to be dead by then. (While some people live beyond age 100, the number who do is not statistically significant.) Consequently, the premium rate for whole life insurance is based on the assumption that the insured will be paying premiums for the whole of life, to age 100. At age 100, the cash value of the policy has accumulated to the point that it equals the face amount of the policy, as it was actuarially designed to do. At that point, the policy has completely matured or endowed. No more premiums are owed; the policy is completely paid up.

For those insureds who live to age 100, the insurance company will issue checks for the full value of their policies. At that point, the policy expires; the contract has been completed. Thus, when whole life is defined as a policy that provides a death benefit whenever death occurs, some qualification is required. Whole life insurance provides a death benefit if death occurs before age 100; if the insured has not died by age 100, the full maturity value of the policy is paid out to the insured as a living benefit and the policy terminates. In either event, age 100 defines the point at which the cash value of the policy equals the face amount (or death benefit amount) of the policy. (See Figure 3.4.)

**FIGURE 3.4   Whole Life Insurance**

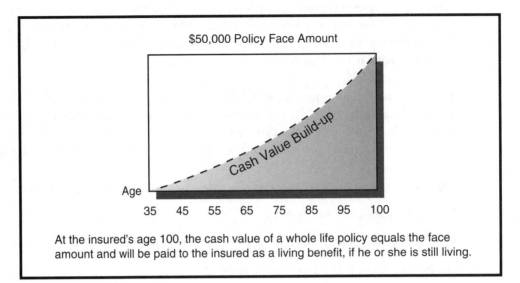

$50,000 Policy Face Amount

Cash Value Build-up

Age

35   45   55   65   75   85   95   100

At the insured's age 100, the cash value of a whole life policy equals the face amount and will be paid to the insured as a living benefit, if he or she is still living.

**Living Benefits**  Another unique feature of whole life insurance is the living benefits it can provide. Through the cash value accumulation build-up in the policy, a policyowner has a ready source of funds that may be borrowed at reasonable rates of interest. These funds may be used for a personal or business emergency, to help pay for a child's education, or to pay off a mortgage. It is not a requirement of the policy that the loan be repaid. However, if a loan is outstanding at the time the insured dies, the amount of the loan plus any interest due will be subtracted from the death benefit before it is paid. Indeed, policy loans are more benefit advances than loans.

In addition, because life insurance is considered property with a quantifiable cash value, it may be used as collateral or security for loans. Also, the policyowner may draw on the cash value to supplement retirement income. Cash values belong to the policyowner. The insurance company cannot lay claim to these values.

## WHOLE LIFE PREMIUMS

As noted, whole life is actuarially designed as if the insured will live to age 100. Accordingly, the premium amount for a whole life policy is calculated, in part, on the basis of the number of years between the insured's age at issue and age 100. This time span represents the full premium-paying period, with the amount of the premium spread equally over that period. This is known as a *level premium basis*. As is the case with level premium term insurance, this approach allows whole life insurance premiums to remain level rather than increase each year with the insured's age. To put it simply, the premium amount is calculated so that in the early years it is more than necessary to meet anticipated claims and expenses and is less than adequate in the later years when the claims likely will be paid. The balanced result is a level amount payable over the entire period.

## BASIC FORMS OF WHOLE LIFE

Just because whole life premiums are calculated as if they were payable to age 100, they do not necessarily have to be paid this way. Whole life is flexible and a number of policy types have been developed to accommodate different premium-paying periods. Three notable forms of whole life plans are *straight whole life*, *limited pay whole life*, and *single-premium whole life*.

**Straight Whole Life** Straight whole life is whole life insurance that provides permanent level protection with level premiums from the time the policy is issued until the insured's  death (or age  100).

**Limited Pay Whole Life** Limited pay whole life policies have level annual premiums that are limited to a certain period (less than life). This period can be of any duration. For example, a 20-pay life policy is one in which premiums are payable for 20 years from the policy's inception, after which no more premiums are owed. A life-paid-up-at-65 policy is one in which the premiums are payable to the insured's age 65, after which no more premiums are owed.

The names of the policies denote how long the premiums are payable.

---

E X A M P L E           A 30-year-old applicant who purchases a life paid-up at 65 policy will pay premiums for 35 years and then have a paid-up policy. If the same applicant buys a 20-pay life policy, he will pay premiums for 20 years and have a paid-up policy at age 50.

Keep in mind that even though the premium payments are limited to a certain period, the insurance protection extends until the insured's death, whenever that may be, or to age 100.

**Single-Premium Whole Life** The most extreme form of limited pay policies is a single-premium policy. A single-premium whole life policy involves a large one-time-only premium payment at the beginning of the policy period. From that point, the policy is completely paid for.

**FIGURE 3.5   Premium Rates per $1,000 of Insurance**

| Issue Age | 1-Year Term | Straight Whole Life | Life Paid-up at 65 | 20-Pay Life |
|---|---|---|---|---|
| 35 | $1.35 | $16.29 | $21.07 | $26.00 |
| 45 | $3.10 | $23.17 | $32.16 | $32.16 |
| 55 | $12.68 | $36.44 | $70.01 | $50.12 |

**Premium Periods** The shorter the premium-paying period, the higher the premium. The same principle applies when a person purchases an item on a credit installment plan—the shorter the payment period, the higher each payment will be. As Figure 3.5 shows, the premium rates at age 35 for a 20-pay life policy are over 1½ times those for a straight life policy, per $1,000 of insurance coverage. This is because the 20-pay life policy has a premium-paying period of 20 years, while the straight life policy assumes a premium-paying period of 65 years, or until age 100.

The length of the premium-paying period also affects the growth of the policy's cash values. The shorter the premium-paying period (and consequently, the higher the premium), the quicker the cash values grow. This is because a greater percentage of each payment is credited to the policy's cash values. By the same token, the longer the premium-paying period, the slower the cash values grow. Figure 3.6 shows how the cash values grow in a 20-pay, a 30-pay, and a straight whole life policy. As this figure also shows, the cash values build up in the limited pay policies faster during

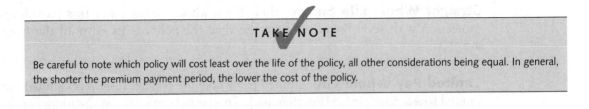

**TAKE NOTE**

Be careful to note which policy will cost least over the life of the policy, all other considerations being equal. In general, the shorter the premium payment period, the lower the cost of the policy.

the premium-paying years than during the non-premium-paying years. After the premium-paying period, the cash values continue to grow, but more slowly, until the policy matures and the cash value equals the face amount, again, at age 100.

FIGURE 3.6   How Cash Values Grow

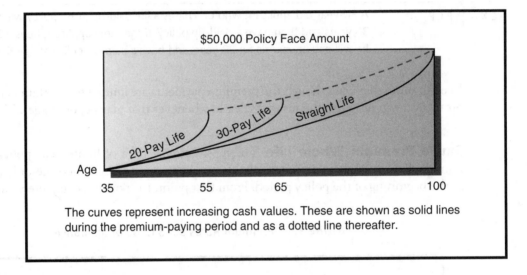

The curves represent increasing cash values. These are shown as solid lines during the premium-paying period and as a dotted line thereafter.

## OTHER FORMS OF WHOLE LIFE

There are many other forms of whole life insurance, most of which are characterized by some variation in the way the premium is paid. Let's review these policies next.

**Modified Whole Life**  Modified whole life policies are distinguished by premiums that are lower than typical whole life premiums during the first few years (usually five) and then higher than typical thereafter. During the initial period, the premium rate is only slightly higher than that of term insurance. Afterward, the premium is higher than the typical whole life rate at age of issue.

**Graded Premium Whole Life**  Similar to modified whole life, graded premium policies also redistribute premiums. Premiums are lower than typical whole life rates during the preliminary period following issue (usually 5 to 10 years) and increase each year until leveling off after the preliminary period. Again, the premium rates are actuarially equivalent to standard whole life.

**T A K E   N O T E**

The purpose of modified whole life policies is to make the initial purchase of permanent insurance easier and more attractive, especially for individuals who have limited financial resources in the present, but the promise of an improved financial position in the future. Actuarially, the premiums are equivalent to standard whole life policies.

## MODIFIED ENDOWMENT CONTRACTS

In 1988, Congress enacted the Technical and Miscellaneous Revenue Act (TAMRA). Among other things, this act revised the tax law definition of a life insurance contract, primarily to discourage the sale and purchase of life insurance for investment purposes or as a tax shelter. By redefining life insurance, Congress effectively created a new class of insurance, known as modified endowment contracts (MECs).

For the producer who sells life insurance and for the consumer who purchases life insurance, the significance of this class of insurance is the way a life policy, if it is deemed an MEC, will be taxed. Historically, life insurance has been granted very favorable tax treatment. Specifically:

- Cash value accumulations are not taxed to the policyowner as they build inside a policy.

- Policy withdrawals are not taxed to the policyowner until the amount withdrawn exceeds the total amount the policyowner paid into the contract.

- Policy loans are not considered distributions and are not taxed to the policyowner unless or until a full policy surrender takes place and then only to the extent that the distribution exceeds what was paid into the policy.

However, for those policies that do not meet the specific test (described below) and consequently are considered MECs, the tax treatment is different,  and it is the policyowners who pay.

If a policy is deemed an MEC and the policyowner receives any amount from it in the form of a loan or withdrawal, that amount will be taxed first as ordinary income and second as return of premium, if there is any gain in the contract over premiums paid. A 10% penalty tax also is imposed on these amounts if they are received before the policyowner's age 59½ and none of the exceptions to the penalty tax apply.

In order to avoid being classified as an MEC, a policy must meet what is known as the *7-pay test*. This test states that if the total amount a policyowner pays into a life contract during its first years exceeds the sum of the net level premiums that would have been payable to provide paid-up future benefits in seven years, the policy is an MEC. And once a policy is classified as an MEC—which it can be at any time during the first seven years—it will remain so throughout its duration.

E X A M P L E

Suppose a policyowner purchased a $100,000 7-year limited pay whole life policy. The scheduled premiums are $7,500 a year, payable for seven years. At the end of that period, the policy will be completely paid up. The first year, the policyowner pays $7,500. The second year, the policyowner pays $8,000. At that point, the policy would become an MEC because the policyowner paid more into the policy than the net level premiums required to provide paid-up benefits in seven years. From that point on, any withdrawals or loans the policyowner takes from that policy will be taxed as income, to the extent there is gain in the policy. Now let's assume that this policyowner paid $7,500 in the first year and $7,000 in the second year. In the third year, he can make an $8,000 payment and not run afoul of the 7-pay test—he still is within the guidelines of the sum of the net level premiums payable. However, if that sum total limit ever is exceeded in those first seven years, the policy will become an MEC.

Making sure that policies meet the definition of life insurance and comply with the 7-pay test is the responsibility of insurers and their actuaries. Agents do not have the time or resources; consumers do not have the knowledge or understanding. However, because the potential for misuse—or even abuse—exists with single-pay, limited pay, and universal life policies, and because consumers may be lured into purchasing insurance for its tax benefits instead of its protection guarantees, producers must be aware of this law and its implications.

# SPECIAL USE POLICIES

In addition to the basic types of life insurance policies—term, whole life, and endowment—there are a number of special use policies insurers offer. Many of these are a combination, or packaging, of different policy types, designed to serve a variety of needs.

## FAMILY PLAN POLICY

The family plan policy is designed to insure all family members under one policy. Coverage is sold in units. A typical plan would insure the family breadwinner for, say, $10,000 or $15,000, the spouse for $3,000 and each child for $1,000. Usually the insurance covering the family head is permanent insurance; that covering the spouse and children is level or decreasing term. These plans generally cover all children currently in the family within certain age limits—for example, older than 14 days and younger than age 21. Children who are born later are covered automatically at no extra premium. The children's coverage usually is convertible without evidence of insurability.

## JOINT LIFE POLICY

A joint life policy is one policy that covers two people. Using some type of permanent insurance (as opposed to term), it pays the death benefit when the first insured dies. The survivor then has the option of purchasing a single individual policy without evidence of insurability. The premium for a joint life policy is less than the premium for two separate policies. The ages of the two insureds are averaged and a single premium is charged for both lives. A variation of the joint life policy is the *last survivor policy*, also known as a *second-to-die policy*. This plan also covers two lives, but the benefit is paid on the death of the second insured. In a last survivor policy, the beneficiary typically is the estate.

## JUVENILE INSURANCE

Insurance written on the lives of children (ordinarily age one day to age 14 or 15 years) is called juvenile insurance. Application for insurance and ownership of the policy rest with an adult such as a parent or guardian. The adult applicant usually is the premium payor as well, until the child comes of age and is able to take over the payments. A payor provision typically is attached to juvenile policies. It provides that, in the event of death or disability of the adult premium payor, the premiums will be waived until the insured child reaches a specified age (such as 25) or until the maturity date of the contract, whichever comes first. A special form of juvenile insurance is the *jumping juvenile* policy. These policies typically are written on children ages 1 to 15 years in units of $1,000, which automatically increase to $5,000—or five times the face amount—at age 21. Although the face amount increases automatically, the premium remains the same and no evidence of insurability is required.

Note that some states limit the amount of life insurance that can be written on a child at an early age. They do so by specifying a maximum that can be in force on a child's life during his early years, such as up to age 5, 10, or 15.

## CREDIT LIFE INSURANCE

Credit life insurance is designed to cover the life of a debtor and pay the amount due on a loan if the debtor dies before the loan is repaid. The type of insurance used is decreasing term, with the term matched to the length of the loan period, though usually limited to 10 years or less, and the decreasing insurance amount matched to the declining loan balance. Credit life sometimes is issued to individuals as single policies, but most often it is sold as Group Credit Life to banks or other lending institutions covering all of the institution's borrowers.

# NONTRADITIONAL LIFE POLICIES

In the 1970s, insurance companies introduced a number of new policy forms, most of which are more flexible in design and provisions than their traditional counterparts. The most notable of these are *adjustable life*, *universal life*, *variable life*, and *variable universal life*.

## ADJUSTABLE LIFE

Adjustable life policies are distinguished by their flexibility, which comes from combining term and permanent insurance concepts into a single plan. The policyowner determines how much face amount protection he needs and how much premium he wants to pay. The insurer then selects the appropriate plan to meet those needs. Or, the policyowner may specify a desired plan and face amount, and the insurer will calculate the appropriate premium. As financial needs and objectives change, the policyowner can make adjustments to his coverage, such as increasing or decreasing the:

■ premium and (or) the premium-paying period; or

■ face amount and (or) the period of protection.

Consequently, depending on the desired changes, the policy can be converted from term to whole life or from whole life to term—from a high premium contract to a lower premium or limited pay contract.

## UNIVERSAL LIFE

Universal life is a variation of whole life insurance, characterized by considerable flexibility. Unlike whole life, with its fixed premiums, fixed face amounts, and fixed cash value accumulations, universal life allows its policyowners to determine the amount and frequency of premium payments and to adjust the policy face amount up or down to reflect changes in needs. Consequently, no new policy need be issued when changes are desired.

Universal life provides this flexibility by unbundling, or separating, the basic components of a life insurance policy—the insurance (protection) element, the savings (accumulation) element, and the expense (loading) element. As with any other life policy, the policyowner pays a premium. Each month, a mortality charge is deducted from the policy's cash value account for the cost of the insurance protection. In addition, an expense, or loading, charge will also be deducted.

As with all insurance policies, the universal life mortality charge increases steadily with age. Actually, universal life technically is defined as term insurance with a policy value fund. Even though the policyowner may pay a level premium, an increasing share of that premium goes to pay the mortality charge as the insured ages.

As premiums are paid and cash values accumulate, interest is credited to the policy's cash value. This interest may be either the current interest rate, declared by the company (and dependent on current market conditions) or the guaranteed minimum rate, specified in the contract. As long as the cash value account is sufficient to pay the monthly mortality and expense costs, the policy will continue in force, whether or not the policyowner pays the premium.

The policyowner can increase or decrease the face amount of the policy, and increases generally require evidence of insurability. A corresponding increase (or decrease) in premium payment is not required, as long as the cash values can cover the mortality and expense costs. By the same token, the policyowner can elect to pay more into the policy, thus adding to the cash value account, subject to certain guidelines that control the relationship between the cash values and the policy's face amount.

Another factor that distinguishes universal life from whole life is the fact that partial withdrawals can be made from the policy's cash value account. (Whole life insurance allows a policyowner to tap cash values only through a policy loan or a complete cash surrender of the policy's cash values, in which case the policy terminates.) Also, the policyowner may surrender the universal life policy for its entire cash value at any time. However, the company probably will assess a surrender charge unless the policy has been in force for a certain number of years.

## UL DEATH BENEFIT OPTIONS

Universal life insurance offers two death benefit options. Under option one, the policyowner may designate a specified amount of insurance. The death benefit equals the cash values plus the remaining pure insurance (decreasing term plus increasing cash values). If the cash values approach the face amount before the policy matures, an additional amount of insurance, called the *corridor*, is maintained in addition to the cash values. (Figure 3.7 illustrates option one.)

Under option two, the death benefit equals the face amount (pure insurance) plus the cash values (level term plus increasing cash values). To comply with the tax code's definition of life insurance, the cash values cannot be disproportionately larger than the term insurance portion. (Figure 3.7 illustrates option two.)

**FIGURE 3.7   Universal Life Death Benefit Options**

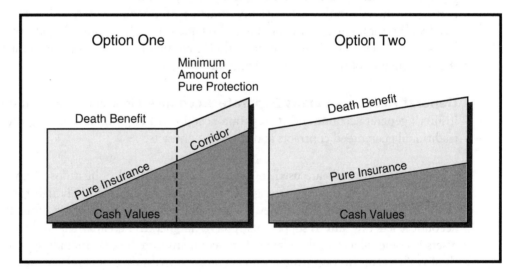

## VARIABLE INSURANCE PRODUCTS

Introduced in the 1970s, variable insurance products added a new dimension to life insurance: the opportunity for policyowners to achieve higher-than usual investment returns on their policy cash values by accepting the risk of the policy's performance. This concept is best explained by a comparison to traditional whole life plans.

Under traditional whole life insurance policies, the insurer guarantees a certain minimum rate of return will be credited to the policies' cash values. This is accomplished because the insurer invests the policyowner's premiums in its general account—an investment account composed of investments carefully selected to match the liabilities and guarantees of the contracts they back. (These investments usually are quite conservative: US government securities and investment-grade bonds are common.) Actually, the premiums paid for life insurance are not, in and of themselves, sufficient to cover the benefits promised in the contract. Rather, they will be sufficient only if the insurer can earn a certain interest rate on the invested values. This makes earnings of crucial importance; the insurer is bound to provide the contractually guaranteed values and benefits whether or not it earns its assumed rate of return. Consequently, with traditional whole life policies, it is the insurer that bears the investment risk. That is why the guaranteed rate of return for traditional whole life policies is quite conservative—typically 3 to 5%.

In contrast, variable insurance products do not guarantee contract values and it is the policyowner who assumes the investment risk. Variable life insurance contracts do not make any promises as to interest rates or minimum cash values. What these products do offer is the potential to realize investment gains that exceed those available with traditional life insurance policies. This is done by allowing policyowners to direct the investment of the funds that back their variable contracts through separate account options. By placing their policy values into separate accounts, policyowners can participate directly in the account's investment performance, which will earn a variable (as opposed to a fixed) return. Functioning on much the same principle as mutual funds, the return enjoyed—or loss suffered—by policyowners through their investment in a separate account is directly related to the performance of the assets underlying the separate account.

**General Accounts versus Separate Accounts** Understanding the distinctions between an insurer's general account and its separate account is key to understanding the difference between traditional guaranteed contracts and variable contracts.

General account assets are used to support the contractual obligations of an insurer's fixed, traditional policies; they represent the general assets of the company. Though they are the foundation of the insurer's policy reserves, they also are subject to the claims of creditors. If an insurer's general account assets ever fail to support its reserve liability, the company is said to be insolvent and the assets become subject to the claims if the company's creditor's—including policyowners. To reduce the likelihood of this occurring, insurers typically invest their general account assets in conservative investment instruments.

Separate accounts are just as their name implies: accounts separate from the insurer's general accounts. Separate accounts are maintained solely for the purpose of allowing policyowners to participate directly in the account's investment performance, and contract values earn a variable, rather than a fixed, return. Also, because they are separate from the insurer's general account, separate accounts are not subject to the claims of the insurer's general creditors. This means that policyowners cannot lose the physical assets underlying their variable contracts in the event of the company's insolvency (though the assets' value can be lost by changes in market conditions). Many consumers today purchase variable contracts for this reason. In addition to being able to participate in this investment performance of the assets underlying their contracts, variable contractholders are assured that their share of those assets never will be compromised, even in the event of company insolvency.

Because of the transfer of investment risk from the insurer to the policyowner, variable insurance products are considered securities contracts as well as insurance contracts. Therefore, they fall under the regulation of both state insurance departments and the Securities and Exchange Commission (SEC). To sell variable insurance products, an individual must hold a life insurance license and a National Association of Securities Dealers (NASD) registered representative's license. Some states also may require a special variable insurance license or special addendum to the regular life insurance license.

Because variable insurance policies are securities, full and fair disclosure must be provided to the prospective policyowner. Therefore, by law, a variable insurance sales presentation cannot be conducted unless it is preceded or accompanied by a prospectus, prepared and furnished by the insurance company and reviewed by the SEC. Also, all other materials used in selling and promoting variable insurance products—direct mail letters, brochures, advertising pieces, and the like—must also have prior approval of the SEC. These requirements provide consumer protection and promote meaningful communication between agents and consumers.

With this introduction in mind, let's look at two types of variable insurance products: *variable life insurance* and *variable universal life insurance*. Keep in mind that while these policies involve investment management and offer the potential for investment gains, they primarily are life insurance policies, not investment contracts. The primary purpose of these plans, like any life insurance plan, is to provide financial protection in the event of the insured's death.

**Variable Life Insurance** Variable life insurance is permanent life insurance with many of the same characteristics of traditional whole life insurance. The main difference, as explained previously, is the manner in which the policy's cash values are invested. With traditional whole life, these values are kept in the insurer's general accounts and invested in conservative investments selected by the insurer to match its contractual guarantees and liabilities. With variable life insurance policies, the policy values are invested in the insurer's separate accounts, which house common stock, bond, money-market, and other securities investment options. Values held in these separate accounts are invested in riskier, but potentially higher-yielding, assets than those held in the general account.

As with any permanent insurance product, the growth of the policy's cash values support the death benefit. In traditional whole life products, that benefit is fixed and guaranteed; with variable life insurance, the benefit rises (and falls) in relation to the performance of the policy's values. There is a minimum guaranteed death benefit; this is equal to the face amount at policy issue and is based on an assumed rate of return, usually 3 to 4%. However, if the separate account growth (and by extension, the cash value growth) exceeds this assumed rate, the result is an elevated death benefit.

Figure 3.8 shows the effect over time of increases—and decreases—in a variable life insurance policy's separate account rate of return. Each year that the actual return exceeds the assumed rate of return (shown in this example as 4%), there is a positive net investment return and the death benefit is increased. In years where the actual return or growth is less than assumed, the death benefit is decreased from any previously attained levels. Note, however, that the death benefit never will drop below the face amount guaranteed at policy issue.

**FIGURE 3.8   Variable Life Death Benefit**

The following graph shows how the investment performance of a variable life insurance policy's values affect the death benefit. Here, the assumed rate of return is 4 percent. If the net investment results were equal to 4 percent throughout the life of the policy, the death benefit would remain the same—that is, the face amount of the policy at issue. However, as is more likely, the actual investment results will vary. A return greater than 4 percent produces a rise in the death benefit; a return less than 4 percent produces a drop in the death benefit from the previous year.

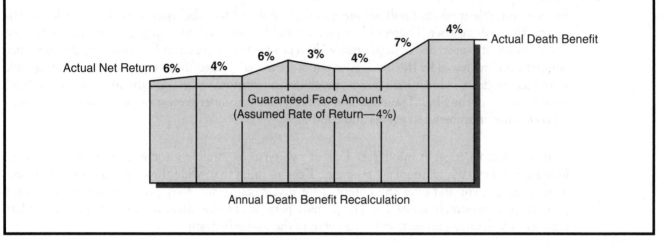

Variable life insurance policyowners can access their policy values through policy loans. However, the amount of the loan is limited—usually 75 to 80% of the cash value. (Compare this to conventional whole life policies, which typically permit loans up to 100 percent of the cash value.) The reason for this restriction is to reduce the possibility that falling returns will cause an outstanding policy loan to become greater than the policy's cash value.

**Variable Universal Life**   Variable universal life (VUL) blends many features of whole life, universal life, and variable life. Premium flexibility, cash value investment control, and death benefit flexibility are key among these features. These features give VUL its unique characteristics and make it responsive to policyowners' needs.

Cash value in a VUL plan is maintained separately from the rest of the plan. At the time of application, the policyowner elects to have his net premiums and cash values allocated to one or more separate account investment options. These accounts usually are mutual funds created and maintained by the insurance company or provided through arrangements between the insurance company and other investment companies. These funds are kept in separate accounts and function independently of the insurance company's assets. Earnings or losses accrue directly to the policyowner's cash value, subject to stated charges and management fees. Policyowners can redirect future premiums and switch accounts periodically, generally once a year, without charge. The result is a life insurance policy that provides policyowners with self-directed investment options.

VUL policies generally offer both a level death benefit or a variable death benefit. Under the level death benefit, the policyowner specifies the total death benefit in the policy. This amount remains constant and does not fluctuate as cash values increase or decrease. Instead, cash values build up within the policy until they reach the corridor, at which time the death benefit will increase to corresponding increases in the cash value. Until that point is reached, however, the cash value simply accumulates, with each increase replacing a corresponding amount of pure insurance needed to keep the death benefit at the specified amount. Under the variable death benefit, the policyowner selects a specified amount of pure insurance coverage. This specified amount remains constant. The death benefit payable at any time is a combination of the specified (or face) amount and the cash value within the policy. Essentially, the cash value is added to the specified amount to create the total death benefit. Under this option, the emphasis is on the potential for both cash value and death benefit growth. This option often is recommended for policyowners who want favorable investment results and additional premiums reflected directly in increased death benefits.

**Loan or Withdrawal?** Partial cash value distributions may be classified as loans or withdrawals; which of the two is chosen depends on several factors.

A loan is just that—the policyowner borrows money from the insurance company, and the insurance company uses the cash value as collateral for the loan. It is withdrawn with the presumption that it will be repaid (with accrued interest). If the loan is not repaid, the amount of future benefits—including the death benefit—will be reduced by the loaned amount (plus accrued interest).

The withdrawl is treated as a permanent withdrawal, thus immediately reducing the death benefit and, of course, the cash value. The withdrawn amount does not accrue interest against future policy values, as it does with a loan.

Generally, only universal life and variable universal life policies, with their inherent policy flexibility, permit withdrawals. Traditional whole life and variable life do not lend themselves to this type of flexibility and, though there may be a few exceptions, they typically provide only for loans.

Cash value withdrawals (as opposed to loans) are recognized as taxable income to the extent they exceed the policyowner's cost basis in the contract. Withdrawals are not taxable up to the owner's basis; withdrawn amounts above basis are taxable.

Like universal life, VUL policies permit partial withdrawals, allowing the owner to tap the cash value without incurring any indebtedness. Policyowners need not repay those funds and no interest is incurred on the amount withdrawn. Withdrawals, of course, affect the policy's future earnings, and their effect on the death benefit depends on the death benefit option in force. Partial withdrawals taken in a policy's early years may be subject to surrender charges (when the insurer is trying to recover the costs of issuing the policy).

# SUMMARY

Today's life insurers offer a vast array of life insurance plans, which are designed to serve various functions and meet different needs. Term insurance, the simplest type of plan, provides pure protection only, for a specified temporary period or term. At the end of the term, the protection expires. If a policyowner desires, he can extend the coverage through two options: the option to renew the term policy for another term and (or) the option to convert the term policy to a whole life, or permanent, plan.

Whole life insurance provides protection for the whole of life and pays a death benefit if the insured dies at any time before age 100. Whole life insurance is characterized by cash values that accumulate over time, eventually reaching a level equal to the policy's face amount at the insured's age 100. At that point, the policy has matured or endowed. Premiums for whole life insurance are level throughout the policy's period and are calculated as though the insured were to pay them until age 100. A large percentage of whole life policies, known as straight life policies, are purchased on this basis. However, if a policyowner desires, the premium-paying period can be limited to a certain age or for a specified number of years; these policies are known as limited pay life policies. The most extreme example of limited pay life is single-premium whole life. Other types of whole life plans—such as modified whole life, graded premium whole life—also provide permanent protection but vary the way in which premiums are paid.

Various special use plans, which combine features of term and whole life into single policies, are available to fit different needs. These include family policies, joint life policies, juvenile insurance, and credit life insurance.

Finally, a number of newer, nontraditional life policies have been introduced over the past decade or so. These policies are characterized in part by increased flexibility and current market returns. Most notable of these newer policy forms are adjustable life, universal life, variable life, and variable universal life.

# UNIT QUIZ

1. Which of the following statements regarding term life insurance is NOT correct?

   A. A three-year renewable policy allows a term policyowner to renew the same coverage for another three years.

   B. A three-year renewable policy allows a term policyowner to increase coverage for the next three years.

   C. An option to convert provides that a term life insurance policy can be exchanged for a permanent one.

   D. Both the option to renew and the option to convert relieve the insured from furnishing evidence of insurability.

2. Which of the following statements describing whole life insurance is NOT correct?

   A. The face amount of the policy stays the same as long as the policy remains in force.

   B. The shorter a premium period is, the faster the cash value will grow.

   C. The policy's cash value decreases each year the policy is in force.

   D. Whole life insurance is designed to mature at age 100.

3. The cash values of life insurance policies belong to which of the following entities?

   A. Policyowner

   B. Insured

   C. Insurer

   D. Beneficiary

4. Which of the following statements regarding basic forms of whole life insurance is NOT correct?

   A. Generally, straight life premiums are payable, at least annually, for the duration of the insured's life.

   B. The owner of a 30-pay life policy will owe no more premiums after the 30th year the policy is in force.

   C. Limited payment life provides protection only for the years during which premiums are paid.

   D. A single-premium life policy is purchased with a large one-time-only premium.

5. Which of the following statements regarding modified endowment contracts (MECs) is CORRECT?

   A. A 1988 revenue act, commonly known as TAMRA, greatly increased the popularity of MECs.

   B. Congress has granted the MEC the most favorable tax status among all life insurance policies.

   C. To avoid being classified as an MEC, a life insurance policy must satisfy the 7-pay test.

   D. According to the 7-pay test, if the total amount a policyowner pays into a life contract during its first seven years is less than the sum of the net level premiums that would have been payable to provide paid-up future benefits in seven years, the policy is an MEC.

6. What type of policy would be the best choice to insure the declining balance on a home mortgage?

   A. Level term

   B. Decreasing term

   C. Whole life

   D. Universal life

7. An insured purchases a $50,000 5-year level term policy. Which of the following statements about this coverage is NOT correct?

   A. The policy provides a straight, level $50,000 of coverage for five years.

   B. If the insured dies at any time during the five years, the beneficiary will receive the policy's face value.

   C. If the insured dies after the specified five years, only the policy's cash value will be paid.

   D. If the insured lives beyond the five years, the policy expires and no benefits are payable.

8. Which of the following is a policy covering two lives that only pays a death benefit when the second insured person dies?

   A. Joint life

   B. Family

   C. Family maintenance

   D. Joint and last survivor

9. Jane, age 35, has just purchased a 20-pay whole life policy. When she turns 55, she will

   A. receive the policy's face amount benefit
   B. have a fully matured policy
   C. cease paying premiums
   D. no longer be covered by the policy

10. At what point does a whole life policy mature or endow?

   A. When the policy's cash value equals the face amount
   B. When premiums paid equal the policy's face amount
   C. When premiums paid equal the policy's cash value
   D. When the policy's cash value equals the loan amount

11. If four individuals, all age 30, purchase the following life insurance policies, and all policies are still in force 10 years later, who will have the largest cash value in his policy?

| | |
|---|---|
| Bob | $100,000 straight whole life |
| Dennis | $100,000 life paid-up at 65 |
| Ralph | $100,000 20-pay life |
| Jack | $100,000 life paid-up at 55 |

   A. Bob
   B. Dennis
   C. Ralph
   D. Jack

# ANSWERS AND RATIONALES TO UNIT QUIZ

1. **B.** An option to renew allows the policyowner to renew the same coverage before the policy's termination date, without having to show evidence of insurability. A three-year renewable policy, therefore, would allow a term policyowner to renew the same coverage for another three years.

2. **C.** The shorter the premium-paying period (and consequently, the higher the premium), the faster the cash values grow in a whole life insurance policy. This is because a greater percentage of each payment is credited to the policy's cash values.

3. **A.** Ownership of a policy's cash value rests solely with the policyowner. A policy's cash value is nonforfeitable; that is, policyowners are assured that they are fully entitled to the accrued cash values of their policies.

4. **C.** Even though premium payments are limited to a certain period, the insurance protection under a limited pay whole life policy extends until the insured's death, or to age 100.

5. **C.** To avoid being classified as a modified endowment contract, a life insurance policy must meet the 7-pay test. According to this test, if the total amount a policyowner pays into a life contract during its first year exceeds the sum of the net level premiums that would have been payable to provide paid-up future benefits in seven years, the policy is an MEC.

6. **B.** Decreasing term insurance is best suited for an individual whose need for protection declines from year to year. It therefore would be a good choice to insure the declining balance on a home mortgage.

7. **C.** If the insured dies after the end of the five-year period, the beneficiary will receive nothing. A term life policy has no cash value.

8. **D.** Under a joint and last survivor policy, two lives are covered but the benefit is paid only on the death of the second insured.

9. **C.** Limited pay whole life policies have level premiums that are limited to a certain period (less than life), after which no more premiums are owed.

10. **A.** Whole life insurance is designed to mature at age 100. At age 100, the cash value of the policy has accumulated to the point that it equals the face amount of the policy, as it was actuarially designed to do. At that point the policy has completely matured or endowed. No more premiums are owed; the policy is completely paid up.

11. **C.** The larger the face amount of the policy, the larger the cash values; the shorter the premium-payment period, the quicker the cash values grow; and the longer the policy has been in force, the greater the build-up in cash values.

# 4

# Life Insurance Policy Provisions, Options, and Riders

### KEY CONCEPTS

- The rights of policyowners
- Standard life insurance provisions
- Nonforfeiture values and options
- Life insurance dividends and dividend options
- Common life insurance riders

Life insurance is property, and policyowners have important rights, as well as responsibilities, inherent in the ownership of this special type of property. Although no standard policy form must be used in life insurance, states have enacted strict guidelines as to what must and must not be included in a policy. As a result, all life insurance policies contain certain standardized policy provisions that identify the rights and obligations of the policyowner and the insurer. Of course, life insurance can be customized to meet the specific needs of the owner through policy riders and options. In this unit, we will examine the standard provisions found in most life insurance contracts as well as some of the common riders and options that can be added to give a life insurance contract its form and flexibility.

## OBJECTIVE

When you complete this unit you should be able to:

■ list and describe the standard provisions in a life insurance policy;

■ describe the most common types of policy exclusions;

■ compare and contrast the three nonforfeiture options—cash surrender, reduced paid-up insurance, and extended term insurance;

■ explain the different options policyowners have for receiving dividends; and

■ list and describe the different types of policy riders.

# RIGHTS OF POLICY OWNERSHIP

Before we discuss specific policy provisions, it is important to mention the rights of ownership that policyowners have. Although there are no provisions in a life insurance policy specifically titled Rights of Ownership, the fact is, owning a life insurance policy does involve important rights. These rights are woven throughout the policy in various clauses and provisions. The most significant rights of ownership include the right to:

■ designate and change the beneficiary of the policy proceeds;

■ select how the death proceeds will be paid to the beneficiary;

■ cancel the policy and select a nonforfeiture option;

■ take out a policy loan, assuming the policy is a whole life or other permanent plan and a cash value exists;

■ receive policy dividends and select a dividend payment option, if it is a participating policy; and

■ assign ownership of the policy to someone else.

The clauses and provisions that set forth these rights will be examined in this and later lessons.

# STANDARD POLICY PROVISIONS

Despite insurance companies' efforts to offer products distinctive from their competitors', insurance policies are more notable for their many similarities than differences. This high degree of uniformity is rooted in the state-level regulation of the industry and the adoption of National Association of Insurance Commissioners (NAIC) guidelines.

We will begin this section with a discussion of the standard provisions that appear in most life insurance contracts, then take a look at some of the common exclusions.

## ENTIRE CONTRACT PROVISION

The entire contract provision, found at the beginning of the policy, states that the policy document, the application (which is attached to the policy), and any attached riders constitute the entire contract. Nothing may be incorporated by reference, meaning that the policy cannot refer to any outside documents as being part of the contract.

---

 E X A M P L E        An insurance company could not claim that a special rider, not attached to the policy but on file in the home office, is part of the policy.

---

The entire contract clause has another important function—it prohibits the insurer from making any changes to the policy, either through policy revisions or changes in the company's bylaws, after the policy has been issued.

## INSURING CLAUSE

The insuring clause, or provision, sets forth the company's basic promise to pay benefits on the insured's death. Generally, this clause is not actually titled as such, but appears on the cover of the policy.

---

 E X A M P L E        A typical insuring clause reads:

The Insurance Company agrees, in accordance with the provisions of this policy, to pay to the beneficiary the death proceeds upon receipt at the Principal Office of due proof of the insured's death prior to the maturity date.

Further, the Company agrees to pay the surrender value to the owner if the insured is alive on the maturity date.

---

## FREE-LOOK PROVISION

The free-look provision, required by most states, gives policyowners the right to return the policy for a full premium refund within a specified period of time, if they decide not to purchase the insurance. Most policies provide for a 10-day free-look period.

**TAKE NOTE**

It is important to note that the free-look period begins when the policy document actually is received by the policyowner, not when the application is signed or when the policy is issued by the insurance company.

**TAKE NOTE**

If an insured dies during the grace period and the premium has not been paid, the policy benefit is payable. However, the premium amount due is deducted from the benefits paid to the beneficiary.

## CONSIDERATION CLAUSE

As we learned in Unit 1, consideration is the value given in exchange for a contractual promise. The consideration clause, or provision, in a life insurance policy specifies the amount and frequency of premium payments that the policyowners must make to keep the insurance in force. Often, the amount and frequency of required premiums are listed on the Schedule or Specifications page. A separate page will provide details on the manner in which premiums must be paid (as well as the consequences of not making a premium payment).

## GRACE PERIOD PROVISION

The grace period provision undoubtedly has saved many life insurance policies from lapsing. If policyowners forget or neglect to pay their premiums by the date they are due, the grace period allows an extra 31 days or one month (possibly less for some industrial policies) during which premiums may be paid to keep policies in force.

## REINSTATEMENT PROVISION

It always is possible that, due to nonpayment of premiums, a policy may lapse, either deliberately or unintentionally. In cases where a policyowner wishes to reinstate a lapsed policy, the reinstatement provision allows him to do so, with some limitations. With reinstatement, a policy is restored to its original status and its values are brought up to date.

Most insurers require the following to reinstate a lapsed policy:

■ all back premiums must be paid;

■ interest on past-due premiums may be assessed;

■ any outstanding loans on the lapsed policy may be required to be paid; and

■ the policyowner may be asked to prove insurability.

In addition, there is a limited period of time in which policies may be reinstated after lapse. This period usually is three years but may be as long as seven years in some cases. A new contestable period usually goes into effect with a reinstated policy, but there is no new suicide exclusion period. (See *Incontestable Clause and Suicide Provision* in this unit.)

## POLICY LOAN PROVISION

State insurance laws require that cash value life insurance policies include a policy loan provision. This means that, within prescribed limits, policyowners may borrow money from the cash values of their policies if they wish to do so.

These loans may not be called by the company and can be repaid at any time by the policyowners. If not repaid by the time the insured dies, the loan balance and any interest accrued are deducted from the policy proceeds at the time of claim. If the policy is surrendered for cash, the cash value available to the policyowner is reduced by the amount of any outstanding loan plus interest.

Loan values and cash surrender values are shown as identical amounts in a policy and often are listed under the single column heading of Cash or Loan Value. (See Figure 4.1.)

### FIGURE 4.1   Table of Guaranteed Values

Face Amount: $100,000                Annual Premium: $2,000

| End of Policy Year | Cash or Loan Value | Reduced Paid-up | Extended Term Years | Extended Term Days |
|---|---|---|---|---|
| 1 | $0 | $0 | 0 | 0 |
| 2 | $50 | $210 | 0 | 66 |
| 3 | $960 | $3,600 | 2 | 290 |
| 4 | $2,150 | $7,250 | 6 | 9 |
| 5 | $4,000 | $12,000 | 8 | 111 |
| 6 | $5,975 | $16,110 | 10 | 147 |
| 7 | $7,210 | $19,880 | 12 | 22 |
| 8 | $9,340 | $23,800 | 14 | 18 |
| 9 | $11,415 | $27,620 | 15 | 312 |
| 10 | $13,005 | $30,990 | 16 | 362 |
| 11 | $14,770 | $34,010 | 17 | 202 |
| 12 | $16,785 | $37,880 | 18 | 116 |
| 13 | $19,430 | $40,940 | 18 | 1 |
| 14 | $23,000 | $43,985 | 17 | 144 |
| 15 | $26,990 | $47,010 | 16 | 302 |
| 16 | $30,215 | $50,600 | 15 | 347 |
| 17 | $34,600 | $53,815 | 15 | 88 |
| 18 | $38,910 | $56,910 | 14 | 117 |
| 19 | $43,020 | $60,010 | 13 | 361 |
| 20 | $47,910 | $63,715 | 13 | 47 |
| Age 65 | $56,770 | $78,700 | 11 | 36 |

This table shows how the guaranteed (nonforfeitable) values are presented in a life insurance policy. These figures reflect the values available to the policyowner at different points in the policy's life for purposes of surrendering the policy for cash, taking out a loan against the policy, purchasing a reduced paid-up policy or purchasing an extended term policy. (See also the sample policy in the Appendix.)

## INCONTESTABLE CLAUSE

The incontestable clause, or provision, provides that after a specified period of time (usually two years from the issue date and while the insured is living), the insurer no longer has the right to contest the validity of the life insurance policy so long as the contract continues in force. This means that after the policy has been in force for the specified term, the company cannot contest a death claim or refuse payment of the proceeds even on the basis of a material misstatement, concealment, or fraud. Even if the insurer learns that an error was deliberately made on the application, it must pay the death benefit at the insured's death if the policy has passed the contestable period.

The incontestable clause applies to the policy face amount, plus any additional death benefit added by rider that is payable in the case of normal death.

It should be noted that there are three situations to which the incontestable clause does not apply. A policy issued under any of these circumstances is not a valid contract, and gives the insurer the right to contest and possibly void the policy at any time:

■ *Impersonation.* When application for insurance is made by one person but another person signs the application or takes the medical exam, the insurer can contest the policy and its claim.

■ *No insurable interest.* If no insurable interest existed between the applicant and the insured at the inception of the policy, the contract is not valid to begin with; as such, the insurer can contest the policy at any time.

■ *Intent to murder.* If it is subsequently proven that the applicant applied for the policy with the intent of murdering the insured for the proceeds, the insurance company can contest the policy and its claim.

## ASSIGNMENT PROVISION

People who purchase life insurance policies commonly are referred to as policyowners rather than policyholders because they actually own their policies and may do with them as they wish. They can even give them away, just as they can give away any other kind of property they own. This transfer of ownership is known as assignment.

The assignment provision in a life insurance contract sets forth the procedure necessary for ownership transfer. This procedure usually requires that the policyowner notify the company in writing of the assignment. The company then will accept the validity of the transfer without question. A policyowner need not have the insurer's permission to assign a policy. The new owner is known as the *assignee*.

---

 **E X A M P L E**      If an individual gave a policy to his church as a don ation, the church would be the assignee. An insurable interest need not exist between the insured and the assignee.

As the owner of the policy, the assignee is granted all the rights of policy ownership, including the right to name a beneficiary. If the assignee does not change the beneficiary designation, the proceeds will be paid to the beneficiary named by the original owner.

**TAKE NOTE**

The assignee has the right to change the beneficiary as long as the original beneficiary designation was revocable. If a policyowner names an irrevocable beneficiary (meaning the beneficiary cannot be changed), he must get the beneficiary's agreement to any assignment.

Within the guidelines set forth for assignments in any given policy, a policyowner generally has two options. Under the first, *absolute assignment*, the transfer is complete and irrevocable, and the assignee receives full control over the policy and full rights to its benefits. Under the second, *collateral assignment*, the policy is assigned to a creditor as security, or collateral, for a debt. If the insured dies, the creditor is entitled to be reimbursed out of the benefit proceeds for the amount owed. The insured's beneficiary then is entitled to any excess of policy proceeds over the amount due the creditor. Once the debt is repaid, the policyowner is entitled to the return of the rights assigned.

## ACCELERATED BENEFITS PROVISION

Accelerated benefits provisions are standard in life insurance policies. They provide for the early payment of some portion of the policy face amount should the insured suffer from a terminal illness or injury. The death benefit, less the accelerated payment, still is payable.

EXAMPLE    A $250,000 policy that provides for a 75% accelerated benefit would pay up to $187,500 to the terminally ill insured, with the remaining $62,500 payable as a death benefit to the beneficiary when the insured dies. An accelerated payment can be made in a lump sum or in monthly installments over a special period, such as one year.

This provision is provided at no increase in premium. Some companies deduct an interest charge from the proceeds paid out to make up for what the company would have earned had the money not been withdrawn from the contract.

## SUICIDE PROVISION

The suicide provision, found in most life policies, protects the company and its policyowners against the possibility that a person might buy an insurance policy and deliberately commit suicide to provide a sum of money for the beneficiary. With this provision, a life insurance policy discourages suicide by stipulating a period of time (usually one or two years from the date of policy issue) during which the death benefit will not be paid if the insured commits suicide. If that happens, however, the premiums paid for the policy will be refunded.

Of course, if an insured takes his own life after the policy has been in force for the period specified in the suicide clause, the company will pay the entire proceeds, just as if death were from a natural cause.

## MISSTATEMENT OF AGE OR GENDER PROVISION

The misstatement of age or gender provision is important because the age and gender of the applicant are critical factors in establishing the premium rate for a life insurance policy. To guard against a misunderstanding about the applicant's age, the company reserves the right to make an adjustment at any time. Likewise, an adjustment is made if an applicant's gender is incorrectly indicated in a policy because, age for age, premium rates for females generally are lower than for males. Normally, such adjustments are made either in the premium charged or in the amount of insurance.

Assume an error in age is discovered after the death of an insured. If the insured was younger than the policy showed, excess premiums would be refunded. On the other hand, if the insured was older than the policy indicated, the amount of benefits would be decreased to whatever the premium paid would have purchased at the correct age.

If an error is discovered while the insured is living, the premium will be adjusted downward if the insured is younger than the policy shows and a refund of the premium overpayments will be made. By the same token, if the insured is older than the policy indicates, the company will reduce the amount of insurance to what it should be for the amount of premium being paid.

## AUTOMATIC PREMIUM LOAN PROVISION

A provision that is now commonly added to most cash value policies is the automatic premium loan. This provision authorizes the insurer to withdraw from the policy's cash value the amount of premium due if the premium has not been paid by the end of the grace period. The amount withdrawn becomes a loan against the cash value, bearing the rate of interest specified in the contract.

Depending on the insurer, this provision may be standard to the contract or added as a rider, with no additional charge to the policyowner.

Note that this provision may be very beneficial for a policyowner who forgets to pay the premium within the grace period or who cannot pay the current premium because of financial difficulties. Most importantly, the policy does not lapse and coverage continues.

If the policyowner allows the automatic premium loan to continually pay the premiums, of course, the policy eventually will lapse when the cash value is reduced to nothing. The owner then would have to reinstate the policy and pay back the loans.

# POLICY EXCLUSIONS

Most life insurance policies contain restrictions that exclude from coverage certain types of risks from coverage. If no exclusions existed, premium rates would be much higher. Exclusions can be stated in the policy itself or attached as riders. The most common types of exclusions include:

■ *War.* This exclusion provides that the death benefit will not be paid if the insured dies as a direct result of war.

■ *Aviation.* This exclusion commonly is found in older policies; very few policies issued today exclude death as a result of commercial aviation. However, some insurers will exclude aviation deaths for other than fare-paying passengers.

■ *Hazardous occupations or hobbies.* Individuals who have hazardous occupations, such as stunt people, or who engage in hazardous hobbies, such as auto racing, may find that their life insurance policies exclude death as a result of their occupation or hobby. Or, these risks may be covered, but an increased, or rated, premium will be charged.

■ *Commission of a felony.* Some contracts will exclude death when it results from the insured committing a felony.

■ *Suicide.* As previously noted, almost all policies exclude payment of the benefit if the insured commits suicide during the specified time period. After that period passes, death by suicide is covered.

# NONFORFEITURE VALUES AND OPTIONS

Earlier we learned that an important feature of whole life insurance is its cash value, which is created in part by the level premium funding method. As a policy matures, cash values grow until, when the policy endows, the cash value equals the face amount of the policy. Though the cash value is an important part of the underlying funding of the policy, the policyowner is entitled to receive the accrued cash value at any time. When a policy is active, the owner can borrow from the cash value. If a policy is lapsed or surrendered, the owner is entitled to the cash surrender value.

The term *nonforfeiture value* refers to the fact that a policy's cash value is not forfeitable. Nonforfeiture options are the ways in which cash values can be paid out to or used by policyowners, if they choose to lapse or surrender their policies.

### NONFORFEITURE OPTIONS

There are three nonforfeiture options from which policyowners can select: *cash surrender, reduced paid-up insurance,* and *extended term insurance.*

**Cash Surrender Option**  If they desire, policyowners may request an immediate cash payment of their cash values when their policies are surrendered. A table of cash surrender values is included in every permanent life insurance policy, as illustrated in Figure 4.1, under the heading Cash or Loan Value. The amount of cash value the policyowner receives is reduced by any outstanding policy indebtedness.

**Reduced Paid-Up Option** A second nonforfeiture option is to take a paid-up policy for a reduced face amount of insurance. By doing this, the policyowner does not pay any more premiums but still retains some amount of life insurance. In essence, the cash value is used as the premium for a single-premium whole life policy, at a lesser face amount than the original policy.

When this option is exercised, the paid-up policy is the same kind as the original, but for a lesser amount of coverage. (See Figure 4.2.)

### FIGURE 4.2    Reduced Paid-up Option

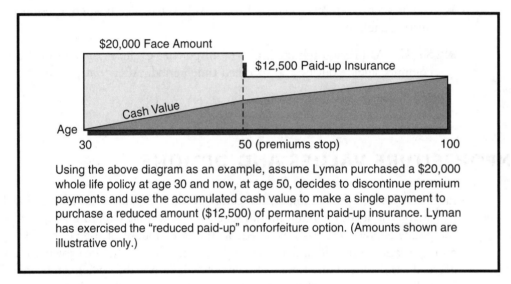

Using the above diagram as an example, assume Lyman purchased a $20,000 whole life policy at age 30 and now, at age 50, decides to discontinue premium payments and use the accumulated cash value to make a single payment to purchase a reduced amount ($12,500) of permanent paid-up insurance. Lyman has exercised the "reduced paid-up" nonforfeiture option. (Amounts shown are illustrative only.)

**Extended Term Option** The third nonforfeiture option is to use the policy's cash value to purchase a term insurance policy in an amount equal to the original policy's face value, for as long a period as the cash value will purchase. When the term insurance expires, no more protection exists. Moreover, all supplemental benefits included with the original policy, such as a term rider or accidental death or disability benefits, are dropped. (See Figure 4.3.)

## POLICY DIVIDENDS

As noted previously, life insurance policies may be either participating or nonparticipating, and it is important to distinguish between the two to understand the source of policy dividends. At any given age, people who buy participating (par) policies normally pay premiums that are slightly higher than premiums paid by those who purchase nonparticipating (nonpar) policies. This is because an extra charge to cover unexpected contingencies is built into premiums for par policies.

At the end of each year, the insurance company analyzes its operations. If fewer insureds have died than was estimated, a *divisible surplus* results and the company can return to the policyowners a part

## FIGURE 4.3   Extended Term Option

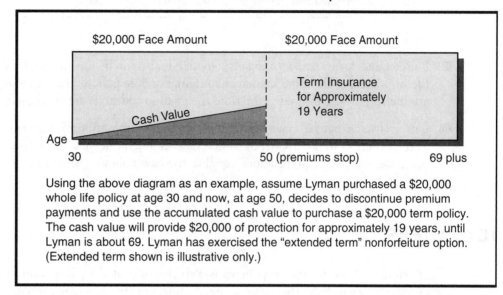

$20,000 Face Amount             $20,000 Face Amount

Cash Value

Term Insurance
for Approximately
19 Years

Age

30                         50 (premiums stop)              69 plus

Using the above diagram as an example, assume Lyman purchased a $20,000 whole life policy at age 30 and now, at age 50, decides to discontinue premium payments and use the accumulated cash value to purchase a $20,000 term policy. The cash value will provide $20,000 of protection for approximately 19 years, until Lyman is about 69. Lyman has exercised the "extended term" nonforfeiture option. (Extended term shown is illustrative only.)

of the premiums paid for participating policies. A company also can issue returns stemming from positive operating or investment income. These payments are called dividends but should not be confused with the dividends paid on stocks.

Because the payment of policy dividends hinges on several unexpected contingencies that will affect the amount of the dividend, policy dividends normally will vary from year to year and cannot be guaranteed.

Thus, when an insurance company gives a policy illustration that includes dividends, it is purely an estimate or approximation of what future dividends might be. To protect life insurance buyers against the misuse of dividend illustrations, most states require life insurance proposals containing a dividend illustration to state clearly that future dividends are not guaranteed.

## DIVIDEND OPTIONS

Policyowners generally are permitted by insurers to utilize their dividends through one of five options:

■ *Take dividends in cash.* When dividends become payable, they usually are paid on policy anniversary dates. Policyowners who elect to take their dividends in cash automatically receive their dividend check after the company approves a dividend.

■ *Apply dividends against premium payments.* Dividends also can be applied directly to the policyowner's premium payments, lowering the owner's out-of-pocket expense.

■ *Allow dividends to accumulate at interest.* A third option is to leave the dividends with the company to accumulate with interest, for withdrawal at any time. Note that while policy dividends are not taxable, any interest paid on them is taxable income in the year the interest is credited to the policy, whether or not it actually is received by the policyowner.

Insurance policy dividends really are a return of part of the premiums paid. As such, policy dividends are not taxable income, unlike corporate dividends, which are reportable for income tax purposes.

■ *Use dividends to buy paid-up additions*. Dividends also can be used to purchase paid-up additions of life insurance, of the same kind as the original or base policy. The premium rate is based on the attained age of the insured at the time the paid-up additions are purchased.

■ *Use dividends to purchase one-year term insurance*. A fifth option, though not utilized as frequently as the others, is to use dividends to purchase as much one-year term insurance as possible or to purchase one-year term insurance equal to the base policy's cash value.

# POLICY RIDERS

The flexibility of life insurance policies is well demonstrated by the ability policyowners have to customize a policy to meet their specific needs. Imagine buying a new car without being able to purchase optional features, such as air conditioning or a CD player. Like new car options, policy riders are available at an extra cost (through increased premiums) but are justified because of the increased value the riders give to the base policy.

Most of the optional riders described below must be selected at the time the policy is applied for. The automatic premium loan rider (if it is an option and not a standard policy feature) is the only optional rider available at no cost to the policyowner. It sometimes can be added after the policy is in force.

### GUARANTEED INSURABILITY RIDER

For an extra premium, the guaranteed insurability rider may be attached to a permanent life insurance policy at the time of purchase. It permits the insured, at specified intervals in the future, to buy specified amounts of additional insurance without evidence of insurability.

Typically, this option allows the insured to purchase additional life insurance at stated policy intervals or ages. The amount of insurance that can be purchased at each option date is subject to minimums and maximums specified in the rider, but the insurance is available at standard premium rates, whether or not the insured still is insurable.

These riders generally allow the insured to buy additional life insurance at three-year intervals, beginning with the policy anniversary date nearest age 22 and terminating at the anniversary date nearest age 40. (Guaranteed insurability options usually do not extend past age 40.) Thus, the option dates listed in the rider are for the insured's ages 22, 25, 28, 31, 34, 37, and 40. The insured normally has 90 days in which to exercise an option to purchase. If no purchase is made within that time, the option for that particular age expires automatically. The expiration of one option will not affect the exercise of future options.

**EXAMPLE**
Assume that an insured purchases a $10,000 ordinary life policy at age 21 with a guaranteed insurability rider. At ages 25, 28, 31, 34, 37, and 40, this insured can exercise the option to add $10,000 of insurance at each of these six dates, even if he has become uninsurable in the meantime, and thereby add up to $60,000 of coverage to the original $10,000 policy.

## WAIVER OF PREMIUM RIDER

The waiver of premium rider provides valuable added security for policyowners. It can prevent a policy from lapsing for nonpayment of premiums while the insured is disabled and unable to work.

Under the waiver of premium, if the company determines that the insured is totally disabled, the policyowner is relieved of paying premiums as long as the disability continues.

Some policies specify that an insured must be totally and permanently disabled for the waiver to take effect. It does not apply to short-term illnesses or injuries. In fact, an insured generally must be seriously disabled for a certain length of time, called the *waiting period* (usually 90 days or six months). The policyowner continues paying premiums during the waiting period. If the insured still is disabled at the end of this period, the company will refund all of the premiums paid by the policyowner from the start of the disability.

The company then continues to pay all premiums that become due while the insured's disability continues. If the insured recovers and can return to work, premium payments then must be resumed by the policyowner. No premiums paid by the company, however, have to be repaid by the policyowner.

Although premiums are waived for a disabled insured, the death benefit remains the same, cash values increase at their normal rate, and dividends for a participating policy are paid as usual. In fact, cash values continue to be available to the policyowner at all times while the insured's disability continues.

## AUTOMATIC PREMIUM LOAN RIDER

The automatic premium loan rider, discussed earlier in this unit, is a standard feature in some life insurance policies; in others, its provisions are added to the policy by rider. In either case, it is available to the policyowner at no additional charge. As noted previously, it allows the insurer to pay premiums from the policy's cash value if premiums have not been paid by the end of the grace period. These deductions from cash values are treated as loans and are charged interest; in time, if the loan is not repaid, the interest also will be deducted from the cash value. Should the insured die, the loan plus interest will be deducted from the benefits payable.

Automatic premium loans provide that, as long as premiums are not paid, the loan procedure will be repeated until the cash value of the policy is exhausted. When the cash value is depleted, the policy lapses.

## PAYOR PROVISION OR RIDER

As noted earlier in the discussion of juvenile insurance, a payor provision usually is available with such policies, providing for waiver of premiums if the adult premium-payor should die or, with some policies, become totally disabled.

Typically, this payor provision, also known as a *death and disability payor benefit*, extends until the insured child reaches a specified age, such as 21 or 25. It is available for a small extra premium, but before it is issued the adult who is to pay the premium usually must show evidence of insurability.

## ACCIDENTAL DEATH BENEFIT RIDER

The accidental death benefit rider (sometimes called a double indemnity provision) provides an additional amount of insurance, usually equal to the face amount of the base policy, if death occurs under stated conditions. Consequently, if the insured died as a result of the stated circumstances, and he had a double indemnity rider, the total benefit paid would be double the policy's face—the benefit payable under the policy plus the same amount payable under the rider. A triple indemnity provision would provide a total death benefit of three times the face amount. Any policy loans are subtracted from the policy's face amount and not from the accidental death riders.

*Accidental death* is strictly defined and it does not include accidents resulting, directly or indirectly, from an ailment or physical disability of the insured. The additional proceeds are paid only if the insured dies as a result of bodily injury from some external, violent, and purely accidental cause. Also, death must occur within a specified time (usually 90 days) following the accident. Deaths that might be considered accidental, such as those resulting from self-inflicted injury, war, or private aviation activities, are excluded.

## RETURN OF PREMIUM RIDER

A return of premium rider provides that in the event of the insured's death within a specified period of time, the policy will pay, in addition to the face amount, an amount equal to the sum of all premiums paid to date. In actuality, this rider does not return premiums but pays an additional benefit equal to premiums paid on the date of death. The policyowner simply is purchasing term insurance that increases as the total amount of premiums paid increases.

## COST OF LIVING RIDER

Some companies offer their applicants the ability to guard against the eroding effects of inflation. A cost of living (COL) or cost of living adjustment (COLA) rider can provide increases in the amount of insurance protection without requiring the insured to provide evidence of insurability. The amount of increase is tied to an increase in an inflation index, most commonly the Consumer Price Index (CPI). Depending on the type of base policy, these riders can take several different forms.

For standard whole life policies, a COL rider usually is offered as an increasing term insurance rider that is attached to the base policy. The COL rider provides for automatic increases in the policy death benefit in proportion to increases in the CPI. Generally there is a maximum percentage increase, such as 5%, allowed in any one year. When the increase becomes effective, the policyowner is billed for the additional coverage.

**TAKE NOTE**

Declines in the CPI are not matched by a decline in the amount of coverage; instead, future increases are held off until the CPI again exceeds its prior high point.

## OTHER INSUREDS RIDER

A rider that is useful in providing insurance for more than one family member is the other insureds rider. Usually this rider is offered as a term rider, covering a family member other than the insured, and is attached to the base policy covering the insured. Sometimes this is called a *children's rider* if it covers only the children; otherwise, it often is referred to as a *family rider*. This type of rider is used in family plan policies.

# SUMMARY

All life insurance policies are characterized by standardized policy provisions that identify the rights and obligations of the policyowner and the insurance company. Many standard provisions are required by state insurance regulators to be included in policies. Other provisions, dealing with exclusions and restrictions of coverage, are optional and can be included at the discretion of the insurer.

Whole life policies generate cash values to which policyowners are entitled. Policyowners may borrow from a policy's cash value or, on lapse or surrender of the policy, select one of three possible nonforfeiture options.

Participating policies share in the divisible surplus of company operations by returning part of the premium to the owner as a policy dividend. There are five dividend options available to policyowners in deciding how to use their policy dividends.

Policyowners can customize their policy to meet their specific insurance needs by including, generally at a cost, one or more policy riders.

# U N I T   Q U I Z

1. In which of the following situations does the incontestable clause apply?

   A. Impersonation of the applicant by another
   B. No insurable interest
   C. Intent to murder
   D. Concealment of smoking

2. If after the death of an insured, but before any death benefits are distributed, the insurance company discovers that the insured was older than stated in the policy, how would it handle the situation?

   A. No adjustment would be made because the contestable period had passed.
   B. The amount of death proceeds would be reduced to reflect the statistically diminished mortality risk.
   C. The amount of death proceeds would be reduced to reflect whatever benefit the premium paid would have purchased at the correct age.
   D. The beneficiary would be required to pay all underpaid back premiums before the death benefit is received.

3. Which of the following allows an extra 31 days or one month (possibly less for some industrial policies) during which premiums may be paid to keep policies in force?

   A. Grace period
   B. Reinstatement clause
   C. Incontestable clause
   D. Waiting period

4. Which of the following statements regarding the assignment of a life insurance policy is NOT correct?

   A. Absolute assignment involves a complete transfer, which gives the assignee full control over the policy.
   B. Under a collateral assignment, a creditor is entitled to be reimbursed out of the policy's proceeds only for the amount of the outstanding credit balance.
   C. Under a collateral assignment, policy proceeds exceeding the collateral amount pass to the insured's beneficiary.
   D. All beneficiaries must expressly approve any assignments of life insurance policies.

5. All of the following are standard life insurance policy nonforfeiture options EXCEPT

   A. cash surrender
   B. one-year term insurance
   C. extended term insurance
   D. reduced paid-up (permanent) insurance

6. Which of the following statements best describes life insurance policy dividends?

   A. They represent earnings to shareowners who hold stock in insurance companies.
   B. They affect the costs of virtually all insurance policies issued today.
   C. They are an intentional return of a portion of the premiums paid.
   D. They provide policyowners with a level, known annual cash inflow.

7. Which life insurance provision allows the policyholder to inspect and, if dissatisfied, to return the policy for a full refund?

   A. Waiver of premium
   B. Facility of payments
   C. Probationary period
   D. Free look

8. If an insurance company determines that the insured is totally disabled, the policyowner is relieved of paying the policy premiums as long as the disability continues. This above statement describes the

   A. premium suspension clause
   B. waiting period exemption
   C. disability income rider
   D. waiver of premium rider

9. A 10-day free-look provision would apply to the first 10 days after the

   A. application has been signed by the applicant
   B. application has been received by the insurer
   C. policy has been issued by the insurer
   D. issued policy has been received by the policyowner

10. Which provision of a life insurance policy states that the application is part of the contract?

    A. Consideration clause
    B. Insuring clause
    C. Entire contract clause
    D. Incontestable clause

11. Ron, the insured under a $100,000 life insurance policy, dies during the grace period. What happens, considering that he has not paid the premium on the policy?

    A. The premium is canceled because the insured died during the grace period.
    B. The amount of the premium is deducted from the policy proceeds paid to the beneficiary.
    C. The premium due, plus a 10% penalty, is charged against the policy.
    D. The beneficiary must pay the premium after the death claim is paid.

12. Which of the following statements about reinstatement of a life insurance policy is NOT correct?

    A. A suicide exclusion period is renewed with a reinstated policy.
    B. When reinstating a policy, the insurer will charge the policyowner for past-due premiums.
    C. When reinstating a policy, the insurer will charge the policyowner for interest on past-due premiums.
    D. A new contestable period becomes effective in a reinstated policy.

13. Leland elects to surrender his whole life policy for a reduced paid-up policy. The cash value of his new policy will

    A. continue to increase
    B. decrease gradually
    C. remain the same as in the old policy
    D. be forfeited

14. If, after an insured dies, it is discovered that he was younger than the policy stated, what will the insurance company do?

    A. Reduce the death benefits
    B. Reduce premiums
    C. Waive the difference
    D. Refund overpaid premiums

15. Which of the following statements about a life insurance policy's cash values is CORRECT?

    A. In many but not all states, policyowners are fully entitled to the accrued cash values of their whole life policies.
    B. When a whole life insurance policy is active, the owner can borrow against the cash value.
    C. Owners of term and whole life insurance are entitled to the cash surrender value when a policy is lapsed or surrendered.
    D. If a policyowner lets his whole life policy lapse, the insurer will be entitled to part of the policy's cash value.

# A N S W E R S   A N D   R A T I O N A L E S   T O   U N I T   Q U I Z

1. **D.** If an applicant did not reveal that he smoked, and the specified time period passed, the insurer cannot contest the validity of the life insurance policy, even though the applicant concealed this material information.

2. **C.** A misstatement of age provision gives the insurer the right to make an adjustment at any time if the applicant's age was stated incorrectly in a policy. Thus, if an insurer discovers that the insured was older than previously thought, it could reduce the amount of death proceeds to reflect whatever benefit the premium paid would have purchased at the correct age.

3. **A.** An insurance policy's grace period allows an extra 31 days or one month during which premiums may be paid to keep a policy in force. The grace period may be less for some industrial policies.

4. **D.** If irrevocable beneficiaries are named under an insurance contract, the policyowner must obtain their consent before assigning the policy. However, consent need not be obtained before a policy is assigned if there are only revocable beneficiaries.

5. **B.** Standard nonforfeiture options include cash surrender options, reduced paid-up options, and an extended term option. A one-year term insurance option does not exist. The extended term option permits the policyowner to use the policy's cash value to purchase a term insurance policy in an amount equal to the original policy's face value, for as long a period as the cash value will purchase.

6. **C.** Insurance policy dividends constitute a return of part of the premiums paid and normally will vary from year to year. They differ from dividends paid on stocks because they do not represent corporate earnings.

7. **D.** The free-look provision gives policyowners the right to return a policy for a full premium refund within a specified period of time, if they decide not to purchase the insurance. This period usually is 10 days.

8. **D.** A waiver of premium rider prevents a policy from lapsing because the insured cannot pay premiums while he is disabled and unable to work. This waiver continues as long as the insured is disabled.

9. **D.** Most policies provide for a 10-day free look provision beginning when the policyowner actually receives the policy document, not when the application is signed or when the insurance company issues the policy.

10. **C.** The entire contract clause states that the insurance policy documents, the application, and any attached riders constitute the entire contract.

11. **B.** If Ron has not paid the premium and dies during the grace period, the policy benefit still is payable. However, the premium amount that was due will be deducted from the benefits paid to his beneficiary.

12. **A.** If a policy is reinstated, a new contestable period usually goes into effect, but there is no new suicide exclusion period.

13. **A.** If Leland surrenders his whole life policy for a reduced paid-up policy, the face value of the new policy remains the same for the life of the policy, and cash values will continue building.

14. **D.** If an insured died but was younger than the policy stated, the insurer will refund overpaid premiums.

15. **B.** When a whole life policy is active, the policyowner can borrow against the cash value. If the policy is lapsed or surrendered, the owner is entitled to the entire cash surrender value. However, the insurer is not entitled to any part of a policy's cash value.

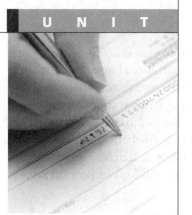

UNIT

# 5

# Life Insurance Premiums and Proceeds

## KEY CONCEPTS

- ■ Allocation of life insurance premiums
- ■ Mortality, interest, and expense factors used in premium calculation
- ■ Life insurance policy proceeds
- ■ Taxation of policy cash values and proceeds
- ■ Section 1035 exchanges
- ■ Life insurance and estate taxes
- ■ Life policy beneficiary designations

83

When people buy life insurance, they must, of course, pay premiums. In this unit, we will examine the three primary factors that affect an insured's premium rates: the mortality charge, interest earnings, and an expense charge. We also will look at some of the other premium factors that come into play when evaluating individual applications for life insurance. After a policy is in force, the owner may surrender it at any time or keep it active by paying premiums. When an insured dies, the policy proceeds can be paid to the beneficiary in a variety of ways, depending on the beneficiary's needs and personal situation. After reviewing the different settlement options a beneficiary may select, we will examine the important topic of life insurance taxation. Specifically, we will look at how premiums, cash values, and life insurance proceeds are taxed.

## OBJECTIVE

When you finish this unit you should be able to:

- explain how mortality, interest, and expenses affect premium rates and list the other factors affecting premiums;

- explain how level premium funding works;

- describe how life insurance premiums, cash values, and proceeds are taxed;

- list and explain the various options for paying death proceeds to beneficiaries; and

- describe the tax treatment of accelerated death benefits, viatical settlements, 1035 exchanges, and policy surrenders.

# LIFE INSURANCE PREMIUMS

The task of determining an insurance company's premium rates rests with the company's actuaries. Actuaries are mathematicians by education who are responsible for bringing together the financial and statistical data that have an influence on life (and health) insurance premium rates. Establishing realistic premium rates is a critical function in any life insurance company. Rates must be high enough to cover the costs of paying claims and doing business, yet low enough so that they are competitive with other insurers' rates.

**FIGURE 5.1    How the Life Insurance Premium Dollar is Used**

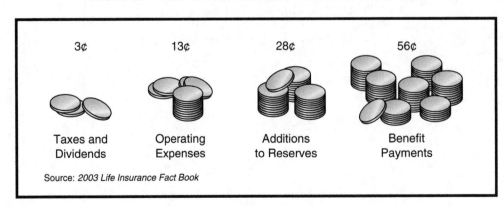

| 3¢ | 13¢ | 28¢ | 56¢ |
| --- | --- | --- | --- |
| Taxes and Dividends | Operating Expenses | Additions to Reserves | Benefit Payments |

Source: *2003 Life Insurance Fact Book*

Life insurance premium rates generally are expressed as an annual cost per $1,000 of face amount.

**EXAMPLE**

One company's rate for a male, age 35, is $13.73. What exactly does this mean? It means that for the particular policy in question (say, a $50,000 participating straight whole life policy), the policyowner, a male who was 35 when he purchased the policy, pays an annual premium of $13.73 for every $1,000 of face amount he purchased, or $686.50 ($13.73 × 50). Because it is a straight whole life policy, this policyowner will pay $686.50 per year for his life (or to age 100, if he lives that long).

# PRIMARY FACTORS IN PREMIUM CALCULATIONS

Three primary factors are considered when computing the basic premium for life insurance: *mortality, interest,* and *expense.* Of these, the mortality factor has the greatest effect on premium calculations (commonly termed *rate-making*). That is, while an insurer's interest and expense factors generally are the same for all of its policyholders, the mortality factor can vary greatly, depending on personal characteristics of individual insureds.

## MORTALITY FACTOR

A basic principle of life insurance is that it must be based on an accurate prediction of mortality, that is, the average number of deaths that will occur each year in each age group. Throughout the years, statistics have been compiled, showing how many and at what ages people generally can be expected to die. Compiled, these statistics become mortality tables, which reflect death rates at each age.

Figure 5.2 is a sample mortality predictions table, taken from the 1980 Commissioner's Standard Ordinary, or CSO, Mortality Table. For easier reading, the starting group has been reduced to 100,000. (The complete CSO table reflects 10,000,000 lives.) Also, only 10-year age intervals are shown, and the ages in between (except age 99) are not included.

Two primary purposes of a mortality table are to indicate: (1) the expectation of life at given ages—the average number of years remaining for a group of persons of the same age and (2) the probability of death—the average number of deaths for a group of persons in given years. Obviously, the significance of mortality predictions to an insurance company is that they provide a basis to estimate how long its insureds will live, how long they will be paying premiums and at what future dates the company will have to pay out benefits. Consequently, the portion of the premium associated with mortality reflects the pure cost of providing death protection. Large insurance companies typically base their rates on their own statistics and experience, or construct their own mortality tables from a data pool based on the experience of many insurers. Actuaries use the experience of several years to determine the mortality data that will be incorporated into premium rates.

The mortality table arbitrarily sets the upper age limit at 100, because statistics show that very few people live to that age. Therefore, for purposes of determining mortality, age 100 is deemed to be the age at which the last person in an original population of 100,000 dies. Whole life insurance will mature or endow at age 100 because insurance is not designed to provide coverage beyond that age.

TAKE NOTE

For a mortality table to be accurate, it must be based on two things—a large cross section of people and a large cross section of time.

## INTEREST FACTOR

When policyowners pay premiums to a life insurance company, the funds do not sit idle in the insurer's vaults. They are combined with other funds and invested to earn interest. Among other things, this interest earned helps hold down the cost of life insurance premiums.

### FIGURE 5.2    1980 CSO Mortality Table

| Age | Number Living at Start of Year | Deaths Within Year |
|---|---|---|
| 0 | 100,000 | 418 |
| 10 | 98,783 | 72 |
| 20 | 97,542 | 185 |
| 30 | 95,800 | 166 |
| 40 | 93,772 | 283 |
| 50 | 89,666 | 602 |
| 60 | 80,842 | 1,300 |
| 70 | 62,742 | 2,479 |
| 80 | 32,745 | 3,237 |
| 90 | 6,458 | 1,432 |
| 99 | 108 | 108 |
| 100 | 0 | 0 |

The figures above are a sampling from the 1980 CSO Mortality Table, showing how many individuals are expected to die within certain years out of a starting group of 100,000. For example, out of 100,000 people, 93,772 are expected to be living at the age of 40; during that 40th year, 283 are expected to die.

Notice the mortality patterns this table reveals. The first year of life is one of relatively high mortality. The mortality rate of 418 deaths during the year out of the original group of 100,000 is not matched again until age 45 (not shown here).

At age 1 (not shown), the number dying is 107, and the rate continues to decline until age 10 (with 72 deaths, it is the lowest in the table). Then begins the climb up. Older teens and young adults face an increased risk of death. But from a rate of 185 deaths at age 20, the mortality actually decreases as this population matures through its 20s. The rate at age 29 is 164, the lowest it will be for the remainder of this population's average life expectancy.

From a high of 3,300 at age 78 (the highest rate in the table), the rate once again begins to decline—a sign that if one can make it this long, the odds of making it to 100 actually improve.

Actuaries know that many people live longer than the average life expectancy. Nonetheless, it is an indisputable fact that everyone dies eventually, so actuaries have set age 100 as the somewhat arbitrary age at which the last person in the original population of 100,000 dies. It is at age 100, therefore, that whole life policies mature or endow.

---

**TAKE NOTE**

There is no reliable basis for predicting future interest rates or trends, therefore a company must remain conservative in its interest assumptions, because it is committed to the interest rate guaranteed in its life insurance policies for as long as those policies remain in force. Interest earnings on invested premiums is the second consideration in premium rate calculations; the higher the assumed rate of interest, the lower the premium rate charged to policyowners.

---

**TAKE NOTE**

An expense factor is computed and included in the premium rates for life insurance. Sometimes the expense factor is called the *loading charge*.

---

An insurer makes two assumptions with regard to interest. First, it assumes that a specific net rate of interest will be earned on all its investments. Actually, some investments will earn more than the assumed rate and some will earn less, so the company selects an average rate for its assumption. The assumed interest rate may seem low (generally, 3½ to 4½%), but it directly affects the premium levels that are guaranteed to policyowners for years into the future. Thus, the assumed rates must be reasonably conservative.

The second assumption made by the company is that one full year's interest will be earned by each premium policyowners pay. Therefore, it must be assumed that all premiums are paid at the beginning of the year.

## EXPENSE FACTOR

The third factor affecting premium rates is expenses. As does any business, an insurance company has various operating expenses. Personnel must be hired and paid; sales forces must be recruited, trained, and compensated; supplies must be purchased; rent must be paid; and buildings must be maintained. Local, state, and federal taxes also must be paid. Each premium must carry its small proportionate share of these normal operating costs.

## NET VERSUS GROSS PREMIUMS

The factors basic to premium calculations—mortality, interest, and expense—are only a portion of the equation. Actuaries use the assumptions underlying these factors and translate them into *net single premium*, *net level premiums*, and *gross premiums*.

The net single premium can be defined as the single amount needed today to fund the future benefit. Basically, it is the amount of premium, when combined with interest, that will be sufficient to pay the future death benefit. However, only rarely do people purchase life insurance with a single premium because of the large cash outlay required. Most pay premiums over a number of years. Thus, the net single premium is converted into net annual level premiums, with some adjustments due to a lesser amount of interest these smaller premiums will earn. Finally, the gross premium is determined, which reflects the addition of the expense factor. The gross premium is what the policyowners are required to pay.

In very general terms, actuaries deduct the assumed interest earnings from the mortality cost. The mortality cost less the assumed interest earnings equals the net premium. The expense factor then is added to the net premium to arrive at the gross premium.

The two key formulas to keep in mind are:

$$\text{Net single premium} = \text{Mortality cost} - \text{Interest}$$

$$\text{Gross premium} = \text{Net single premium} + \text{Expense}$$

## OTHER PREMIUM FACTORS

The preceding discussion focused on the three primary factors underlying all life insurance premiums. When evaluating individual applications for life insurance, other premium factors come into play, all of which influence mortality to one degree or another:

- *Age.* As we have seen, the age of an individual has a direct bearing on mortality, and mortality is figured directly into premium calculations. The older the insured, the greater the mortality risk.

- *Gender.* The gender of the applicant also has a bearing on mortality. Experience has shown that, on the average, women live five or six years longer than men. Statistically, then, they are considered better life insurance risks than men, and their premium rates are lower than those for men.

- *Health.* Another factor influencing mortality is the health of the applicant. Obviously, those in poorer health represent a higher risk than those in good health.

- *Occupation or avocation.* An applicant's occupation or avocation also can affect mortality. Those employed in hazardous occupations pose a greater risk to an insurer, as do those who engage in dangerous hobbies.

- *Habits.* An individual's personal habits also may influence the premium rate he will be assessed. Habits such as smoking or overeating adversely affect health and may increase the risk of death.

Factors such as these are considered carefully by insurance company underwriters, whose job it is to evaluate and select risks. In those cases where an individual applicant represents a higher-than-normal risk to the insurer due to one or more of these personal characteristics, he is known as a substandard risk. Of course, insurers can reject a substandard risk, and some applicants are denied. However, another way to treat a substandard case is to adjust the premium to reflect the increased risk. This approach is known as *rating.*

# LEVEL PREMIUM FUNDING

As mentioned earlier, the age of an insured has direct influence on the mortality charge—the higher the age, the higher the mortality charge. Because the mortality charge has a direct impact on the amount of premium, it stands to reason that as a person ages, the premium rate for that person should increase.

As discussed, life insurance is issued with premiums calculated and payable on a level basis for the policy's life. If the policy is a term policy, the premiums are level for the duration of the term; if the

> ### TAKE NOTE
>
> There is a slight extra charge when premiums are not paid annually, as all gross premiums are calculated on an annual basis. The extra charge is to cover the additional paperwork and to make up for interest lost by the company because it does not have the full annual premium to invest in advance.

policy is a whole life policy, the premiums are level for life or, in the case of a limited pay policy, for the duration of the premium-paying period.

Under the level premium funding method, the insured pays more than the insurance protection requires in the policy's early years; in the policy's later years, when the increasing mortality charge normally would increase the premium to a very high level, the excess paid in the early years is used to help fund the additional cost now required.

Interest plays an important role in this process. The excess funds paid in the early years will earn interest, thus making it possible to keep the actual premium level lower than if interest were not considered.

## MODES OF PREMIUM PAYMENT

Policyowners ordinarily may pay their premiums under one of four modes: annually, semiannually, quarterly, or monthly. On any policy anniversary date (or at other times, if company rules permit) a policyowner may change from one payment mode to another, provided the payment is not less than a minimum specified by the company.

The more often a premium becomes due, the more expensive the mode of the premium will be for the insurance company to administer. The insurer passes these costs on to the policyowner.

## TAX TREATMENT OF PREMIUMS

As a general rule, premiums paid for personal life insurance policies by individual policyowners are considered to be personal expenses and, therefore, are not deductible from gross income. Also, premiums paid for business life insurance usually are not deductible.

EXAMPLE    ABC Corporation purchased a key-person life insurance policy on the life of its president. The premiums are not deductible by the corporation.

# TAX TREATMENT OF CASH VALUES

The yearly increase in the cash value of a whole life insurance policy is not taxed during the period it accumulates inside the policy. If the cash value is taken out while the insured still is living—for example, as retirement income—a portion of each retirement income payment is received tax free, because it represents a return of principal. Let's look at this in more detail. With regard to the taxation of surrendered cash values, a policyowner is allowed to receive tax free an amount equal to what he paid into the policy over the years in the form of premiums. The sum of the premiums paid is known as the policyowner's *cost basis*. However, when the accumulated cash value exceeds the premiums paid—when the cash value is greater than the policyowner's cost basis—the difference is taxable.

**EXAMPLE**   At the age of 65, Mel decides to surrender his whole life policy and take the $28,000 accumulated cash value in a lump sum. He paid a total of $19,000 in premiums over the years. The difference between his cost basis and the accumulated value ($28,000 − $19,000 = $9,000) will be treated as taxable income in the year Mel actually receives it.

As long as a policy is not surrendered, the cash value continues to accumulate tax free. There never is a tax imposed on the policyowner, even if the cash value exceeds the cost basis, as long as the cash value remains in the policy.

# LIFE INSURANCE POLICY PROCEEDS

One thing that distinguishes life insurance from other forms of insurance is that a life insurance policy kept in force long enough is inevitably going to pay a benefit. When this benefit is payable due to the death of the insured, it is known as the policy's death proceeds.

### DEATH BENEFITS

The death proceeds of a life insurance policy can be paid out in a variety of ways. The choice is up to the policyowner, as a right of ownership, or he may leave the decision to the beneficiary.

The variety of options insurers offer makes the selection fairly easy, because the decision usually rests on whether the beneficiary will need the entire amount at once or as income payable over time. There are five settlement options available: *lump-sum, interest-only, fixed-period, fixed-amount,* and *life income*.

**Lump-Sum Cash Option** Many years ago, all life insurance policy proceeds were paid out in single lump-sum cash settlements. Today, this option still is available, though not used to the extent of some of the others.

**Interest-Only Option**   Under the interest only option, the proceeds are left on deposit with the insurance company. The account works similar to a money market account, where the beneficiary may make partial surrenders (ie. to pay funeral expenses), may leave all the money in the account, or may take all the funds similar to the lump sum cash option. The beneficiary may also choose to utilize all or some of the proceeds in another settlement option. The death proceeds are not taxable but all interest credited to the account is taxable.

**Fixed-Period Option**   Under the fixed-period (or fixed-time) option, the company pays the beneficiary equal amounts of money at regular intervals over a specified period of years. This option pays out both principal (proceeds) and the interest earned. The amount of each installment payment is determined by the length of the desired period of income. Thus, the longer the period of income, the smaller each payment will be. Conversely, the shorter the period, the larger each payment amount. (See Figure 5.3.)

**FIGURE 5.3 Fixed-Period Option**

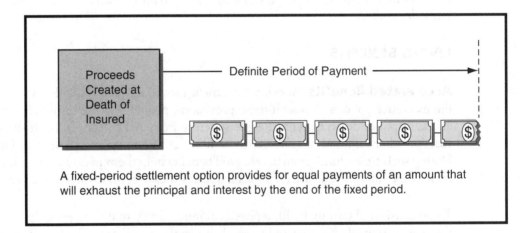

Proceeds Created at Death of Insured

Definite Period of Payment

A fixed-period settlement option provides for equal payments of an amount that will exhaust the principal and interest by the end of the fixed period.

**Fixed-Amount Option**   Under a fixed-amount option, the policy proceeds plus interest are used to pay out a specified amount of income at regular intervals for as long as the proceeds last. The policyowner or beneficiary requests the size of payment desired. The amount of each income payment is fixed, and the duration of the payment period varies according to the payment amount. (See Figure 5.4.)

## FIGURE 5.4 Fixed-Amount Option

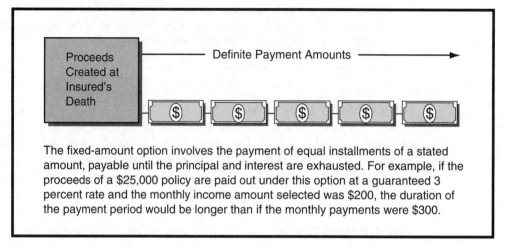

The fixed-amount option involves the payment of equal installments of a stated amount, payable until the principal and interest are exhausted. For example, if the proceeds of a $25,000 policy are paid out under this option at a guaranteed 3 percent rate and the monthly income amount selected was $200, the duration of the payment period would be longer than if the monthly payments were $300.

**Life Income Options** Under a life income option, of which there are many, the beneficiary receives a guaranteed income for life—no matter how long he lives. This unique concept is successful because the principal and interest of life insurance proceeds are paid out together, with the amount of payment actuarially calculated and guaranteed to last a lifetime. Even if the principal is depleted, income payments will continue, so long as the primary beneficiary lives. Essentially, the insurance company uses the death benefit to purchase a single payment immediate annuity for the beneficiary. As you will learn later, the purpose of annuities is to provide an income stream for the duration of an individual's life.

## LIVING BENEFITS

**Accelerated Benefits** Accelerated benefit provisions are standard in most individual and group life insurance policies. Through these provisions, people who are terminally or chronically ill have access to policy death benefits. People suffering from AIDS, cancer, heart disease, Alzheimer's disease, or other terminal or severe chronic illnesses often experience devastating financial hardship. During such times, funds from accelerated benefits help them maintain their independence and dignity. These funds usually are used for such necessities as rent, food, and medical services.

To be considered terminally ill, a physician must certify that the person has an illness or condition that can reasonably be expected to result in death in two years. To be considered chronically ill, a licensed health care practitioner must have certified within the previous 12 months that the person (1) is unable to perform, without substantial assistance, at least two activities of daily living for at least 90 days due to a loss of functional capacity; (2) has a similar level of disability as defined by regulations; or (3) requires substantial supervision to protect the person from threats to health and safety because of severe cognitive impairment.

**Viatical Settlements** Through viatical settlements, individuals with a terminal illness or severe chronic illness sell their life insurance policies to viatical companies. The viatical company will require the policy to have been in force beyond the contestable period. The price viatical companies pay for policies depends on the insured's life expectancy and the cost of future premiums. The NAIC has adopted model guidelines for fair payment. Under these guidelines, insureds receive anywhere from 50% to 80% of the policy face value. When a viatical company purchases a policy, it becomes the policyowner and is responsible for paying premiums. The company receives the death benefit when the insured dies.

Under HIPAA, the proceeds from the sale of life insurance by a chronically or terminally ill individual to a qualified viatical settlement provider are exempt from federal income tax, as are accelerated death benefits.

# TAX TREATMENT OF PROCEEDS

To understand the taxation of life insurance proceeds, remember one basic principle: death benefits paid under a life insurance policy to a named beneficiary are free of federal income taxation. However, interest paid by an insurance company on death benefit proceeds left with the company is taxable income, just as interest payments any financial institution makes are taxable.

## PROCEEDS PAID AT THE INSURED'S DEATH

When an insured dies, life insurance policy proceeds paid as a lump-sum death benefit to a beneficiary are exempt from federal income tax. The amount paid under a double indemnity provision and the benefits from any paid-up additions to a life insurance policy also are tax exempt.

When proceeds are paid out to an individual on an installment basis—as is the case with the fixed-amount, fixed-period, or life income options—a portion of each payment consists of principal and a portion consists of interest. The portion of the proceeds attributed to interest is taxable; the remaining portion is received tax free.

When the insurance company holds the death proceeds of a policy under the interest-only option, the interest credited is taxable to the beneficiary as ordinary income. When the principal amount is finally paid out, it still represents tax-free income.

**Transfer for Value Rule** In certain cases another tax provision, called the transfer for value rule, applies. If a policy is transferred by assignment or otherwise for valuable consideration (i.e., the policy is sold to another party) and the insured dies, the person who then owns the policy will be taxed on the excess of the proceeds over the consideration paid, including any premiums paid by the transferee.

## PROCEEDS PAID DURING THE INSURED'S LIFETIME

There are three reasons why an insured policyowner might receive proceeds from (or by reason of) a life insurance policy while he still is living: as a result of a policy surrender, as accelerated benefits, or as payment received in a viatical settlement. Let's review the tax treatment of such proceeds paid during the insured's lifetime.

**TAKE NOTE**

Remember that the policyowner's cost basis is figured as total premiums paid, less policy dividends received, less any policy loan, and less extra premiums paid for supplementary benefits, such as waiver of premium or accidental death benefits.

**TAKE NOTE**

If a life insurance policy is exchanged for another life insurance policy, the policies must be on the life of the same insured. Thus, if Tim exchanged a policy insuring only his life for a policy that insured the lives of both himself and his wife, this exchange would not qualify as a tax-free exchange under Section 1035. To constitute a nontaxable exchange, Tim would have to exchange his current policy for one insuring his life only.

**Policy Surrender**  As noted earlier in this unit under Tax Treatment of Cash Values, the taxation of accumulated values received when a policyowner surrenders a policy is determined by his cost basis. Only the excess of such proceeds over the cost of the policy is taxable.

**Accelerated Death Benefits and Viatical Arrangements**  Accelerated death benefits generally are not included in a terminally or chronically ill person's income. A terminally or chronically ill person also can assign or sell a life policy to a viatical settlement provider and not pay federal taxes on amounts received. These provisions remove tax barriers for policyowners who need access to policy values because of terminal or chronic illness.

## 1035 POLICY EXCHANGES

Another provision of the Internal Revenue Code pertains to life insurance policies that are exchanged or transferred for another like-kind policy. Typically, when an individual realizes a gain on a financial transaction, that gain is taxed. As we just learned, if a policyowner surrenders a life insurance policy and receives the cash value, he will realize a gain to the extent that the cash value exceeds the amount of premiums paid. That gain is considered ordinary income and is fully taxable. However, if a policy is exchanged for another, Section 1035 of the Tax Code stipulates that no gain (or loss) will be recognized. Consequently, the transaction is not subject to any tax. The following kinds of exchanges are allowed under this provision:

■  a life insurance policy for another life insurance policy, or annuity contract; and

■  an annuity contract for another annuity contract.

## LIFE INSURANCE AND THE INSURED'S ESTATE

When an insured dies, the value of any life insurance policy he owned is included in his gross estate for federal estate tax purposes. State death taxes also may be payable. The proceeds payable at death to a beneficiary, as explained previously, are not subject to federal income tax. Any accumulated policy dividends, although exempt from income tax, also are included in the insured's gross estate for federal estate tax purposes.

# LIFE INSURANCE BENEFICIARIES

One of a policyowner's most important rights is the ability to name the beneficiary of his life insurance policy. In most cases, an individual is selected to be the sole or proportional beneficiary of a life insurance policy. There may be one named individual or more than one. For example, a policyowner could designate his wife as the sole beneficiary or designate that she receive half the proceeds of his policy with the remainder to be split equally between his two children. Designating a trust as the beneficiary of a life insurance policy means that the proceeds will be paid to the trust for the ultimate benefit of and use by another. Trusts are managed by trustees, who have the fiduciary responsibility to oversee and handle the trust and its funds for its beneficiaries. Naming a charity as the beneficiary of a life insurance policy is another commonly accepted practice.

## TYPES OF BENEFICIARY DESIGNATIONS

A number of ways to classify beneficiary designations exist: by the order of succession (or preference); by the number named; by line of descent; or by whether or not the designation(s) can be changed. A discussion of these various types of designations follows. In any event, it is important to select and arrange beneficiary designations carefully, because once they are in effect, the insurance company must follow them to the letter.

**Order of Succession** It always is possible that a beneficiary to a life insurance policy may predecease the insured. To meet this contingency, policyowners are encouraged to designate *primary*, *secondary*, and, occasionally, *tertiary* beneficiaries.

*Primary Beneficiaries*. A primary beneficiary is the party designated to receive the proceeds of a life insurance policy when they become payable. There may be more than one primary beneficiary, and how the proceeds are to be split is up to the policyowner.

*Secondary (Contingent)*. Beneficiaries A secondary beneficiary also may be named and stands second in line to receive the proceeds of a life insurance policy if the primary beneficiary dies before the insured. Secondary beneficiaries are entitled to policy proceeds only if no primary beneficiaries are living. Secondary beneficiaries also are known as *contingent* or *successor* beneficiaries.

*Tertiary (Contingent)*. Beneficiaries A tertiary beneficiary stands third in line to receive the proceeds of a life insurance policy, in cases where all primary and secondary beneficiaries predecease the insured.

**More Than One Beneficiary per Category** Policyowners may name more than one beneficiary in any category, whether the category is primary, secondary, or tertiary. When they do so, however, they should specify the percentage or dollar amount of the proceeds that each is to receive. Most companies recommend that each beneficiary's share be indicated as a fraction. For example, "one-half to my wife, Shirley Dawn Brown; one-fourth to my son, Curtis Rodney Brown; one-fourth to my daughter, Mary Lee Brown. In the event of the death of any beneficiary, his or her share shall be divided equally between the survivors or all shall go to the sole survivor."

**TAKE NOTE**

If no beneficiary is named, or if all primary and contingent beneficiaries are deceased at the time of the insured's death, the proceeds are paid to the policyowner or to his or her estate, if the policyowner is deceased.

**TAKE NOTE**

The revocable beneficiary designation is used in the vast majority of life insurance contracts today. Note that the insured may change a revocable beneficiary at any time and any number of times during the term of the policy.

**Distribution by Descent**   When life insurance policy proceeds are to be distributed to a person's descendents, a *per stirpes* or a *per capita* approach generally is used. The term *per capita* means *per person* or *by head*. A *per capita* distribution means that a policy's proceeds are paid only to the beneficiaries who are living and have been named in the policy. In short, the *per capita* beneficiary claims proceeds in his or her own right, while the *per stirpes* beneficiary receives the proceeds through the rights of another. Today, the *per stirpes* method of distribution is by far the more common approach.

**Changing a Beneficiary**   Beneficiary designations are classified according to whether they can be changed after a policy is issued. Recall that the right to change beneficiary designations is a right of ownership. It is a right the policyowner may retain or relinquish. The terms used to indicate this right are *revocable* and *irrevocable* beneficiary.

*Revocable Beneficiary.* When beneficiaries are designated revocable, the policyowner may change the designation at any time. It also means that the policyowner remains the complete owner of the policy. The policyowner can make policy changes whenever needed or desired. A revocable beneficiary has no vested claim on the policy or its proceeds as long as the insured (or policyowner, if different) is living.

*Irrevocable Beneficiary.* When a beneficiary is designated irrevocable, the policyowner gives up the right to change the beneficiary. For all practical purposes, the policy is owned by both the policyowner and the beneficiary. An irrevocable beneficiary has a vested right in the policy, and the policyowner cannot exercise any right that would affect the vested rights of the beneficiary without the beneficiary's consent. For instance, a policyowner cannot borrow from the policy, assign the policy, or surrender it without the written consent of the beneficiary.

# SUMMARY

There are three primary factors in a life insurance premium. The mortality charge has the greatest influence in making one insured's premium different from another insured's, assuming the two people represent different risks to the insurance company. The mortality charge is reduced by expected interest earnings, which is the second premium factor; these two factors constitute the net premium. The insurer's cost of doing business is recouped partly through an expense charge, the third premium factor, which, when added to the net premium, equals the gross premium.

Life insurance premiums generally are not tax deductible. Life insurance proceeds can be paid out in a variety of ways. The standard means of paying a death benefit is in a lump sum. However, either the policyowner or the beneficiary can select another settlement option as an alternate method of paying a policy's proceeds.

Life insurance death benefits are paid without income tax consequence, with one exception. If the transfer for value rule applies, the recipient of the proceeds will be taxed on a portion of the proceeds that exceeds the amount paid for the policy.

Federal income taxes are payable on interest earnings credited to a policy on either death benefit proceeds or policy dividends that have been left with the company.

# U N I T   Q U I Z

1. Mr. Williams names his son, John, a beneficiary of his life insurance policy. What designation should he use if he wants to make sure that John's children would receive John's share of the life insurance policy proceeds should John predecease his father?

   A. *Per capita*
   B. All my children
   C. *Per stirpes*
   D. Grandchildren

2. What is the beneficiary designation that can only be changed with the beneficiary's written agreement?

   A. Revocable beneficiary
   B. Wife of the insured
   C. *Per stirpes*
   D. Irrevocable beneficiary

3. A mortality table would reveal which of the following pieces of information?

   A. That there is no death rate for persons age 99
   B. Who will die in any given year
   C. The average number of deaths that will occur each year in any age group
   D. That the death rate normally is higher in the lower age groups

4. All of the following are primary premium factors EXCEPT

   A. expense
   B. interest
   C. dividends
   D. mortality

5. Which of the following statements pertaining to life insurance premiums is CORRECT?

   A. Premium rates usually are lower for men than women.
   B. The most significant factor in premium rate calculation is interest.
   C. Harold and Billy, both age 25, each buy a whole life policy from the same company. However, Harold has a participating policy, while Billy's policy is nonparticipating. Harold will pay a higher premium.
   D. Lucy, who is substantially overweight, has applied for a life insurance policy. Her weight may affect her insurability but not the amount of premium on her policy.

6. Art, the owner and insured under a $75,000 life policy, is killed in an accident. He had paid total premiums of $26,000. How much of the death benefit will be included in his gross estate for estate tax purposes?

   A. $0
   B. $26,000
   C. $49,000
   D. $75,000

7. With regard to the situation described in Question 5, how much of the $75,000 death benefit that was paid to Art's wife in a lump sum is taxable income to her?

   A. $0
   B. $26,000
   C. $49,000
   D. $75,000

8. Assume the following persons buy identical life insurance policies from the same company. Who will pay the lowest premium, if all have standard ratings?

   A. Linda, age 28
   B. Thomas, age 28
   C. Louise, age 40
   D. Joe, age 45

9. Sarah, age 65, the owner of a $150,000 whole life policy, decides to surrender the policy and take the $90,000 cash value in a lump sum. Over the years, she has paid a total of $54,000 in premiums. How much, if any, of the payment will be taxed?

   A. $0
   B. $36,000
   C. $54,000
   D. $90,000

10. Under which option does the insurer hold the death proceeds for a specified period of time and pay the beneficiary a guaranteed rate of interest on the proceeds at regular intervals?

   A. Fixed-period
   B. Interest-only
   C. Fixed-amount
   D. Life income

11. Bill names his church as the beneficiary of his $300,000 life insurance policy. When Bill dies, who is responsible for the income taxes payable on the lump-sum proceeds received by the church?

   A. His estate
   B. His church
   C. No income tax is payable on the death proceeds
   D. His estate and the beneficiary share the tax liability equally

12. Which of the following factors is most important when computing basic premiums for life insurance?

   A. Expense
   B. Interest
   C. Mortality
   D. Reserves

13. Which of the following statements about accelerated death benefits and viatical settlements is NOT correct?

   A. A terminally ill person receives accelerated death benefits tax free.
   B. An insured who sells an insurance policy to a viatical company usually receives 100% of the policy's face value.
   C. A chronically ill person receives funds from a viatical settlement tax free.
   D. Accelerated benefit provisions are standard in most individual and group life insurance policies.

14. Which of the following statements about the taxation of insurance proceeds is NOT correct?

   A. Accumulated dividends are exempt from income tax.
   B. A beneficiary will not be taxed on insurance proceeds paid as a lump sum death benefit.
   C. A policyowner who receives the cash value for a surrendered policy must pay capital gains tax on any gain.
   D. Generally, no gain or loss is realized when one insurance policy is exchanged for another.

15. Ralph owns a $50,000 nonpar whole life policy. Its cash value has accumulated to $15,000, and he has paid a total of $9,500 in premiums. If he surrenders the policy for its cash value, how will it be taxed?

   A. He will receive the $15,000 tax free.
   B. He will receive $5,500 tax free; the $9,500 balance is taxable as income.
   C. He will receive $9,500 tax free; the $5,500 balance is taxable as income.
   D. He will receive the $15,000 as taxable income.

# ANSWERS AND RATIONALES TO UNIT QUIZ

1. **C.** Mr. Williams should use the *per stirpes* distribution method. Under this method, if John predeceased his father, John's share of the insurance proceeds would be passed down to his children in equal shares. If John's father designated the proceeds to be distributed *per capita*, John's children would not receive any of the proceeds. Instead, the other primary beneficiaries would receive John's share.

2. **D.** When a beneficiary is designated irrevocable, the policyowner can change the beneficiary designation only with the beneficiary's consent. This is because an irrevocable beneficiary has a vested right in the policy and the policyowner cannot exercise any right that would affect the beneficiary without the beneficiary's consent.

3. **C.** A mortality table is used to compute life insurance premiums. Mortality tables show the average number of deaths that will occur each year in each age group.

4. **C.** The three primary factors used to compute basic premiums for life insurance include mortality, interest, and expense. The amount of dividends does not affect an insurance policy's premium rates.

5. **C.** Because participating life insurance policies pay dividends, they are more expensive than nonparticipating policies, which do not pay dividends.

6. **D.** When Art dies, the entire value of the life insurance policy he owned ($75,000) is included in his gross estate for federal estate tax purposes. However, the proceeds will not be subject to income tax.

7. **A.** At Art's death, the $75,000 of insurance proceeds paid as a lump-sum death benefit to Art's wife will not be subject to federal income tax. If she had chosen another settlement option instead (such as fixed-amount, fixed-period, or life income options), a portion of each payment would consist of principal and interest. The portion attributed to interest would be taxable while the remaining part would be tax free.

8. **A.** Linda will pay the lowest premium. Of all these individuals, Linda and Thomas are the youngest. The younger the insured, the less the mortality risk; conversely, the older the insured, the greater the mortality risk. However, Linda's premium will be lower than Thomas's because she is a woman. Generally, the average woman lives longer than the average man. As a result, women are considered better insurance risks than men and usually have lower premium rates.

9. **B.** If Sarah surrenders her policy, she can receive the amount she paid into the policy (i.e., her premiums) tax free. However, because the accumulated cash value exceeds the amount of premiums she paid, the difference between these two amounts is taxable. In Sarah's case, the taxable portion would be calculated by taking the difference between her cost basis and the policy's accumulated value ($90,000 − $54,000 = $36,000).

10. **B.** Under an interest-only option, the insurance company holds the death proceeds for a specified period of time and, at regular intervals, pays the beneficiary a guaranteed rate of interest on the proceeds.

11. **C.** When Bill dies, the proceeds paid to the church as a lump-sum death benefit are exempt from federal income tax. This is true whether the beneficiary is a person or a charitable organization.

12. **C.** Of the three primary factors that are considered when computing the basic premium for life insurance—mortality, interest, and expense—the mortality factor has the greatest effect on premium calculations. This is because while an insurer's interest and expense factors generally are the same for all of its policyholders, the mortality factor can vary greatly depending on the personal characteristics of individual insureds.

13. **B.** When an insured sells a life insurance policy to a viatical company, he or she will receive from 50 to 80% of the policy face value.

14. **C.** If a policyowner surrenders a life insurance policy and receives the cash value, he or she will realize a gain to the extent that the cash value exceeds the amount of premiums paid. However, that gain is considered ordinary income, not capital gain, and is fully taxable.

15. **C.** A policyowner is allowed to receive tax free an amount equal to what he or she paid into the policy over the years in the form of premiums.

# 6

# Life Insurance Underwriting and Policy Issue

## KEY CONCEPTS

- Life insurance needs and uses
- Insurable interest in life insurance
- The life policy application process
- Reports used in the underwriting process
- Policy effective dates and contract delivery

As we have seen, there are many types of life insurance available to consumers. In this unit, we will consider the methods used to calculate the amount of life insurance needed, and study the many ways life insurance may be used by individuals and businesses. To determine who is qualified to purchase life insurance and who is not, insurance company underwriters must engage in a process called risk selection. This involves reviewing each applicant to determine whether or not and on what basis it will accept an application for insurance. In many cases the underwriter places much weight on the agent's or broker's recommendations. In this unit, we will examine how the underwriting process works, and look at the agent's role in this process. We also will discuss what happens after underwriting is finished, namely, how policies are issued and delivered.

## OBJECTIVE

When you complete this unit you should be able to:

- explain the two major methods for calculating life insurance needs;

- explain how life insurance is used by individuals and businesses;

- define underwriting and explain its purpose;

- list and describe the most common sources of underwriting information;

- explain the agent's role in the underwriting process; and

- describe the agent's role after a policy has been issued.

# LIFE INSURANCE NEEDS

For most people, the best solution to the adverse financial consequences that result when a breadwinner dies is to have an adequate amount of life insurance. Without question it remains the most efficient way to guarantee a family's or business's continued financial integrity. Accurately determining the proper amount of life insurance requires the consideration of a number of factors, including the planned uses for the insurance, the client's long-range goals, and the ways insurance may or may not be able to help meet those goals. Two basic approaches are used today to help insurance buyers and producers determine the proper amount of life insurance.

The *human life value* approach attempts to measure the value of an individual's life and express it as a dollar amount that determines the death benefit of a life policy. Through this approach, the producer, working with the client, determines the average annual earnings of an insured and how much of those earnings are used to support their dependents. The resulting figure is multiplied by the number of years the insured anticipates working, and a death benefit is recommended. For example, Diane makes an average of $50,000 per year; $35,000 is devoted to the care and maintenance of her family. If she anticipates working 20 more years, the human life value approach would support $700,000 worth of life insurance ($35,000 × 20 years).

The *needs approach*, more commonly used today, determines how much insurance protection a person should have by analyzing their existing assets and liabilities and considering the financial needs and objectives of the insured. The difference between what is owned now (or what will ultimately be available) and what is needed in terms of funds then is used by the producer in recommending an insurance program that may employ term insurance, permanent insurance, annuities, or a combination of all three.

# PERSONAL AND BUSINESS USES OF LIFE INSURANCE

Life insurance is used by individuals and families to provide financial protection. When a family loses a loved one, the consequences can be devastating emotionally and monetarily. Life insurance may be used to provide a final expense fund (funeral expenses), payoff existing debt (home mortgage, auto loans), provide an education fund for dependent children, and provide a steady stream of income allowing the family to maintain its normal standard of living. As we work, we attempt to build retirement savings. For this reason, retirement income needs should also be considered by individuals purchasing life insurance.

## BUSINESS USES FOR LIFE INSURANCE

Continued financial well-being for families depends not only on income from breadwinners but also on the continued good health of the businesses in which they are engaged. So life insurance also plays an important role in the business world. The reasons for buying life insurance for business uses are the same as those for buying personal insurance—in one word, protection.

When people buy insurance for personal reasons, their families are concerned; when they buy it for business reasons, their employees, their associates, and their families are involved. Life insurance is used in businesses in a variety of ways:

- As *a funding medium*. For example, life insurance can be used to fund a business continuation (buy-sell) agreement to transfer ownership between partners or stockholders or to fund a deferred compensation plan.

- As *a form of business interruption insurance*. Life insurance cannot prevent the interruption of business activity caused by death or disability; however, it can indemnify the business for losses created by these interruptions.

- As *an employee benefit*. Life insurance can protect employees and their families from the financial problems of death, disability, illness, and retirement.

**Partnership Buy-Sell Plans**  By law, partnerships are dissolved automatically upon the death of a partner. Thus, it is vital that a binding buy-sell agreement be established by the partners while they are living. Under such an agreement, the interest of any partner who dies will be sold to and purchased by the surviving partners. The price (or a formula to determine one) is agreed upon in advance and stipulated in the buy-sell plan. When properly executed—and funded with life insurance—a partnership buy-sell plan benefits all parties involved, and no uncertainty as to the outcome exists. The deceased has agreed beforehand to the sale of his interest. The surviving partners know they will have a legal right to buy, and the deceased's family and heirs are certain that the partnership interest will be disposed of at a fair price. Two kinds of partnership insured buy-sell agreements exist: the *cross-purchase plan* and the *entity plan*.

*Cross-purchase plans* are used by small partnerships. With these plans, each partner owns, is the beneficiary of, and pays the premiums for life insurance on the other partner or partners in an amount equal to his share of the purchase price. *Partnership entity plans* are used by large partnerships. Under the entity buy-sell plan, the business itself—the partnership—owns, pays for, and is the beneficiary of the policies that insure the lives of the individual partners. The partnership is a party to the buy-sell agreement. With an entity plan, when a partner dies, his interest is purchased from his or her estate by the partnership. This interest then is divided among the surviving partners in proportion to their own interest.

**Key-Person Insurance**  Another important use of life insurance is to protect a business against interruptions caused by the loss of one of its valuable assets—a key employee or key executive. When an individual dies, the primary function of life insurance is to offset the economic loss. When an insured key person dies, the insurance beneficiary is the business itself.

**Deferred Compensation Plans**  *Deferred compensation plans* are a popular way for businesses to provide an important benefit for their owners or for select employees. Basically, a deferred compensation plan is an arrangement whereby an employee (or owner) agrees to forgo some portion of his current income (such as annual raises or bonuses) until a specified future date, typically retirement. Life insurance is a popular funding vehicle for deferred compensation plans, in that the amounts deferred are used to pay premiums on cash value life insurance. At retirement, the cash values are available to the employee to supplement income. If the employee dies before retirement, his beneficiary receives the policy's proceeds.

# THE PURPOSE OF UNDERWRITING

Insurance companies would like nothing more than to be able to sell their policies to anyone wishing to buy them. However, they must exercise caution in deciding who is qualified to purchase insurance. Issuing a policy to someone who is uninsurable is an unwise business decision that can easily mean a financial loss for the company.

Each insurer sets its own standards as to what constitutes an insurable risk versus an uninsurable risk, just as each insurer determines the premium rates it will charge its policyowners. Every insurance applicant is reviewed individually by a company underwriter to determine if he or she meets the standards established by the company to qualify for its life insurance coverage.

## INSURABLE INTEREST

As discussed in Unit 1, insurable interest is extremely important in life insurance. Without this requirement, people could purchase life insurance and the policy would be nothing more than a wagering contract. As we have established, an insurable interest exists when the death of the insured would have a clear financial impact on the policyowner. (See Figure 6.1.) Individuals are presumed to have an insurable interest in themselves. Therefore, when the applicant and proposed insured are the same person, there is no question that insurable interest exists. Questions are raised, however, with third-party contracts—those in which the applicant is not the insured.

It bears repeating that with life insurance, an insurable interest must exist only at the policy inception; it need not exist when the policy proceeds actually are paid. Thus, a policyowner could assign a life policy to someone who has no insurable interest in the insured, and the assignment nonetheless would be valid.

## INSURABILITY

Once the underwriter determines that insurable interest exists, he must next determine the applicant's insurability. The underwriting process is the way an underwriter determines insurability.

TAKE NOTE

Some relationships automatically are presumed to qualify as having an insurable interest—spouses, parents, children, and people in certain business relationships. In most other cases, the burden is on the applicant to show that an insurable interest exists.

**FIGURE 6.1   What Constitutes Insurable Interest?**

Though laws differ slightly from state to state, in general the following types of relationships automatically carry insurable interest:

- An individual has an insurable interest in his or her life.

- A husband or wife has an insurable interest in his or her spouse.

- A parent has an insurable interest in his or her child.

- A child has an insurable interest in a parent or grandparent.

- A business has an insurable interest in the lives of its officers, directors and key employees.

- Business partners have an insurable interest in each other.

- A creditor has an insurable interest in the life of a debtor, but only to the extent of the debt.

# THE UNDERWRITING PROCESS

The underwriting process is accomplished by reviewing and evaluating information about an applicant and applying what is known about the individual against the insurer's standards and guidelines for insurability and premium rates.

Underwriters have several sources of underwriting information available to help them develop a risk profile of an applicant. The number of sources checked usually depends on several factors, most notably the size of the requested policy and the risk profile developed after an initial review of the application. The larger the policy, the more comprehensive and diligent the underwriting research. Regardless of the policy size, if the application raises questions in the underwriter's mind about the applicant, that also can trigger a review of other sources of information.

## THE APPLICATION

The application for insurance is the basic source of insurability information. Regardless of what other sources of information the underwriter may draw from, the application—the first source of information to be reviewed—will be evaluated thoroughly. Thus, it is the agent's responsibility to see that an applicant's answers to application questions are recorded fully and accurately. There are three basic parts to a typical life insurance application: *Part I—General, Part II—Medical*, and *Part III—Agent's Report*.

**Part I—General**   Part I of the application asks general questions about the proposed insured, including name, age, address, birth date, sex, income, marital status, and occupation. Also to be indicated here are details about the requested insurance coverage:

- type of policy;

- amount of insurance;

- name and relationship of the beneficiary;

- other insurance the proposed insured owns; and

- additional insurance applications he has pending.

Other information sought may indicate possible exposure to a hazardous hobby, foreign travel, aviation activity, or military service. Whether the proposed insured smokes also is indicated in Part I.

**Part II—Medical**   Part II focuses on the proposed insured's health and asks a number of questions about the health history of not only the proposed insured but also his family. This medical section must be completed in its entirety for every application. Depending on the proposed policy face amount, this section may or may not be all that is required in the way of medical information. The individual to be insured may be required to take a medical exam.

**Part III—Agent's Report**   Part III of the application often is called the agent's report. This is where the agent reports his personal observations about the proposed insured. Because the agent represents the interests of the insurance company, he is expected to complete this part of the application fully and truthfully.

In this important section, the agent provides firsthand knowledge about the applicant's financial condition and character, the background and purpose of the sale, and how long the agent has known the applicant.

The agent's report also usually asks if the proposed insurance will replace an existing policy. If it will, most states demand that certain procedures be followed to protect the rights of consumers when policy replacement is involved.

## THE MEDICAL REPORT

A policy often is issued on the basis of the information provided in the application alone. Most companies have set nonmedical limits, meaning that applications for policies below a certain face amount (perhaps $50,000 or even $100,000) will not require any additional medical information other than what is provided by the application. However, for larger policies (or smaller policies when the applicant is older than a certain age) a medical report may be required to provide further underwriting information.

Medical reports must be completed by a qualified person, but that person does not necessarily have to be a physician. Many companies accept reports completed by a paramedic or a registered nurse. Usually the applicant can select the physician or paramedic facility to perform the exam; insurers also are prepared to recommend paramedic facilities where the exam can be given. In almost all cases, the expense for the exam is borne by the insurance company.

When completed, the medical report is forwarded to the insurance company, where it is reviewed by the company's medical director or a designated associate.

## THE MEDICAL INFORMATION BUREAU

Another source of underwriting information that focuses specifically on an applicant's medical history is the Medical Information Bureau (MIB). The MIB is a nonprofit central information agency established by a number of insurance companies to aid in the underwriting process and is supported by more than 600 member insurance companies.

The MIB's purpose is to serve as a reliable source of medical information concerning applicants and to help disclose cases where an applicant either forgets or conceals pertinent underwriting information, or submits erroneous or misleading medical information with fraudulent intent. The MIB operations help to hold down the cost of life insurance for all policyowners through the prevention of misrepresentation and fraud.

This is how the system works: If a company finds that one of its applicants has a physical ailment or impairment listed by the MIB, the company is pledged to report the information to the MIB in the form of a code number. By having this information, home office underwriters will know that a past problem existed should the same applicant later apply for life insurance with another member company. The information is available to member companies only and may be used only for underwriting and claims purposes.

## INSPECTION REPORTS

Inspection reports usually are obtained by insurance companies on applicants who apply for large amounts of life insurance. These reports contain information about prospective insureds, which is reviewed to determine their insurability. Insurance companies normally obtain inspection reports from national investigative agencies or firms.

The purpose of these reports is to provide a picture of an applicant's general character and reputation, mode of living, finances, and exposure to abnormal hazards. Investigators or inspectors may interview employees, neighbors, and associates of the applicant as well as the applicant.

Inspection reports ordinarily are not requested on applicants who apply for smaller policies, although company rules vary as to the sizes of policies that require a report by an outside agency.

## CREDIT REPORTS

Some applicants may prove to be poor credit risks, based on information obtained before a policy is issued. Thus, credit reports obtained from retail merchants' associations or other sources are a valuable underwriting tool in many cases.

Applicants who have questionable credit ratings can cause an insurance company to lose money. Applicants with poor credit standings are likely to allow their policies to lapse within a short time, perhaps even before a second premium is paid. An insurance company can lose money on a policy that is lapsed quickly, because the insurer's expenses to acquire the policy cannot be recovered in a short period of time. It is possible, then, that home office underwriters will refuse to insure persons who have failed to pay their bills or who appear to be applying for more life insurance than they reasonably can afford.

## THE FAIR CREDIT REPORTING ACT OF 1970

To protect the rights of consumers for whom an inspection report or credit (or consumer) report has been requested, Congress enacted the Fair Credit Reporting Act (FCRA) in 1970. As previously mentioned, this federal law applies to financial institutions that request these types of consumer reports, including insurance companies.

The FCRA established procedures for the collection and disclosure of information obtained on consumers through investigation and credit reports; it seeks to ensure fairness with regard to confidentiality, accuracy, and disclosure. The FCRA is quite extensive. Included in it are the following important requirements pertaining to insurers:

- Applicants must be notified (usually within three days) that the report has been requested. The insurer also must notify the applicant that he can request disclosure of the nature and scope of the investigation. If the applicant requests such disclosure, the insurer must provide a summary within five days of the request.

- The consumer must be provided with the names of all people contacted during the preceding six months for purposes of the report. People contacted who are associated with the consumer's place of employment must be identified as far back as two years.

- If, based on an inspection or consumer report, the insurer rejects an application, the company must provide the applicant with the name and address of the consumer reporting agency that supplied the report.

- If requested by the applicant (more formally, the consumer), the consumer reporting agency—not the insurance company—must disclose the nature and substance of all information (except medical) contained in the consumer's file. The FCRA does not give consumers the right to see the actual report, although most reporting agencies do provide copies of the report routinely, if requested.

- If the applicant/consumer disagrees with information in his file, he can file a statement giving his opinion on the issue.

## CLASSIFICATION OF APPLICANTS

Once all the information about a given applicant has been reviewed and evaluated, the underwriter seeks to classify the risk that the applicant poses to the insurer. In a few cases, an applicant represents a risk so great that he is considered uninsurable and his application will be rejected.

> **TAKE NOTE**
>
> Some substandard applicants are rejected outright; others will be accepted for coverage but with an increase in their policy premium.

However, the vast majority of insurance applicants fall within an insurer's underwriting guidelines and accordingly will be classified as a *standard risk*, *substandard risk*, or *preferred risk*.

**Standard Risk**  *Standard risk* is the term used for individuals who fit the insurer's guidelines for policy issue without special restrictions or additional rating. These individuals meet the same conditions as the tabular risks on which the insurer's premium rates are based.

**Substandard Risk**  A substandard risk is one below the insurer's standard or average risk guidelines. An individual can be rated as substandard for number of reasons: poor health, a dangerous occupation, or attributes or habits that could be hazardous.

**Preferred Risk**  Many insurers today reward exceptionally good risks by assigning them to a preferred risk classification. Preferred risk premium rates generally are lower than standard risk rates. Personal characteristics that contribute to a preferred risk rating include not smoking, weight within an ideal range, and favorable cholesterol levels.

# FIELD UNDERWRITING PROCEDURES

As noted earlier, an agent plays an important role in underwriting. As a field underwriter, he initiates the process and is responsible for many important tasks: proper solicitation, completing the application thoroughly and accurately, obtaining appropriate signatures, collecting the initial premium, and issuing a receipt. Each of these tasks is vitally important to the underwriting process and policy issue.

## PROPER SOLICITATION

As a representative of the insurer, an agent has the duty and responsibility to solicit good business. This means that an agent's solicitation and prospecting efforts should focus on cases that fall within the insurer's underwriting guidelines and represent profitable business to the insurer. At the same time, the agent has a responsibility to the insurance-buying public to observe the highest professional standards when conducting insurance business. All sales solicitations should be open and aboveboard, with the agent identifying the insurer he represents and the reason for the call clearly. In addition, good sales practices avoid high pressure tactics and are aimed at helping applicants select the most appropriate policies to meet their needs.

False advertising is prohibited as an unfair trade practice in all states. In this context, *advertising* encompasses almost any kind of communication used to promote the sale of an insurance policy.

**E X A M P L E**   Descriptive literature, sales aids, slide shows, prepared group talks, brochures, sales illustrations, and policy illustrations all are considered advertising.

All advertising must be truthful. Insurance products should be described properly and accurately, without exaggerating benefits or minimizing drawbacks.

Sales presentations must not be deceptive. What is a deceptive sale? Any presentation that gives a prospect or client the wrong impression about any aspect of an insurance policy or plan is deceptive. Any presentation that does not provide complete disclosure to a prospect or client is deceptive. Any presentation that includes misleading or inconclusive product comparisons is deceptive.

## COMPLETING THE APPLICATION

As mentioned earlier, the application is one of the most important sources of underwriting information, and it is the agent's responsibility to see that it is completed fully and accurately. Statements made in the application are used by insurers to evaluate risks and decide whether or not to insure the life of the applicant. Such statements are considered representations: statements an applicant represents as being substantially true to the best of his knowledge and belief but which are not warranted to be exact in every detail. Representations must be true only to the extent that they are material to the risk.

If an insurer rejects a claim based on a representation, it bears the burden of proving materiality. Representations are considered fraudulent only when they relate to a matter material to the risk and when they were made with fraudulent intent.

Several signatures are required to complete an application, and to overlook a needed signature will cause delay in issuing a policy. Each application requires the signatures of the proposed insured, the policyowner (if different from the insured), and the agent who solicits the application. Moreover, a form authorizing the insurance company to obtain investigative consumer reports or medical information from investigative agencies, physicians, hospitals, or other sources generally must be signed by the proposed insured and the agent as witness.

**Changes in the Application**  The application for insurance must be completed accurately, honestly, and thoroughly, and it must be signed by the insured and witnessed. When attached to the insurance policy, the application becomes part of the legal contract between the insurer and the insured. Consequently, the general rule is that no alterations of any written application can be made by any person other than the applicant without the applicant's written permission.

When an applicant makes a mistake in the information he has given to an agent in completing the application, the applicant can have the agent correct the information, but the applicant must initial the correction. If the company discovers a mistake, it usually returns the application to the agent, who then corrects the mistake with the applicant and has the applicant initial the change. If the company accepts an application and then, before the policy's incontestable clause takes effect, discovers incorrect or incomplete information in it, the company may rescind or cancel the contract.

## INITIAL PREMIUM AND RECEIPTS

It is generally in the best interests of both the proposed insured and the agent to have the initial premium (or a portion of it) paid with the application. For the agent, this usually will help solidify the sale and may accelerate the payment of commissions on the sale. The proposed insured benefits by having the insurance protection become effective immediately, with some important restrictions.

### FIGURE 6.2   Conditional Receipts

When a conditional receipt is given, the applicant and the company form what might be called a *conditional contract*—contingent upon conditions that exist at the time the application is signed (or when the medical exam is completed, if required). In providing early coverage, the insurer conditionally assumes the risk and will provide coverage from the specified date, on the condition that the applicant is approved for policy issue.

For example, assume an agent sells a $50,000 nonmedical life insurance policy to Matthew, who hands the agent his signed application with a check for the first premium. In turn, Matthew receives from the agent a conditional receipt for the premium. Two days later, Matthew becomes seriously ill and enters the hospital. So long as the company finds that Matthew qualifies for the policy as applied for, the company will issue the policy, regardless of his condition in the hospital. In fact, if Matthew died before the policy was issued, but was qualified at the time of application, his beneficiary still would receive the $50,000 death benefit.

However, in this example, if the company's underwriter determined that Matthew was uninsurable, and thus rejected the application, then there is no coverage, even during the period when the receipt was effective.

On the other hand, if a premium deposit is not paid with the application, the policy will not become valid until the initial premium is collected.

Applicants who pay a premium deposit with the application are entitled to a premium receipt. It is the type of receipt given that determines exactly when and under what conditions an applicant's coverage begins. The two major types of receipts are *conditional receipts* and *binding receipts* (sometimes called *temporary insurance agreements*).

**Conditional Receipts**   The most common type of premium receipt is the conditional receipt. A conditional receipt indicates that certain conditions must be met for the insurance coverage to go into effect.

The conditional receipt provides that coverage is effective when the applicant pays the initial premium—on the condition that the applicant proves to be insurable—either on the date the application was signed or the date of the medical exam, if one is required.

Companies usually impose a limit on the amount of coverage provided under a conditional receipt (generally $100,000 or less). Therefore, even if the applicant is applying for a policy with a much higher face amount, the insurer usually will restrict the conditional coverage to a specified limit.

**Binding Receipts**  Under the binding receipt (or temporary insurance agreement), coverage is guaranteed, even if the proposed insured is found to be uninsurable, until the insurer rejects the application formally. Because the underwriting process often can take several weeks or longer, this can place the company at considerable risk. Accordingly, binding receipts often are reserved only for a company's most experienced agents.

Like the conditional receipt, a binding receipt typically stipulates a maximum amount that would be payable during the special protection period.

## POLICY EFFECTIVE DATE

The policy effective date—the date the policy goes into effect—is another important factor that must be addressed in any life insurance sale. The effective date is important for two reasons: it identifies when the coverage is effective and establishes the date by which future annual premiums must be paid.

If a receipt (either conditional or binding) was issued in exchange for the payment of an initial premium deposit, the date of the receipt generally will be noted as the policy effective date in the contract.

If a premium deposit is not given with the application, the policy effective date usually is left to the discretion of the insurer. Often, it will be the date the policy is issued by the insurance company. However, the policy will not be truly effective until it is delivered to the applicant, the first premium is paid, and a statement of continued good health is obtained.

**Back Dating**  As we have learned, the premiums required to support a life insurance policy are determined, in part, by the insured's age. If an applicant can be treated by the insurance company as being a year younger, the result can be a lifetime of slightly lower premiums. Thus, it is understandable that applicants might want to back date a policy, making it effective at an earlier date than the present, in order to save age.

First of all, the insurer must allow back dating. Second, the company usually will impose a time limit on how far back a policy can be back dated (typically six months, the limit imposed by most states' laws). More importantly, the policyowner is required to pay all back-due premiums and the next premium is due at the back-dated anniversary date (which can be as close as six months in the future).

# POLICY ISSUE AND DELIVERY

After the underwriting is complete and the company has decided to issue the policy, other departments in the company assume the responsibility for issuing the policy. Once issued, the policy document is sent to the sales agent for delivery to the new policyowner. The policy usually is not sent directly to the policyowner, because as an important legal document, it should be explained by the sales agent to the policyowner.

**FIGURE 6.3   From Application to Policy Delivery**

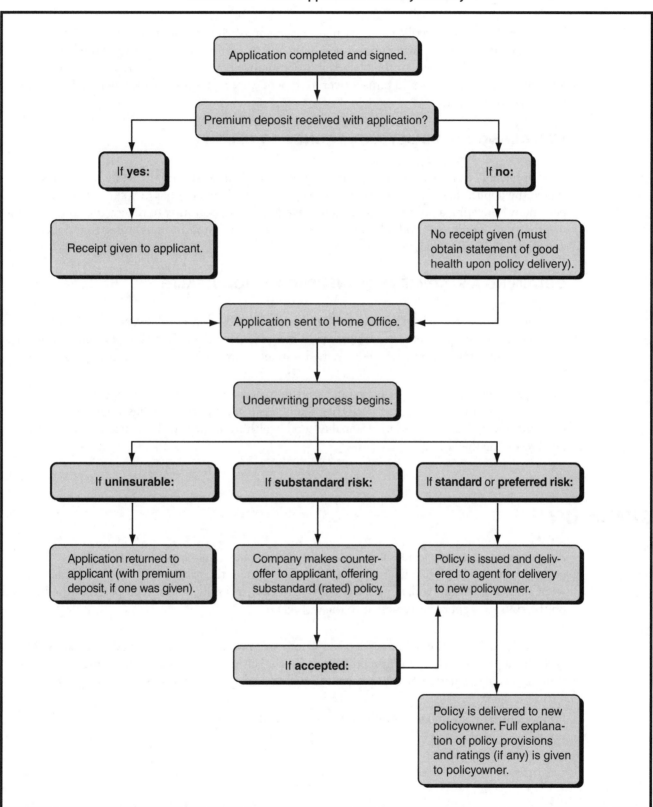

## CONSTRUCTIVE DELIVERY

From a legal standpoint, policy delivery may be accomplished without physically delivering the policy into the policyowner's possession. Constructive delivery, which satisfies the legal interpretation of delivery, is accomplished if the insurance company intentionally relinquishes all control over the policy and turns it over to someone acting for the policyowner, including the company's own agent.

## EXPLAINING THE POLICY AND RATINGS TO CLIENTS

Most applicants will not remember everything they should about their policies after they have signed the application. This is another reason agents should deliver policies in person. Only by personally delivering a policy does the agent have a timely opportunity to review the contract and its provisions, exclusions, and riders. In fact, some states (and most insurers) insist that policies be delivered in person for this very reason.

## OBTAINING A STATEMENT OF INSURED'S GOOD HEALTH

In some instances, the initial premium will not be paid until the agent delivers the policy. In such cases, common company practice requires that, before leaving the policy, the agent must collect the premium and obtain from the insured a signed statement attesting to his continued good health.

The agent then is to submit the premium with the signed statement to the insurance company. Because there can be no contract until the premium is paid, the company has a right to know that the policyowner has remained in reasonably good health from the time he signed the application until receiving the policy.

# SUMMARY

An insurance company decides if it is going to issue a policy to an applicant during the underwriting process. The underwriter seeks to determine if the proposed insured is insurable and, if so, at standard, substandard, or preferred rates. Underwriters assign rates to proposed insureds, based on the risks the applicants represent to the insurers.

The effective date of the policy depends on whether or not an initial premium deposit was paid with the application (thus requiring the agent to issue either a conditional or binding receipt) as well as the date requested by the applicant (policies can be back dated in some situations).

Policy delivery is an important responsibility of the sales agent.

# U N I T   Q U I Z

1. Underwriting is a process of
   A. selection and issue of policies
   B. evaluation and classification of risks
   C. selection, reporting, and rejection of risks
   D. selection, classification, and evaluation of risks

2. Which of the following statements about a life insurance policy application is CORRECT?
   A. The names of both the insured and the beneficiary are indicated on the application.
   B. If an applicant's age is shown erroneously on a life insurance application as 28 instead of 29, the result may be a premium quote that is higher than it should be.
   C. The size of the policy being applied for does not affect the underwriting process.
   D. The agent's report in the application must be signed by the agent and the applicant.

3. If a medical report is required on an applicant, it is completed by
   A. a home office underwriter
   B. a paramedic or examining physician
   C. the agent
   D. the home office medical director

4. Which of the following statements about the Medical Information Bureau (MIB) is CORRECT?
   A. The MIB is operated by a national network of hospitals.
   B. Information obtained by the MIB is available to all physicians.
   C. The MIB provides assistance in the underwriting of life insurance.
   D. Applicants may request that MIB reports be attached to their policies.

5. Which of the following statements regarding the Fair Credit Reporting Act (FCRA) is CORRECT?
   A. Applicants must be notified within a short period of time that their credit report has been requested.
   B. If an applicant for insurance is rejected based on a consumer report, the name of the reporting agency must be kept confidential.
   C. If requested to do so, the insurance company must provide the actual consumer report to the applicant.
   D. Consumer reports are final in nature and cannot be disputed by an applicant.

6. Which of the following statements about the classification of applicants is NOT correct?
   A. A substandard applicant never can be rejected outright by the insurer.
   B. Applicants who are preferred risks have premium rates that generally are lower than standard rate risks.
   C. An individual can be rated as a substandard risk because of a dangerous occupation.
   D. A standard applicant fits the insurer's guidelines for policy issue without special restrictions.

7. Which of the following statements about the Fair Credit Reporting Act is CORRECT?
   A. It prohibits insurance companies from obtaining reports on applicants from outside investigative agencies.
   B. It provides that consumers have the right to question reports made about them by investigative agencies.
   C. It applies to reports about applicants that are made by insurance agents to their companies.
   D. It prohibits insurance companies from rejecting an application based on a credit report.

8. Generally, the party who delivers an insurance policy to the new policyowner is the
   A. insurance company's home office
   B. sales agent
   C. state insurance commissioner's office
   D. underwriter

9. Who performs the function of risk selection in determining an individual's insurability for policy issue?
   A. Actuary
   B. Agent
   C. Fiduciary
   D. Underwriter

10. What is the basic source of information for life insurance underwriting and policy issue?
    A. Consumer reports
    B. Medical Information Bureau
    C. Application
    D. Physician reports

# ANSWERS AND RATIONALES TO UNIT QUIZ

1. **D.** Underwriting is the process of reviewing the many characteristics that make up an applicant's risk profile to determine if the applicant is insurable at standard or substandard rates. It therefore can be considered a process of selection, classification, and evaluation of risks.

2. **A.** In the application, the proposed insured must provide details about the requested insurance, including the type of policy, amount of insurance, name and relationship of the beneficiary, other insurance owned, and any additional insurance applications that are pending.

3. **B.** A physician, paramedic, or registered nurse typically can complete a medical report on an applicant.

4. **C.** The Medical Information Bureau is a nonprofit central information agency that aids in the underwriting process. Its purpose is to provide reliable medical information concerning applicants and to help disclose cases where an applicant either forgets or conceals pertinent underwriting information or fraudulently submits erroneous or misleading medical information.

5. **A.** If an insurance company requests an inspection or credit report, the applicant must be notified (usually within three days) that the report has been requested.

6. **A.** Some substandard applicants can be rejected outright while others will be accepted for coverage but with an increase in their policy premium.

7. **B.** If an applicant disagrees with information in his MIB file, he can file a statement giving his opinion on the issue.

8. **B.** Once a policy has been issued, the insurer sends the policy to the sales agent for delivery to the new policyowner. It usually is not sent directly to the policyowner.

9. **D.** Risk selection is performed by insurance company underwriters.

10. **C.** The application for insurance is the basic source of insurability information. It is the first source of information to be reviewed, and it is reviewed thoroughly.

# 7

# Annuities

## KEY CONCEPTS

- The difference between annuities and life insurance
- Annuities as a retirement savings and retirement income vehicle
- Annuity payout options
- Annuity investment options
- Taxation of annuities

As noted in our discussion of life insurance, a beneficiary can choose among several different options for receiving the proceeds from a life insurance policy. One option is the life income option, which actually consists of about half a dozen choices. Beneficiaries who select this option receive an important guarantee: they can never outlive the income provided under the contract.

When a beneficiary selects a life income option, he actually is using the proceeds to purchase an annuity and selecting an annuity payout option. Annuities provide a way to receive a stream of income for a guaranteed period of time, a period that most typically is defined in terms of the recipient's life. In this unit, we examine how annuities can be structured to meet a person's financial needs and also look at the different payout options available. Finally, we will examine the different ways in which annuities typically are used and how payments are taxed.

## OBJECTIVE

When you complete this unit you should be able to:

- explain how annuities can be funded and the differences between immediate and deferred annuities;

- list and explain the various annuity payout options;

- compare and contrast fixed and variable annuities;

- explain how annuity payments are taxed using the exclusion ratio; and

- identify how annuities are used by individuals, in qualified plans and in structured settlements.

# PURPOSE AND FUNCTION OF ANNUITIES

An annuity is a mathematical concept that is quite simple in its most basic definition. Start with a lump sum of money, pay it out in equal installments over a period of time until the original fund is exhausted, and you have an annuity. An annuity simply is a vehicle for liquidating a sum of money. Of course, in practice the concept is more complex. An important factor not mentioned above is interest. The sum of money that has not yet been paid out is earning interest, and that interest also is passed on to the income recipient, or the *annuitant*.

Anyone can provide an annuity. By knowing the original sum of money (the principal), the length of the payout period, and an assumed rate of interest, it is a fairly simple process to calculate the payment amount. Actuaries have constructed tables of annuity factors that make this process even easier.

 **EXAMPLE**     The present value interest factor for a $1 annuity (a formal name for one of the afore-mentioned tables; see Figure 7.1) shows that the factor for a 20-year annual payment of $1, based on a 7% interest factor, is 10.59. This means that if a person set aside $10.59, and could earn 7% interest while the fund was being depleted, an annual income of $1 could be paid for 20 years. The income recipient would receive a total of $20 for the original $10.59 invested in the annuity.

Other tables solve for related problems (for example, how long income can be paid for any given amount of principal). The basic underlying principle, however, is the same in every case—the amount of an annuity payment depends on three factors: starting principal, interest, and income period.

One important element is absent from this simple definition of an annuity, and it is the one distinguishing factor that separates life insurance companies from all other financial institutions. While anyone can set up an annuity and pay income for a stated period of time, only life insurance companies can do so and guarantee income for the life of the annuitant.

Because of their experience with mortality tables, life insurance companies are uniquely qualified to combine an extra factor into the standard annuity calculation. Called a survivorship factor, it is, in concept, very similar to the mortality factor in a life insurance premium calculation. Thus, it provides insurers with the means to guarantee annuity payments for life, regardless of how long that life lasts.

**FIGURE 7.1   Present Value of $1 Payable**

The following is a present value annuity table that shows the amount which, if deposited today at 7 percent interest, would produce an annual income of $1 for the specified number of years. In other words, this table reflects the value today of a series of payments tomorrow. For example, the present value of $1 payable for 25 years, at 7 percent interest, is $11.65. This means that $11.65 deposited today at 7 percent interest would generate a payment of $1 for 25 years.

| Years | Present Value (at 7 percent) | Years | Present Value (at 7 percent) |
|---|---|---|---|
| 5 | $4.10 | 30 | $12.40 |
| 10 | $7.02 | 35 | $12.94 |
| 15 | $9.10 | 40 | $13.33 |
| 20 | $10.59 | 45 | $13.60 |
| 25 | $11.65 | 50 | $13.80 |

In more practical terms, suppose you wanted to know how much money you should have on hand at age 65 to generate $5,000 a year in income for 10 years, assuming you could earn 7 percent interest while the fund was being paid out. The present value of $1 payable for 10 years is $7.02; therefore, the present value of $10,000 payable for 10 years is $70,200 ($10,000 × $7.02).

## ANNUITIES VERSUS LIFE INSURANCE

It is important to realize that annuities are not life insurance contracts. In fact, it can be said that an annuity is a mirror image of a life insurance contract—they look alike but actually are exact opposites.

Whereas the principal function of a life insurance contract is to create an estate (an estate being a sum of money) by the periodic payment of money into the contract, an annuity's principal function is to liquidate an estate by the periodic payment of money out of the contract. Life insurance is concerned with how soon one will die; life annuities are concerned with how long one will live.

It is easy to see the value of annuities in fulfilling some important financial protection needs. Their role in retirement planning should be obvious; guaranteeing that an annuitant cannot outlive the payments from a life annuity has brought peace of mind to countless people over the years. Annuities can play a vital role in any situation where a stream of income is needed for only a few years or for a lifetime.

## ANNUITY BASICS

An annuity is a cash contract with an insurance company. Unlike life insurance products, where policy issue and pricing are based largely on mortality risk, annuities primarily are investment products. Individuals purchase or fund annuities with a single sum amount or through a series of periodic payments. The insurer credits the annuity fund with a certain rate of interest, which currently is not taxable to the annuitant. In this way, the annuity grows. The ultimate amount that will be available for payout is, in part, a reflection of these factors. Most annuities guarantee a death benefit payable in the event the annuitant dies before payout begins; however, it usually is limited to the amount paid into the contract plus interest credited.

With any annuity, there are two distinct time periods involved: the accumulation period and the payout or annuity period. The accumulation period is that time during which funds are being paid into the annuity in the form of payments by the contract holder and interest earnings credited by the insurer. The payout or annuity period refers to the point at which the annuity ceases to be an accumulation vehicle and begins to generate benefit payments on a regular basis.

## STRUCTURE AND DESIGN OF ANNUITIES

Annuities are flexible in that the purchaser has a number of options that enable her to structure and design the product to best suit his needs:

- Funding method—single lump-sum payment or periodic payments over time

- Date annuity benefit payments begin—immediately or deferred until a future date

- Investment configuration—a fixed (guaranteed) rate of return or a variable (non-guaranteed) rate of return

- Payout period—a specified term of years or for life, or a combination of both

Let's take a closer look at each of these options. (They are illustrated in graphic form in Figure 7.2.)

## FUNDING METHOD

An annuity begins with a sum of money, called the principal. Annuity principal is created (or funded) in one of two ways: immediately with a single premium or over time with a series of periodic premiums.

**Single Premium**   Annuities can be funded with a single, lump-sum premium, in which case the principal is created immediately.

**E X A M P L E**   An individual nearing retirement whose financial priority is retirement income could surrender his whole life policy and use the cash value as a lump-sum premium to fund an annuity.

**FIGURE 7.2**   **Annuities Classification Chart**

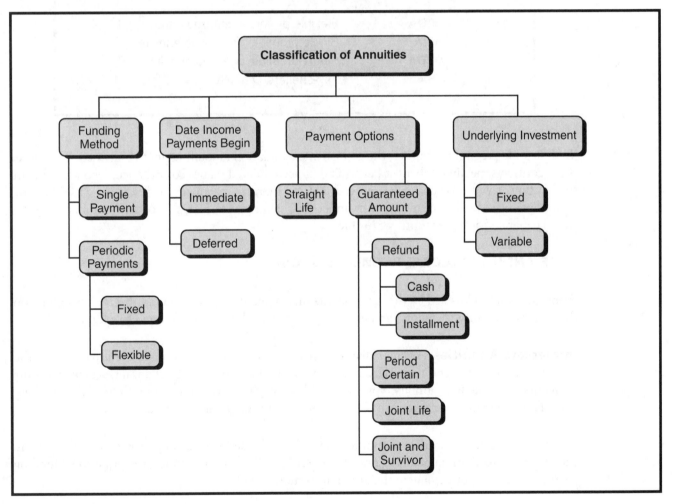

> ### TAKE NOTE
>
> The income flow from immediate annuities can be either fixed or variable. Under a fixed immediate annuity, the annuitant is guaranteed an income flow without risk of market fluctuations affecting the amount of the income. The insurance company absorbs the market risk associated with the investment of the annuity funds. In contrast, a variable immediate annuity transfers the investment risk to the annuitant. This means that once an income stream is created, the payments can increase or decrease depending on the performance of the underlying investments.

**Periodic Payments** Annuities also can be funded through a series of periodic premiums that, over time, will create the annuity principal fund. At one time, it was common for insurers to require that periodic annuity premiums be fixed and level, much like insurance premiums.

#### FIGURE 7.3    Types of Annuities

| | |
|---|---|
| FPDA | Flexible-premium deferred annuity |
| SPIA | Single-premium immediate annuity |
| SPDA | Single-premium deferred annuity |
| TSA | Tax-sheltered annuity |

With flexible premium annuities, the ultimate accumulation amount cannot be defined. Therefore, these contracts specify the benefit per $1,000 of accumulated value. For instance, a contract might specify that it will provide for guaranteed lifetime monthly payments of $5.06 per $1,000 at the annuitant's age 65. This means that a contract that has grown to $100,000 on the annuitant's age 65 would generate $506 per month for his life.

## DATE ANNUITY INCOME PAYMENTS BEGIN

Annuities can be classified by the date the income payments to the annuitant begin. Depending on the contract, annuity payments can begin immediately or they can be deferred to a future date.

**Immediate Annuities** An immediate annuity is designed to make its first benefit payment to the annuitant at one payment interval from the date of purchase. Because most annuities make monthly payments, an immediate annuity typically would pay its first payment one month from the purchase date. Thus, an immediate annuity has a relatively short accumulation period.

As you might guess, immediate annuities can only be funded with a single payment and often are called single-premium immediate annuities, or SPIAs. An annuity cannot accept periodic funding payments and pay out income to the annuitant simultaneously.

**Deferred Annuities** Deferred annuities provide income payments at some specified future date. Unlike immediate annuities, deferred annuities can be funded with periodic payments over time. Periodic payment annuities commonly are called flexible premium deferred annuities, or FPDAs. Deferred annuities also can be funded with single premiums, in which case they are called single-premium deferred annuities.

**T A K E   N O T E**

Surrender charges for most annuities are of limited duration, applying only during the first five to eight years of the contract. However, for those years in which surrender charges are applicable, most annuities provide for an annual free withdrawal, which allows the annuity owner to withdraw up to a certain percentage, usually 10%, of his annuity account with no surrender charge applied.

**T A K E   N O T E**

The straight life income annuity pays the most income per month, in comparison with the other annuity payout options.

Most insurers charge contract holders for liquidating deferred annuities in the early years of the contract. These surrender charges cover the costs associated with selling and issuing contracts as well as costs associated with the insurer's need to liquidate underlying investments at a possibly inappropriate time.

Insurance companies impose restrictions on how far into the future income benefit payments may be deferred. Typically, deferred annuities must be annuitized (that is, converted from the accumulation mode to an income paying mode) before the annuity owner reaches a maximum age, such as 75 years.

## ANNUITY PAYOUT OPTIONS

Just as life insurance beneficiaries have various settlement options for the disposition of policy proceeds, so too do annuitants have various income payout options to specify how an annuity fund is to be paid out. In fact, selecting any of the life income options as a life insurance settlement is the same as using the policy proceeds to purchase a single-premium immediate annuity and selecting an annuity income option.

**Straight Life Income Option**   A straight life income annuity option (often called a life annuity or a straight life annuity) pays the annuitant a guaranteed income for his lifetime. When the annuitant dies, no further payments are made to anyone. If the annuitant dies before the annuity fund (the principal) is depleted, the balance, in effect, is forfeited to the insurer. It is used to provide payments to other annuitants who live beyond the point where the income they receive equals their annuity principal. (See Figure 7.4.)

**FIGURE 7.4 Life Income Option**

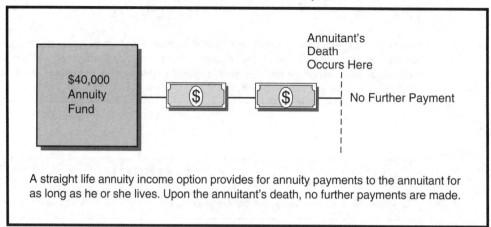

A straight life annuity income option provides for annuity payments to the annuitant for as long as he or she lives. Upon the annuitant's death, no further payments are made.

**Life with Period Certain Option** Also known as the life income with term certain option, this payout approach is designed to pay the annuitant an income for life but guarantees a definite minimum period of payments. (See Figure 7.5.)

E X A M P L E

If an individual has a life and 10-year certain annuity, he is guaranteed payments for life or 10 years, whichever is longer. If the individual receives monthly payments for six years and then dies, his beneficiary will receive the same payments for four more years. Of course, if the annuitant died after receiving monthly annuity payments for 10 or more years, his beneficiary would receive nothing from the annuity.

**FIGURE 7.5 Life with Period Certain Option**

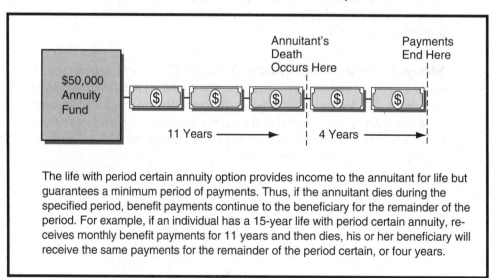

The life with period certain annuity option provides income to the annuitant for life but guarantees a minimum period of payments. Thus, if the annuitant dies during the specified period, benefit payments continue to the beneficiary for the remainder of the period. For example, if an individual has a 15-year life with period certain annuity, receives monthly benefit payments for 11 years and then dies, his or her beneficiary will receive the same payments for the remainder of the period certain, or four years.

**Joint and Full Survivor Option**   The joint and full survivor option provides for payment of the annuity to two people. If either person dies, the same income payments continue to the survivor for life. When the surviving annuitant dies, no further payments are made to anyone. (See Figure 7.6.)

FIGURE 7.6   **Joint and Survivor Option**

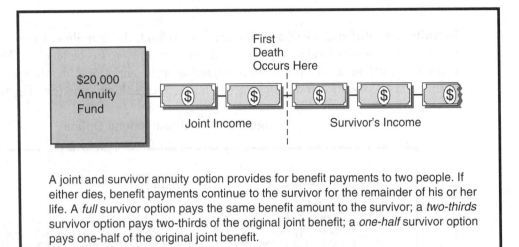

A joint and survivor annuity option provides for benefit payments to two people. If either dies, benefit payments continue to the survivor for the remainder of his or her life. A *full* survivor option pays the same benefit amount to the survivor; a *two-thirds* survivor option pays two-thirds of the original joint benefit; a *one-half* survivor option pays one-half of the original joint benefit.

## PAYMENTS TO BENEFICIARIES

When a beneficiary is eligible to receive annuity proceeds under "period certain" options, they may receive the proceeds in one of two ways:

**Cash Refund Option**   A cash refund option provides a guaranteed income to the annuitant for life and, if the annuitant dies before the annuity fund (the principal) is depleted, a lump-sum cash payment of the remainder is made to the annuitant's beneficiary. Thus, the beneficiary receives an amount equal to the beginning annuity fund less the amount of income already paid to the deceased annuitant. (See Figure 7.7.)

FIGURE 7.7   **Cash Refund Option**

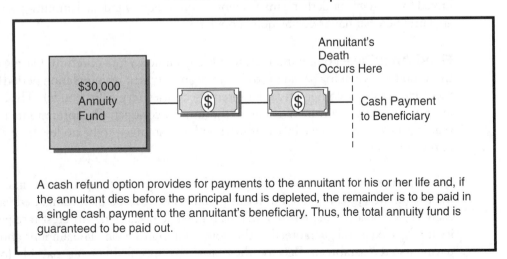

A cash refund option provides for payments to the annuitant for his or her life and, if the annuitant dies before the principal fund is depleted, the remainder is to be paid in a single cash payment to the annuitant's beneficiary. Thus, the total annuity fund is guaranteed to be paid out.

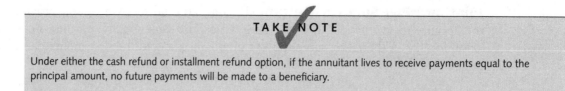

TAKE NOTE

Under either the cash refund or installment refund option, if the annuitant lives to receive payments equal to the principal amount, no future payments will be made to a beneficiary.

**Installment Refund Option** Like the cash refund, the installment refund option guarantees that the total annuity fund will be paid to the annuitant or to his beneficiary. The difference is that under the installment option, the fund remaining at the annuitant's death is paid to the beneficiary in the form of continued annuity payments, not as a single lump sum. (See Figure 7.8.)

**FIGURE 7.8  Installment Refund Option**

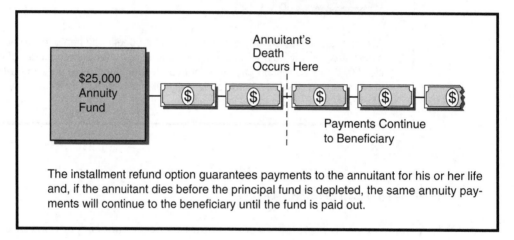

The installment refund option guarantees payments to the annuitant for his or her life and, if the annuitant dies before the principal fund is depleted, the same annuity payments will continue to the beneficiary until the fund is paid out.

## INVESTMENT CONFIGURATION

Annuities also can be defined according to their investment configuration, which affects the income benefits they pay. The two classifications are fixed annuities, which provide a fixed, guaranteed accumulation or payout, and variable annuities, which attempt to offset inflation by providing a benefit linked to a variable underlying investment account. Equity indexed annuities, a type of fixed annuity, are fairly new but have become quite popular.

**Fixed Annuities** Fixed annuities provide a guaranteed rate of return. During the period in which the annuitant is making payments to fund the annuity (the accumulation period), the insurer invests these payments in conservative, long-term securities (typically bonds). This, in turn, allows the insurer to credit a steady interest rate to the annuity contract. The interest rate payable for any given year is declared in advance by the insurer and is guaranteed to be no less than a minimum specified in the contract.

When converted to a payout mode, fixed annuities provide a guaranteed fixed benefit amount to the annuitant, typically stated in terms of dollars per $1,000 of accumulated values (such as $7 for each $1,000 of accumulated value). This is possible because the interest rate payable on the annuity funds is fixed and guaranteed at the point of annuitization. The amount and duration of benefit payments are guaranteed. Because they provide a specified benefit, payable for life (or any other

> ### TAKE NOTE
>
> A fixed annuity typically has two interest rates: a minimum guaranteed rate and a current rate. The current rate is what the insurer credits to the annuity on a regular schedule (typically each year); the current rate never will be lower than the minimum rate, which the insurer guarantees. In this way, the accumulation of funds in a fixed annuity is certain and the contract owner's principal is secure.

period the annuitant desires), fixed annuities can offer security and financial peace of mind. On the other hand, because the benefit amount is fixed, annuitants may see the purchasing power of their payments decline over the years due to inflation.

**Equity Indexed Annuities** The equity indexed annuity is another type of annuity product. These annuities have most of the features of fixed annuity contracts, except that the interest credited to the annuity owner's account is tied to a stock market related (equity) index, such as the Standard & Poor's 500 Index. However, unlike variable annuities, an equity indexed annuity cannot decrease in value. Besides having a fixed minimum guarantee (somewhat similar to a fixed annuity), the value of an annuity owner's account can only increase because of stock market appreciation. If the market is flat or declining, the account value will not decrease in value. Once interest has been credited to an equity indexed annuity, it cannot be lost.

**Variable Annuities** In unit 3, we discussed variable life insurance. The same underlying principles of variable life insurance apply to variable annuities. As is true with variable life, variable annuities shift the investment risk from the insurer to the contract owner. If the investments supporting the contract perform well, the owner probably will realize investment growth that exceeds what is possible in a fixed annuity. However, the lack of investment guarantees means that the variable annuity owner can see the value of his annuity decrease in a depressed market or in an economic recession.

Variable annuities invest deferred annuity payments in an insurer's separate accounts, as opposed to an insurer's general accounts, which allow the insurer to guarantee interest in a fixed annuity. Because variable annuities are based on nonguaranteed equity investments, such as common stock, a sales representative who wants to sell such contracts must be registered with the National Association of Securities Dealers (NASD) and also hold a state insurance license.

To accommodate the variable concept, a new means of accounting for both annuity payments and annuity income was required. The result is the accumulation unit (which pertains to the accumulation period) and the annuity unit (which pertains to the income payout period).

**Accumulation Units** In a variable annuity, during the accumulation period, contributions made by the annuitant, less a deduction for expenses, are converted to accumulation units and credited to the individual's account. The value of each accumulation unit varies, depending on the value of the underlying stock investment.

EXAMPLE

Assume that the accumulation unit initially is valued at $10, and the holder of a variable annuity makes a payment of $200. This means she has purchased 20 accumulation units. Six months later, she makes another payment of $200, but during that time, the underlying stocks have declined and the value of the accumulation unit is $8. This means that the $200 payment now will purchase 25 accumulation units. As the value of the account rises and falls, the value of each accumulation unit rises and falls.

**Annuity Units**   At the time the variable annuity benefits are to be paid out to the annuitant, the accumulation units in the participant's individual account are converted into annuity units. At the time of initial payout, the annuity unit calculation is made and, from then on, the number of annuity units remains the same for that annuitant. The value of one annuity unit, however, can and does vary from month to month, depending on investment results.

---

**EXAMPLE**

An annuitant has 1,000 accumulation units in her account by the time she is ready to retire, and these units have been converted into 10 annuity units. She always will be credited with 10 annuity units—that number does not change. What does change is the value of the annuity units, in accordance with the underlying stock. Assume when she retired, each annuity unit was valued at $40. That means her initial benefit payment is $400 (10 × $40). As long as the value of the annuity unit is $40, her monthly payments will be $400. But what if the value of the stock goes up and her annuity unit value becomes $45? Her next monthly payment will be $450 (10 × $45).

The theory has been that the payout from a variable annuity over a period of years will keep pace with the cost of living and thus maintain the annuitant's purchasing power at or above a constant level. As with fixed annuities, the variable annuity owner has various payout options from which to choose. These options usually include the life annuity, life annuity with period certain, unit refund annuity (similar to a cash refund annuity), and a joint and survivor annuity.

---

# INCOME TAXATION OF ANNUITY BENEFITS

Annuity benefit payments are a combination of principal and interest. Accordingly, they are taxed in a manner consistent with other types of income: the portion of the benefit payments that represents a return of principal (i.e., the contributions made by the annuitant) are not taxed. However, the portion representing interest earned on the declining principal is taxed. The result, over the benefit payment period, is a tax-free return of the annuitant's investment and the taxing of the balance.

Though a detailed discussion of how to compute the taxable portion of an annuity payment is beyond the scope of this text, the basics are not difficult to understand. An exclusion ratio is applied to each benefit payment the annuitant receives:

$$\frac{\text{Investment in the contract}}{\text{Expected return}} = \text{Exclusion ratio}$$

The investment in the contract is the amount of money paid into the annuity; the expected return is the annual guaranteed benefit the annuitant receives, multiplied by the number of years of his life expectancy. The resulting ratio is applied to the benefit payments, allowing the annuitant to exclude a like percentage from income.

---

TA**✓**KE NOTE

A 10% penalty tax is imposed on withdrawals from a deferred annuity before age 59½. Withdrawals after age 59½ are not subject to the 10% penalty tax, but still are taxable as ordinary income.

---

TA**✓**KE NOTE

An annuity contract cannot be exchanged tax free for a life insurance contract. This is not an acceptable exchange under Section 1035.

---

Deferred annuities accumulate interest earnings on a tax-deferred basis. While no taxes are imposed on the annuity during the accumulation phase, taxes are imposed when the contract begins to pay its benefits (in accordance with the exclusion ratio just described). To discourage the use of deferred annuities as short-term investments, the Internal Revenue Code imposes a penalty (as well as taxes) on early withdrawals (and loans) from annuities. Partial withdrawals are treated first as earnings income (and are thus taxable as ordinary income); only after all earnings have been taxed are withdrawals considered a return of principal.

## 1035 CONTRACT EXCHANGES

As discussed in Unit 5, Section 1035 of the Internal Revenue Code provides for tax-free exchanges of certain kinds of financial products, including annuity contracts. Recall that no gain will be recognized (meaning no gain will be taxed) if an annuity contract is exchanged for another annuity contract or if a life insurance or endowment policy is exchanged for an annuity contract.

# USES OF ANNUITIES

Annuities have a variety of uses. They are suited to a variety of circumstances that require a large sum of money to be converted into a series of payments over a set time, particularly a lifetime. Now let's look at some of the common uses of annuities.

## INDIVIDUAL USES

The principal use of an annuity is to provide income for retirement. The advantage of the structured, guaranteed life income provided by annuities for retirement purposes is obvious and is one of the primary reasons the annuity is so popular. Many individuals, especially those in retirement, may be reluctant to use the principal of their savings, fearing it may become depleted. However, if they choose to conserve the principal, they run the risk of never deriving any benefit from it at all—and ultimately are obliged to pass it on to others at their deaths. An annuity is designed to liquidate principal—but in a structured, systematic way that guarantees it will last a lifetime.

Besides being able to guarantee a lifetime income, annuities make excellent retirement products because they are conservative in nature, reliable, and flexible enough to meet nearly all needs. As

**TAKE NOTE**

While annuities are designed to create and accumulate income for retirement, they can be used for other purposes as well. For instance, they can be used to create and accumulate funds for a college education. Annuities serve a variety of purposes for which a stream of income is needed for a few years or a lifetime.

**TAKE NOTE**

In addition to TSAs and IRAs, annuities are an acceptable funding mechanism for other qualified plans, including pensions and 401(k) plans.

accumulation vehicles, they offer safety of principal, tax deferral, diversification, competitive yields (enhanced by tax deferral), and liquidity. As distribution vehicles, they offer a variety of payout options, which can be structured to conform to certain payment amounts or certain payment periods. They can cover one life or two. They can be arranged so that a beneficiary will receive a benefit if the annuitant dies before receiving the full annuity principal.

## QUALIFIED ANNUITY PLANS

A qualified plan is a tax-deferred arrangement established by an employer to provide retirement benefits for employees. The plan is qualified by reason of having met government requirements. A qualified annuity is an annuity purchased as part of a tax-qualified individual or employer-sponsored retirement plan, such as an individual retirement account (IRA), which will be discussed in Unit 8, a tax-sheltered annuity (TSA), or other IRS-recognized plans.

A TSA is a special type of annuity plan reserved for nonprofit organizations and their employees. It also is known as a 403(b) plan or a 501(c)(3) plan, because it was made possible by those sections of the Internal Revenue Code. For many years, the federal government, through its tax laws, has encouraged specified nonprofit charitable, educational, and religious organizations to set aside funds for their employees' retirement. Regardless of whether the money actually is set aside by the employers for the employees of such organizations or the funds are contributed by the employees through a reduction in salary, such funds may be placed in TSAs and are excludable from the employees' current taxable income.

Upon retirement, payments received by employees from the accumulated savings in tax-sheltered annuities are treated as reportable income. However, as the total annual income of the employees likely is less after retirement, the tax to be paid by such retirees likely is less than while they were working. Furthermore, the benefits can be spread out over a specified period of time or over the remaining lifetime of the employee so that the amount of tax owed on the benefits in any one year generally will be small.

## STRUCTURED SETTLEMENTS

Annuities also are used to distribute funds from the settlement of lawsuits or the winnings of lotteries and other contests. Such arrangements are called structured settlements.

Court settlements of lawsuits often require the payment of large sums of money throughout the rest of the injured party's life. Annuities are perfect vehicles for these settlements because they can be tailored to meet the needs of the claimant. Annuities also are suited for distributing the large awards people win in state lotteries. These awards usually are paid out over a period of 10 or 20 years. Because of the extended payout period, the state can advertise large awards and then provide for the distribution of the award by purchasing a structured settlement from an insurance company at a discount. The state can get the discounted price because a $1 million award distributed over a 20-year period is not worth $1 million today. Trends indicate that significant growth can be expected from both these markets for annuities.

# SUMMARY

Annuities are suited ideally for providing peace of mind to anyone who is concerned about receiving income for life. The exact opposite of the life insurance concept, annuities start with a large fund and reduce it through a series of payments. Life insurance companies are the only financial institutions that can guarantee annuity payments will be made to the annuitant for life. Like beneficiaries of life insurance policies, annuitants have a variety of payout options as to how they can receive their annuity benefit payments.

While many annuitants find comfort in the guarantees of a traditional fixed annuity, many others prefer the potential investment gains possible with equity indexed annuities or variable annuities. Because variable annuities are recognized by the Securities and Exchange Commission as an investment, people who want to sell them must be licensed by and registered with the NASD. All states also require salespeople to hold a valid life insurance license to sell any type of annuity.

# U N I T   Q U I Z

1. Which of the following statements regarding annuities is NOT correct?

   A. Generally, annuity contracts issued today require fixed, level funding payments.
   B. Annuities are sold by life insurance agents.
   C. An annuity is a periodic payment.
   D. Annuitants can pay the annuity premiums in lump sums.

2. What annuity payout option provides for lifetime payments to the annuitant but guarantees a certain minimum term of payments, whether or not the annuitant is living?

   A. Installment refund option
   B. Life with period certain
   C. Joint and survivor
   D. Straight life income

3. Which of the following statements regarding annuity payout options is NOT correct?

   A. Under a straight life annuity option, all annuity payments stop when the annuitant dies.
   B. In a cash refund annuity, upon the annuitant's death, the beneficiary always receives an amount equal to the beginning annuity fund.
   C. A period certain annuity guarantees a definite number of payments.
   D. Joint and survivor annuities guarantee payments for the duration of two lives.

4. James died after receiving $180 monthly for six years from a $25,000 installment refund annuity. His wife, Lucy, as beneficiary, now will receive the same monthly income until her payments total

   A. $2,160
   B. $12,040
   C. $12,960
   D. $25,000

5. Annuity payments are taxable to the extent that they represent interest earned rather than capital returned. What method is used to determine the taxable portion of each payment?

   A. Exclusion ratio
   B. Marginal tax formula
   C. Surtax ratio
   D. Annuitization ratio

6. Before he died, Gary received a total of $9,200 in monthly income payments from his $15,000 straight life annuity. He also was the insured under a $25,000 life insurance policy that named his wife, Darlene, as primary beneficiary. Considering the two contracts, Darlene would receive death benefits totaling

   A. $15,000
   B. $25,000
   C. $30,800
   D. $40,000

7. When a cash value life insurance policy is converted into an annuity in a nontaxable transaction, that event generally is known as a

   A. rollover
   B. 1035 exchange
   C. modified endowment
   D. pension enhancement

8. Joanna and her husband, Tom, have a $40,000 annuity that pays them $200 a month. Tom dies and Joanna continues receiving the $200 monthly check as long as she lives. When Joanna dies, the company ceases payment. This is an example of what kind of annuity?

   A. Installment refund
   B. Joint and full survivor
   C. Life
   D. Cash refund

9. Which kind of the following statements about variable annuities is NOT correct?

   A. Individuals selling variable annuities must be registered with the NASD.
   B. The contract owner, rather than the insurer, bears the investment risk.
   C. Once a variable annuity contract has been annuitized, the amount of annuity income will not fluctuate.
   D. During the accumulation period, the annuitant's contributions are converted to accumulation units and credited to his account.

# ANSWERS AND RATIONALES TO UNIT QUIZ

1. **A.** Years ago, insurers typically required that annuity premiums be fixed and level. Today, annuitants have much more flexibility as to when and how much they pay into their annuity contracts.

2. **B.** The life with period certain payout option pays the annuitant an income for life and guarantees a definite minimum period of payments regardless of whether the annuitant is living.

3. **B.** In a cash refund option, the annuitant receives a guaranteed income for life, and, if he dies before the principal is depleted, the annuitant's beneficiary will receive a lump-sum cash payment of the remainder. The beneficiary will receive an amount equal to the beginning annuity fund less the amount of income that already has been paid to the annuitant.

4. **B.** Under an installment refund option, the total annuity fund is paid to the annuitant or to his beneficiary. If James received $180 a month for six years before he died, he would have received a total of $12,960 ([$180 × 12] × 6). As beneficiary, his wife will receive the remaining balance of the annuity ($25,000 − $12,960 = $12,040) in monthly annuity payments.

5. **A.** The taxable portion of each annuity payment is determined by using the exclusion ratio. This ratio is determined by dividing the investment in the contract (the amount of money paid into the annuity) by the expected return.

6. **B.** Under Gary's straight life annuity, he will receive a guaranteed income only during his lifetime. At his death, no further payments are made to anyone. Darlene therefore will receive only $25,000, the proceeds paid to her as beneficiary of his life insurance policy.

7. **B.** A life insurance policy can be exchanged for an annuity in a nontaxable transaction known as a 1035 exchange.

8. **B.** Joanna and Tom have a joint and full survivor annuity. The joint and full survivor option provides for payment of an annuity to two people. At either person's death, the same income payments continue to the survivor for life. When the surviving annuitant dies, no further payments are made.

9. **C.** Even after a variable annuity contract has been annuitized, the amount of annuity income will fluctuate. This is because the value of one annuity unit can and will vary from month to month, depending on investment results.

# 8

# Social Security and Retirement Plans

## KEY CONCEPTS

- Social Security benefits
- Retirement planning considerations
- Qualified versus nonqualified plans
- Large employer plans
- Small employer plans
- Individual retirement accounts

Social Security is a government insurance program providing for the basic needs of individuals facing financial hardship. The program provides a variety of benefits but falls short of meeting all of the needs most of us face later in life. To meet the financial challenges of retirement, individuals must take the initiative and begin preparing early if they want full security down the road. This preparation involves maintaining adequate life insurance to meet the costs of death, enough health insurance to cover illnesses, and a well-planned retirement program to ensure a desired standard of living when employment income ceases. For many individuals, saving through an employer-sponsored plan or a personal plan likely is the most effective way to accumulate retirement assets.

## OBJECTIVE

When you complete this unit you should be able to:

- explain how Social Security benefits are determined;

- describe the kinds of benefits provided by Social Security;

- compare and contrast qualified and nonqualified plans;

- explain the basic ERISA concepts of participation, coverage, vesting, funding, and contributions;

- identify the basic features of 401(k) plans, tax-sheltered annuities, and Section 457 plans;

- list and describe the different types of qualified plans available to small employers; and

- explain the differences between traditional IRAs, Roth IRAs, and education IRAs.

# SOCIAL SECURITY

The Social Security program, administered at the federal level by the Social Security Administration, more formally is called OASDI. This acronym aptly identifies the types of protection provided under the program: Old Age (retirement), Survivors (death benefits), and Disability Insurance.

The Social Security system was enacted in 1935—in the throes of the Great Depression—for one purpose: to provide basic protection for all working Americans against the financial problems brought on by death, disability, and aging. That remains the primary objective of Social Security. Its purpose always has been to augment—not replace—a sound personal insurance plan.

Americans are entitled to participate in the program's benefits, provided they meet basic eligibility requirements. With few exceptions, most gainfully employed people are covered by Social Security and are, or will be, eligible for the program's benefits. It is estimated that more than 45 million Americans currently are receiving benefits under the system.

### HOW SOCIAL SECURITY BENEFITS ARE DETERMINED

The amount of benefits to which a worker is entitled under Social Security is based on his earnings over the years. There is a direct relationship between the amount of FICA taxes paid and the level of benefits earned. Workers who pay the maximum FICA tax over their lifetimes will receive higher benefits than those who pay less than the maximum. However, the FICA tax is not necessarily applied to all of a worker's earnings; the FICA tax is assessed only up to a maximum amount of earnings (known as the maximum taxable wage base).

Benefits are based upon one's Primary Insurance Amount (PIA). The PIA actually is the amount equal to the worker's full retirement benefit at age 65 (benefits are reduced for early retirement) or benefits to a disabled worker. Benefits payable to workers and their spouses and dependents usually are expressed as a percentage of the worker's PIA. For example, a person who elects to retire at age 62 with Social Security retirement benefits will receive benefits equal to 80 percent of his PIA.

### SOCIAL SECURITY DISABILITY AND DEPENDENT BENEFITS

Social Security provides disability benefits to eligible individuals incapable of performing any form of gainful employment within the national economy. Their disability must be expected to last for a minimum of 12 months. Once a person has qualified for benefits, he/she is subject to a five-month waiting period. Benefits begin on the first day of the sixth month.

Additionally, dependents (spouse/children) are eligible to receive Social Security benefits when a worker has died or becomes disabled. The spouse or children may receive benefits expressed as a percentage of the deceased or disabled worker's benefit. A surviving spouse without children can begin drawing benefits at age 60 (full benefits at age 65). A surviving spouse with children under age 16 is eligible for additional benefits until the youngest child reaches age 16. The time between the youngest child's 16th birthday, and the surviving spouse's 60th birthday is called the "blackout period"—a period of time during which no benefits are available to the surviving spouse. Dependent children may receive benefits until age 18 (or 19 if attending high school full time).

# RETIREMENT PLANS

Many kinds of retirement plans exist, each designed to fulfill specific needs. Life insurance companies play a major role in the retirement planning arena, as the products and contracts they offer provide ideal funding or financing vehicles for both individual and employer-sponsored plans.

# QUALIFIED VERSUS NONQUALIFIED PLANS

Retirement plans can be divided into two categories: *qualified plans* and *nonqualified plans*. Qualified plans, by design or by definition, meet certain requirements established by the federal government and, consequently, receive favorable tax treatment:

- Employer contributions to a qualified retirement plan are considered a deductible business expense, which lowers the business's income taxes.

- The earnings of a qualified plan are exempt from income taxation as they accumulate in the plan.

- Employer contributions to a qualified plan currently are not taxable to the employee in the years they are contributed but are taxable when they are paid out as a benefit and, typically, when the employee is retired.

- Contributions to an individual qualified plan, such as an individual retirement account (IRA) or annuity, are deductible from income under certain conditions.

- Employee contributions to certain types of employer plans, such as 401(k) plans, are not included in the employee's gross income, which lowers his income taxes.

If a plan does not meet the specific requirements the federal government sets forth, it is termed a nonqualified plan and, thus, is not eligible for favorable tax treatment.

---

**E X A M P L E**    Bill, age 42, decides he wants to start a retirement fund. He opens a new savings account at his local bank, deposits $150 a month in that account and vows not to touch that money until he reaches age 65. Although his intentions are good, they will not qualify his plan. The income he deposits and the interest he earns still are taxable every year.

---

In this unit our discussion will focus on qualified retirement plans, both individual and employer-sponsored.

# QUALIFIED EMPLOYER RETIREMENT PLANS

## BASIC CONCEPTS

Many of the basic concepts associated with qualified employer plans can be traced to the Employee Retirement Income Security Act of 1974, commonly called ERISA. The purpose of ERISA is to protect the rights of workers covered under an employer-sponsored plan.

ERISA imposes a number of requirements that retirement plans must follow to obtain IRS approval as a qualified plan eligible for favorable tax treatment. While an in-depth discussion of these requirements is beyond the scope of this text, the basic concepts of *participation, coverage, vesting, funding,* and *contributions* should be noted.

**Participation Standards**    All qualified employer plans must comply with minimum participation standards designed to determine employee eligibility. In general, employees who have reached age 21 and have completed one year of service must be allowed to enroll in a qualified plan. Or, if the plan provides for 100% vesting upon participation, they may be required to complete two years of service before enrolling.

**Coverage Requirements**    The purpose of coverage requirements is to prevent a plan from discriminating against rank-and-file employees in favor of the elite—shareholders, officers, and highly compensated employees—whose positions often enable them to make basic policy decisions regarding the plan. The IRS will subject qualified employer plans to coverage tests to determine if they are discriminatory. A qualified plan cannot discriminate in favor of highly paid employees in its coverage provisions or in its provisions for contributions and benefits.

**Vesting Schedules**   All qualified plans must meet standards that set forth the employee vesting schedule and nonforfeitable rights at any specified time. Vesting means the right each employee has to his fund; benefits that have vested belong to the employee even if he terminates employment before retirement.

**FIGURE 8.1   Vesting Schedules for Qualified Plans**

To meet qualification standards, an employer retirement plan must provide for a *vesting schedule,* which sets forth the time period by which an employee-participant becomes entitled to nonforfeitable benefits under the plan. In general, two schedules are available:

| 1. Cliff Vesting | Years of Service | Vested Percentage | 2. Graded Vesting | Years of Service | Vested Percentage |
|---|---|---|---|---|---|
| | 1 | 0 | | 1 | 0 |
| | 2 | 0 | | 2 | 0 |
| | 3 | 0 | | 3 | 20 |
| | 4 | 0 | | 4 | 40 |
| | 5 | 100 | | 5 | 60 |
| | | | | 6 | 80 |
| | | | | 7 | 100 |

As an alternative, a plan can provide for a different vesting schedule, as long as it is no less favorable to the participants than those above.

*Note:* For plans that include matching employer contributions, two new schedules are required: 3-year cliff vesting and 2- to 6-year graduated vesting. Under the former, a participant is 100 percent vested in employer matching contributions after three years. Under the latter, the participant is gradually vested in 20 percent increments, and is 100 percent vested in six years.

The new vesting schedules apply only to employer matching contributions in defined contribution plans. For all other types of plans and employer contributions, the 5-year and 7-year schedules continue to apply.

**Funding Standards**   For a plan to be qualified, it must be funded. In other words, there must be real contributions on the part of the employer, the employee, or both, and these funds must be held by a third party and invested. The funding vehicle is the method for investing the funds as they accumulate. Federal minimum funding requirements are set to ensure that an employer's annual contributions to a pension plan are sufficient to cover the costs of benefits payable during the year, plus administrative expenses.

**Contributions** Qualification standards regarding the amount and type of contributions that can be made to a plan vary, but all plans must restrict the amount of contributions that can be made for or accrue to any one plan participant.

## DEFINED CONTRIBUTION PLANS

The provisions of a defined contribution plan address the amounts currently going into the plan and identify the participant's vested (nonforfeitable) account. These predetermined amounts contributed to the participant's account accumulate to a future point (such as retirement) and the final fund available to any one participant depends on total amounts contributed, plus interest and dividends earned.

## CASH OR DEFERRED ARRANGEMENTS (401(k) PLANS)

A popular form of qualified employer retirement plan is commonly known as the 401(k) plan, whereby employees can elect to take a reduction in their current salaries by deferring amounts into a retirement plan. These plans are called cash or deferred arrangements because employees cannot be forced to participate; they may take their income currently as cash, or defer a portion of it until retirement, with favorable tax advantages. These plans are used by for-profit organizations.

The amounts deferred are not included in the employees' gross incomes and earnings credited to the deferrals grow tax free until distribution. Typically, 401(k) plans include matching employer contributions: for every dollar the employee defers, for example, the employer will contribute 50 cents.

The maximum annual amount an employee could defer in 2007 was $15,500. This amount is indexed for inflation and will vary from year to year as follows:

| Year | Contribution Limit |
|------|--------------------|
| 2004 | $13,000 |
| 2005 | $14,000 |
| 2006 | $15,000 |
| 2007 | $15,500* |

\* The $15,500 limit is indexed for inflation in $500 increments after 2006.

## TAX-SHELTERED ANNUITIES (403(b) PLANS)

Another type of employer retirement plan is the tax-sheltered annuity, or 403(b) plan. This was explained in our discussion of annuities, but it is appropriate to review it here.

A tax-sheltered annuity is a special tax-favored retirement plan available only to certain groups of employees. Tax-sheltered annuities may be established for the employees of specified nonprofit charitable, educational, religious, and other 501(c)(3) organizations, including teachers in public school systems. Such plans generally are not available to other kinds of employees.

Funds are contributed by the employer or by the employees (usually through payroll deductions) to tax-sheltered annuities and, thus, are excluded from the employees' current taxable income.

# QUALIFIED PLANS FOR THE SMALL EMPLOYER

Before 1962, many small business owners found that their employees could participate in, and benefit from, a qualified retirement plan, but the owners themselves could not. Self-employed individuals were in the same predicament. The reason was that qualified plans had to benefit employees. Because business owners were considered employers, they were excluded from participating in a qualified plan.

The Self-Employed Individuals Retirement Act, signed into law in 1962, rectified this situation by treating small business owners and self-employed individuals as employees, thus enabling them to participate in a qualified plan, if they chose to do so, just as their employees. The result was the Keogh or HR-10 retirement plan.

## KEOGH PLAN (HR-10)

A Keogh plan is a qualified retirement plan designed for unincorporated businesses that allows the business owner (or partner in a business) to participate as an employee.

## SIMPLIFIED EMPLOYEE PENSION (SEP)

Another type of qualified plan suited for the small employer is the simplified employee pension (SEP) plan. Due to the many administrative burdens and the costs involved with establishing a more complex plan as well as maintaining compliance with ERISA, many small businesses have been reluctant to set up retirement plans for their employees. SEPs were introduced in 1978 specifically for small businesses to overcome these cost, compliance, and administrative hurdles.

Basically, an SEP is an arrangement whereby an employee (including a self-employed individual) establishes and maintains a traditional IRA to which the employer contributes (employees do not contribute to the plan). Employer contributions are not included in the employee's gross income. A primary difference between a SEP and an IRA is the much larger amount that an employer can contribute each year to a SEP—currently, up to 25% of the employee's compensation or $45,000 per year (2007).

In accordance with the rules that govern other qualified plans, SEPs must not discriminate in favor of highly compensated employees with regard to contributions or participation.

## SIMPLE PLAN

Known as a Savings Incentive Match Plan for Employees, or SIMPLE plan, these arrangements allow eligible employers to set up tax-favored retirement savings plans for their employees without addressing many of the usual (and burdensome) qualification requirements.

**TAKE NOTE**

In place of the dollar-for-dollar matching contributions, an employer can choose to make nonelective contributions of 2% of compensation on behalf of each eligible employee. Only the first $200,000 of the employee's compensation can be taken into account when determining the contribution limit.

SIMPLE plans are available to small businesses (including tax-exempt and government entities) that employ no more than 100 employees who received at least $5,000 in compensation from the employer during the previous year. In addition, to establish a SIMPLE plan, the employer must not have a qualified plan in place.

A SIMPLE plan may be structured as an IRA or as a 401(k) cash or deferred arrangement. Under these plans, employees who elect to participate may defer up to a specified amount each year (up to $10,500 in 2007) and the employer then makes a matching contribution, dollar-for-dollar, up to an amount equal to 3% of the employee's annual compensation. All contributions to a SIMPLE IRA or SIMPLE 401(k) plan are nonforfeitable; the employee is vested immediately and fully. Taxation of contributions and their earnings is deferred until funds are withdrawn or distributed.

# INDIVIDUAL RETIREMENT PLANS

In much the same way that it encourages businesses to establish retirement plans for their employees, the federal government provides incentives for individuals to save for their retirement by allowing certain kinds of plans to receive favorable tax treatment. Individual retirement accounts (IRAs) are the most notable of these plans. Available IRAs include the traditional tax-deductible IRA and the traditional non-tax-deductible IRA, as well as the Roth IRA, and the Coverdell IRA. The Roth and Coverdell IRAs were created by the Taxpayer Relief Act of 1997. Both of these IRAs require nondeductible contributions but offer tax-free earnings and withdrawals.

## TRADITIONAL IRA

An IRA is a means by which individuals can save money for retirement and receive a current tax break. Basically, the amount contributed to an IRA accumulates and grows tax deferred. IRA funds are not taxed until they are taken out at retirement. In addition, depending on the individual's earnings and whether or not he is covered by an employer-sponsored retirement plan, the amount he contributes to a traditional IRA may be fully or partially deducted from current income, resulting in lower current income taxes.

**IRA Participation**  Anyone under age 70½ who has earned income may open a traditional IRA and contribute each year an amount up to the contribution limit or 100% of compensation, whichever is less. (The limit is $4,000 in 2007, and $5,000 in 2008.) A non-wage-earning spouse is allowed to open an IRA and contribute up to the contribution limit each year.

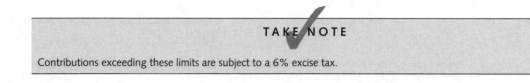

After 2008, the contribution limit will be adjusted annually for inflation. These limits will also apply to any combined contributions that might be made to a traditional IRA and a Roth IRA.

Also beginning in 2002, persons who are age 50 and older were allowed to make "catch-up" contributions to their IRAs, above the scheduled $4,000 or $5,000 limit, enabling them to save even more for retirement. These catch-up payments can be either deductible or made to a Roth IRA. The additional catch-up amount allowed in 2007 and beyond is $1,000.

**Deduction of IRA Contributions**  In many cases, the amount an individual contributes to a traditional IRA can be deducted from his income in the year it is contributed. The ability of an IRA participant to take a deduction for his contribution rests on two factors:

■  whether or not he is covered by an employer-sponsored retirement plan; and

■  the amount of income he makes.

Individuals who are not covered by an employer-sponsored plan may contribute up to the annual limit to a traditional IRA and deduct the full amount of the contribution from their current income, no matter what their income level. Married couples who both work and have no employer-sponsored plan can contribute and deduct up to a combined total of $8,000 in 2007 to any and all of their IRAs.

Individuals who are covered by an employer-sponsored plan are subject to different rules regarding deductibility of traditional IRA contributions. For them, the amount of income they make is the determining factor: the more they make, the less IRA deduction they can take.

**Traditional IRA Withdrawals**  Because the purpose of an IRA is to provide a way to accumulate retirement funds, a number of rules discourage IRA owners from withdrawing these funds before retirement. By the same token, traditional IRA owners are discouraged from sheltering their accounts from taxes perpetually by rules that mandate when the funds must be withdrawn.

Traditional IRA owners must begin to receive payment from their accounts no later than April 1 following the year in which they reach age 70½. The law specifies a minimum amount that must be withdrawn every year. Failure to withdraw the minimum amount can result in a stiff penalty tax on the difference between the amount that should have been withdrawn and the amount that was actually withdrawn.

**TAKE NOTE**

Do not confuse contribution deductibility with the ability to make contributions. Again, anyone under age 70½ who has earned income (as well as his or her non-wage-earning spouse) can contribute to a traditional IRA. However, level of income and participation in an employer plan may affect the traditional IRA owner's ability to deduct the contributions.

With a few exceptions, any distribution from a traditional IRA before age 59½ will have adverse tax consequences. In addition to income tax, the taxable amount of the withdrawal will be subject to a 10% penalty (similar to that imposed on early withdrawals from deferred annuities). Early distributions taken for any of the following reasons or circumstances will not be assessed the 10% penalty:

- if the owner dies or becomes disabled;
- if the owner is faced with a certain amount of qualifying medical expenses;
- to pay for higher education expenses;
- to cover first-time home purchase expenses (up to $10,000);
- to pay for health insurance premiums while unemployed;
- if the distribution is taken in equal payments over the owner's lifetime; or
- to correct or reduce an excess contribution.

At retirement, or any time after age 59½, a traditional IRA owner can elect to receive either a lump-sum payment or periodic installment payments from his fund. IRA distributions are taxed in much the same way as annuity benefit payments are taxed. That is, the portion of an IRA distribution that is attributed to nondeductible contributions is received tax free; the portion that is attributed to interest earnings or deductible contributions is taxed. The result is a tax-free return of the IRA owner's cost basis and a taxing of the balance.

If an IRA owner dies before receiving full payment, the remaining funds in the deceased's IRA will be paid to the named beneficiary.

## ROTH IRA

In 1997, a new kind of IRA was introduced: the Roth IRA. Roth IRAs are unique in that they provide for back-end benefits. No deduction can be taken for contributions made to Roth IRAs, but the earnings on those contributions are entirely tax free when they are withdrawn.

An amount up to the contribution limit for the year ($4,000 in 2007, $5,000 in 2008) can be contributed to a Roth IRA for any one eligible individual. Active participant status is irrelevant—an individual can contribute to a Roth regardless of whether he is covered by an employer plan or maintains and contributes to other IRA accounts. (Note, however, that the annual limit on contributions applies collectively to both traditional and Roth IRAs. No more than this amount can be contributed in any year for any account or combination of accounts.)

Unlike traditional IRAs, which are limited to those people under age 70½, Roth IRAs impose no age limits. At any age, an individual with earned income can establish a Roth and make contributions. On the other hand, Roth IRAs subject participants to earnings limitations which traditional IRAs

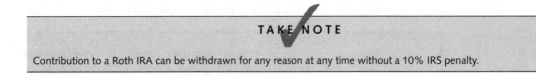

do not. High income earners may not be able to contribute to a Roth IRA because the maximum annual contribution that can be made begins to phase out for individuals whose modified adjusted gross incomes reach certain levels. Above these limits, no Roth contributions are allowed.

**Qualified Roth Withdrawals** Withdrawals from Roth IRAs are either qualified or nonqualified. A qualified withdrawal provides for the full tax advantage that Roths offer: tax-free distribution of earnings. To be a qualified withdrawal, two requirements must be met:

■ the funds must have been held in the account for a minimum of five years; and

■ the withdrawal must occur for one of the following reasons:

— the owner has reached age 59½;

— the owner dies;

— the owner becomes disabled; or

— the distribution is used to purchase a first home.

If these requirements are met, no portion of the withdrawal is subject to tax.

**Nonqualified Roth Withdrawals** A nonqualified withdrawal does not meet the previously discussed criteria. Because Roth contributions are made with after-tax dollars, only the *earnings* on those contributions are subject to taxation. Furthermore, they are taxed only when those earnings are removed from the account without having met the above requirements.

If the owner of the Roth IRA is younger than 59½ when the withdrawal is taken, it will be considered premature and (if it does not qualify as an exception to the premature distribution rule) the earnings will be assessed a 10% penalty.

**No Required Distribution** Unlike traditional IRAs, Roth IRAs do not require mandatory distributions. No minimum distribution requirement exists for the account owner—the funds can remain in the account as long as the owner desires. In fact, the account can be left intact and passed on to heirs or beneficiaries.

**FIGURE 8.2   Taxation of Earnings Distributed from a Roth IRA**

| Type of Distribution | Roth IRA Held Less Than 5 Years | | Roth IRA Held 5 Years or More | |
|---|---|---|---|---|
| | Earnings Taxed | 10% Penalty | Earnings Taxed | 10% Penalty |
| Pre 59½ | Yes | Yes | Yes | Yes |
| Pre 59½, but distribution due to death, disability, or for a first home purchase | Yes | No | No | No |
| Post 59½ | Yes | No | No | No |

## COVERDELL IRA (COVERDELL EDUCATION SAVINGS ACCOUNT)

Education IRAs, or education savings accounts, are special investment accounts that allow individuals and families to fund formal education expenses on a tax-favored basis.

Beginning in 2002, education IRAs are exempt from tax as long as they are used for qualified education expenses of the account's beneficiary, such as tuition, tutoring, books, room and board, computer equipment, uniforms, extended day program costs, and any other supplies required for attendance at any public or private elementary or secondary school, as well as at any college, university, vocational school, or other postsecondary educational institution.

Education IRAs were originally designed to fund higher education expenses of a designated beneficiary by allowing after-tax (nondeductible) contributions to accumulate on a tax-deferred basis. When distributions are taken from an education IRA, the earnings portion of the distribution is excluded from income to the extent it is used to pay qualified education expenses. Earnings are taxed when they are not used to pay qualified education expenses, and then they are also subject to a 10% penalty.

Contributions to education IRAs are not deductible, currently are limited to $2000 each year per child, and must be made before the beneficiary turns 18. If the child for whom an account has been established does not use the funds for education, or if there are any amounts remaining in an account when the beneficiary reaches age 30, remaining funds can be rolled over to another education IRA benefiting another family member with no penalty. Any IRA distributions that are not used to pay for a beneficiary's education expenses will be included in the recipient's income and will be subject to a 10% penalty.

Nothing prevents more than one individual from contributing to an education IRA. The annual limit applies to each beneficiary only. Consequently, parents and grandparents can contribute to a single account, so long as the annual limit is not exceeded in any year. Excess contributions will still be subject to a 6% excise penalty.

### ROLLOVER IRA

Normally, benefits withdrawn from any qualified retirement plan are taxable the year in which they are received. However, certain tax-free rollover provisions of the tax law provide some degree of portability when an individual wishes to transfer funds from one plan to another, specifically to a rollover IRA.

Essentially, rollover IRAs provide a way for individuals who have received a distribution from a qualified plan to reinvest the funds in a new tax deferred account and continue to shelter those funds and their earnings from current taxes. Rollover IRAs are used by individuals who, for example, have left one employer for another and have received a complete distribution from their previous employer's plan or by those who had invested funds in an individual IRA of one kind and want to roll over to another IRA for a higher rate of return.

A distribution from some employer plans may result in an automatic 20% federal tax withholding. Plan participants can avoid this by completing a "direct rollover" in which the employer distributes the money directly to another IRA or qualified plan without the plan participant actually taking physical receipt of the distribution. If a plan participant does take receipt of the distribution, he/she has 60 days from the date of distribution to roll over some or all of the distribution to another IRA or qualified plan. If all or a portion of the distribution is not rolled over, the part that is not rolled over will be taxed as ordinary income and subject to a 10% penalty.

## SUMMARY

Social Security is a government insurance program designed to provide wage loss benefits to the disabled, death benefits to dependents, and retirement income to retirees. As the retirement income offered by Social Security fails to fully address the needs of many people, it is important that people employ additional tools in preparing for retirement.

Individuals prepare for the financial challenges of retirement in a variety of ways. They may be covered under any one (or more) of a variety of employer-sponsored qualified retirement plans, including defined benefit and defined contribution pension plans, 403(b) plans, simplified employee pension (SEP) plans, SIMPLE plans, Keogh plans, and 401(k) plans. Even if they are not covered under an employer-sponsored plan, individuals can save for retirement with a traditional or Roth individual retirement account (IRA) or annuity.

## U N I T   Q U I Z

1.  Which of the following statements does NOT describe the purpose of Social Security correctly?

    A.  It provides a source of income for a meaningful standard of living during retirement.
    B.  It provides basic protection against financial problems accompanying death, disability, and retirement.
    C.  It augments a sound personal insurance plan.
    D.  It provides retirement and survivor benefits to a worker and his family.

2.  All of the following employed persons who have no employer-sponsored retirement plan would be eligible to set up and contribute to a traditional IRA EXCEPT

    A.  Miriam, age 26, secretary
    B.  Brent, age 40, medical technician
    C.  Jack, age 60, plumber
    D.  Edna, age 72, nurse

3.  Which of the following statements regarding Roth IRAs is NOT correct?

    A.  They provide for tax-free accumulation of funds.
    B.  They limit contributions each year.
    C.  They mandate distributions no later than age 70½.
    D.  They are not available to those in the upper-income tax brackets.

4.  Which of the following statements does NOT describe correctly the tax advantages of a qualified retirement plan?

    A.  The earnings of a qualified plan are exempt from the employee's current income taxation.
    B.  Employer contributions to a qualified plan are considered a deductible business expense.
    C.  An employee's contribution to his retirement plan is included in ordinary income.
    D.  Earnings from a qualified retirement plan are taxable when paid out as a benefit.

5.  Vesting can be best described as which of the following?

    A.  The time at which a worker meets the eligibility requirements for plan participation.
    B.  The age at which an employee must begin to make withdrawals from retirement plans.
    C.  The right of an employee's spouse to be accounted for in the employee's qualified plan benefits.
    D.  The employee's right to funds or benefits contributed by the employer.

6.  All of the following statements about SIMPLE plans are correct EXCEPT

    A.  an employer may establish a SIMPLE plan if another qualified plan is not already in place
    B.  they can be structured as an IRA or as a 401(k) cash or deferred arrangement
    C.  employers must make a matching contribution, dollar-for-dollar, up to 2% of each employee's annual compensation
    D.  only employers with no more than 100 employees can establish SIMPLE plans

7.  Which of the following statements about 401(k) plans is CORRECT?

    A.  All of a company's employees must participate in the plan.
    B.  An employee's deferred contributions become nonforfeitable according to the plan's vesting schedule.
    C.  Employer contributions are included in an employee's income for the year.
    D.  As of 2007, the limit on employee deferrals to a 401(k) plan was $15,500 per year.

8.  Bob owns a traditional IRA and a Roth IRA. What is the maximum combined amount that he can contribute to both accounts in 2007 without being penalized?

    A.  $1,000
    B.  $3,000
    C.  $4,000
    D.  $6,000

9. After a family's breadwinner dies, the *blackout period* generally can be defined as the period
   A. during which children are living at home
   B. that begins when the youngest child turns 16 and ends when the surviving parent retires
   C. during which children are in school
   D. from the surviving parent's retirement to death

10. All of the following benefits are available under Social Security EXCEPT
    A. welfare
    B. death
    C. old age or retirement
    D. disability

# ANSWERS AND RATIONALES TO UNIT QUIZ

1. **A.** The purpose of Social Security is to provide basic protection to all working Americans against the financial problems caused by death, disability, and aging. It is not designed to provide a source of income for a meaningful standard of living during retirement.

2. **D.** Anyone under age 70½ may open a traditional IRA. Because Edna is 72 years old, she is not eligible to set up and contribute to a traditional IRA.

3. **C.** Unlike traditional IRAs, Roth IRAs do not require mandatory distribution. There is no minimum distribution requirement, and the account owner may leave funds in the account as long as desired. In fact, the account can be left intact and passed on to heirs or beneficiaries.

4. **C.** An employee's contributions to an individual qualified plan are deductible from income under certain conditions.

5. **D.** Vesting means the right each employee has to his retirement fund. Benefits that have vested belong to the employee even if he terminates employment prior to retirement. Although an employee always has a 100% vested interest in benefits that he has contributed, an employer's contributions will vest according to a vesting schedule established by law.

6. **C.** With a SIMPLE plan, an employer has two options for making contributions. First, it can make a matching contribution of up to 3%, dollar-for-dollar, of an employee's annual compensation. Alternatively, it can make nonelective contributions of 2% of compensation on behalf of each eligible employee.

7. **D.** In 2007, an employee could defer up to $15,500 to his 401(k) plan account.

8. **C.** Although Bob can own a traditional and Roth IRA and make contributions to both, he can contribute no more than $4,000 total in 2007.

9. **B.** The *blackout period* is the time during which no Social Security benefits are payable to a surviving spouse. This period begins when the youngest child reaches age 16 and continues until the spouse retires.

10. **A.** Social Security provides death benefits, old age or retirement benefits, and disability benefits to eligible workers. Social Security is an entitlement program, not a welfare program.

# 9

# Introduction to Health Insurance

## KEY CONCEPTS

- Types of accident and health insurance
- Individual versus group insurance
- Basic Medical and Major Medical plans
- Limited plans
- Service providers

The terms *health and accident insurance*, *accident and sickness insurance*, and *health insurance* are used interchangeably in the health insurance industry, from state to state and company to company. But no matter how this type of insurance is referred to in the industry, it all means the same thing to consumers—a critically important type of insurance that provides financial protection from the high costs of illness and injury.

In this unit we will take a look at the types of health insurance plans that exist, the providers of health insurance coverages, policy provisions, underwriting standards, and more. This unit is designed to provide an overview of the broad field of health insurance, focusing on the basics.

## OBJECTIVE

When you complete this unit you should be able to:

- explain the main features of medical expense insurance, disability income insurance, and accidental death and disability insurance;

- describe the typical ways in which individuals and families purchase health insurance;

- explain the main ways in which health insurance differs from life insurance;

- describe the different types of coverage available under basic medical expense plans;

- explain the difference between supplementary major medical and comprehensive major medical plans;

- explain the concepts of coinsurance, stop-loss features, and preexisting conditions;

- describe the main features of hospital indemnity policies and limited risk policies; and

- describe the major types of service providers, including HMOs and PPOs.

# BASIC FORMS OF HEALTH INSURANCE COVERAGE

Health insurance (as it will be called in this text) refers to the broad field of insurance plans that provide protection against the financial consequences of illness, accidents, injury, and disability.

Within the broad field of health insurance, three distinct categories of health coverage exist: *medical expense insurance*, *disability income insurance*, and *accidental death and dismemberment insurance*. Each of these coverages will be discussed in detail in subsequent lessons, but an introduction is appropriate here.

**FIGURE 9.1   Health Coverages and What They Provide**

| Type of Coverage | Provisions and Benefits |
|---|---|
| Medical Expense Insurance | Provides benefits for the cost of medical care. Depending on the type of policy (and its specific provisions), coverage can range from limited (coverage for hospital costs only, for example) to very broad (coverage for all aspects of medical services and care). |
| Disability Income Insurance | Provides a specified periodic income to the insured—usually on a monthly basis—in the event he or she becomes disabled. |
| Accidental Death and Dismemberment Insurance | Provides a lump-sum payment in the event the insured dies due to an accident or suffers the loss of one or more body members due to an accident. |

## MEDICAL EXPENSE INSURANCE

Medical expense insurance provides financial protection against the cost of medical care by reimbursing the insured, fully or in part, for these costs. It includes many kinds of plans that cover hospital care, surgical expenses, physician expenses, medical treatment programs, outpatient care, and the like. Medicare supplement insurance and long-term care insurance, two types of health insurance coverage designed for the elderly, also are examples of medical expense insurance plans and are discussed in detail later in the book.

## DISABILITY INCOME INSURANCE

Disability income insurance is designed to provide a replacement income when wages are lost due to a disability. As such, it does not cover the medical expenses associated with a disability; rather, it provides the disabled insured with a guaranteed flow of periodic income payments while he is disabled.

## ACCIDENTAL DEATH AND DISMEMBERMENT (AD&D) INSURANCE

Accidental death and dismemberment insurance (AD & D) is the purest form of accident insurance, providing the insured with a lump-sum benefit amount in the event of accidental death or dismemberment under accidental circumstances.

Within each of these three categories are many forms and variations of coverage that have evolved to meet unique insurance needs. Each of these basic coverages, as well as the many types of health insurance providers, will be discussed in later lessons. They are introduced here to help acquaint you with the health insurance field in general.

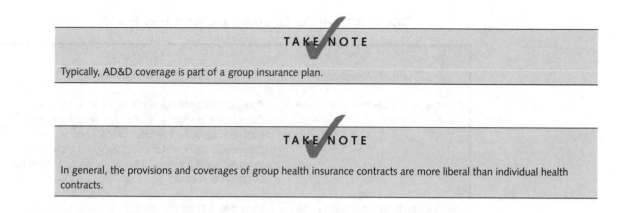

TAKE NOTE

Typically, AD&D coverage is part of a group insurance plan.

TAKE NOTE

In general, the provisions and coverages of group health insurance contracts are more liberal than individual health contracts.

## HOW HEALTH INSURANCE IS PURCHASED

As is the case with life insurance, health insurance is available to individuals and families through individual plans and policies or group plans and policies.

*Individual health insurance* is issued by commercial insurers and service organizations as contracts between the insured and the company. Though all companies have standard policies for the coverages they offer, most allow an individual to select various options or benefit levels that will meet his needs most precisely. Individual health contracts require an application, and the proposed insured usually must provide evidence of insurability.

*Group health insurance*, also issued by commercial insurers and service organizations, provides coverage under a master contract to members of a specified group. Group health plans are available to employers, trade and professional associations, labor unions, credit unions, and other organizations. Insurance is extended to the individuals in the group through the master contract, usually without individual underwriting and usually without requiring group members to provide evidence of insurability. The employer or the association is the policyowner and is responsible for premium payments. The employer may pay the entire premium or may require some contribution from each member to cover the insurance cost. Each group member is an *insured* and is issued a certificate of coverage.

Health insurance also is provided through state and federal government programs. At the state level, Medicaid is available to assist low-income individuals in meeting the costs of medical care. The federal government offers health insurance protection through Medicare and OASDI disability provisions, components of the Social Security system.

## CHARACTERISTICS OF HEALTH INSURANCE

Though closely related to life insurance in purpose, health insurance differs from it in several important ways. A review here of the distinguishing characteristics of health insurance will set the stage for the more in-depth discussion to follow in later units.

## RENEWABILITY PROVISIONS

Life insurance (particularly whole life insurance) and annuities are characterized by their permanence; the policies cannot be canceled by the insurer unless the policyowner fails to make a required premium payment. Even term life policies are guaranteed effective for the duration of the term, as long as premiums are paid. Health insurance is not as permanent in nature. Health insurance policies may contain any one of a wide range of renewability provisions, which define the rights of the insurer to cancel the policy at different points during the life of the policy. The distinguishing characteristics of each type will be covered later, but, in general, the more advantageous the renewability provisions are to the insured, the more expensive the coverage.

## PREMIUM FACTORS

Like life insurance, health insurance is funded by the regular payment of premiums. Unlike life insurance, however, relatively few payment options are available with a health policy. For instance, health policies do not offer any sort of limited payment option, as one would find with, say, a 10-pay or paid-up- at-65 life policy. Health insurance policies are paid for on a year-by-year basis. Health premiums can be paid under one of several different payment modes, including annual, semiannual, quarterly, and monthly.

Various factors enter into premium calculations for health insurance. These include interest, expense, types of benefits, and morbidity. Morbidity is the expected incidence of sickness or disability within a given age group during a given period of time; it is to health insurance what mortality is to life insurance. Other health insurance premium factors are claims experience and the age, sex, and occupation of the insured.

## RESERVES

Reserves are set aside by an insurance company and designated for the payment of future claims. Part of each premium is designated for the reserves.

Two types of health insurance reserves are *premium reserves* and *loss* (or *claims*) *reserves*. Premium reserves reflect the liability of the insurer for losses that have not occurred but for which premiums have been paid. Reserves earmarked as loss (or claims) reserves represent the insurer's liability for losses that have occurred but for which settlement is not yet complete. The details of how reserves are handled and recorded by the company are very technical. State laws dictate the minimum requirements for reserves for both life and health insurance. The annual statements required by state insurance departments break down a company's reserves in considerable detail.

## CLAIMS

The role of the health insurance claims examiner differs somewhat from that of the life insurance claims examiner. In the case of life insurance, most claims are fairly well defined: the amount of insurance coverage is readily determined by the policy and benefits are payable if the insured has died. With health insurance, though, the claims process is not as clearly defined. Medical expense insurance, for example, typically is based on a *reimbursement contract*, meaning that the benefit an insured receives is not fixed but instead is dependent on the amount of the loss. Its purpose is to reimburse the insured for the amount of loss sustained (within limits). This is in contrast to life insurance, AD&D, and disability income insurance, which all are *valued contracts*—they pay the amount stated in the contract if a defined event, such as death or disability, occurs.

The health claims examiner also must decide if, in fact, a loss actually has occurred. This is especially challenging in disability income cases, where a subjective assessment of disability can create misunderstandings.

# MEDICAL EXPENSE INSURANCE

When people speak of their health insurance, they usually are referring to insurance that protects against the costs of medical care. Medical expense insurance, which is available in several different forms, reimburses policyowners for part or all of the costs of obtaining medical care. It is a vital form of insurance considered by many to be the one type of insurance they cannot do without.

Medical expense insurance provides financial protection against the cost of medical care for accidents and sickness. In this broad context, medical care includes hospital care, physician services, surgical expenses, drugs, nursing and convalescent care, diagnostic treatment, laboratory services, rehabilitative services, dental care, physical therapy—in short, all medical treatment and services. The extent to which a given medical expense policy covers medical care—the specific types of services and treatments covered and the benefits provided—depends on the policy. In general, medical expense insurance is available through one of two different policy plans: *basic medical insurance* or *major medical insurance*. Basic medical insurance limits coverage to select types of medical care. Major medical insurance, which can work either as a supplement to a basic plan or as a comprehensive stand-alone plan, provides broader, more complete coverage.

### REIMBURSEMENT VERSUS INDEMNITY APPROACH

Medical expense plans typically pay benefits as a reimbursement of actual expenses, although some benefits are paid as fixed indemnities, regardless of the actual loss.

---

 E X A M P L E

Karl owns a reimbursement-type medical expense policy that pays a maximum benefit of $200,000. He is hospitalized for 10 days and incurs covered medical expenses totaling up to $10,000. The policy would provide benefits of $10,000—the expenses incurred.

**EXAMPLE**   Doris owns an indemnity-type medical expense policy that provides a $100-per-day benefit for each day of hospitalization. She is hospitalized for 10 days, incurring medical expenses of $10,000. Her policy will indemnify her by providing benefits of $1,000: 10 days at $100 per day. Indemnity medical expense policies do not pay expenses or bills; they merely provide the insured with a stated benefit amount for each day he is confined to a hospital as an inpatient. The money may be used by the insured for any purpose.

With this foundation, we are ready to take a look at the two kinds of medical expense insurance policies: *basic* and *major medical*. Many types of plans fall within these two categories.

# BASIC MEDICAL EXPENSE PLANS

Basic medical expense insurance sometimes is called first dollar insurance because, unlike major medical expense insurance, it provides benefits up front, without requiring the insured to satisfy a deductible first. For many years it was the leading type of medical expense insurance sold, but today it is overshadowed by major medical insurance. This is due largely to the fact that basic medical expense policies limit the type and duration of services covered and dollar amounts that will be paid (or reimbursed) to the insured. Major medical plans are not as limiting.

### BASIC HOSPITAL EXPENSE

Basic hospital expense insurance reimburses policyowners for the cost of hospital confinement. (Many policies today also provide coverage for outpatient care if it is provided in lieu of hospitalized care.) Basic hospital policies cover costs associated with daily room and board and other miscellaneous expenses.

### BASIC SURGICAL EXPENSE

Basic surgical expense policies provide coverage for the cost of a surgeon's services, whether the surgery is performed in the hospital or out. The surgeon's fees, anesthesiologist's fees, and any postoperative care generally are included in the coverage.

### BASIC PHYSICIANS' (NONSURGICAL) EXPENSE

Basic physicians' expense insurance provides benefits for nonsurgical physicians' services. Examples of services covered include office visits and the care by a physician while the insured is hospitalized for a nonsurgical reason. Benefits usually are based on the indemnity approach.

**E X A M P L E**     A plan might pay a flat fee of $50 per visit (not to exceed the actual charge, if less).

These policies typically carry a number of exclusions, such as x-rays, drugs, and dental treatment.

# MAJOR MEDICAL EXPENSE PLANS

Major medical expense insurance, often called simply major medical, has made it possible for many people to achieve substantial protection against the high cost of medical care. It offers broad coverage under one policy, and is available on both an individual basis and a group basis.

The services and supplies covered under a major medical policy must be performed or prescribed by a licensed physician and necessary for the treatment of an insured's illness or injury. The benefit period may be defined on a calendar-year basis or may be specified as a two- to five-year period. Major medical policies provide total maximum lifetime benefits to individual insureds from $250,000 to $1 million or more.

Major medical expense insurance usually picks up where basic medical expense insurance leaves off, in one of two ways: as a supplement to a basic plan or as a comprehensive stand-alone plan.

## SUPPLEMENTARY MAJOR MEDICAL

A supplementary major medical plan covers expenses not included under a basic plan. It also provides coverage for expenses that exceed the dollar maximums specified in the basic policy as well as those expenses no longer covered by the basic plan because the benefits have been exhausted.

With a supplemental plan, major medical coverage is coordinated with various basic medical expense coverages, picking up where the basic plan leaves off.

**E X A M P L E**     A basic plan may provide for hospital room and board benefits for a maximum of 45 days. If that basic plan were supplemented with a major medical plan, the supplementary major medical plan would cover hospital room and board expenses beginning on the 46th day. Or, if a basic plan provides a maximum benefit of $1,500 for a specific surgical procedure and the actual cost of the procedure was $2,000, a major medical supplement would cover the additional $500.

In addition, because of the broad coverage associated with most major medical supplements, a supplement likely will cover expenses that are either beyond the scope of the basic plan or excluded from its coverage.

## COMPREHENSIVE MAJOR MEDICAL

The second type of major medical plan is the comprehensive major medical plan. Comprehensive plans are distinguished by the fact that they cover virtually all medical expenses—hospital expenses, physician and surgeon expenses, nursing care, drugs, physical therapy, diagnostic x-rays and laboratory services, medical supplies and equipment, transfusions, and more—under a single policy.

Major medical plans, whether supplementary or comprehensive, typically include two important features: *deductibles* and *coinsurance*. Both of these features require the insured to absorb some of the cost of his medical expenses, thus allowing the insurer to avoid small claims and keep the cost of premiums down. By contrast, a basic medical plan usually does not include either a deductible or coinsurance; instead it imposes limitations in the form of maximum benefit amounts that will be paid.

## DEDUCTIBLES

A deductible is a stated initial dollar amount that the individual insured is required to pay before insurance benefits are paid.

 EXAMPLE    If a plan has a flat $250 annual deductible, the insured is responsible for the first $250 of medical expenses every year. Covered expenses exceeding $250 then are paid by the major plan (subject to any coinsurance).

**Flat Deductible**  A flat deductible is a stated amount that the insured must pay before policy benefits become payable.

 EXAMPLE    If an insured has a policy with a $500 deductible and incurs $2,000 of covered medical expenses, he must pay $500 toward the total. The insurer then will base its payments on the remaining $1,500.

Quite often, policies will include a family deductible, usually equal to three times the individual deductible amount. In a family of four, for example, if three members each satisfied the individual deductible in one year, no deductible would be applied to medical expenses incurred by the fourth member.

## COINSURANCE

Coinsurance, or percentage participation, is another characteristic of major medical policies. It is, simply, a sharing of expenses by the insured and the insurer. After the insured satisfies the deductible, the insurance company pays a high percentage of the additional (covered) expenses—usually 75 or 80%—and the insured pays the remainder.

**EXAMPLE**

Joe has an 80%/20% major medical policy, with a $200 flat annual deductible. This year, he incurs $1,200 in medical expenses, all of which are covered by his policy. The responsibility for payment would be as follows:

| | |
|---|---:|
| Total expenses: | $1,200 |
| Deductible Joe pays: | −200 |
| Basis for insurer's payment: | $1,000 |
| | × .80 |
| Amount insurer pays: | $ 800 |
| Coinsurance amount Joe pays: | $ 200 |

Thus, the insurer will pay 80% of the charges after the deductible has been satisfied, or $800. Joe must pay the $200 deductible and 20% of the remaining expenses, for a total cost share of $400.

Now let's assume that Joe experiences two separate medical problems this year. The first, which required hospitalization and surgery, totaled $7,500. Under his major medical policy, Joe submitted his claim and paid his $200 deductible. The policy would pay 80% of the charges above the deductible, or $5,840; Joe is responsible for the remaining $1,460. Three months later, Joe incurs another round of medical expenses amounting to $900. Because his policy stipulates a flat annual deductible, which Joe has paid already, the policy will base its 80% payment on the full $900; Joe must pay the remaining 20%, or $180.

Coinsurance provisions are effective throughout the duration of a policy.

## STOP-LOSS FEATURE

To provide a safeguard for insureds, most major medical policies contain a stop-loss feature that limits the insured's out-of-pocket expenses. Once the insured has paid a specified amount toward his covered expenses—usually $1,000 to $2,000—the company pays 100% of covered expenses. How a stop-loss cap is defined depends on the policy. For instance, one policy may stipulate that the contract will cover 100% of eligible expenses after the insured incurs $1,000 in out-of-pocket costs. Another policy may specify that the coinsurance provision applies only to the next $5,000 of covered expenses after the deductible is paid, with full coverage for any remaining expenses.

**EXAMPLE**

Bill has a major medical policy with a stop-loss feature. It calls for a $500 deductible, followed by an 80%/20% coinsurance on the next $5,000 in covered expenses. Amounts above that are fully absorbed by the policy. If Bill were to incur hospital and surgical bills of $20,000 this year, this is how payment would be assigned:

| | |
|---|---:|
| Total expenses: | $20,000 |
| Deductible Bill pays: | − 500 |
| | $19,500 |
| Coinsurance Bill pays (20% of the next $5,000 in expenses): | − 1,000 |
| Amount insurer pays: | $18,500 |

Thus, with a $500 deductible and $1,000 in coinsurance for the next $5,000, Bill's plan provides for a maximum out-of-pocket expenditure by the insured of $1,500.

> **TAKE NOTE**
>
> A hospital indemnity plan may provide the insured $100 a day for every day he is confined in a hospital irrespective of the actual expenses incurred. The insured can apply the benefits to any purpose.

## PREEXISTING CONDITIONS

Another feature characteristic of most major medical policies is the exclusion for preexisting conditions. For individual plans, a preexisting condition is an illness or physical condition that existed before the policy's effective date and one that the applicant did not disclose on the application. (A condition that is noted on the application may be excluded by rider or waiver.) Consequently, medical costs incurred due to a preexisting condition are excluded from coverage under plans that contain this exclusion. However, the exclusion applies for only a limited time. After that time limit passes, any existing conditions no longer are considered preexisting and will be covered in full, subject to any other policy limitations.

# OTHER TYPES OF MEDICAL EXPENSE COVERAGE

As we've discussed, basic medical expense plans and major medical expense plans are the two primary kinds of health policies that provide coverage for accidents and illness. However, a discussion of medical expense plans would not be complete without mentioning a couple of other plans, most notably *hospital indemnity policies* and *limited risk* (or *dread disease*) *policies*.

## HOSPITAL INDEMNITY POLICY

A hospital indemnity policy simply provides a daily, weekly, or monthly indemnity of a specified amount based on the number of days the insured is hospitalized.

This insurance has been available for many years but has been promoted more heavily in recent years largely due to rapidly increasing health care costs. Many companies can offer high benefit indemnity plans at reasonable premiums because underwriting and administration are greatly simplified and claim costs are not affected by increases in medical costs.

Benefits may run as high as $4,500 per month, based on a daily hospital confinement benefit of $150, and some are even higher. Maximum benefit periods range from about six months to several years or for a lifetime. Benefits are payable directly to the insureds and may be used for any purpose. Hospital indemnity policies also usually are exempt from most state laws that apply to specific kinds of insurance contracts.

## DREAD DISEASE/LIMITED RISK POLICIES

Policies that provide medical expense coverage for specific kinds of illnesses are known as limited risk or dread disease policies. They are available primarily due to the high costs associated with certain illnesses, such as cancer or heart disease. Note, however, that some states prohibit the sale of these policies, because they invite questionable sales and marketing practices that take advantage of people's fear of these diseases.

# SERVICE PROVIDERS

Service providers are not insurers per se; rather, they operate on the principle that their subscribers (the term used in place of policyholders) receive medical care services as a result of their payment of premiums. Subscribers typically are not billed for services rendered by a medical care provider. Instead, the care provider—who has entered into an agreement with the service organization to provide medical care—is paid by the service organization directly.

## BLUE CROSS AND BLUE SHIELD

Blue Cross and Blue Shield are voluntary not-for-profit health care service organizations. Blue Cross offers prepayment plans designed to cover hospital services. Blue Shield covers surgical expenses and other medical services performed by physicians.

In the past few years, most Blue Cross and Blue Shield plans merged into single plans. Unlike commercial insurance companies, Blue Cross and Blue Shield organizations have contractual arrangements with hospitals and physicians. These contracts provide for payments for services rendered to subscribers with agreed-upon rates or fee schedules.

## HEALTH MAINTENANCE ORGANIZATION (HMO)

A Health Maintenance Organization (HMO) is another type of organization offering comprehensive prepaid health care services to its subscribing members. HMO participants can be members under a group insurance plan [as an individual, or through family members].

HMOs are distinguished by the fact that they not only finance health care services for their subscribers on a prepayment basis but also organize and deliver the health services. Subscribers pay a fixed periodic fee to the HMO (as opposed to paying for services only when needed) and are provided with a broad range of health services, from routine doctor visits to emergency and hospital care. This care is rendered by physicians and hospitals that participate in the HMO. HMOs are known for stressing preventive care, with the objective of reducing the number of unnecessary hospital admissions and duplication of services.

Two basic types of HMOs exist: an open-panel HMO and a closed-panel HMO.

- *Open-panel HMO.* An open-panel HMO is characterized by a network of physicians who work out of their own private offices and participate in the HMO on a part-time basis.

- *Closed-panel HMO.* A closed-panel HMO is represented by a group of physicians who are salaried employees of the HMO and work out of its facilities.

## PREFERRED PROVIDER ORGANIZATION (PPO)

Another relatively new type of health insurance provider is the preferred provider organization (PPO). A preferred provider organization is a collection of health care providers, such as physicians, hospitals, and clinics who offer their services to certain groups at prearranged prices. In exchange, the group refers its members to the preferred providers for health care services. Unlike HMOs, preferred provider organizations usually operate on a fee-for-service-rendered basis, not on a prepaid basis. Members of the PPO select from among the preferred providers for needed services. Also in contrast to HMOs, PPO health care providers normally are in private practice. They have agreed to offer their services to the group and its members at fees that typically are less than what they normally charge. In exchange, because the group refers its members to the PPO, the providers broaden their patient and service base.

## SUMMARY

This unit introduced the important field of health insurance. Many hybrid plans offer health protection in three different forms: medical expense, disability income, and accidental death and dismemberment. Health insurance is available to individuals and families on an individual basis, through a group plan or through the federal government. It is distinguished by many factors, including its provisions for renewability, premium factors, whether or not the contract is participating, reserves, and its claims procedures. The need for medical expense insurance—health care insurance in current vernacular—is greater today than at any time in the past because of the high cost of medical care. Basic medical expense insurance, once the predominant form of health insurance, now is overshadowed by major medical insurance in terms of premium dollars and total coverage. Offered as individual and group policies, medical expense insurance is an indispensable part of a total insurance portfolio.

# UNIT QUIZ

1. All of the following are basic forms of health insurance coverage EXCEPT
   A. medical expense
   B. limited pay health
   C. disability income
   D. accidental death and dismemberment

2. When a medical expense policy pays benefits on an indemnity basis, it pays
   A. a certain percentage of whatever the hospital room charges are
   B. for total hospital expenses, less a deductible
   C. a flat amount per day for hospital room and board
   D. only for surgery and miscellaneous hospital expenses

3. If the coinsurance feature in a major medical insurance policy is 75/25 with a $100 deductible, how much of a $2,100 bill would the insured pay?
   A. $100
   B. $500
   C. $600
   D. $1,500

4. HMOs are known for stressing which of the following?
   A. Preventive care
   B. Health care and services on a fee-for-services-rendered basis
   C. Health care and services in hospital settings
   D. Health care and services to government employees

5. Which of the following statements is NOT true of PPOs?
   A. A PPO is a group of health care providers, such as doctors, hospitals, and ambulatory health care organizations, that contracts with a group to provide their services.
   B. PPOs operate on a prepaid basis.
   C. PPO members select from among the preferred providers for needed services.
   D. PPOs offer their services to the group and its members at fees that are less than what they normally charge.

6. Leonard owns a major medical health policy which requires him to pay the first $200 of covered expenses each year before the policy pays its benefits. The $200 is the policy's
   A. coinsurance amount
   B. deductible
   C. stop-loss amount
   D. annual premium

7. Basic surgical expense policies generally provide coverage for all of the following EXCEPT
   A. anesthesiologist services
   B. surgeon services
   C. postoperative care
   D. miscellaneous expenses, such as lab fees and x-rays

8. A stop-loss feature in a major medical policy specifies the maximum
   A. benefit amount the policy provides each year
   B. benefit amount the policy provides in a lifetime
   C. amount the insured must pay in premiums
   D. amount the insured must pay toward covered expenses

# ANSWERS AND RATIONALES TO UNIT QUIZ

1. **B.** Three distinct categories of basic health insurance coverage exist: medical expense, disability income, and accidental death and dismemberment.

2. **C.** Under a medical expense policy, when benefits are paid on an indemnity basis, the policy will pay a flat amount per day for hospital room and board.

3. **C.** In an insurance policy with a 75/25 coinsurance feature and a $100 deductible, the insured would pay $600 of a $2,100 bill. This would be calculated as follows: $100 deductible plus $500 (25% of $2,000, the remaining amount of the bill).

4. **A.** HMOs stress preventive care to reduce the number of unnecessary hospital admissions and duplication of services.

5. **B.** Unlike HMOs, PPOs usually operate on a fee-for-service-rendered basis, not a prepaid basis.

6. **B.** A deductible is a stated initial dollar amount that the individual insured is required to pay before insurance benefits are paid.

7. **D.** Miscellaneous expenses are covered under basic hospital expense policies. These extras include drugs, x-rays, anesthesia, lab fees, dressings, use of the operating room, and supplies.

8. **D.** To provide a safeguard for insureds, many major medical policies contain a stop-loss feature that limits the insured's out-of-pocket expenses. This means that once the insured has paid a specified amount toward his covered expenses—usually $1,000 to $2,000—the company pays 100% of covered expenses after that point.

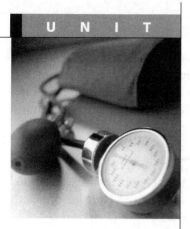

# 10

# Disability Income Insurance/AD&D Policies

## KEY CONCEPTS

- The role of disability insurance
- Different measures used to define total disability
- At-work benefits
- Policy provisions and riders
- Accidental Death and Dismemberment policies

The risk associated with disability is not only the loss of income; there is also the additional cost of caring for a disabled breadwinner who can no longer work. And when a disability is permanent, the financial consequences can be just as severe as those resulting from death. This unit describes the role disability income insurance plays in a well-planned insurance program and explains the features typically found in disability policies.

This unit also discusses accidental death and dismemberment (AD&D) insurance, which pays benefits when an accidental injury results in death or dismemberment. AD&D policies are widely used in group insurance plans, but AD&D coverage may also be included as a rider to a basic life or health insurance policy.

## OBJECTIVE

When you complete this unit you should be able to:

- explain how the percent-of-earnings and flat amount methods are used to determine the amount of disability income benefits;

- compare and contrast the *any occupation* and *own occupation* definitions of total disability;

- describe how partial disability benefits are determined;

- list and describe the standard provisions typically found in a disability income policy;

- list and describe the different types of riders that may be purchased with disability income policies;

- explain the purpose of accidental death and dismemberment insurance and the types of benefits that typically are payable;

- explain the difference between policies that base benefits on injuries due to accidental means versus accidental results; and

- compare and contrast limited risk policies and special risk policies and give an example of each type of policy.

# DISABILITY INCOME BENEFITS

The benefits paid under a disability income policy are in the form of monthly income payments. Unlike life insurance, which insurers will issue for almost any amount, the amount of disability income benefits applied for is based upon the applicant's actual income. Insurers typically place a ceiling on the amount of disability income protection they will issue on any one applicant, defined in terms of the insured's earnings. And with few exceptions, this benefit ceiling is less than the insured's regular income.

Insurers use two methods to determine the amount of benefits payable under their disability income policies. The first method determines the benefit using a percentage of the insured's predisability earnings and takes into account other sources of disability income.

**TAKE NOTE**

Without a benefit ceiling, a disabled insured could conceivably receive as much income as he did while working, with little incentive to return to work and much incentive to prolong the disability.

**TAKE NOTE**

The percent of earnings approach typically is used in group disability income plans. The flat amount method is more common in individual plans.

EXAMPLE

An individual earning $2,000 a month may be limited by Company A to a monthly benefit of 60% of income, or $1,200. If that individual already has an existing disability income policy from Company X that provides for $400 in monthly income, the amount payable by Company A would be limited to $800 each month.

Some policies that use the percent-of-earnings formula provide a benefit that varies with the length of the disability. For instance, the benefit amount may equal 100% of the insured's predisability earnings for the first month and then reduce the benefit amount to 70% thereafter.

The second method used to establish disability benefits is the flat amount method. Under this approach, the policy specifies a flat income benefit amount that will be paid if the insured becomes totally disabled. Normally, this amount is payable regardless of any other income benefits the insured may receive.

## DISABILITY DEFINED

An insured must be totally disabled before benefits under a disability income policy are payable. What constitutes total disability varies from policy to policy. The insured must meet the definition set forth in his policy. Basically, there are two definitions: *any occupation* or *own occupation*.

**Any Occupation** The any occupation definition of total disability requires the insured to be unable to perform any occupation for which he is reasonably suited by reason of education, training, or experience to qualify for disability income benefits.

**Own Occupation** The own occupation definition of total disability requires that the insured be unable to work at his own occupation as a result of an accident or sickness.

Disability income policies often qualify total disability in two stages, using both the own occupation and any occupation definitions. These policies will provide initial benefits based on the own occupation definition for a specified period of time (for example, during the first two years of the disability), then change the qualifying basis to the any occupation definition.

**Presumptive Disability** Most policies today contain a presumption of disability provision. Basically, this provision specifies certain conditions that automatically qualify the insured for the full

**TAKE NOTE**

Obviously from a policyowner's point of view, an own occupation disability income policy is more advantageous—it also is more expensive.

**TAKE NOTE**

From the insured's viewpoint, the "any occupation" definition is more restrictive than the "own occupation" definition. The insurer is less likely to pay a benefit—the insured's disability must prevent him from engaging in *any* reasonably suitable occupation.

**TAKE NOTE**

Normally, partial disability benefits are payable only if the policyowner first has been totally disabled. This benefit is intended to encourage disabled insureds to get back to work, even on a part-time basis, without fear that they will lose all their disability income benefits.

benefit, because the severity of the conditions presumes the insured is totally disabled even if he is able to work. Presumptive disabilities include blindness, deafness, loss of speech, loss of two hands, two feet or one hand, and one foot.

**EXAMPLE**

If Janet has a stroke and loses her ability to speak she has suffered a presumptive disability and would be entitled to total disability benefits for the rest of her policy's benefit period.

## AT WORK BENEFITS

The exception to the total disability requirement is a policy that also pays benefits in the event of a partial disability. It is not uncommon for disability income policies to make provision for partial disability, either as part of the basic coverage or as an optional rider for an additional premium. By most definitions, partial disability is the inability of the insured to perform one or more important duties of his job or the inability to work at that job on a full-time basis, either of which results in a diminished income.

The amount of benefit payable when a policy covers partial disabilities depends on whether the policy stipulates a *partial amount* or a *residual amount*.

**Partial Disability Benefit** A flat amount benefit is a set amount stated in the policy. Usually this amount is 50% of the full disability benefit.

E X A M P L EHelen, who has a disability income policy with an own occupation definition, is injured severely after falling down a flight of stairs. She is unable to work for four months, during which time her disability income policy pays a full benefit. After four months she is able to return to work, but only on a part-time basis, earning substantially less than she did before her injury. If her policy did not contain a partial disability provision, her benefits would cease entirely because she no longer meets the definition of totally disabled. However, if her policy provides for partial disability benefits to be paid as a flat amount, she will be able to work on a part-time basis and continue to receive half of her disability benefits.

**Residual Amount Benefit**   A residual amount benefit is based on the proportion of income actually lost due to the partial disability, taking into account the fact that the insured is able to work and earn some income. The benefit usually is determined by multiplying the percentage of lost income by the stated monthly benefit for total disability.

E X A M P L EIf the insured suffered a 40% loss of income because of the partial disability, the residual benefit payable would be 40% of the benefit that the policy would provide for total disability. This percentage is subject to change as the disabled insured's income varies.

Insurers require proof of an insured's total or partial disability before they will pay benefits. To be eligible for benefits, the disabled insured must be under the care of a physician.

## CAUSE OF DISABILITY

Another important aspect of disability income policies is the way in which they define the cause of disability. How a disability occurs is an important consideration for disability income policies, as well as any other kind of policy covering injury due to accident.

Generally, disability income policies state that benefits are payable when injuries are either caused by external, violent, and accidental means, or result in accidental bodily injury.

Policies that use the *accidental means provision* require that the cause of the injury must have been unexpected and accidental. Policies that use the accidental bodily injury provision require that the result of the injury—in other words, the injury itself—has to be unexpected and accidental. This also is known as the *results provision*.

E X A M P L EJim, the insured, took an intentional dive off a high, rocky ledge into a lake. He struck his head on some rocks and was partially paralyzed. If his policy had an accidental means provision, the benefits probably would not be payable because the cause of his injury—the dive—was intentional. However, if his policy had an accidental bodily injury (or results) provision, benefits would be payable because the result of the accident—his injury—was unintentional and accidental.

**TAKE NOTE**

A disability income probationary period applies to sickness only; it does not apply to accidents. Whereas a person may be able to anticipate a sickness-related disability (after a visit to the doctor, for example), it is not possible to anticipate an accident.

Today, most disability income policies (and other policies providing accident protection) use the accidental bodily injury or results provision, which is far less restrictive than the accidental means provision. In fact, many states now require all accident-based insurance benefits to be based on the accidental bodily injury provision.

# DISABILITY INCOME POLICY PROVISIONS

In addition to specifying the amount of benefit payable and the circumstances under which a benefit is payable (plus complying with required provisions standards), disability income policies contain a number of other important provisions. The most notable of these are as follows.

## PROBATIONARY PERIOD

The probationary period specified in a disability insurance policy is the period of time that must elapse following the effective date of the policy before benefits are payable. It is a one-time-only period that begins on the policy's effective date and ends 15 or 30 days after the policy has been in force. The purpose of the probationary period is to exclude preexisting sicknesses from coverage and provide a guidepost in borderline cases when there is a question as to whether an insured became ill before or after the effective date of the policy. Just as important, it helps protect the insurer against adverse selection, because those who know they are ill are more likely to try to obtain insurance coverage.

## ELIMINATION PERIOD

Similar in concept to a deductible, the elimination period is the time immediately following the start of a disability when benefits are not payable. Elimination periods eliminate claims for short-term disabilities for which the insured usually can manage without financial hardship and save the insurance company from the expense of processing and settling small claims. This, in turn, helps keep premiums down. The longer the elimination period, the lower the premium for comparable disability benefits. An elimination period can be compared to a deductible because both are cost-sharing devices that can have a direct bearing on the amount of premium required of the policyowner.

## BENEFIT PERIOD

The benefit period is the maximum length of time that disability income benefits will be paid to the disabled insured. The longer the benefit period, the higher the cost of the policy. For individual policies, there are basically two types of benefit periods and accordingly they serve to classify a disability income policy as either short term or long term. Individual short-term policies provide benefits for six months to two years, after which payments cease. Individual long-term policies are characterized by benefit periods of more than two years, such as 5, 10, or 20 years. In some cases, a long-term policy will provide for benefits until the insured reaches age 65. The classifications of short term and long term are not necessarily the same for individual and group plans.

## RECURRENT DISABILITY PROVISION

It is not unusual for a person who experienced a total disability to recover and then, weeks or months later, undergo a recurrence of the same disability. Most policies provide for recurrent disabilities by specifying a period of time during which the recurrence of a disability is considered a continuation of the prior disability. The most common period is six months.

---

**EXAMPLE**    Rachel has a short-term disability policy that stipulates a new benefit-paying period begins if the insured is disabled, recovers, returns to work for six months and then becomes disabled again. Rachel is totally disabled and off work from January 15 to April 15, when she returns to work. She is stricken again the same year and is off work from September 1 to November 10. Rachel's policy would resume paying benefits, classifying her recurrence as a continuation of her prior disability, because her return to work did not last six months. She would not be subject to a new elimination period.

## NONDISABLING INJURY

Frequently, a person covered by a disability income policy will suffer an injury that does not qualify for income benefits. Many such policies include a provision for a medical expense benefit that pays the actual cost of medical treatment for nondisabling injuries that result from an accident. The benefit generally is limited to a percentage of the weekly or monthly income benefit specified in the policy. It is payable to eligible insureds in lieu of other benefits under the policy.

# DISABILITY INCOME POLICY RIDERS

As is true with life insurance policies, disability income policies may be purchased with riders or options that will enhance their value to the insured. Some of the more common riders are discussed below.

## WAIVER OF PREMIUM RIDER

A waiver of premium rider is a valuable provision because it exempts the policyowner from paying the policy's premiums during periods of total disability. To qualify for the exemption, the insured must experience total disability for more than a specified period, commonly three or six months. In some cases, the waiver applies retroactively to the original date of disability and any premiums paid for that period are refunded.

## SOCIAL INSURANCE RIDER

The Social Security rider, sometimes called the social insurance substitute rider, provides for the payment of additional income when the insured is eligible for social insurance benefits, but those benefits

---

**TAKE NOTE**

The waiver of premium generally does not extend past the insured's age 60 or 65. When the waiver is added, policy premiums are adjusted upward to cover the additional risk. Premiums then are reduced when the waiver is dropped due to the insured reaching the specified age limit.

---

have not yet begun, have been denied, or have begun in an amount less than the benefit amount of the rider. Usually covered under the definition social insurance are disability benefits from Social Security as well as state and local government programs or workers' compensation programs.

When applying for the rider, the applicant states the amount of benefit expected from Social Security and any other programs for which he might be eligible. Of course, the level of expected benefits must be realistic in light of the applicant's earnings level. When total disability strikes, the applicant must show that social insurance benefits have been applied for. After the Social Security Administration (or comparable administrative body of a state or local program) determines the benefit payable, the difference between the actual benefit and the expected benefit listed in the rider is payable as an additional disability income benefit.

### COST OF LIVING ADJUSTMENT (COLA) RIDER

The cost of living adjustment (COLA) rider links the monthly or weekly benefit payable under a disability policy to changes in the Consumer Price Index (CPI). The rider makes adjustments to benefits payable *after* the disability payments have begun.

### GUARANTEED INSURABILITY RIDER

This option guarantees the insured the right to purchase additional amounts of disability income coverage at predetermined times in the future without evidence of insurability. The guarantee may be contingent upon the insured meeting an earnings test prior to each purchase—a condition stipulated by the insurer to avoid overinsurance.

Most guaranteed insurability riders require the insured to exercise the option for additional coverage before reaching a specific age.

# AD&D POLICIES

Accidental death and dismemberment insurance is the primary form of pure accident coverage. As such, it serves a somewhat limited purpose: it provides a stated lump-sum benefit in the event of accidental death or in the event of loss of body members due to accidental injury. This latter event includes loss of hands or feet or the loss of sight in one or both eyes.

# AD&D BENEFITS

Because an AD&D policy pays a specified benefit to the insured in the event of accidental death or dismemberment due to accidental injury, it is necessary for the policy to make distinctions between these two contingencies and to define the benefits accordingly. Consequently, AD&D policies make benefits payable in the form of a principal sum and a capital sum.

**Principal Sum**   The principal sum under an AD&D policy is the amount payable as a death benefit. It is the amount of insurance purchased—$10,000, $25,000, $50,000, $100,000, or more. The principal sum represents the maximum amount the policy will pay.

**Capital Sum**   The capital sum paid under an AD&D policy is the amount payable for the accidental loss of sight or accidental dismemberment. It is a specified amount, usually expressed as a percentage of the principal sum, that varies according to the severity of the injury.

## ACCIDENTAL MEANS VERSUS ACCIDENTAL RESULTS

By way of a review, policies that base their benefit payments on accidental means require that both the cause and the result of an accident must be unintentional. Policies that use the more liberal accidental results definition stipulate that only the injury resulting from an accident must be unintentional.

EXAMPLE

If Ted, the insured under an AD&D policy, intentionally jumps from the roof of his house after fixing his antenna (instead of climbing down the ladder) and so severely injures his leg that it must be amputated, he would be paid the appropriate percentage of the capital sum only if his policy used the results definition. If his policy used the means definition, no benefit would be payable because Ted intentionally performed the action (the jump) that resulted in the injury.

Most states require that policies that provide any form of accident benefit, as do AD&D policies, base the definition of accident on the results definition, not the means definition.

# OTHER FORMS OF AD&D

Accidental death and dismemberment coverage is made available in a variety of ways. It can be purchased by individuals as a single policy or it may be a part of an individual disability income policy. Quite typically, however, it is an aspect of a group insurance plan—either group life or group health—or it may in and of itself constitute a group plan. Usually, AD&D benefits are payable whether the injury resulted on or off the job.

By their very nature, AD&D policies are somewhat narrow, providing benefits only in the event of death or dismemberment due to an accident. There is another type of AD&D coverage, even more narrow in scope, that provides protection against accidental death or dismemberment only in the event of certain specified accidents. Travel accident policies are one such contract.

## TRAVEL ACCIDENT POLICIES

Travel accident policies set forth a specific risk and provide benefits to cover death or dismemberment due to that risk. For example, an aviation policy provides benefits for accidental death or dismemberment if death or injury results from an aviation accident during a specified trip. Travel accident covers most kinds of travel accidents, but only for a specified period of time, such as one year.

# SUMMARY

Often called "the forgotten need," disability income insurance is an important part of a complete insurance program. Monthly or weekly benefits are paid when the insured is totally disabled, as determined by either the any occupation or the more liberal own occupation definition. If the policy includes "at work" provisions, benefits may be payable if the insured is able to work only part time or suffers a less-than-total disability. Another feature of disability income policies is that they define the cause of a disabling accident on an accidental means or accidental results basis.

Disability income contracts are characterized by probationary periods, which exclude preexisting sickness from immediate coverage, and elimination periods, which specify the time after the start of a disability when benefits are not payable, thereby excluding very short-term disabilities from coverage. Like life insurance, disability income policies may be purchased with policy riders that can increase their value to the insured.

Accidental death and dismemberment insurance (AD&D) represents the purest form of accident coverage. It provides a stated sum benefit in the event of accidental death or accidental loss of one or more body members or accidental loss of sight. The benefit payable in the event of death is known as the principal sum; the benefit payable in the event of dismemberment or loss of sight is the capital sum.

Like all policies that provide accident benefits, AD&D policies must define the term accident on either a means basis (in which both the cause and the result of the accident must be unintentional) or on a results basis (requiring only that the injury itself be accidental). Most states stipulate the use of the results definition.

AD&D coverage may be purchased as an individual policy but usually is part of a larger group life or health plan. In some cases, it is offered as a separate group plan. Specialized forms of AD&D coverage, known as limited risk and special risk insurance, provide accident protection in the event of specified limited risks, such as travel or aviation.

# U N I T   Q U I Z

1. Which of the following riders provides for changes in the benefit payable based on changes in the consumer price index (CPI)?

   A. Guaranteed insurability
   B. Cost of living adjustment
   C. Social Security
   D. Waiver of premium

2. Benefit periods for individual short-term disability policies typically vary from

   A. 1 to 12 months
   B. 3 months to 3 years
   C. 6 months to 2 years
   D. 1 to 5 years

3. Sidney has a monthly benefit of $2,500 for total disability under a residual disability income policy. If Sidney suffers a 40% loss of his predisability income, how much will his benefit be?

   A. $0
   B. $1,000
   C. $1,500
   D. $2,500

4. What is the initial period of time specified in a disability income policy that must pass, after a policy is in force, before a loss due to sickness can be covered?

   A. Preexisting term
   B. Probationary period
   C. Temporary interval
   D. Elimination period

5. The amount payable as a death benefit in an accidental death and dismemberment policy is known as the

   A. primary amount
   B. capital sum
   C. indemnity amount
   D. principal sum

6. Theodore received a $15,000 cash benefit from his $50,000 accidental death and dismemberment policy for the accidental loss of one eye. The amount he received could be identified as the policy's

   A. principal sum
   B. secondary sum
   C. capital sum
   D. contingent amount

7. Paul has an accidental death and dismemberment policy that paid him $100,000 after he was injured in a skydiving accident. His policy bases its benefit payments on accidental

   A. means
   B. results
   C. methods
   D. means and methods

8. A waiver of premium provision may be included with which kind of health insurance policy?

   A. Hospital indemnity
   B. Major medical
   C. Disability income
   D. Basic medical

# ANSWERS AND RATIONALES TO UNIT QUIZ

1. **B.** A cost of living adjustment rider provides for indexing monthly or weekly disability benefits to changes in the Consumer Price Index.

2. **C.** Individual short-term disability policies typically have benefit periods ranging from 6 months to 2 years, after which payments stop. In contrast, individual long-term policies provide for benefit periods of more than two years.

3. **B.** Sidney's benefit under his residual disability income policy will be determined by multiplying the percentage of lost income by the stated monthly benefit for total disability. Because he suffered a 40% loss of income, the residual benefit payable would be 40% of the policy's benefit (40% × $2,500), or $1,000.

4. **B.** The probationary period is the period of time that must elapse before benefits due to sickness become payable. It is a one-time-only period that ends 15 or 30 days after the policy has been in force. Its purpose is to exclude preexisting sicknesses from coverage.

5. **D.** The principal sum under an AD&D policy is the amount payable as a death benefit. It is the amount of insurance purchased and represents the maximum amount the policy will pay.

6. **C.** The $15,000 cash benefit Theodore received for the accidental loss of one eye is the policy's capital sum. This is the amount payable for the accidental loss of sight or accidental dismemberment. It is a specified amount that usually is expressed as a percentage of the principal sum and varies according to the severity of the injury.

7. **B.** Paul's AD&D policy bases its benefit payments on accidental results. Policies using this definition stipulate that only the injury resulting from an accident must be unintentional. If Paul's policy used the accidental means definition, it would not pay any benefits because Paul intentionally performed the action (skydiving) that resulted in injury.

8. **C.** A waiver of premium rider generally is included with guaranteed renewable and noncancelable individual disability income policies. It is a valuable provision because it exempts the policyowner from paying the policy's premiums during periods of total disability.

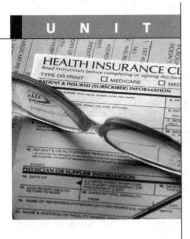

# 11

# Individual Health Insurance Policy Provisions

## KEY CONCEPTS

- Standardization and the NAIC
- Mandatory provisions protecting consumers
- Optional provisions
- Conversion privileges for individual health policies
- Common exclusions
- Renewability provisions

### TAKE NOTE

Because these provisions are to be followed in substance, insurers may employ different wording from that of the law, as long as the protection is provided and is no less favorable to the insured than the law stipulates.

Health insurance is characterized by a number of mandatory provisions that must be included in the contract. These provisions were developed by the National Association of Insurance Commissioners (NAIC) to protect the rights of individual health insurance consumers. In this unit, we will review the 12 mandatory provisions and 11 optional provisions that the NAIC developed to add uniformity to health insurance contracts. This unit also will discuss some of the more common exclusions and restrictions found in health policies as well as typical renewability provisions that allow the insurer to continue or discontinue coverage.

### OBJECTIVE

When you complete this unit you should be able to:

■  list and describe the 12 mandatory policy provisions for individual health insurance contracts;

■  list and describe the 11 option policy provisions for individual health insurance contracts;

■  explain the purpose of the insuring clause, consideration clause, conversion privilege for dependents, and free-look provision in a health insurance contract;

■  identify the typical exclusions that are not covered by health insurance policies; and

■  list and describe the five types of renewability provisions found in health insurance policies.

## NAIC MODEL HEALTH INSURANCE POLICY PROVISIONS

In 1950, the National Association of Insurance Commissioners (NAIC) developed a model Uniform Individual Accident and Sickness Policy Provisions Law. Almost all states have adopted this model law or similar legislation or regulations.

The purpose of the NAIC law was to establish uniform or model terms, provisions, and wording standards for inclusion in all individual health insurance contracts or all contracts that provide insurance against loss resulting from sickness, bodily injury or death by accident, or both. The result was 12 mandatory policy provisions and 11 optional policy provisions.

Similar to a life insurance contract, a health insurance contract obligates the insurer to pay the insured (or a beneficiary) a stipulated benefit under circumstances specified in the contract. The specifics of the benefit and the requisite circumstances are set forth in the contract's provisions. Let's take a look at these provisions.

**TAKE NOTE**

Depending on the state, the minimum grace periods that may be specified typically are seven days for policies with weekly premium payments, 10 days for policies with premiums payable on a monthly basis, and 31 days for other policies. Some states, however, require a standard grace period of 31 days, regardless of the frequency of premium payment or policy term.

## TWELVE MANDATORY POLICY PROVISIONS

In accordance with the NAIC model law, there are 12 mandatory provisions that must be in all health insurance contracts. These are as follows:

**Entire Contract** Like its counterpart in a life insurance policy, the entire contract provision in a health insurance policy protects the policyowner in two ways. First, it states that nothing outside of the contract—which includes the signed application and any attached policy riders—can be considered part of the contract; that is, nothing can be incorporated by reference. Second, it assures the policyowner that no changes will be made to the contract after it has been issued, even if the insurer makes policy changes that affect all policy sales in the future.

**Time Limit on Certain Defenses** Under the time limit on certain defenses provision, the policy is incontestable after it has been in force a certain period of time, usually two years. This is similar to the incontestable clause in a life insurance policy. However, unlike life policies, a fraudulent statement on a health insurance application is grounds for contest at any time, unless the policy is guaranteed renewable, in which case it cannot be contested for any reason after the contestable period expires.

Another part of this provision concerns any preexisting conditions (conditions that existed before the policy's effective date) an insured may have. Under the provision, the insurance company cannot deny a claim on the basis of a preexisting condition after expiration of the stated contestable period—unless such preexisting condition has been excluded specifically from the policy by name or description.

**Grace Period** Per the grace period provision, the policyowner is given a number of days after the premium due date during which time the premium payment may be delayed without penalty and the policy continues in force.

**Reinstatement** Under certain conditions, a policy that has lapsed may be reinstated. Reinstatement is automatic if the delinquent premium is accepted by the company or its authorized agent and the company does not require an application for reinstatement.

If a company does require such an application, it may or may not approve the application. If it takes no action on the application for 45 days, the policy is reinstated automatically. To protect the company against adverse selection, losses resulting from sickness are covered only if the sickness occurs at least 10 days after the reinstatement date.

**Notice of Claim** The notice of claim provision describes the policyowner's obligation to the insurer to provide notification of loss within a reasonable period of time. Typically, this period is

20 days after the occurrence or a commencement of the loss, or as soon thereafter as is reasonably possible. If the loss involves disability income payments that are payable for two or more years, the disabled claimant must submit proof of loss every six months. Such proof may be submitted to either the company or an authorized agent of the company.

**Claim Forms** It is the company's responsibility to supply a claim form to an insured within 15 days after receiving notice of claim. If it fails to do so within the time limit, the claimant may submit proof of loss in any form, explaining the occurrence, the character, and the extent of the loss for which the claim is submitted.

**Proof of Loss** After a loss occurs, or after the company becomes liable for periodic payments (for example, disability income benefits), the claimant has 90 days in which to submit proof of loss. The claim will not be affected in any way, however, if it is not reasonably possible for the claimant to comply with the 90-day provision.

**Time of Payment of Claims** The time of payment of claims provision provides for *immediate* payment of the claim after the insurer receives notification and proof of loss. If the claim involves disability income payments, they must be paid at least monthly, if not at more frequent intervals specified in the policy.

**Payment of Claims** The payment of claims provision in a health insurance contract specifies how and to whom claim payments are to be made. Payments for loss of life are to be made to the designated beneficiary. If no beneficiary has been named, death proceeds are to be paid to the deceased insured's estate. Claims other than death benefits are to be paid to the insured.

**Physical Exam and Autopsy** The physical exam and autopsy provision entitles a company, at its own expense, to make physical examinations of the insured at reasonable intervals during the period of a claim. In the case of death, the insurer has the right to conduct an autopsy on the body of the insured, provided it is not forbidden by state law.

**Legal Actions** The insured cannot take legal action against the company in a claim dispute until after 60 days from the time the insured submits proof of loss. The same rule applies to beneficiaries. Also, if legal action is to be taken against the company, it must be done within a certain time after proof of loss is submitted (usually two or three years).

FIGURE 11.1    NAIC Uniform Health Insurance Policy Provisions

| Mandatory Provisions | Optional Provisions |
|---|---|
| 1. Entire Contract | 1. Change of Occupation |
| 2. Time Limit on Certain Defenses | 2. Misstatement of Age |
| 3. Grace Period | 3. Other Insurance in This Insurer |
| 4. Reinstatement | 4. Insurance with Other Insurer |
| 5. Notice of Claims | 5. Insurance with Other Insurers |
| 6. Claims Forms | 6. Relation of Earnings to Insurance |
| 7. Proof of Loss | 7. Unpaid Premiums |
| 8. Time of Payment of Claims | 8. Cancellation |
| 9. Payment of Claims | 9. Conformity with State Statutes |
| 10. Physical Exam and Autopsy | 10. Illegal Occupation |
| 11. Legal Actions | 11. Intoxicants and Narcotics |
| 12. Change of Beneficiary | |

TAKE NOTE

These benefit and premium changes take effect at the time the insured changes occupations. If a change in jobs is discovered after a disability begins, the changes are made retroactively.

**Change of Beneficiary**  The insured, as policyowner, may change the beneficiary designation at any time, unless a beneficiary has been named irrevocably. So long as the insured reserves the right to change beneficiaries, he also may surrender or assign the policy without obtaining the consent of the beneficiary.

## ELEVEN OPTIONAL PROVISIONS

There are 11 optional health policy provisions, and companies may ignore them or use only those that are needed in their policy forms. The provisions pertaining to "other insurance in this insurer," "insurance with other insurers," and "relation of earnings to insurance" seldom are used. They were intended to deal with the problem of overinsurance but generally proved to be ineffective.

**Change of Occupation**  The change of occupation provision sets forth the changes that may be made to premium rates or benefits payable should the insured change occupations. Many insurers include this provision in their disability income policies because an individual's occupation has a direct bearing on his risk profile, and one's risk profile has a direct bearing on premium charges. Consequently, this provision allows the insurer to reduce the maximum benefit payable under the policy if the insured switches to a more hazardous occupation, or to reduce the premium rate charged if the insured changes to a less hazardous occupation.

**Misstatement of Age**  The misstatement of age provision allows the insurer to adjust the benefit payable if the age of the insured was misstated when application for the policy was made. Benefit amounts payable in such cases will be what the premiums paid would have purchased at the correct age. The older the applicant is, the higher the premium would be; therefore, if the insured was older at the time of application than is shown in the policy, benefits would be reduced accordingly. The reverse would be true if the insured were younger than listed in the application; in this instance, the insurer will refund excess premiums paid.

**Other Insurance in This Insurer**  The purpose of the other insurance in this insurer provision is to limit the company's risk with any individual insured. Under this provision, the total amount of coverage to be underwritten by a company for one person is restricted to a specified maximum amount, regardless of the number of policies issued. Premiums that apply to any such excess of coverage must be returned to the insured or the insured's estate.

**Insurance with Other Insurer**  In attempting to deal with the potential problem of overinsurance, the insurance with other insurer provision states that benefits payable for "expenses incurred" will be prorated in cases where the company accepted the risk without being notified of other existing coverage for the same risk. When premiums are paid that exceed the amount needed to cover what the company determines it will pay, the excess premiums must be refunded to the policyowner.

TAKE NOTE

Any premiums paid for the excess coverage are refunded.

**Insurance with Other Insurers** Similar to the above, the insurance with other insurers provision calls for the prorating of benefits that are payable on any basis other than "expenses incurred." It also provides for a return of premiums that exceed the amount needed to pay for the company's portion of prorated benefits.

**Relation of Earnings to Insurance** If disability income benefits from all disability income policies for the same loss exceed the insured's monthly earnings at the time of disability (or the average monthly earnings for two years preceding disability), the relation of earnings provision states that the insurer is liable only for that proportionate amount of benefits as the insured's earnings bear to the total benefits under all such coverage.

**Unpaid Premiums** If there is an unpaid premium at the time a claim becomes payable, the amount of the premium is to be deducted from the sum payable to the insured or beneficiary.

**Cancellation** Though prohibited in a number of states, the provision for cancellation gives the company the right to cancel the policy at any time with five days' written notice to the insured. It also provides that the insured may cancel the policy anytime after the policy's original term has expired. Any unearned premium is to be refunded to the insured. If a claim is pending at the time of cancellation, the claim cannot be affected by the cancellation. (See also *Renewability Provisions*, later in this unit.)

**Conformity with State Statutes** Any policy provision that conflicts with state statutes in the state where the insured lives at the time the policy is issued automatically is amended to conform with the minimum statutory requirements.

**Illegal Occupation** The illegal occupation provision specifies that the insurer is not liable for losses attributed to the insured's commission of, or being connected with, a felony or participation in any illegal occupation.

**Intoxicants and Narcotics** The insurer is not liable for any loss attributed to the insured while intoxicated or under the influence of narcotics, unless such drugs were administered on the advice of a physician.

## OTHER HEALTH INSURANCE POLICY PROVISIONS

The 12 mandatory provisions and 11 optional provisions just described comprise the substantive elements of individual health insurance policies. However, a number of other very important clauses and provisions should be noted.

**Insuring Clause** Generally, the insuring clause is a broad statement on the first page of the health policy, stipulating conditions under which benefits are to be paid. While these critical provisions vary considerably in health insurance contracts, they basically represent a company's promise to pay benefits for specific kinds of losses resulting from sickness or accidents. They usually specify that benefits are subject to all provisions and exclusions stated in the policy.

**Consideration Clause** The consideration clause states the amount and frequency of premium payments. If the first premium has not been paid—even though the application has been completed and signed by the applicant—the necessary consideration is partially lacking.

Frequently, the consideration clause also lists the effective date of the contract and defines the initial term of the policy. In addition, it may specify the insured's right to renew the policy.

**Conversion Privilege for Dependents** A single health policy may insure one person, or more than one if the applicant is an adult family member and the others to be covered are members of his family. Thus, additional persons who may be insured include the husband, wife, dependent children, or others dependent on the adult applicant. To be eligible, children must meet certain age requirements.

Generally, children of the insured are eligible for coverage under a family policy until they attain a specified age, usually age 19 or, if they are in school full time, age 23. Adopted children, stepchildren, and foster children usually are eligible for coverage. As long as a policy is in force, coverage for a child generally continues until the child marries or reaches the limiting age. However, a number of states have enacted special laws that require insurers to retain as insureds under the parent's individual health policy any child who reaches the limiting age but is dependent on the insured and incapable of self-support because of mental or physical impairment.

Attaining a minimum age, such as 14 days, may be required for coverage. However, legislation in some states mandates that health policies insuring family members also provide coverage for newborn children from the date of birth. Typically, such legislation permits the insurer to require that notice of the child's birth be given and an application and additional premium be submitted within a specified period.

If the insurance on a covered individual is terminated because he no longer fits the policy definition of a family member, that person has a right to take out a conversion policy without evidence of insurability.

EXAMPLE      Faye divorces Stanley and thus no longer can be covered under his family policy. She has a right to obtain a conversion policy. When their children reach the limiting age for children's coverage, they also will be eligible for a conversion policy.

**TAKE NOTE**

Any preexisting condition that the insured has disclosed clearly in the application usually is not excluded or, if it is, the condition is named specifically in an excluding waiver or rider.

**Free-Look Provision** Most states mandate that their health insurance policies contain a free-look provision permitting policyowners either 10 or 20 days in which to examine their new policies at no obligation. If they decide not to keep their policies, they may return them within the prescribed time limit and receive full refunds of premiums paid.

# COMMON EXCLUSIONS OR RESTRICTIONS

Health insurance policies frequently cite a number of exclusions or conditions that are not covered. The common ones are injuries due to war or an act of war, self-inflicted injuries, and those incurred while the insured is serving as a pilot or crew member of an aircraft.

Other exclusions are losses resulting from suicide, riots, or the use of drugs or narcotics. Losses due to injuries sustained while committing a felony, or attempting to do so, also may be excluded.

## PREEXISTING CONDITIONS

As we have learned, medical expense and disability income policies usually exclude paying benefits for losses due to preexisting conditions pertaining to illness, disease, or other physical impairments. For purposes of issuing individual health policies, insurers consider a preexisting condition to be one that the insured contracted (or one that was manifested) before the policy's effective date. Consequently, in the event the insured did not cite the condition on the application specifically and the insurer did not exclude the condition from coverage expressly, the preexisting condition provision would serve to exclude the condition nonetheless. However, such exclusions are subject to the "time limit on certain defenses" provision.

## WAIVERS FOR IMPAIRMENTS

The majority of health policies are standard and are issued as applied for. However, a few people have an existing impairment that increases the risk and so are required to pay an extra premium. A few people are uninsurable and must be declined. Others, however, fall in between and would not be able to obtain health insurance if waivers were not in use. Waivers usually are stated in simple language. For example: "This policy does not cover or extend to any disability resulting directly or indirectly from..." A waiver is dated and bears the signature of an officer of the company and, in many cases, the applicant. This usually is called an impairment rider.

If the insured's condition improves, the company may be willing to remove the waiver. Meanwhile, the person at least has health protection from other hazards that he otherwise could not obtain.

> **TAKE NOTE**
>
> The impairment rider allows for coverage despite a preexisting condition, when such coverage might not otherwise be available to the insured, or only at prohibitive cost.

# RENEWABILITY PROVISIONS

One of the distinguishing features of health insurance policies is the provisions they contain that allow the insurer to continue or discontinue coverage. Known as renewability provisions, they vary from policy to policy. Generally, the more favorable the renewability provision is to the insured policyholder, the higher the premium.

## NONCANCELABLE POLICIES

A noncancelable, or noncan policy, cannot be canceled, nor can its premium rates be increased under any circumstances; these rates are specified in the policy. The term of most noncancelable policies is to the insured's age 65. Noncan provisions most commonly are found in disability income policies; they rarely are used in medical expense policies.

## GUARANTEED RENEWABLE POLICIES

The renewal provision in a guaranteed renewable policy specifies that the policy must be renewed, as long as premiums are paid, until the insured reaches a specified age, such as 60 or 65. Premium increases may be applied, but only for the entire class of insureds; they cannot be assessed to individual insureds.

## CONDITIONALLY RENEWABLE POLICIES

A conditionally renewable policy allows an insurer to terminate the coverage, but only in the event of one or more conditions stated in the contract. Usually, the premium for conditionally renewable policies may be increased, if such an increase applies to an entire class of policies.

## OPTIONALLY RENEWABLE POLICIES

The renewability provision in an optionally renewable policy gives the insurer the option to terminate the policy on a date specified in the contract. Furthermore, this provision allows the insurer to increase the premium for any class of optionally renewable insureds. Usually termination or premium increases take place on policy anniversary dates or premium due dates.

## CANCELABLE POLICIES

The renewability provision in a cancelable policy allows the insurer to cancel or terminate the policy at any time, simply by providing written notification to the insured and refunding any advance premium that has been paid. Cancelable policies also allow the insurer to increase premiums.

## SUMMARY

To protect the rights of individual health insurance policyholders, the NAIC developed a set of 12 mandatory and 11 optional policy provisions. These provisions help assure consumers that the health policies they buy will meet at least a minimum level of standards. Other provisions, though not categorized as required or optional, are equally important. Of special note are the renewability provisions—absent from life insurance policies, but an essential feature of health policies.

# UNIT QUIZ

1. Which of the following is the usual grace period for a semi-annual premium policy?

   A. 7 days
   B. 20 days
   C. 31 days
   D. 60 days

2. All of the following are required uniform provisions in individual health insurance policies EXCEPT

   A. change of occupation
   B. grace period
   C. entire contract changes
   D. reinstatement

3. Under the misstatement of age provision in a health insurance policy, what can a company do if it discovers that an insured gave a wrong age at the time of application?

   A. Cancel the policy
   B. Increase the premium
   C. Adjust the benefits
   D. Assess a penalty

4. The conformity with state statutes provision in a health insurance policy stipulates that any policy provision that conflicts with the statutes of the state where the insured resides is

   A. to be submitted to the insurance commissioner for approval
   B. cause for the insured's policy to be voided
   C. automatically amended to conform to the minimum requirements of the state's statutes
   D. to be rewritten if the policy is returned to the company

5. Which section of a health insurance policy specifies the conditions, times, and circumstances under which the insured is NOT covered by the policy?

   A. Coinsurance provision
   B. Coverages
   C. Insuring clause
   D. Exclusions

6. Which kind of health insurance policy assures renewability up to a specific age of the insured, although the company reserves the right to change the premium rate on a class basis?

   A. Noncancelable
   B. Guaranteed renewable
   C. Optionally renewable
   D. Cancelable

7. According to the notice of claims provision in a health insurance policy, a claimant normally must notify the insurance company of loss within how many days after the loss occurs?

   A. 10
   B. 20
   C. 40
   D. 60

8. Which of the following types of health insurance policies prevents the company from changing the premium rate or modifying the coverage in any way?

   A. Optionally renewable
   B. Noncancelable
   C. Guaranteed renewable
   D. Cancelable

9. After an insurer receives a notice of claim, it must supply a claim form to the insured within how many days?

   A. 10
   B. 15
   C. 20
   D. 30

10. Which of the following is a standard optional provision for health policies?

   A. Grace period
   B. Physical exam and autopsy
   C. Change of beneficiary
   D. Misstatement of age

# ANSWERS AND RATIONALES TO UNIT QUIZ

1. **C.** A semi-annual premium policy usually has a 31-day grace period in which the policyowner can pay the premium due. For policies with weekly premium payments, the grace period is seven days, and policies with monthly premiums have 10-day grace periods.

2. **A.** The grace period, entire contract changes, and reinstatement provisions are mandatory uniform provisions. The change of occupation provision sets forth the changes that may be made to premium rates or benefits payable if the insured changes occupations. This provision is optional.

3. **C.** The misstatement of age provision allows the insurer to adjust the benefit payable if the insured's age was misstated when the policy application was made. The benefit amounts payable in such cases will be what the premiums paid would have purchased at the correct age.

4. **C.** Any policy provision that conflicts with the statutes of the state where the insured resides will be amended automatically to conform with the minimum statutory requirements.

5. **D.** The exclusions section of a health insurance policy specifies the conditions, times, and circumstances under which the insured is not covered by the policy. Common exclusions include injuries due to war and self-inflicted injuries.

6. **B.** In a guaranteed renewable policy, the renewal provision states that the policy must be renewed, as long as premiums are paid, until the insured reaches a specified age, such as 60 or 65. Premiums may be increased, but only for the entire class of insureds.

7. **B.** A policyowner typically must notify the insurer within 20 days after a loss has occurred.

8. **B.** A noncancelable policy prevents the insurance company from canceling or modifying the coverage or changing the premium rate.

9. **B.** After an insurer receives a notice of claim, it must supply a claim form to the insured within 15 days. If it fails to do so, the claimant may submit proof of loss in any form, explaining the occurrence, character, and extent of the loss for which the claim is submitted.

10. **D.** Misstatement of age is one of 11 optional policy provisions. Companies may ignore them or use them in their policy forms.

12

# Group Life and Health Insurance

## KEY CONCEPTS

- Group insurance compared to individual policies
- Eligible groups and individual participation
- Continuation of coverage and conversion privileges
- Coordination of group insurance benefits
- Types of group insurance
- The difference between MSAs and HSAs
- Taxation of group insurance

Up to this point, we have focused our discussion on individual insurance plans, policies, and underwriting. However, there is another important category of insurance: group insurance. Group insurance provides life and health insurance coverage for a number of people under one contract. Because business owners generally recognize that employee benefits—or the lack of them—vitally affect their businesses in numerous ways, they usually are quick to realize the importance of group insurance. Like individual insurance coverage, a group plan can be tailored to meet the employer's needs.

By its very nature, group insurance has several features that set it apart from individual plans, including the nature of the contract, the cost of the plan, the form of premium payments, and eligibility requirements. In this unit, we will look at the principles of group life and health insurance.

## OBJECTIVE

When you complete this unit you should be able to:

- list and describe the principal characteristics of group health insurance;

- explain how group insurance differs from individual insurance plans;

- describe the types of groups eligible for group insurance coverage and the various plans insurers may offer them;

- explain the general underwriting factors that are considered when issuing a group health insurance policy;

- compare and contrast group and individual medical expense, disability income, and AD&D insurance;

- explain the rights given to terminated employees under COBRA;

- explain the tax treatment of group health premiums and benefits;

- explain how group life insurance benefits are determined under the earnings, employment position, and flat benefit schedules;

- explain how group life insurance premiums and proceeds are taxed; and

- identify and describe the main characteristics of credit life insurance, multiple employer trusts, and multiple employer welfare arrangements.

# PRINCIPLES OF GROUP INSURANCE

The basic principle of group insurance is that it provides insurance coverage for a number of people under a single master contract or master policy. Because a group policy insures a group of people, it is the group—not each individual—that must meet the underwriting requirements of the insuring company.

---

**TAKE NOTE**

When an employer pays all of the premium, the plan is a noncontributory plan because the employees are not required to contribute to premium payments. If a group plan requires its members to pay a portion of the premium, it is a contributory plan.

---

**TAKE NOTE**

Group insurance involves experience rating, which is a method of establishing a premium for the group based on the group's previous claims experience. The larger and more homogeneous the group, the closer it comes to reflecting standard mortality and morbidity rates.

---

Group insurance most typically is provided by an employer for its employees as a benefit. In these cases, the employer is the applicant and contract policyholder. The employees, as group members, are not parties to the contract—in fact, they are not even named in the contract. Instead, each employee who is eligible to participate in the plan fills out an enrollment card and is given a certificate of insurance, which summarizes the coverage terms and explains the employee's rights under the group contract. A list of individual employees covered under the contract is maintained by the insurer.

In most cases, it is the policyholder—the employer—that selects the type of insurance coverage the group will have and determines the amount of coverage the contract will provide for covered group members. In addition, the employer typically pays all or a portion of the premium.

To individual members covered by a group life or health insurance plan, the function the insurance serves is identical to an individual plan. In the case of group life, should the covered member die, his beneficiary will receive a stated amount in death proceeds. In the case of group health, should the covered member become ill or disabled, the plan will provide a stated benefit amount to help cover the corresponding medical costs or replace income lost due to the disability. Thus, the purpose of group life and health plans is the same as individual life and health plans. However, group plans have a number of features that set them apart from individual plans.

## MASTER POLICY

As noted, the foremost distinction of a group plan is that it insures a number of people under one contract. Because of this, individual underwriting and individual evidence of insurability are generally not required. When it comes to underwriting, the insurer looks at the group as a whole, not at the health, habits, or characteristics of individual members.

## LOW COST

Another characteristic of group insurance is that, per unit of benefits, it is available at lower rates than individual insurance, due primarily to the lower administrative, operational, and selling expenses associated with group contracts. And because most employers pay all or part of the group premium, individual insureds are able to have insurance coverage for far less than what they normally would pay for an individual or personal plan.

### FLOW OF INSUREDS

Group insurance is distinguished by a flow of insureds, entering and exiting under the policy as they join and leave the group. In fact, for it to operate effectively, group insurance requires a constant influx of new members into the group to replace those who leave, and to keep the age and health of the group stable.

# ELIGIBLE GROUPS

What kinds of groups are eligible for group insurance coverage? Generally, almost any kind of natural group—those formed for a purpose other than to obtain insurance—will be considered by an insurer.

Insurable groups most typically fall into one of the following categories:

- single-employer groups;
- labor unions;
- trade associations;
- creditor and debtor groups; and
- fraternal organizations.

In years past, only groups of a certain size, such as 50 or more, were eligible for group insurance. Today, in accordance with NAIC guidelines that do not set a minimum size limit, insurers often issue coverage to groups with as few as 10 (or even fewer) members.

It is important to note, however, that once a group policy is issued, insurers usually require that a certain number or percentage of eligible members must participate to keep the coverage in force.

### ELIGIBILITY OF GROUP MEMBERS

By its very nature, group insurance provides for participation by virtually all members of a given insured group. Whether or not an individual member chooses to participate usually depends on the amount of premium he must pay, if the plan is contributory. If the plan is noncontributory and the employer pays the entire premium, full participation is the general rule.

On the other hand, employers and insurers are allowed some latitude in setting minimum eligibility requirements for employee participants. For instance, employees must be full-time workers and actively at work to be eligible to participate in a group plan. If the plan is contributory, the employee must authorize payroll deductions for his share of premium payments. In addition, a probationary period may be required for new employees, which means they must wait a certain period of time (usually from one to six months) before they can enroll in the plan.

The probationary period is designed to minimize the administrative expense involved with those who remain with the employer only a short time. The probationary period is followed by the enrollment period, the time during which new employees can sign up for the group coverage. If an employee does not enroll in the plan during the enrollment period (typically 31 days), he may be required to provide evidence of insurability if he wants to enroll later. This is to protect the insurer against adverse selection.

**Underwriting Practices**   Generally, the approach in underwriting group health plans is the same as underwriting group life plans: the insurer evaluates the group as a whole, rather than individuals within the group. Based on the group's risk profile, which is measured against the insurer's selection standards, the group is either accepted or rejected.

However, there are some changes taking place with regard to underwriting group medical expenses plans, especially for small groups. Whereas for large group medical plans it is common to accept all currently eligible members and new members coming into the group, this is not necessarily true for smaller groups. In smaller groups, the presence of even one bad risk can have a significant impact on the claims experience of the group. Consequently, most insurers today reserve the right to engage in individual underwriting to some degree with groups they insure.

# GROUP HEALTH INSURANCE

## CONVERSION PRIVILEGES

Group health plans that provide medical expense coverage universally contain a conversion privilege for individual insureds, which allows them to convert their group certificate to an individual medical expense policy with the same insurer, if and when they leave their employment. Insurers are permitted to evaluate the individual and charge the appropriate premium, be it a standard rate or substandard rate; however, an individual cannot be denied coverage, even if he has become uninsurable.

The conversion must be exercised within a given period of time, usually 30 or 31 days, depending on the state (31 days in Minnesota). During this time, the individual remains insured under the group plan, whether or not a conversion ultimately takes place. Conversion privileges generally are reserved for those who were active in the group plan during the preceding three months.

## PREEXISTING CONDITIONS

In the past, group health insurance plans typically excluded a person from coverage because of preexisting conditions. A preexisting condition generally was defined as any condition for which a participant received treatment at any time during the three months before the effective date of the group coverage. Group plans also specified when a condition would stop being considered preexisting.

However, the Health Insurance Portability and Accountability Act (HIPAA) has changed the rules governing preexisting conditions for group health plans. On July 1, 1997, HIPAA limited the ability of employer-sponsored groups and insurers to exclude individuals on the basis of preexisting medical conditions. The exclusion for preexisting conditions now is limited to conditions for which medical advice or treatment was recommended or received within the six-month period ending on the enrollment date. However, the exclusion can extend for no more than 12 months (18 months for late enrollees).

**TAKE NOTE**

This exclusion period must be reduced by one month for each that the employee was covered at a previous job. For example, if an employee had prior group health coverage for eight months, he would be subject to only a four-month exclusion period when he changes jobs. Thereafter, the employee's new plan must cover all of his medical problems. In contrast, if the employee was covered by a group health plan for 12 straight months, the new plan could not invoke the preexisting condition exclusion at all. It must cover the new employee's medical problems as soon as he enrolls in the plan.

## COORDINATION OF BENEFITS

The purpose of the coordination of benefits (COB) provision, found only in group health plans, is to avoid duplication of benefit payments and overinsurance when an individual is covered under more than one group health plan. The provision limits the total amount of claims paid from all insurers covering the patient to no more than the total allowable medical expenses.

**EXAMPLE**

An individual who incurs $700 in allowable medical expenses would not be able to collect any more than $700, no matter how many group plans he is covered by.

The COB provision establishes the primary plan, that is, the plan that is responsible for providing the full benefit amounts as it specifies. Once the primary plan has paid its full promised benefit, the insured may submit the claim to the secondary provider for any additional benefits payable. In no case, however, will the total amount the insured receives exceed the costs incurred, or the total maximum benefits available under all plans. Coordinating benefits is appropriate for married couples, when each is covered by an employer group plan.

**EXAMPLE**

John and Cindy, a married couple, each are participants in their own company's health plan and also are covered as dependents under their spouse's plan. John's plan would specify that it is the primary plan for John; Cindy's plan would be his secondary plan. Likewise, Cindy's plan would specify that it is the primary plan for Cindy; John's plan would be her secondary plan.

## COBRA CONTINUATION OF BENEFITS

Participants in group medical expense plans are protected by a federal law that guarantees a continuation of their group coverage if their employment is terminated for reasons other than gross misconduct. Practically, the law protects employees who are laid-off but not those who are fired for cause.

This law, known as the Consolidated Omnibus Budget Reconciliation Act of 1985 (or COBRA), requires employers with 20 or more employees to continue group medical expense coverage for terminated workers (as well as their spouses, divorced spouses, and dependent children) for up to 18 months (or 36 months, in some situations) following termination.

**COBRA Continued Coverage for Former Employees** The following events would qualify for extended medical expense coverage under COBRA for a terminated employee:

- Employment is terminated (for other than gross misconduct): 18 months of continued coverage (or up to 29 months if disabled)

- Employee's hours are reduced (resulting in termination from the plan): 18 months of continued coverage (or up to 29 months if disabled)

- Employee dies: 36 months of continued coverage for dependents

- Dependent child no longer qualifies as dependent child under the plan: 36 months of continued coverage

- Employee becomes eligible for Medicare: 36 months of continued coverage

- Employee divorces or legally separates: 36 months of continued coverage for former spouse

The law does not require the employer to pay the cost of the continued group coverage; the terminated employee can be required to pay the premium, which may be up to 102% of the premium that otherwise would be charged. (The additional two percent is allowed to cover the insurer's administrative expenses.) The schedule of benefits will be the same during the continuation period as under the group plan.

## GROUP DISABILITY INCOME PLANS

Group disability income plans differ from individual plans in a number of ways. Individual plans usually specify a flat income amount, based on the person's earnings, determined at the time the policy is purchased. In contrast, group plans usually specify benefits in terms of a percentage of the individual's earnings.

Like individual plans, group disability can include short-term plans or long-term plans. The definitions of short term and long term, however, are different for group and individual.

Group short-term disability plans are characterized by maximum benefit periods of rather short duration, such as 13 or 26 weeks. Benefits typically are paid weekly and range from 50 to 100% of the individual's income.

Group long-term disability plans provide for maximum benefit periods of more than two years, occasionally extending to the insured's retirement age. Benefit amounts usually are limited to about 60% of the participant's income.

If an employer provides both a short-term plan and a long-term plan, the long-term plan typically begins paying benefits only after the short-term benefits cease. Often, long-term plans use an *own occupation* definition of total disability for the first year or two of disability and then switch to an *any occupation* definition.

Most group disability plans require the employee to have a minimum period of service, such as 30 to 90 days, before he is eligible for coverage. In addition, most group plans include provisions making their benefits supplemental to workers' compensation benefits, so that total benefits received do not exceed a specified percentage of regular earnings. In some cases, group disability plans actually limit coverage to nonoccupational disabilities, because occupational disabilities normally qualify for workers' compensation benefits.

## GROUP AD&D

Accidental death and dismemberment insurance is a very popular type of group coverage, frequently offered in conjunction with group life insurance plans. It also may be provided as a separate policy, in which case it normally is paid for entirely by the employee.

## MEDICAL SAVINGS ACCOUNTS/HEALTH SAVINGS ACCOUNTS

Medical Savings Accounts (MSAs) and Health Savings Accounts (HSAs) were designed to provide a tax break to health care consumers covered under a high-deductible medical plan. These accounts enable individuals to set aside funds on a tax-advantaged basis to help defray health care costs. As the accounts have much in common, we will compare and contrast the features of each.

Available from January 1, 1997 through 2003, MSAs were primarily designed for self-employed individuals and small employers. MSAs were discontinued in 2004; while existing accounts could be maintained, no new accounts could be established. They have been replaced by the HSA.

|  | Medical Savings Account | Health Savings Account |
|---|---|---|
| Available to any size employer? | No—50 or fewer | Yes |
| Funding? | Either employer or employee, but not both. Unused balance carries forward. Funds are portable after termination of employment. Contributions are generally tax deductible. | Employer, employee, or both. Unused balance carries forward. Funds are portable after termination of employment. Contributions are generally pretax or tax deductible. |
| Tax treatment of withdrawals? | Money withdrawn for medical expenses is tax free. Nonmedical withdrawals are taxed (plus a 15% penalty, if taken before age 65). | Money withdrawn for medical expenses is tax free. Nonmedical withdrawals are taxed (plus a 10% penalty if taken before age 65). |

# TAX TREATMENT OF GROUP HEALTH PLANS

As an incentive for employers to provide health insurance benefits to their employees, the federal government grants favorable tax treatment to group plans. Let's briefly review this treatment.

## TAXATION OF GROUP HEALTH PREMIUMS

Employers are entitled to take a tax deduction for premium contributions they make to a group health plan, as long as the contributions represent an ordinary and necessary business expense. By the same token, individual participants do not include employer contributions made on their behalf as part of their taxable income.

As a general rule, individual premium contributions to a group health plan are not tax deductible. Only when unreimbursed medical expenses—expenses that can include any individual contributions to a group medical plan—exceed 7.5% of an individual's adjusted gross income can a tax deduction be taken. The deduction is limited to the amount exceeding 7.5% of adjusted gross income.

## TAXATION OF GROUP HEALTH BENEFITS

Any benefits an individual receives under a medical expense plan are not considered taxable income, because they are provided to cover losses the individual incurred. It is a somewhat different story with disability income plans, however. Disability benefit payments that are attributed to employee contributions are not taxable, but benefit payments that are attributed to employer contributions are taxable.

 **EXAMPLE**   Anne is a participant in a contributory group disability income plan in which her employer pays two-thirds of the premium and Anne pays one-third. Her employer qualifies for a tax deduction for its share of the premium and, as is true with employer contributions to all group health plans, Anne is not taxed on those contributions. The premium portion that Anne pays does not qualify for a tax deduction for her.

Now assume Anne becomes disabled and receives disability income benefits of $900 a month. One-third of the monthly benefit—$300—would be tax free, because it is attributed to the premium she paid; the remaining two-thirds of the payment—$600—would be taxable income, because it is attributed to the premium her employer paid.

# GROUP LIFE INSURANCE

Today, approximately 40% of life insurance in force in the United States is group life insurance, and billions of dollars more are purchased every year. In fact, as far as coverage amounts go, group life insurance is the fastest growing life insurance line. According to the American Council of Life Insurance *1999 Life Insurance Fact Book*, at the end of 1998, group life insurance in force in the United States totaled more than $5.73 trillion. This represents an 8.6% increase in one year and is nearly twice the amount in force at the end of 1988. More and more, employees look to their group coverage to provide the foundation for their life insurance programs.

## TYPES OF GROUP LIFE PLANS

There are many types of group life plans that insurers offer employers. The appropriate choice depends on the employer's objectives, needs, and resources. Group life can be either term or permanent.

**Group Term Life**  Most group life plans are term plans, which use annual renewable term (ART) insurance as the underlying policy. This gives the insurer the right to increase the premium each year (based on the group's experience rating), and it gives the policyholder the right to renew coverage each year. As is characteristic of ART policies, coverage can be renewed without evidence of insurability. The prevalent use of ART insurance is another reason for the low cost of group insurance.

**Group Permanent Life**  Some group life plans are permanent plans, using some form of permanent or whole life insurance as the underlying policy. The most common types of permanent group plans are *group ordinary, group paid-up,* and *group universal life*.

Group ordinary insurance is any type of group life plan—and there are many variations—that uses cash value life insurance. In some cases, the employees are allowed to own the cash value portion of the policy if they contribute to the plan. In other instances, an employee's termination results in the forfeiture of the cash value, which then is used to help fund the plan for the remaining employees.

With group paid-up plans, a combination of term and whole life insurance is used. Usually the employer pays for the term portion of the plan, and employee contributions are used to purchase units of single-premium whole life. The sum of the employees' paid-up insurance and the employer-paid term insurance (usually decreasing term, to offset the annually increasing amount of paid-up insurance) equals the amount of life insurance the employees are entitled to under the plan. At retirement or termination, employees possess their paid-up policies.

A growing number of group life plans use universal life insurance policies, due to the flexibility these policies provide. The underlying policy contains the same features as individual universal life, but the policy is administered in much the same way as any group ordinary policy.

**Taxation of Group Life Premiums and Proceeds**  To encourage employers to provide employee benefits—such as a group life insurance plan—the federal government has granted these plans favorable tax treatment. First, an employer may deduct the group plan premiums as a business expense. Second, the employee does not have to report the employer paid premiums as income as long as the insurance coverage is $50,000 or less. (Employees who are provided with more than $50,000 of coverage must declare the premiums paid by the employer for the excess coverage as taxable income.)

Proceeds paid under a group life plan to a deceased employee's beneficiary are exempt from income taxation if they are paid in a lump sum. If the proceeds are paid in installments consisting of principal and interest, the interest portion is taxed.

For a group life insurance plan to receive favorable tax treatment, the government imposes some requirements to ensure that rank-and-file employees are not discriminated against in favor of select key employees. Basically, these requirements apply to eligibility and the type and amount of benefits provided.

Regarding eligibility, the requirements are that:

■ the plan must benefit at least 70% of all employees; or

■ at least 85% of all participating employees must not be key employees.

Regarding benefits, the requirements state that, again, the plan cannot discriminate in favor of key employees. For example, the amount of life insurance provided to all employees must bear a uniform relationship to their level of compensation or position.

If a group life insurance plan fails to meet these nondiscrimination requirements, the cost of the first $50,000 of coverage—normally excluded from gross income—will be included in a key employee's gross income for tax purposes. Rank-and-file employees are not so penalized.

## CONVERSION TO INDIVIDUAL PLAN

Once coverage becomes effective for an individual under a group life plan, it remains effective until he leaves the employer group or the plan is terminated. Most group life policies contain a conversion provision that allows individual insured members to convert to an individual plan without evidence of insurability if their employment is terminated. Usually, the employee has a limited period of time following termination (typically 31 days) in which to exercise the conversion privilege. This means that the group coverage will continue in force for the terminated employee for the duration of the conversion period, even if no conversion takes place.

EXAMPLE            If a group-insured ex-employee were to die within 31 days after termination of employ-
                   ment, the group insurance death benefit would be payable to his beneficiary.

Most group conversion provisions require the individual to convert to a permanent policy, as opposed to term. The premium for the new policy is based on the individual's attained age at the time of conversion.

With portable group term life insurance, all of the ported policies are pooled together rather than remaining in the employer's plan. The rates, therefore, are more like group rates and are much lower than individually sold coverage. In contrast, most group conversion provisions require the individual to convert to a whole life policy, as opposed to term. As a result, the policy's rates will mirror individual rates and generally will be much higher.

## GROUP CREDIT LIFE INSURANCE

Group credit life insurance is another form of group insurance. A type of decreasing term insurance, it is issued by insurance companies to creditors to cover the lives of debtors in the amounts of their respective loans. Typically, it is provided through commercial banks, savings and loan associations, finance companies, credit unions, and retailers.

If an insured dies before his loan is repaid, the policy proceeds are paid to the creditor to settle the remaining loan balance. Unlike regular group life insurance, premiums for group credit life may be paid wholly by the individual insureds. State laws, which vary, generally set a maximum amount of group credit life insurance per individual creditor (generally the creditor must have a minimum of 100 debtors per year) and limit the amount of insurance per borrower, which may not exceed the amount of indebtedness. Debtors cannot be forced to take the coverage from any particular insurance company but have the right to choose their insurers.

## MULTIPLE EMPLOYER TRUSTS AND MULTIPLE EMPLOYER WELFARE ARRANGEMENTS

A method of marketing group benefits to employers who have a small number of employees is the multiple employer trust (MET). METs may provide either a single type of insurance (such as health insurance) or a wide range of coverages (such as, life, medical expense, and disability income insurance). In some cases, alternative forms of the same coverage are available (such as comprehensive health insurance or basic health insurance).

An employer who wants to get coverage for employees from a MET first must become a member of the trust by subscribing to it. The employer is issued a joinder agreement, which spells out the relationship between the trust and the employer and specifies the coverages to which the employer has subscribed. An employer need not subscribe to all the coverages offered by a MET.

A MET may either provide benefits on a self-funded basis or fund benefits with a contract purchased from an insurance company. In the latter case, the trust, rather than the subscribing employers, is the master insurance contract holder. In either case, the employees of subscribing employers are provided with benefit description (certificates of insurance) in a manner similar to the usual group insurance agreement.

In addition to alternative methods of funding benefits, METs can be categorized according to how they are administered, that is, whether by an insurance company or a third-party administrator.

**TAKE NOTE**

There also is another type of MET called a multiple employer welfare arrangement (MEWA). It covers union employees, is self-funded, and has tax-exempt status. Employees covered under an MEWA are required by law to have an "employment related common bond."

# SUMMARY

Group health insurance—like group life insurance—is evidenced by one master contract that covers multiple lives. Virtually any health insurance product available as an individual contract also is available under the group umbrella. Thus, medical expense insurance, disability income insurance, and accidental death and dismemberment insurance all are common group plans.

Of utmost concern to insurance regulators is that employees be protected from loss of their insurance coverage if their job is terminated. Accordingly, nearly all states have provisions in their insurance laws that require group life and medical expense policies to provide a conversion option to terminating participants. The federal government also has exercised its regulatory prerogative by passing laws, like COBRA, that protect terminated employees.

Group insurance is a way to provide insurance coverage for a number of individuals under one master policy. It generally is purchased by an employer as a benefit for employees. Usually the employer pays all or a portion of the premium on behalf of its employees. Employer-pay-all plans are known as noncontributory plans; plans that require partial premium contributions from employees are contributory plans.

When a group plan initially is installed, all employees who meet the eligibility requirements are eligible for coverage. Individual underwriting usually is not done; instead, the insurer looks at the characteristics of the group as a whole. New employees who are hired after the plan is in effect usually are subject to a probationary period before they are allowed to enroll.

Most group life insurance plans are term plans that use annually renewable term insurance as the underlying policy. Permanent group life plans include group ordinary, group paid-up, and group universal life. The amount of life insurance coverage individual employees receive is determined by the employer based on earnings, employment position, or flat benefit schedule.

Other types of group plans are group credit life, multiple employer trusts, and multiple employer welfare arrangements.

# UNIT QUIZ

1. Dan is a participant in his company's group health plan. One of the plan's provisions specifies that, in the event he is eligible for benefits under another policy, his group plan will serve as the primary plan. What is this provision called?

   A. Excess coverage
   B. Coordination of benefits
   C. Other insurance with this insurer
   D. Double indemnity

2. The purpose of COBRA requirements concerns

   A. coordination of health benefits
   B. continuation of health insurance
   C. Medicare supplement coverage
   D. nondiscrimination in group health plans

3. Sally is covered by her employer's non-contributory group disability income plan, the premium for which is $50 a month. If she were to become disabled and receive $1,000 a month, how much of each benefit payment would be taxable income to her?

   A. $0
   B. $50
   C. $950
   D. $1,000

4. The minimum number of persons to be insured under a group health insurance plan is established by

   A. the NAIC
   B. state law
   C. federal law
   D. the employer

5. As it pertains to group health insurance, COBRA stipulates that

   A. retiring employees must be allowed to convert their group coverage to individual policies
   B. terminated employees must be allowed to convert their group coverage to individual policies
   C. group coverage must be extended for terminated employees up to a certain period of time at the employee's expense
   D. group coverage must be extended for terminated employees up to a certain period of time at the employer's expense

6. When a group disability insurance plan is paid entirely by the employer, benefits paid to disabled employees are

   A. taxable income to the employee
   B. deductible income to the employee
   C. deductible business expenses to the employer
   D. taxable income to the employer

7. All of the following are characteristics of group health insurance plans EXCEPT

   A. their benefits are more extensive than those under individual plans
   B. the parties to a group health contract are the employer and the employees
   C. employers may require employees to contribute to the premium payments
   D. the cost of insuring an individual is less than what would be charged for comparable benefits under an individual plan

8. All of the following statements regarding Medical Savings Accounts are true EXCEPT

   A. contributions may be made by employer or employee, but not both
   B. money withdrawn from an MSA for non-medical purposes before 59½ is subject to a 10% penalty
   C. unused contributions to an MSA remain in the account and grow tax-deferred
   D. MSAs are not available to large employers

9. What type of term contract is typically used in group life insurance?

   A. Annually Renewable Term
   B. Optionally Renewable Term
   C. Decreasing Term
   D. 10-Pay Term

# ANSWERS AND RATIONALES TO UNIT QUIZ

1. **B.** A coordination of benefits provision establishes which plan is the primary plan when an insured is covered by another health plan.

2. **B.** COBRA requires employers to continue group medical expense coverage for terminated workers (and their families) for up to 36 months after termination.

3. **D.** Because Sally does not contribute toward the cost of the premium for the group disability income plan, all of the benefits she receives will be attributed to the premium her employer paid. As a result, she will have to report all of her monthly benefits ($1,000) as taxable income.

4. **B.** State laws specify the minimum number of persons to be covered under a group policy. One state may stipulate 15 persons as a minimum number, while another state may require a minimum of 10. (Ten is the most typical minimum requirement.)

5. **C.** COBRA requires employers with 20 or more employees to continue group medical expense coverage for terminated workers (as well as their spouses, divorced spouses, and dependent children) for up to 18 months (or 36 months, in some situations) following termination. However, the terminated employee can be required to pay the premium, which may be up to 102% of the premium that would otherwise be charged.

6. **A.** Disability benefit payments that are attributed to employee contributions are not taxable, but benefit payments that are attributed to employer contributions are taxable.

7. **B.** The contract for coverage is between the insurance company and the employer, and a master policy is issued to the employer.

8. **B.** Nonmedical withdrawals from an MSA before age 65 are subject to a 15% penalty. MSAs are available to small employers and self-employed persons; contributions can be made by an employer (or employee), and unused money remains in the account growing taxdeferred.

9. **A.** Most group life contracts are established as an Annually Renewable Term policy.

# 13

# Government and Senior Insurance Plans

## KEY CONCEPTS

- Insurance needs among seniors
- The role of government insurance
- Medicare, Medicare supplement policies, and Medicaid
- The purpose and characteristics of Long-Term Care insurance

This unit addresses the insurance needs of seniors. Some of these needs are met by government-sponsored plans such as Medicare and Medicaid. Medicare covers medical expenses of people who are age 65 or older or who are on Social Security because of disability. Medicaid reimburses hospitals and other healthcare providers for providing care to needy and low-income people who cannot pay their own medical expenses.

Medicare coverage is by no means comprehensive, however, and many Medicare recipients supplement their health coverage with Medicare supplement policies that pick up coverage where Medicare leaves off. In addition, neither Medicare nor Medicare supplements covers chronic conditions requiring long-term custodial care. As a result, many people purchase long-term care insurance to finance this level of care.

## OBJECTIVE

When you complete this unit you should be able to:

- explain the types of coverage available under Medicare Part A and Part B;

- identify the different health plan options available under the Medicare+Choice Program;

- explain the purpose of Medicaid and how it differs from Medicare;

- explain the purpose of Medicare supplement policies and describe the types of coverage they provide;

- list and describe the different types of coverage provided under long-term care policies;

- identify the basic provisions and typical limits and exclusions found in most long-term care policies; and

- explain the tax treatment of long-term care benefits.

# ORIGINAL MEDICARE PLAN

The Original Medicare Plan consists of two parts: Medicare Part A and Medicare Part B. Medicare Part A is compulsory hospitalization insurance (HI) that provides specified in-hospital and related benefits. It is compulsory in that all workers covered by Social Security finance its operation through a portion of their FICA taxes and automatically are provided with benefits once they qualify for Social Security benefits.

Medicare Part B is a voluntary program designed to provide supplementary medical insurance (SMI) to cover physician services, medical services, and supplies not covered under Part A. Those who desire the coverage must enroll and pay a monthly premium. Medicare Part B is financed by monthly premiums from those who participate and by tax revenues.

## MEDICARE PART A COVERAGES

Medicare Part A provides coverage for inpatient hospitalization and post-hospital skilled facility care and home care. For the first 60 days of hospitalization during any one benefit period, Medicare pays for all covered services, except for an initial deductible. Covered services include semiprivate room, nursing services, and other inpatient hospital services.

For the 61st through the 90th day of hospitalization, Medicare pays a reduced amount of the covered services. The patient is responsible for a daily copayment.

This 90-day hospitalization coverage is renewed with each benefit period. A benefit period starts when a patient enters the hospital and ends when the patient has been out of the hospital for 60 days. If a patient reenters a hospital before the end of a benefit period, the deductible is not reapplied, but the 90-day hospital coverage period is not renewed. However, if the patient reenters a hospital after a benefit period ends, a new deductible is required and the 90-day hospital coverage period is renewed.

Medicare patients also have a lifetime reserve of 60 days of hospital coverage. If a patient is hospitalized longer than 90 days in a benefit period, he can tap into the 60-day reserve. The lifetime reserve is a one-time benefit; it does not renew with a new benefit period. If a patient is hospitalized and taps into the reserve days, he is required to pay a higher copayment. If a patient is hospitalized beyond the 60th lifetime reserve day, thereby exhausting the reserve, he is responsible for all hospital charges.

FIGURE 13.1   What Medicare Covers

| *Part A* | *Part B* |
|---|---|
| • Inpatient hospital services, including semiprivate room and board and nursing services | • Physicians' and surgeons' services, whether in a hospital, clinic or elsewhere |
| • Posthospital skilled nursing care, in an accredited care facility | • Medical and health services, such as X-rays, diagnostic lab tests, ambulance services, medical supplies, medical equipment rental and physical and occupational therapy |
| • Posthospital home health services, including nursing care, therapy and part-time home health aides | |
| • Hospice benefits for the care of terminally ill patients (to the exclusion of all other Medicare benefits, except for physician services) | |
| • Inpatient psychiatric care, on a limited basis | |

In addition, Part A provides benefits for skilled nursing facility care, hospice care, home health services, and, to a limited degree, inpatient psychiatric care. In all cases, Part A covers only those services that are medically necessary and only up to amounts deemed reasonable by Medicare.

Part A covers the costs of care in a skilled nursing facility as long as the patient was first hospitalized for three consecutive days. Treatment in a skilled nursing facility is covered in full for the first 20 days. From the 21st to the 100th day, the patient must pay the daily copayment. No Medicare benefits are provided for treatment in a skilled nursing facility beyond 100 days.

**TAKE NOTE**

Medicare Part A deductibles and copayments are applied per benefit period, not on an annual basis.

**TAKE NOTE**

Some preventive services, such as mammograms and flu shots, also are covered. However, Medicare Part B does not cover routine physical exams, eyeglasses, dental care, hearing aids, most prescription drugs, orthopedic shoes, or routine foot care.

## MEDICARE PART B COVERAGES

For those who desire, additional coverage is available under Medicare Part B for physician services, diagnostic tests, physical and occupational therapy, medical supplies, and the like.

Part B participants are required to pay a monthly premium and are responsible for an annual deductible. After the deductible, Part B will pay 80% of covered expenses, subject to Medicare's standards for reasonable charges.

### PRIMARY PAYOR AND SECONDARY PAYOR

Anyone aged 65 who is eligible for Medicare and who works for an employer of 20 or more employees is entitled to the same health insurance benefits as the employer offers to younger employees. In these cases, the employer sponsored plan is the primary payor and Medicare is the secondary payor. This means that Medicare pays only those charges that the employer-sponsored plan does not cover. This also applies to any disabled Medicare enrollee who also is covered by an employer-provided health care plan as a current employee or as a family member of an employee, but only if the employer plan covers 100 or more employees.

# MEDICARE+CHOICE PROGRAM

While Medicare is facing many challenges, the most pressing are the financial pressures resulting from changing demographics. Today, and in the future, the number of people becoming eligible for Medicare will increase rapidly and the number of workers paying taxes to support Medicare will decrease.

In 1997, Congress passed a law to reduce the financial strain on Medicare funds and provide Medicare beneficiaries with a variety of new health plan options. The original Medicare Plan and Medicare supplement insurance (discussed later), which is purchased from private insurance companies, still are available. However, new options are available through what is called the Medicare+Choice Program. These options include a variety of Medicare managed care choices, a private-fee-for-service plan (PFFS), and a Medicare Medical Savings Account Plan (MSA).

## MANAGED CARE SYSTEM

Medicare's managed care system consists of a network of approved hospitals, doctors, and other health-care professionals who agree to provide services to Medicare beneficiaries for a set monthly payment from Medicare. The health care providers receive the same fee every month, regardless of the actual services provided. As a result of this arrangement, health care providers try to manage care in such a way that they achieve a balance between budgetary and health care concerns.

## PRIVATE FEE-FOR-SERVICE PLAN

Another Medicare+Choice option is a private-fee-for-service plan (PFFS). This type of plan offers a Medicare-approved private insurance plan. Medicare pays the plan for Medicare-covered services, while the PFFS plan determines, up to a limit, how much the care recipient will pay for covered services. The Medicare beneficiary is responsible for paying the difference between the amount Medicare pays and the PFFS charges.

## MEDICAL SAVINGS ACCOUNT

Medicare beneficiaries have the most control over their health care expenditures with Medicare Medical Savings Accounts (MSAs). A Medicare+Choice MSA consists of two parts: a high-deductible insurance policy (the policy) and a savings account (the account). The policy pays for at least all Medicare-covered items and services after an enrollee meets the annual deductible. Medicare pays the premium for the policy and deposits the difference between the premium and the fixed amount Medicare allots for each Medicare+Choice enrollee in the individual's account. Money in the account may earn interest or dividends and can be withdrawn tax free to pay for services covered under the Medicare benefit package, as well as services listed as qualified medical expenses in the Internal Revenue Code. MSA funds can also be used to buy long-term care insurance.

# MEDICAID

Medicaid is a government-funded, means-tested program designed to provide health care to poor people of all ages. The goal of Medicaid is to offer medical assistance to those whose income and resources are insufficient to meet the costs of necessary medical care. Individuals claiming benefits must prove they do not have the ability or means to pay for their own medical care.

Applicants must complete a lengthy questionnaire, disclosing all assets and income. To qualify for Medicaid, a person must be poor or become poor. Such people frequently include children born to low-income parents, babies born addicted to drugs, AIDS patients, and the indigent elderly.

Individual states design and administer the Medicaid programs under broad guidelines established by the federal government. On average, the federal government contributes about 56 cents for every Medicaid dollar spent; however, the amount contributed may be lower or higher. State governments contribute the balance and the extent of coverage and the quality of services vary widely from state to state.

### QUALIFYING FOR MEDICAID NURSING HOME BENEFITS

Unlike Medicare, Medicaid does provide for custodial care or assisted care in a nursing home. However, as explained earlier, individuals claiming a need for Medicaid must prove that they cannot pay for their own nursing home care. In addition, the potential recipient must:

- be at least age 65, blind, or disabled (as defined by the recipient's state);

- be a US citizen or permanent resident alien;

- need the type of care that is provided only in a nursing home; and

- meet certain asset and income tests.

## MEDICARE SUPPLEMENT POLICIES

As is apparent from the discussion of Medicare in the previous unit, Medicare leaves many gaps in its coverage. With its structure of limited benefit periods, deductibles, copayments, and exclusions, the coverage it provides is limited at best. To help fill these gaps, private insurance companies market Medicare supplement insurance policies to consumers. Medicare supplement (or Medigap) policies are designed to pick up coverage where Medicare leaves off.

### QUALIFYING FOR MEDIGAP COVERAGE

People age 65 or older who enroll in Medicare Part B are afforded a six-month open enrollment period for purchasing a Medicare supplement policy. They may select any of the Medigap policies available in their state and cannot be denied coverage because of health problems. In fact, insurers may not discriminate in the pricing of the policy or condition the issuance of the policy on good health.

In general, people under age 65, disabled, and enrolled in Medicare Part B are not eligible for open enrollment unless their state mandates otherwise.

## PROTECTING THE CONSUMER

The standardization of Medigap policies was intended to help consumers understand what these policies cover and, more importantly, what they do not cover. Consumers now are encouraged to do some comparison shopping before they purchase a Medicare supplement policy. Prospective insureds should compare benefits, coverage limitations, exclusions, and premiums of several insurers before they buy a policy. In many cases, policies that provide the same coverage will not necessarily have the same premiums.

As further protection for the consumer, purchasers have the option of reviewing their policies and canceling the coverage. Consumers can receive a refund of their premium if they notify the insurer within a specified number of days after the policy is delivered. In most states, this free-look period is 30 days, but some states have shorter periods.

# LONG-TERM CARE POLICIES

Americans are living longer, and many can expect to live a substantial portion of their lives in retirement. That's the good news. The bad news is, although statistics regarding longevity for older Americans may be improving, many individuals over age 65 still have to deal with poor health during their retirement years. As people age, they consume a larger proportion of health care services because of chronic illness, such as Alzheimer's disease, heart disease, and stroke. The cost of the extended day-in, day-out care some older people need can be staggering: as much as $60,000 or $70,000 each year or more for nursing home care and upwards of $1,500 a month—or more—for aides who come to one's home.

As beneficial as Medicare and Medicare supplement insurance are to the elderly in protecting them against the costs of medical care, neither of these programs covers long-term custodial or nursing home care. Medicaid covers some of the costs associated with long-term care, but a person is ineligible for Medicaid until he is practically destitute. How can these costs be paid? The solution for many is long-term care insurance.

## WHAT IS LONG-TERM CARE?

You often will see nursing home care referred to as long-term care. However, long-term care (LTC) refers to a broad range of medical, personal, and environmental services designed to assist individuals who have lost their ability to remain completely independent in the community. Although care may be provided for short periods of time while a patient is recuperating from an accident or illness, LTC refers to care provided for an extended period of time, normally more than 90 days. And, depending on the severity of the impairment, assistance may be given at home, at an adult care center, or in a nursing home.

TAKE NOTE

Activities of daily living (ADLs) provide an excellent means to assess an individual's need for nursing home care, home health care, or other health-related services. A policy should indicate what number and type of ADLs will be used to trigger benefits. When the insured cannot perform these ADLs independently, benefits will be paid to cover expenses for assistance with those activities.

## WHAT IS LONG-TERM CARE INSURANCE?

Long-term care insurance is a relatively new type of insurance product. However, more and more insurance companies are beginning to offer this coverage as the need for it grows. It is similar to most insurance plans in that the insured, in exchange for a certain premium, receives specified benefits in the event he requires LTC, as defined by the policy. Most LTC policies pay the insured a fixed dollar amount for each day he receives the kind of care the policy covers, regardless of what the care costs.

Insurers offer a wide range of benefit amounts, ranging from, for example, $40 each day to $500 or more each day for nursing home care. The daily benefit for at-home care can be a percentage of the nursing home benefit. Many policies include an inflation rider or option to purchase additional coverage, enabling the policies to keep pace with increases in LTC costs.

## LONG-TERM CARE COVERAGES

As individuals age, they are likely to suffer from acute and (or) chronic illnesses or conditions. An acute illness is a serious condition, such as pneumonia or influenza, from which the body can recover fully with proper medical attention. The patient also may need some assistance with chores for short periods of time until recovery and rehabilitation from the illness are complete.

Some people will suffer from chronic conditions, such as arthritis, heart disease, or hypertension, that are treatable but not curable illnesses. When chronic conditions such as diabetes or heart disease initially appear, many people ignore the inconvenience or pain they cause. Over time, however, a chronic condition frequently goes beyond being a nuisance and begins to inhibit a person's independence.

Typically, the need for LTC arises when physical or mental conditions, whether acute or chronic, impair a person's ability to perform the basic activities of daily living—eating, toileting, transferring, bathing, continence, and dressing. This is the risk that long-term care insurance is designed to protect.

The kinds of services and support associated with long-term care are provided at three levels: institutional care, home-based care, and community care. The appropriate level of care depends, of course, on the individual's medical or health care needs. Within each of these broad levels are many types of care, any or all of which may be covered by a long-term care insurance policy. Typical types of coverages are explained below.

**Skilled Nursing Care** Skilled nursing care is continuous around-the-clock care provided by licensed medical professionals under the direct supervision of a physician. Skilled nursing care is usually administered in nursing homes.

**Intermediate Nursing Care** Intermediate nursing care is provided by registered nurses, licensed practical nurses, and nurse's aides under the supervision of a physician. Intermediate care is provided in home or in nursing homes for stable medical conditions that require daily, but not 24-hour, supervision.

**Custodial Care** Custodial care provides assistance in meeting daily living requirements, such as bathing, dressing, getting out of bed, toileting, etc. Such care does not require specialized medical training, but it must be given under a doctor's order. Custodial care usually is provided by nursing homes but also can be given by adult day care centers, by respite centers, or at home.

**Home Health Care** Home health care is care provided in the insured's home, usually on a part-time basis. It can include skilled care (such as nursing, rehabilitative, or physical therapy care ordered by a doctor) or unskilled care (such as help with cooking or cleaning).

**Adult Day Care** Adult day care is designed for those who require assistance with various activities of daily living, while their primary caregivers (usually family or friends) are absent. These day care centers offer skilled medical care in conjunction with social and personal services, but custodial care usually is their primary focus.

**Respite Care** Respite care is designed to provide a short rest period for a family caregiver. There are two options: either the insured is moved to a full-time care facility, or a substitute care provider moves into the insured's home for a temporary period, giving the family member a rest from his caregiving activities.

**Continuing Care** A fairly new kind of LTC coverage, continuing care coverage, is designed to provide a benefit for elderly individuals who live in a continuing care retirement community. Retirement communities are geared to senior citizens' full-time needs, both medical and social, and often are sponsored by religious or nonprofit organizations. It provides independent and congregate living and personal, intermediate, and skilled nursing care and attempts to create an environment that allows each resident to participate in the community's life to whatever degree desired.

**LTC Policy Provisions And Limits** As we have stated, a number of LTC policies are on the market today, each characterized by some distinguishing feature or benefit that sets it apart from the rest. However, there are enough similarities to allow us to discuss the basic provisions of these policies and their typical limits or exclusions.

**LTC Services** Qualified LTC services are defined as the necessary diagnostic, preventive, therapeutic, curing, treating, mitigating, and rehabilitative services, and maintenance or personal care services that are required by a chronically ill individual, and are provided under a plan of care set forth by a licensed health care practitioner.

**Qualifying for Benefits** When LTC policies first were introduced, insurers frequently required at least three days of prior hospitalization or skilled nursing home stays before the LTC policy benefits were triggered. The benefit trigger is an event or condition that must occur before policy benefits become payable. As a result of the 1996 Health Insurance Portability Accountablility Act (HIPAA), prior hospitalization no longer can be used as a benefit trigger; instead, the individual must be diagnosed as chronically ill.

Diagnosis of chronic illness can be made on two levels: physical and (or) cognitive. The physical diagnosis of a chronically ill individual is one who has been certified as being unable to perform at least two activities of daily living. A long-term care policy must take into account at least five of these ADLs. In addition, an individual would be considered chronically ill if he requires substantial supervision to protect his health or safety owing to severe cognitive impairment and this condition was certified within the previous 12 months.

**Benefit Limits** Almost all LTC policies set benefit limits, in terms of how long the benefits are paid or how much the dollar benefit will be for any one covered care service or a combination of services. Maximum dollar amounts vary considerably from policy to policy. Maximum coverage periods also vary.

In fact, with LTC policies, it is not unusual for one policy to include separate maximum coverage periods for nursing home care and home health care.

**FIGURE 13.2   The Impairment Continuum—Activities of Daily Living**

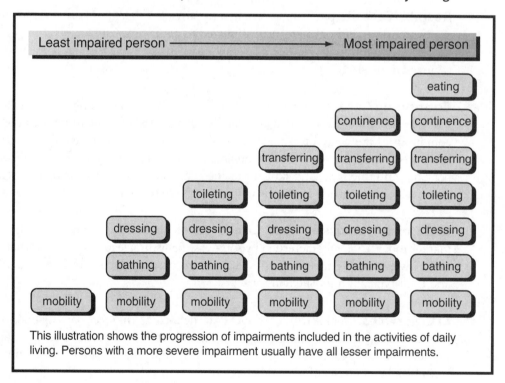

TAKE NOTE

Maximum coverage periods extend anywhere from two to six years. Some policies offer unlimited lifetime coverage.

**Age Limits**  LTC policies typically set age limits for issue, with an average age of about 58. However, some newer policies can be sold to people up through age 89. Many policies also set a minimum purchase age, with an average of age 50. Some companies have a minimum purchase age of 18.

**Renewability**  As a result of HIPAA, all long-term care policies sold today must be guaranteed renewable or better. This means the insurance company cannot cancel the policy and must renew coverage each year, as long as premiums are paid. A guaranteed renewable policy allows the insurer to raise premiums, but only for entire classes of insureds.

**Probationary Periods**  LTC probationary periods can range from 0 to 365 days, and many insurers give the insured the option of selecting the period that best serves his needs. The probationary period (also known as the elimination period) serves as a deductible. The longer the probationary period, the lower the premium.

**Specified Exclusions**  Most LTC policies exclude coverage for drug and alcohol dependency, acts of war, self-inflicted injuries, and nonorganic mental conditions. Organic cognitive disorders, such as Alzheimer's disease, senile dementia, and Parkinson's disease, almost always are included.

**Premiums**  The cost for an LTC policy is based on a number of factors: the insured's age and health, the type and level of benefits provided, the inclusion or absence of a deductible or probationary period and the length of that period, and whether or not options or riders are included with the policy (such as the option to purchase additional coverage in the future or the inflation-adjustment rider, which increases the policy's coverage to match inflation levels automatically).

## SUMMARY

The Original Medicare Plan provides hospital and medical expense insurance protection to those aged 65 and older, to those of any age who suffer from chronic kidney disease, or to those who are receiving Social Security disability benefits. Medicaid is a joint federal and state program to pay health care expenses for the poor. To qualify for Medicaid benefits, an individual must meet certain asset and income limitation tests. However, even if a person qualifies for Medicaid, finding an adequate nursing home is difficult because Medicaid does not to pay for the full cost of care. Medicaid patients are limited in choice regarding which nursing home they go to.

Medicare supplement or Medigap policies are designed to make up for what Medicare doesn't cover and also are becoming increasingly popular. As beneficial as Medicare and Medicare supplement insurance are to the elderly in protecting them against the costs of medical care, long-term care insurance still is needed to offer a broad range of medical and personal services to individuals who need assistance with daily activities for an extended period of time.

# U N I T   Q U I Z

1. Which of the following statements pertaining to Medicare is CORRECT?

   A. Bob is covered under Medicare Part B. He submitted a total of $1,100 of approved medical charges to Medicare after paying the required deductible. Of that total, Bob must pay $880.

   B. Each individual covered by Medicare Part A is allowed one 90-day benefit period per year.

   C. For the first 90 days of hospitalization, Medicare Part A pays 100% of all covered services, except for an initial deductible.

   D. Medicare Part A is provided automatically when a qualified individual applies for Social Security benefits.

2. Under Medicare Part B, the participant must pay all of the following EXCEPT

   A. an annual deductible
   B. a per benefit deductible
   C. 20% of covered charges above the deductible
   D. a monthly premium

3. Which of the following statements about Medicare Part B is NOT correct?

   A. It is a compulsory program.
   B. It covers services and supplies not covered by Part A.
   C. It is financed by monthly premiums.
   D. It is financed by tax revenues.

4. All of the following conditions typically are covered in a long-term care insurance policy EXCEPT

   A. Alzheimer's disease
   B. senile dementia
   C. alcohol dependency
   D. Parkinson's disease

5. Which of the following statements about Medicare supplement (Medigap) policies is NOT correct?

   A. Medigap policies supplement Medicare benefits.
   B. Medigap policies cover the cost of extended nursing home care.
   C. Medigap policies pay most, if not all, Medicare deductibles and copayments.
   D. Medigap policies pay for some health care services not covered by Medicare.

6. Which of the following is NOT a typical type of long-term care coverage?

   A. Skilled nursing
   B. Home health
   C. Hospice
   D. Residential

7. Medicaid is primarily designed to pay the health care expenses of a person who

   A. cannot qualify for health insurance
   B. has no assets
   C. recently turned age 65 and retired from their job
   D. is not eligible for group health insurance at work

8. Which of the following people would be most likely to qualify as a chronically ill individual under the terms of a typical long-term care insurance policy?

   A. A person who cannot bathe or dress oneself without the assistance of another person
   B. Someone who is unable to drive a motor vehicle and is having problems with continence
   C. A person who is unable to cook meals independently
   D. A person who has been hospitalized for minor surgery

# ANSWERS AND RATIONALES TO UNIT QUIZ

1.  **D.** When an individual turns age 65, Medicare Part A is available and is provided automatically when he applies for Social Security benefits.

2.  **B.** Under Medicare Part B, a participant must pay a monthly premium and an annual deductible. Once the deductible has been met, Part B will pay 80% of covered expenses and the participant must pay the remaining 20%.

3.  **A.** Medicare Part B is an optional program that provides additional coverage for physician services, diagnostic tests, physical and occupation therapy, medical supplies, and the like.

4.  **C.** Most long-term care policies exclude coverage for drug and alcohol dependency. Organic cognitive disorders, such as Alzheimer's disease, senile dementia, and Parkinson's disease, almost always are included.

5.  **B.** Medigap policies do not cover the cost of extended nursing home care.

6.  **C.** Long-term care services are designed for senior citizens, and hospice services are for terminally ill persons and their families.

7.  **B.** Medicaid is a government entitlement program intended for impoverished people with no assets.

8.  **A.** Long-term care policies qualify bathing and dressing as activities of daily living.

# 14

# Property and Casualty Contract Terms and Definitions

## KEY CONCEPTS

- Property versus casualty insurance products
- Common property insurance provisions
- Property insurance peril forms
- Named peril versus open-peril policies
- Common liability insurance provisions
- Negligence and liability

Standardization has played a large role in the development of property and casualty insurance products, and contracts are often based on established forms used throughout the industry. Nevertheless, some terms are used exclusively in property insurance, others are typical of casualty insurance, and some are used in both areas. This unit introduces students to the terms, definitions, and provisions that are commonly used in these kinds of policies. Later units will cover the types of property and casualty policies that are available to consumers.

## OBJECTIVE

When you complete this unit, you should be able to:

■ describe the various types of insurance and their purposes;

■ explain the operation of various insurance policy provisions;

■ define some of the important terms insurance policies contain; and

■ distinguish between property and casualty insurance provisions.

# PROPERTY INSURANCE

Property insurance protects against losses due to fire and other causes, such as windstorm, hail, or theft, to items of real and personal property. Such insurance is designed primarily to protect against direct financial loss resulting from damage to or destruction of the property itself, but also may include consequential losses that result from damage to property. The major types of property insurance follow:

■ *Fire and allied (related) lines insurance.* Covers property at specified locations; and

■ *Marine insurance.* Protects against loss of property in the course of transportation—in other words property not at a specific location (sometimes referred to as *floaters*). Marine insurance is further divided:

— *Ocean marine.* Covers all types of oceangoing vessels, cargo (import and export shipments), and shipowner's liability; and

— *Inland marine.* Covers domestic shipments; instruments of transportation and communication such as bridges, tunnels, and radio towers; and personal property floater risks.

# CASUALTY INSURANCE

Casualty insurance was developed after fire and marine insurance. It is a broad term that encompasses all types of coverage that are not part of property or marine insurance. Liability insurance, one of the major components of the casualty insurance category, pays for loss due to the insured's negligence. This negligence may come from some responsibility imposed by law or assumed by contract. The insurance company makes the payment to a third party on behalf of the insured. Casualty insurance also includes personal automobile protection, workers' compensation, burglary, robbery, theft, and fidelity and surety bonds.

**Package Policies**  Before 1950, insurance was written on a monoline basis. In other words, a company wrote only one line of coverage, either property or liability. This was due to the fact that insurers were authorized as either property or casualty companies. Starting in the 1950s, and following changes in state laws, insurance companies began writing package policies that combined property coverages with liability. Policies that include several types of insurance are multiple-lines or simply multi-lines.

## PROPERTY AND CASUALTY CLASSIFICATIONS

The person who owns an office building and the person who owns a home face many of the same property risks, such as fire, lightning, wind, and theft, as well as liability arising from negligent conduct. Nevertheless, some differences in the risks exist. Therefore, insurance policies also are categorized as commercial lines (business) and personal lines (nonbusiness).

Many of the insuring agreements, conditions, and exclusions in the two categories, or lines of insurance, are similar; however, certain features are unique to each. Unique property descriptions or causes of loss found in specific contracts will be presented as various policies are described later in this text.

## PROVISIONS COMMON TO PROPERTY AND CASUALTY INSURANCE

We will now look at provisions found in most P & C policies. Provisions are like the ingredients in a recipe. They are added to the contract when it's drafted. Provisions and conditions are terms that may be used interchangeably. In fact, provisions are typically listed within the Conditions section of a P & C policy. Some of the contract provisions that might be found in either a property or casualty policy include the following.

### LIMIT OF LIABILITY

The limit of liability is the maximum amount an insurance company will pay in case of a loss; sometimes it is referred to as the policy's face amount. Despite a maximum amount payable for a loss, a policy may impose internal or sub-limits of insurance—such as $2,000 for loss by theft of firearms in a homeowner's policy, regardless of larger limits of insurance on the home and personal property.

**Property Insurance**  In property insurance, the limit of liability is stated as a single dollar amount. A homeowner's policy that insures the house for $100,000 will pay no more than $100,000 for damage or destruction of the house (less the appropriate deductible). This limit applies for any one occurrence, with no limit on how many times the company may have to pay for separate occurrences during the policy period.

**Liability Insurance**  In liability insurance, a policy may cover several categories of claims stemming from different types of activity of the insured: bodily injury (BI) liability, property damage (PD) liability, personal injury liability, and advertising injury. The policy will pay no more than the stated amount per occurrence. The limit of insurance for bodily injury, property damage, advertising injury, or personal injury may be expressed as one amount (a combined single limit), such as $300,000 per occurrence for bodily injury, property damage, or both combined. Or it may be expressed as a split limit, such as 100/300/50, which indicates $100,000 per person and $300,000 per occurrence for bodily injury and $50,000 per occurrence for property damage.

**Aggregate Limits** A policy also may have an annual aggregate limit, which is the maximum amount the policy will pay in any one policy period (typically one year) for all occurrences. This aggregate limit may be for one coverage or all coverages under the policy.

**Limits Per Occurrence** The limit of liability (whether per occurrence or aggregate) applies regardless of the number of:

- persons or organizations insured under the policy;

- persons or organizations who have sustained injury or damage; or

- claims made or suits brought because of injury or damage.

Thus, if someone names an insured and his spouse in a claim under a homeowner's policy, the limit of insurance applies to that one occurrence, not separately to both the insured and the spouse. The most an insurance company will pay on any loss is the amount of the loss or the policy limit, whichever is lower.

## DEDUCTIBLES

In most cases, a deductible clause is included in a policy. This clause requires the insured to pay a small portion of the loss, with the insurance company paying the remainder. Companies include deductibles for two reasons: (1) to place a certain amount of responsibility on the insured to minimize losses and avoid hazards and (2) to avoid paying small claims that are disproportionately expensive to handle.

It is important to remember that when a loss occurs, any deductible is subtracted after the loss payment is estimated. If the loss is less than the deductible, no payment is made. For example, assume an insured has a homeowner's policy with a $250 deductible. A small fire causes damages totaling $200. In this case, the insured would pay for the damages and collect nothing from the insurer. If, however, the damages were $2,000, the insured would pay the $250 deductible and the insurer would pay the remaining $1,750.

Deductibles in liability insurance are relatively uncommon, except for larger accounts.

## ACCIDENT

An *accident* is a sudden, unforeseeable, unintended event causing loss or damage. An accident must be identifiable as to a specific time and place. The explosion of a steam boiler in an apartment building, a collision between two vehicles, and a slip and fall in a retail store are all examples of accidents.

## OCCURRENCE

The term *occurrence* includes an accident as well as continuous or repeated exposure to the same conditions, which results in injury to persons or damage to property neither expected nor intended from the insured's standpoint. For example, if a contractor damages a gas pipe, causing it to leak, and people working in the area are injured after inhaling the fumes, this is an occurrence.

## CANCELLATION

*Cancellation* occurs when the insurance company or the insured terminates a contract before its normal expiration. Termination is carried out in accordance with provisions in the contract, by mutual agreement or by statute, and must comply with various time limits and notification requirements set by state law.

**Refund of Premium**   Refund of premium after cancellation may be on a *short rate or pro rata* basis, depending on which party canceled the policy. The portion of the premium the insurer retains is called the earned premium. The portion refunded to the policyholder is the *unearned premium* or *return premium*. Premiums are calculated by three methods, as described below.

*Pro Rata Cancellation.* Prorating the premium is the method used to calculate the premium refund when the insurance company initiates cancellation. Under this method, the premium refund equals the premium paid for the unexpired term of the policy. In other words, the insured pays premium for the period he had coverage and gets a full refund for the period he did not have coverage.

*Short Rate Cancellation.* Short rate is the method used when a policyholder cancels his policy before it reaches its natural expiration. In this case, the company pays a return premium less than the pro rata part that remains unearned. The insured pays a penalty of roughly 10% of the unearned premium for canceling early. This amount withheld from the return premium is designed to compensate the insurer for its policy issuance and administrative expenses.

*Flat Cancellation.* When a policy is terminated on its effective date, it is called a flat cancellation. The entire premium is refunded to the policyholder.

## RENEWAL AND NONRENEWAL

**Renewal**   Renewal is the continuation of a policy about to expire. This may be accomplished by issuance of a new policy, a renewal receipt, or a certificate, to take effect upon expiration of the prior policy. Though a new policy number may be issued, the coverage is considered continuous and, thus, a renewal.

**Nonrenewal**   Nonrenewal means that the insurance company will not renew or continue the policy beyond the expiration date.

Most states have laws with specific requirements governing the sending of either a notice of nonrenewal or an offer of renewal when the renewal offer is for a policy with less favorable provisions than the original policy. State laws specify the contents of such nonrenewal notices.

# PROPERTY INSURANCE POLICY PROVISIONS

## BASIS OF PAYMENT FOR LOSS OF THE INSURED PROPERTY

A policy may pay the insured on the basis of the following:

- *Actual cash value* (ACV)—the sum of money required to pay for damage to or loss of property. This sum is the property's current replacement cost minus depreciation caused by obsolescence or wear and tear to the property. ACV also may be defined as the current fair market value (FMV) in some states.

- *Replacement cost*—the full amount necessary to replace or repair the damaged property to its condition before the loss. Replacement cost is generally more than the actual cash value because the insurer settles without a deduction for depreciation. Generally, however, the insured must in fact replace the property with like kind, quality, and quantity before the claim is fully recovered.

## VACANCY AND UNOCCUPANCY

The use to which a building is put also affects coverage. Different risks arise when a building is occupied, unoccupied, or vacant.

- *Occupied*—A building that is being used is considered occupied. For example, a building with a bank or a retail store is an occupied building.

- *Unoccupied*—A building is unoccupied if no one is currently in it, but furnishings are present and the occupants intend to return, such as when a family takes a vacation.

- *Vacant*—A building that is not currently being used and does not have enough furnishings to function in its normal capacity is considered vacant.

Certain policies or specific coverages may become ineffective if a building has been unoccupied or vacant for a specified period of time. Some of these restrictions will be noted as specific policies are reviewed.

## COINSURANCE

When applied to real property insurance, a coinsurance clause requires a policyholder to carry insurance equal to a specified percentage of the total value of the property being insured.

---

 E X A M P L E        If property is valued at $100,000 and the coinsurance clause is 80%, the policyholder must carry at least $80,000 of coverage to satisfy the coinsurance clause requirement.

Because property losses typically are only partial losses, property owners are inclined to carry just partial insurance on their property. To distribute the cost of insurance more equitably among insureds, however, many companies include coinsurance clauses requiring policyholders to carry minimum amounts of insurance. A reduced rate is granted on a policy that carries a coinsurance clause. However, if the insured fails to maintain the required insurance and a loss occurs, the insurance company imposes a penalty. The insured becomes a *coinsurer* in the loss and must participate in the loss.

Note that the insured must agree to *maintain* insurance at least equal to the stated percentage of the value of the insured property. This means that the amount of insurance must equal or exceed the required percentage *at the time of loss*. If this requirement has not been met, the insured may not fully recover the loss even though the loss is for less than the policy amount.

The following coinsurance formula is used to determine the amount that an insurance company will pay for a covered loss:

$$\frac{\text{Amount of Insurance Carried}}{\text{Amount of Insurance Required}} \times \text{Loss} - \text{Deductible (if any)} = \text{Amount Paid}$$

The calculation for the example above would be as follows:

$$\frac{\$40,000}{\$80,000 \ (80\% \text{ of } \$100,000)} \times \$10,000 - \$250 = \$4,750$$

## Application of the Coinsurance Formula and Deductible

Assume that an insured owns an office building valued at $200,000. His insurance policy carries an 80% coinsurance clause. Therefore, according to the clause, the insured must maintain a policy for at least $160,000 ($200,000 × 80% = $160,000).

The following examples illustrate how the coinsurance formula affects the claim settlement when the insured suffers a fire loss of $100,000.

---

**EXAMPLE**

$$\frac{\text{Amount Carried}}{\text{Amount Required}} \times \text{Loss} - \text{Deductible} = \text{Amount Paid}$$

*Example 1*

| | |
|---|---|
| Property Value (ACV) | $200,000 |
| Coinsurance | 80% |
| Insurance Carried | $160,000 |
| Loss | $100,000 |

$$\frac{\$160,000}{\$160,000} \times \$100,000 = \$100,000 \text{ settlement}$$

*Example 2*

| | |
|---|---|
| Property Value (ACV) | $200,000 |
| Coinsurance | 80% |
| Insurance Carried | $160,000 |
| Deductible | $500 |
| Loss | $100,000 |

$$\frac{\$160,000}{\$160,000} \times \$100,000 - \$500 = \$99,500 \text{ settlement}$$

*Example 3*

| | |
|---|---|
| Property Value (ACV) | $200,000 |
| Coinsurance | 80% |
| Insurance Carried | $100,000 |
| Deductible | $500 |
| Loss | $100,000 |

$$\frac{\$100,000}{\$160,000} \times \$100,000 = \$62,500$$

$$\$62,500 - \$500 = \$62,000 \text{ settlement}$$

Note: The insured is penalized for being underinsured when the loss occurred. In addition to the $500 deductible, the insured must pay the remaining $37,500 the insurance company won't pay, for a total of $38,000 in out-of-pocket expenses.

*Example 4*

| | |
|---|---|
| Property Value (ACV) | $200,000 |
| Coinsurance | 80% |
| Insurance Carried | $250,000 |
| Deductible | $500 |
| Loss | $100,000 |

*If the amount carried equals or exceeds the amount required, it is not necessary to use the coinsurance formula on the loss.*

Note: The insurer pays a settlement of $99,500 because the insured cannot collect more than the actual loss. Remember, the purpose of insurance is not to enrich the insured, but to indemnify the insured, or to "make whole" by returning the insured property to the condition it was in before the loss.

## SUBROGATION AND INSURER'S RIGHT TO RECOVER PAYMENT

When a company pays the insured for a loss for which some person other than the policyholder is responsible, the insurer has the right to recover its loss from the negligent party. This is the right of subrogation. The insurer steps into the insured's place to take legal action against the negligent party but only to the extent of the amount the insurance company paid to the insured. The insurance company also may recover the insured's deductible, but it has no responsibility to do so. The insured must do everything necessary to secure these rights for the insurer and must do nothing after a loss to impair these rights.

This principle is designed to prevent the insured from collecting from the insurance company, then taking his own legal action against the party who caused the loss and collecting from that party as well. This violates the principle of indemnity.

## PRO RATA LIABILITY

If more than one insurance company has a policy covering the same property (building, auto for physical damage, etc.), or if two or more policies apply to a liability claim, each company prorates its payment for the loss. This also may be expressed as a clause in the contract that reads: "The company's share is the proportion that its limit of liability bears to the total of all applicable limits whether collectible or not." This usually is found in the Other Insurance section of the contract.

**TAKE NOTE**

Subrogation allows an insurance company to collect damages paid to the insured from a negligent third party.

EXAMPLE

| | | | |
|---|---|---|---|
| Total Insurance | $1,000,000 | | |
| Loss | | $300,000 | |

Proportionate Share Policy

| | Limits | | Share of Loss |
|---|---|---|---|
| Company A | $ 500,000 | (½) | $150,000 |
| Company B | $ 250,000 | (¼) | $ 75,000 |
| Company C | $ 250,000 | (¼) | $ 75,000 |
| | $1,000,000 | | $300,000 |

Each company pays only its share. If one company is insolvent, the other companies will pay only their pro rata share of the loss. They will not pay the insolvent company's share.

## PAIR AND SET CLAUSE

The *pair and set clause* in an insurance contract establishes the conditions that apply when a single item of a pair or set is lost or destroyed. The clause generally provides that the insurer (1) may repair or replace the lost part, thereby restoring the pair or set to its value before the loss, or (2) may elect to pay the difference between the actual cash value of the property before the loss and after the loss. This provision is designed to prevent the insured from collecting for a total loss when only part of a pair or set is the subject of the loss.

EXAMPLE

If only one of a pair of diamond earrings is lost, the insurer may elect to replace the lost earring or pay the difference between the value of the pair and the residual value of the single earring. Only the insurer may determine the method of settlement.

## RIGHT OF SALVAGE/ABANDONMENT

An insurance company has the right to any *salvage* when it settles a loss. The company may take possession of the damaged property and pay the insured the appropriate value of the loss. It then can sell or otherwise dispose of this salvage property to reduce the claim's overall cost. However, the insured *cannot* require the company to take the salvage, nor can he abandon the property to the insurer.

**EXAMPLE** In the case of an auto accident, the insurance company may *total the vehicle* by paying the actual cash value to the policyholder. The company then becomes the legal owner of the salvage (in this case, the damaged car) and may dispose of it as the company sees fit. In some cases, the salvage actually is sold to the insured.

## BURGLARY

*Burglary* is defined as the breaking and entering into the premises of another with felonious, wrongful, or criminal intent to take property and with visible sign of forced entry. By definition, burglary involves forcible entry.

## ROBBERY

*Robbery* is the felonious, wrongful, or criminal taking, either by force or by fear of force, of the personal property of another. This act of forcibly taking property from someone commonly is known as a *hold-up*.

## THEFT

*Theft* is any act of stealing, including larceny, burglary, and robbery. In general, it is the taking of someone else's property without the owner's permission. *Larceny* is the unlawful taking of the personal property of another without his consent and with the intent to deprive him of the ownership or use of that property.

## MYSTERIOUS DISAPPEARANCE

*Mysterious disappearance* is the disappearance of insured property in an unexplained manner. An example would be noting one day that a stone is missing from your ring or discovering that the watch you put on your dresser three days ago isn't there. Mere loss of property, such as an article dropped from a boat, is not included in this definition because the disappearance is not mysterious. This coverage is included under a limited number of policies or endorsements.

## INFLATION GUARD/AUTOMATIC INCREASE IN INSURANCE

Property polices may include automatically or by endorsement a provision whereby insurance limits are increased to compensate for inflation. For example, the limit of insurance on a building may be increased at the end of a given period of time, say quarterly, or even daily, based on a fixed percentage determined at the beginning of the policy term. This provision is designed to prevent underinsurance that occurs when the replacement cost or actual cash value of property increases due to inflation.

## INHERENT VICE

*Inherent vice* is a defect or cause of loss arising out of the nature of certain goods. For example, a star sapphire might become cloudy over time, or the rubber moldings on a car might deteriorate after awhile if the car is kept in a very warm climate. Losses due to inherent vice are usually not covered by property insurance policies.

## PERIL/CAUSE OF LOSS

Peril, the actual cause of a loss, is identified or referred to in the policy. Perils include such events as fire, wind, hail, collision with another car, and the like.

**Specified or Named Peril Policy**   A named peril policy provides coverage only if a loss is caused by one of the perils specifically named or identified in the policy, such as fire, wind, or hail. If a peril is not listed, it is not covered. The policy may also specifically exclude certain causes of loss or certain property. Policies also can exclude perils only under certain conditions or cover them only under certain conditions.

---

**E X A M P L E**   Vandalism is a covered cause of loss in most property insurance policies. However, coverage for vandalism often is excluded when a building has been vacant for more than 60 days preceding the loss.

---

When a policy is issued on a named peril basis, the burden of proof in the event of loss rests with the insured. He must demonstrate that the loss was caused by one of the listed perils to have coverage.

**Open Perils or Special form Policy**   The insuring agreement of an open perils policy is stated in very broad terms: the policy provides coverage for risks of direct physical loss or damage except from those causes of loss specifically excluded, such as intentional losses, earthquake, and the like. Because the intent of most property policies is to provide a broad array of coverages, it is easier to identify those few situations in which coverage will not apply than the reverse. For an open perils policy, the burden of proof in the event of a loss is on the insurer. To deny coverage, the insurer must demonstrate that the cause of loss was one of the listed exclusions.

## PROPERTY INSURANCE PERIL FORMS

There are three main peril forms used in property insurance. The first two peril forms (Basic and Broad form) are named-peril forms. The third, Special form is an open-peril form. We will refer to these peril forms throughout the remaining units of this book. The standardized approach that is employed through peril forms originated from the New York Standard Fire policy. Developed in New York state in 1943, the Standard Fire Policy allowed for consistency among insurance companies and the property contracts they provide. The Standard Fire Policy insured against hostile fire, lighting, and removal (preservation of property), and settled claims on an actual cash value basis.

**Basic Form—Named Peril Coverage**   Basic form—named peril coverage (WCSHAVVER) begins by including the three perils (fire, lightning, and removal) from the standard fire policy and adds the following:

- ■ Windstorm (winds from a thunderstorm, tornado, hurricane, etc.)— contents are only covered if the building was damaged first;

- ■ Civil commotion—uprising involving a large number of people;

- ■ Smoke damage—smoke that is sudden and accidental in nature. (No coverage for industrial smoke and agricultural smudging);

- ■ Hail—contents are only covered if the building was damaged first;

- Aircraft—includes self-propelled missiles and spacecraft;

- Vehicles;

- Vandalism and malicious mischief;

- Explosion—steam boiler explosion is specifically excluded from commercial property policies; and

- Riot—violent action by two or more people.

**Broad Form—Named Peril Coverage** Board form—named peril coverage automatically includes all the basic form perils already discussed and adds the following:

- weight of ice, snow, or sleet (doesn't cover ice dams);

- collapse—abrupt falling down or caving in of a building (doesn't cover collapse caused by earth movement);

- falling objects—roof or wall must be damaged before contents are covered;

- power surge—does not provide coverage for electronic components that are part of appliances, computers, or other electronic equipment;

- pipes freezing or bursting—must attempt to maintain heat in the building or drain the water system;

- overflow of a water system—must be internal plumbing contained within the home;

- volcanic eruption—smoke, lava, and ashes covered, but not tremors and land shock waves; and

- sudden and accidental tearing apart of a heating system—includes cracking, burning, or bulging.

**Special Form—Open Peril/All-Risk Coverage** Special form—open peril/all-risk coverage provides coverage against all forms of direct physical damage but also provides a list of exclusions, including the following:

- power outage off premises;

- inherent defects/intentional acts;

- maintenance—mechanical/electrical breakdown;

- building code/ordinance;

- war/nuclear;

- flood and ground water;

- wear and tear, rust and mold;

- earth movement;

- smog;

- birds;

- insects;

- rodents; and

- domestic animals.

**TAKE NOTE**

The term "all risk" should not be used in any written or oral communication with an insured. This has become insurance industry shorthand for an open perils or a special form policy, but the term can be misleading to a policyholder who might expect his policy to cover every type of loss situation.

**Coverage for Theft**   is included under all homeowner policies. Mysterious disappearance is not covered. Theft coverage must be purchased separately under many commercial property policies.

# LIABILITY INSURANCE PROVISIONS

Liability insurance is designed to pay damages on behalf of the insured to others who have been injured or had property damaged as a result of an action or inaction by the insured. This responsibility may (1) arise out of negligence, (2) be imposed by law, or (3) be assumed by contract.

## TYPES OF INJURY OR DAMAGE ARISING FROM LIABILITY

**Bodily Injury**   As used in liability insurance, bodily injury means bodily harm, sickness, or disease, including required care, loss of services, loss of income, and death that results therefrom to a person other than the insured.

**Property Damage**   For purposes of liability insurance, property damage means injury to, destruction of, or loss of use of tangible property. It also may include loss of use of tangible property that has not been physically injured.

**Personal Injury**   As used in liability insurance, personal injury means injury to one's mental or emotional well-being arising out of one or more of the following offenses:

- false arrest, detention or imprisonment, or malicious prosecution;
- libel, slander, or defamation of character; or
- invasion of privacy, wrongful eviction, or wrongful entry.

**Advertising Injury**   Advertising injury is injury arising out of any of the following:

- oral or written publication of material that slanders or libels a person or an organization or that disparages a person's or an organization's goods, products, or services;
- oral or written publication of material that violates a person's right of privacy;
- misappropriation of advertising ideas or style of doing business; or
- infringement of copyright, title, or slogan.

> **TAKE NOTE**
>
> The four types of injury that arise from liability—bodily injury, property damage, personal injury, and advertising injury—represent the coverage typically provided by a personal or business liability policy.

## RIGHT AND DUTY TO DEFEND

The insurer has the right and duty to defend any claim or suit against the insured seeking damages payable under the policy, even though the suit's allegations may be groundless, false, or fraudulent. The insurer may investigate and settle any claim or suit as it deems expedient. The insurer is not obligated to pay any claim or judgment or to defend any suit after the applicable limit of the insurer's liability has been exhausted by payment of judgments or settlements.

**Supplementary Payments**    The insurer pays, in addition to the applicable limit of liability, costs to defend and provide first aid as common to liability insurance. This amount is paid outside of the limits of liability. Other supplementary payments may include:

- bonds—cost of judicial bonds (bail and appeal);

- aid—first aid expenses at the scene of an accident with no limit;

- interest—interest on judgments against the insured with no limit;

- loss of earnings—wage loss while assisting the insurer in the defense or investigation of a claim (amount will vary by policy);

- expenses incurred at the request of the insurer—paid with no limit; and

- defense and investigation costs—paid with no limit.

## NEGLIGENCE AND LIABILITY

Wrongs that an individual may commit can be classified into two categories. The first is a *public wrong* or a *criminal act*. This is a wrong against society, such as murder or arson, that is punishable by the courts.

The second type of wrong that an individual can commit is a *private or civil wrong*, which is an infringement by one person on the rights of another individual. This infringement also is called a *tort*.

**EXAMPLE**    You have the right to drive down the street in your car. You do not have the right to drive at an excessive speed (criminal wrong) and strike another vehicle or pedestrian (tort), causing injury or damage.

These rights and duties arise from *common law*, case law (rulings by judges or court decisions), the constitution, legislative statute, or regulation. Remedies for persons whose rights are infringed upon include direct reasonable action or judicial and civil action, which may include a monetary award, an injunction, or restitution.

**Negligence**  The legal doctrine of *negligence* is based on the principal that every person has a duty to act carefully toward others and in a manner that does not injure others. Negligence arises from the failure of a person to fulfill this duty. It is the failure to do something that a reasonable person under similar circumstances would do. It also is the act of doing something that a reasonable person under similar circumstances would *not* do.

**Contributory Negligence**  Just as people have a duty to act carefully toward others to avoid injuring them, people also have a duty to protect themselves from injury. In some states, a person who is sued for negligence may raise the defense of *contributory negligence*, arguing that the plaintiff's own negligence was a proximate cause of his injury.

**Comparative Negligence**  Most states have *comparative negligence* statutes, under which the extent of a person's negligence is measured in terms of a percentage. A person who suffered personal injury or property damage may sue to recover the costs of the damage. If the person sues another party for money damages and wins, the amount of the award will be reduced by the percentage of that person's own comparative fault, or negligence. Some states will apportion the award strictly according to these percentages.

## SUMMARY

The earliest forms of property insurance include fire and marine insurance. Casualty products include general liability, auto insurance, workers' compensation, crime coverage, and bonds. The product lines are further divided among personal and commercial lines. There are many provisions common to property and liability insurance policies.

Property and liability insurance is often combined into a single, package policy. Peril forms dictate the kinds of losses a property policy will handle. While named-peril policies list the perils that are covered by the contract, open-peril policies will cover any losses not specifically excluded by the contract.

# U N I T   Q U I Z

1. If an insured suffered a loss of one earring from a pair, the insurance company probably would offer to settle in which of the following ways?

   A. Pay the entire value of the pair of earrings
   B. Pay a portion of the total value
   C. Pay ¹⁄₁₀ of the value on the basis that one earring remains
   D. Pay nothing because the entire set was not lost

2. An insured owns a commercial building with a value of $100,000. He takes out an insurance policy for $60,000 with an 80% coinsurance clause and later suffers a $12,000 loss. Based on this information, he will be paid

   A. $7,200
   B. $9,000
   C. $9,600
   D. $12,000

3. Which of the following is the purpose of coinsurance?

   A. To encourage an insured to carry insurance equal to a high percentage of his property's value
   B. To allow rate credits for high amounts of insurance
   C. To punish an insured for not knowing the insurable value of a building
   D. To make an insured share in every loss to encourage loss control

4. A limit in a liability policy that includes coverage under both bodily injury and property damage is called a(n)

   A. single limit
   B. blanket limit
   C. aggregate limit
   D. combined single limit

5. Which of the following describes an aggregate limit?

   A. Maximum amount payable in any policy year
   B. Maximum amount of insurance that can be purchased
   C. Limit that applies to bodily injury claims
   D. Maximum amount of any occurrence

6. Under a property insurance policy, the insured receives what type of payment that takes into account physical depreciation?

   A. Replacement cost
   B. Market value
   C. Actual cash value
   D. Appraised value

7. For insurance purposes, when a building is completely void of any furnishings or equipment, it is considered

   A. vacant
   B. unoccupied
   C. occupied
   D. abandoned

8. A clause in a policy that automatically adjusts the amount of insurance when building costs increase is called a(n)

   A. inflation guard
   B. escalation clause
   C. building cost modifier
   D. agreed value clause

9. Advertising injury involves which of the following?

   A. Oral or written publication of material that slanders or libels a person or an organization
   B. Oral or written material that violates a person's right of privacy
   C. Misappropriation of advertising ideas or style of doing business
   D. All of the above

10. The inability to recover damages when a person is partially responsible for his own injuries or damage is a legal doctrine called

    A. last clear chance
    B. negligence per se
    C. comparative negligence
    D. contributory negligence

11. Which of the following statements best describes subrogation?

    A. The insurer claims the insured's right to sue a third party.
    B. The insurer claims the right to collect damages from the insured.
    C. The insured claims the right to collect from a third party.
    D. The insurer claims the right to collect from a third party.

12. Company X and Company Y each carry $100,000 Building and Personal property coverage on a building. If there is a $10,000 loss, how much would each company pay?

    |   | Company X | Company Y |
    |---|---|---|
    | A. | $0 | $10,000 |
    | B. | $5,000 | $5,000 |
    | C. | $10,000 | $10,000 |
    | D. | $10,000 | $0 |

13. Which of the following statements best describes open-peril policies?

    A. The insurer will pay for any type of damage a property sustains.
    B. The insurer will pay only for losses from the specific perils listed.
    C. The insurer will pay only for those losses specifically excluded by the policy.
    D. The insurer will not provide coverage for those perils specifically excluded by the policy.

14. All of the following perils are covered by basic peril form EXCEPT

    A. windstorm
    B. pipes freezing or bursting
    C. hail
    D. fire

15. Monica owns a $150,000 home. She carries two insurance policies on it; Company A insures $100,000 and Company B insures $50,000. If she suffers a loss to her home of $9,000, how much will Company A pay her?

    A. $9,000
    B. $6,000
    C. $4,500
    D. $3,000

# ANSWERS AND RATIONALES TO UNIT QUIZ

1. **B.** A policy's pair and set clause takes into account the value of the items before the loss and their residual value following the loss, providing payment to the insured of a portion of the total value.

2. **B.** A building valued at $100,000 requires insurance of $80,000 (80% of $100,000) to comply with the coinsurance provision. Because in this case the insured purchased only $60,000 of coverage, the insurer will pay $60,000/$80,000 or (¾) of each loss. Three-fourths of $12,000 is $9,000.

3. **A.** Because most losses are small, insureds may be inclined to carry only minimal insurance, resulting in rate inequities. Through the use of a coinsurance clause, insurance companies encourage policyholders to carry an amount of insurance closer to the full value of their properties.

4. **D.** A liability policy that contains one limit for two types of losses, such as bodily injury and property damage, is called a *combined single limit.*

5. **A.** The maximum amount that a liability policy will pay in a given policy period, regardless of the number of claims submitted, is the aggregate limit.

6. **C.** The definition of actual cash value is replacement cost of the property minus physical deterioration.

7. **A.** A building that is without enough furnishings to conduct the operations for which it is intended is considered vacant.

8. **A.** An inflation guard often is added to a property insurance policy to offset the increases that occur in building costs during the policy year.

9. **D.** Advertising injury involves each of the items listed as well as infringement of copyright, title, or slogan.

10. **D.** Through the defense of contributory negligence, any negligence on the part of the injured party that contributed to his own injury will defeat or reduce the amount that the injured party can collect.

11. **A.** Property and liability policies include a condition referred to as subrogation, which is designed to keep the insured from being able to collect twice for the same loss. If the insured receives a settlement from his insurer and also has a right to recover against a third party who negligently caused the loss, the policy indicates that this right of recovery is transferred to the insurer.

12. **B.** The Commercial Property Conditions, which is part of the Building and Personal Property Coverage Form, provides that the insured may have other insurance that is subject to the same plan, terms, conditions, and provisions as this insurance. If there are other applicable policies, each policy will pay the pro rata share that its limit of liability bears to the total limit of liability of all policies. Thus, if Company X and Company Y each provide $100,000 of coverage (a total of $200,000), each share is half of the loss. Therefore, each will pay half of the $10,000 loss, or $5,000.

13. **D.** Open peril policies will cover all losses except those specifically excluded under the contract.

14. **B.** Pipes freezing or bursting are covered as a broad form (not basic) peril.

15. **B.** When two policies will cover the same loss, each company will pay their proportional (pro-rated) share of the claim. In this example, Company A insures ⅔ of the property's value, and will pay ⅔ of the claim.

# 15

# Homeowners Policies

## KEY CONCEPTS

- The pre-packaged nature of the homeowners policy
- Eligibility requirements
- Persons and property insured through the homeowners policy
- Property coverages, exclusions, conditions, and endorsements
- Liability coverages, exclusions, conditions, and endorsements

Following the passage of multiple-line legislation, the homeowners policy was introduced to provide a package or bundle of coverages that owners of residential property typically need. This was meant to be a single, indivisible contract that provides the coverage every homeowner requires. Policies for tenants of rented buildings and condominium unit owners followed, each designed for the unique exposures they presented.

A homeowners policy is relatively inflexible, meaning the coverages and limits have been predetermined and may be changed only by endorsement to the policy. Despite this inflexibility, homeowners policies offer the following advantages to policyholders:

- broader protection;
- single policy document;
- lower cost;
- one agent and insurance company; and
- single expiration date.

## OBJECTIVE

When you complete this unit, you should be able to:

- identify the types of policies available under the homeowners program and compare them in terms of covered property, covered causes of loss, and loss settlement provisions;
- determine who is an insured under a homeowners policy;
- determine whether coverage would apply to a specific situation under Section I—Property—of the homeowners policy;
- describe endorsements to Section I of the homeowners policy; and
- determine whether coverage would apply to a specific situation under Section II—Liability—of the Homeowners Policy;
- describe endorsements to Section II of the homeowners policy; and
- identify the method of providing coverage for owners of mobile homes.

# HOMEOWNERS COVERAGE

The homeowner policies used by most insurers today are standardized contracts developed by the Insurance Services Office (ISO). ISO is a private, non-profit organization that develops and provides standardized and state-specific forms, rates, and inspections for its members. Insurers will often purchase the rights to use an ISO policy, and then alter the policies. Throughout this and subsequent units, we will examine the standard ISO policies in use. While your own company may employ a modified version of these contracts, your license exam will test the standard forms.

Currently, four different forms are available for homeowners and one each for tenants and condominium owners. To be eligible for coverage under one of the homeowners policy forms, a dwelling must be (1) occupied by the owner (owner-occupied) and (2) a one-family or two-family building. Minnesota allows 1–4 unit residential structures to be insured through HO contracts with the condition that one unit is owner occupied.

*Coverage Parts for HO-1, HO-2, HO-3, HO-8*

### Section I—Property Coverage Form

|  | HO-1 and HO-8 | HO-2 and HO-3 |
|---|---|---|
| Coverage A  Dwelling | Declared Value | Declared Value |
| Coverage B  Other Structures/ Appurtenant Structures | 10% of Coverage A | 10% of Coverage A |
| Coverage C  Personal Property | 50% of Coverage A | 50% of Coverage A |
| Coverage D  Loss of Use | 10% of Coverage A | 30% of Coverage A |

### Section II—Liability Coverage

|  |  |
|---|---|
| Coverage E  Personal Liability | Minimum all forms $100,000 |
| Coverage F  Medical Payments | Minimum all forms $1,000 |

*Coverage Parts for Tenant and Condominium Owners Forms*

### Section I—Property Coverage Form

|  | HO-4 Tenant | HO-6 Condo |
|---|---|---|
| Coverage A  Dwelling | Not Covered | Declared Value |
| Coverage B  Other Structures | Not Covered | Part of Coverage A |
| Coverage C  Personal Property | $6,000 minimum | $6,000 minimum |
| Coverage D  Loss of Use | 30% of Coverage C | 50% of Coverage C |

### Section II—Liability Coverage

|  |  |
|---|---|
| Coverage E  Personal Liability | Same as for Other Forms |
| Coverage F  Medical Payments | Same as for Other Forms |

The four forms are:

- HO-1 Basic Form (withdrawn from use in many states);

- HO-2 Broad Form;

- HO-3 Special Form; and

- HO-8 Modified Form for Special Risks (based on value or construction).

The HO-1 Basic Form is not purchased with enough regularity to support its continued use. Therefore, it has been withdrawn from use in many states and replaced by HO-8. The HO-8 policy is intended for owners of dwellings who do not wish, or find it difficult to insure, their older properties on a replacement cost basis because replacement cost would far exceed the market value. In addition, the form can be used for homes of unusual construction that may be difficult to value. Losses are settled on an actual cash value basis, and coverages are similar but in some cases more restrictive than an HO-1 Basic Form. Additional restrictions apply on theft coverage and property away from the premises.

An HO-5 Comprehensive Form was eliminated due to the substitution of an endorsement added to the HO-3 that duplicated the coverage this separate form provided. This endorsement and its application to the HO-3 are discussed below.

The forms for coverage for tenants and condominium owners are:

■ HO-4 Tenant's or Renter's; and

■ HO-6 Condominium Owner's (also includes town home owners).

Homeowners policies have two major coverage sections. Section I contains the property insurance and in many ways is similar to the coverages of the dwelling program. Section II of the homeowners program provides personal liability and medical payments to others coverages. Unlike the dwelling policies, however, a homeowners policy is an indivisible package of coverage, so all policies contain both sections. The pricing of a homeowners policy is determined largely by the limit selected for Coverage A Dwelling. In fact, the insured is not asked to determine limits for other coverages under the policy because they are percentages of the Coverage A (or Coverage C) limit.

## POLICY PROVISIONS AND REQUIREMENTS

**Risks Not Eligible** Certain risks are not eligible for coverage by any of the forms, though coverage can be obtained through other means.

■ Farms: A farmowners policy can be used.

■ Mobile homes: These can be covered by endorsement to a homeowners policy, by mobile home-owners policy, or by dwelling form.

■ Buildings that are not owner-occupied: These can be covered by another policy designed to fit the use to which the owner puts the property.

**Definitions** The following terms arise in the context of these policies.

■ *Bodily injury* means bodily harm, sickness, or disease, including death that results from these and care or loss of services.

■ *Business* includes a trade, a profession, or an occupation.

■ *Occurrence* means an accident, including repeated or continuous exposure to harmful conditions that results in bodily injury or property damage.

■ *Property damage* means physical injury to or loss of use or destruction of tangible property.

■ *Residence employee* means a domestic employee of the insured on the residence premises or off premises if not related to a business.

■ *Residence premises* means the single-family dwelling, other structures or grounds insured or the part of any other building where the insured resides and that is shown in the declarations. It also includes a two-four family dwelling when the insured resides in one unit if that dwelling is shown in the declarations. (This definition is modified in the HO-6.)

**Persons Insured/Insured** For Section I—Property, the insured is the person named on the declarations page and:

■ a spouse if she resides in the same household; and

■ residents of the household who are relatives of the named insured (including full-time students under age 24), or other persons younger than age 21 and in the insured's care.

For Section II—Liability, an insured also includes:

■ any animal owned by the insured or other persons as described above;

■ watercraft, as described in the policy, owned by the insured or other persons as described above; and

■ any person legally responsible for this animal or watercraft, but not someone who has custody in the course of business, such as a veterinarian, or without the owner's consent, such as a thief.

**Insured Location** The insured location is specifically defined on the declarations page and can be any of the following:

■ Residence premises as defined;

■ Other premises described in the declarations and used by the insured as a residence;

■ Premises acquired by the named insured or a spouse during the policy term and used by the insured as a residence;

■ Nonowned premises at which an insured temporarily resides or occasionally rents to an insured for other-than-business use;

■ Vacant land, other than farmland the insured owns or rents;

■ Land the insured owns or rents on which a dwelling is being built as a residence for the insured; or

■ The insured's individual or family cemetery plots or burial vaults.

# THE 2000 ISO HOMEOWNERS POLICY

## SECTION I—PROPERTY

In a homeowners policy, Section I defines the limits payable to the insured for covered loss of property. This coverage is referred to as Coverage A: Dwelling, Coverage B: Other Structures, Coverage C: Personal Property, and Coverage D: Loss of Use.

**Coverage A: Dwelling** A covered structure is any

■ dwelling on the residence premises, including structures attached to the dwelling (such as an attached garage); or

■ materials and supplies located on or next to the premises that are intended for use in the construction, alteration, or repair of the building.

The homeowners policy specifically excludes land, including the land on which the dwelling is located.

**Coverage B: Other Structures** Other structures on the premises include those set apart from the dwelling by clear space, such as detached garages, fences, swimming pools, or storage sheds. Structures connected to the dwelling by only a fence, utility wire, or similar connection are considered unattached.

Excluded from coverage are buildings used in whole or in part for business purposes and buildings rented to anyone other than a tenant, except if used only for private garage purposes.

**Coverage C: Personal Property** Covered personal property includes:

- personal property the insured owns or uses that is located anywhere in the world;

- personal property of others at the insured's request while it is on the portion of the residence premises the insured occupies;

- personal property of a guest or residence employee when it is located in any residence the insured occupies; and

- personal property usually located in a secondary residence (limited to 10% of Coverage C).

Personal property not covered includes:

- articles described and insured separately elsewhere in this or another policy;

- animals, birds, and fish;

- motor vehicles, unless used to maintain the premises or assist the handicapped; this exclusion would apply to

  — automobiles,

  — motorcycles,

  — ATVs,

  — go-carts,

  — golf carts (liability is covered in Section II when the golf cart is used to play golf on a golf course), and

  — owned snowmobiles;

- aircraft and parts, except model or hobby aircraft;

- property of renters, boarders, or other tenants unrelated to the insured;

- property in an apartment the insured rents to others

- property rented or held for rental to others away from the residence premises; and

- credit cards or fund transfer cards, except as provided under Additional Coverages.

Special loss limits, maximums, and aggregates of certain property apply (they do not increase the Coverage C limit):

- $200 on money, bullion, bank notes, and the like;

- $1,500 on securities, deeds, valuable papers, manuscripts, tickets, personal records, and stamps;

- $1,500 on watercraft, including trailers, motors, and equipment in storage;

- $1,500 on trailers other than those used with watercraft;

- $1,500 on furs, watches, jewelry, and precious and semiprecious stones (*theft only*);

- $2,500 on firearms (*theft only*);

- $2,500 on silverware, goldware (both solid and plated), and pewterware (*theft only*);

- $2,500 on business property on the residence premises;

- $500 on business property away from the residence premises; and

- $1,500 for personal electronics in a vehicle.

Special provisions for theft coverage are as follows:

- Theft coverage is included on all forms and applies to Coverages A, B, and C.

- Theft is defined as loss of property from a known place under circumstances in which a probability of theft exists. Mysterious disappearance is not included in the definition of theft.

**Coverage D: Loss of Use**  Coverage D provides protection when the residence cannot be used because of an insured loss. For that part of the residence premises where the insured resides, the following may be applied at the insured's choice:

- the necessary increase in additional living expense the insured incurred in order to continue his normal standard of living following a loss by an insured peril;

- coverage for prohibited use if the insured cannot use the dwelling for two weeks because of a loss to a neighboring premises by a peril insured against in this policy; or

- the fair rental value of that part of the premises where the insured resides. For that part of the premises rented or held for rental to others, the fair rental value may be applied.

---

**EXAMPLE**    The cost to relocate to a hotel while fire damage is being repaired is covered as an additional living expense because it represents an extraordinary expense to the insured, over and above the normal mortgage payment.

The coverage period is limited to the:

- shortest time required to repair or replace the insured property; and

- time required for the insured to move into permanent housing.

## SECTION I—ADDITIONAL COVERAGES

The ISO homeowners policy provides the following extensions of coverage:

- *Ordinance or law*—10% of Coverage A limits available to cover increased costs of repair or reconstruction due to zoning laws or building ordinances that require upgrades after a loss.

■ *Debris removal*—the cost to remove debris after a loss, including ash, dust, or particles from a volcanic eruption that has caused direct loss to a building or property. If the applicable limits have been exhausted, the insurer will pay an additional 5% (of applicable limits) towards debris removal.

■ *Reasonable repairs*—the reasonable cost of necessary repairs made solely to protect property from further damage.

■ *Trees, shrubs, and other plants*—5% of the limit on Coverage A, subject to a maximum of $500 for any one tree, shrub, or plant. This applies only to the limited specified perils of fire, lightning, explosion, riot, or civil commotion, aircraft, vehicles not owned or operated by a resident of the premises, vandalism, or malicious mischief or theft.

■ *Fire department service charge*—up to $500 for liability assumed for fire department charges to save or protect covered property from a peril insured against, if the fire department is from another community. No deductible applies.

■ *Building additions and alterations*

— HO-4 covers the insured's interest in additions, alterations, fixtures, improvements, or installments as an extension of Coverage C, but not to exceed 10% of coverage C.

— HO-6 grants $1,000 for additions, alterations, and betterments.

■ *Credit card, fund transfer card, forgery, and counterfeit money*—covered to a maximum of $500 if the card is stolen or the insured accepts counterfeit money unknowingly.

■ *Property removed*—covers loss to property while being removed from a premises endangered by a peril insured against for up to 30 days.

■ *Loss assessment*—up to $1,000 for any loss assessment charged against the named insured because of loss to property owned collectively by a corporation or an association.

## EXCLUSIONS TO SECTION I

The general exclusions applicable to the property coverage under the homeowners forms include the following:

■ *Ordinance or law.* Coverage does not apply to the enforcement of any law or ordinance that regulates the construction, repair, or demolition of a building or another structure unless that coverage is provided specifically elsewhere in the policy.

■ *Earth movement.* Excluded are earthquakes, including the land shock waves or earth movement caused by a volcanic eruption, landslide, mine subsidence, mudflow, and earth sinking, rising, or shifting. Coverage is provided if a fire or explosion follows, but only for the damage the ensuing loss causes.

■ *Water damage.* Coverage does not apply to loss due to flood, surface water, waves, tidal water, overflow of a body of water, or the spray from any of these situations, whether or not wind-driven. Coverage also does not apply to water that backs up through sewers or drains or that overflows from a sump, nor to water below the surface of the ground that seeps or leaks through buildings or other structures.

■ *Power failure.* A utility failure off the residence premises is not covered unless an insured peril results on the residence premises, and then coverage applies only to that ensuing loss.

■ *Neglect.* The insured must use reasonable means to protect covered property from further damage. Failure to do so results in denial of the claim.

■ *War.*

■ *Nuclear hazard.*

## CONDITIONS TO SECTION I

When a loss has occurred, the insured has certain duties to the insurer. The insurer can exercise numerous options in settling the claim.

■ The insured's duties after a loss include reporting claims, obtaining police reports for theft losses, preparing inventories, displaying damaged property, and submitting to examination under oath.

■ Settlement for a loss to a pair or set is based on the difference between the value of the pair or set before the loss and the value after the loss.

■ Glass replacement is settled based on replacement with safety glazing materials.

■ Appraisal is required if a dispute occurs as to the amount of a loss.

■ Other insurance provisions require settlement on a pro rata basis if two or more policies apply to the same loss.

■ A suit against the insurer may be commenced only after compliance with all policy conditions and within 2 years of the loss.

■ An insurer has the option of repairing or replacing damaged or destroyed property if it gives the policyholder notice within 30 days of the claim.

■ Loss payments are to be made within 60 days of receiving proof of loss.

■ The policy does not allow abandonment of property to the insurer.

■ A mortgage or loss payable clause provides certain rights to lienholders of property, including the right to make premium payments and receive claim payments, even if the insured causes a loss intentionally.

■ A no-benefit-to-bailee provision means that an individual or organization that has insured property in care, custody, or control is not an insured under this policy.

■ Recovered property, at the insured's option, can be turned over to the insured, in which case the insurer adjusts the settlement made previously with the insured.

**Deductibles** Each of the forms contains a standard deductible clause of $250. Other deductibles are available. The deductible is applied once against any loss Coverages A, B, or C covers and applies per occurrence.

**Valuation-Recovery Considerations/Loss Settlement** Replacement cost applies to all buildings (except those covered by HO-8) and will be paid up to the *lesser* of the:

■ policy limit;

■ replacement cost of that part of the building damaged on the same premises; or

■ necessary amount actually spent to repair or replace the property.

If an insured fails to carry coverage of at least 80% of replacement cost, he  is responsible for part of the loss. This insurance-to-value provision is calculated by using this formula:

Policy Limit

Replacement Cost × 80% × Loss (– Deductible) = Amount Covered

Failure to carry insurance of at least 80% of the replacement cost value (insurance-to-value clause) results in the payment of the *greater* of the:

■ actual cash value; or

■ result from dividing the amount of insurance on the building by 80% of the replacement cost of the building, then multiplying that amount by the actual cost to repair or replace the damaged part of the building, then subtracting the deductible.

**EXAMPLE**

If a home's replacement cost at the time of a loss is $100,000, the insured must carry a limit of at least $80,000 to receive a replacement cost settlement. If the limit is $75,000, the company pays either the quotient of $75,000 divided by 80,000 for the replacement cost of the loss or the actual cash value, whichever is greater.

Personal property and other items are settled on an actual cash value basis.

## ENDORSEMENTS TO SECTION I

Endorsements to the property portion of the homeowners policy include the following:

■ *Special personal property coverage.* This is perhaps the most important of the homeowners policy endorsements. The endorsement may be attached to an HO-3 policy only, and when added converts the Coverage C causes of loss from broad to special form. This endorsement eliminated the need for the HO-5 form, which provided the same coverage.

■ *Personal property replacement cost.* Without endorsement, losses to personal property are settled on an actual cash value basis. This endorsement changes the valuation basis for Coverage C to replacement cost, with few exceptions.

■ *Other structures—increased limits.* This endorsement allows an increase in the Coverage B limit beyond the 10% provided automatically.

■ *Scheduled personal property.* Broader coverage for personal jewelry, furs, cameras, musical instruments, silverware, fine art, golf equipment, and stamp or coin collections may be provided by attaching an endorsement instead of writing a separate personal articles floater policy. Articles must be described and insured on a full value basis.

■ *Increased limit on business property.* If the insured maintains a home office, the $2,500 special loss limit for business property may be inadequate. This endorsement allows an increase in the limit, but does not apply to property pertaining to a business conducted on the residence premises or to property in storage or held as a sample for sale or delivery after a sale.

- *Earthquake*. If coverage is desired for earthquake, this endorsement should be attached to the homeowners policy.

- *Water back-up and sump overflow*. Unendorsed homeowners policies exclude coverage for water that backs up through sewers and drains or that overflows from a sump. This important coverage can be purchased with this endorsement. Coverage is limited to $5,000. A separate $250 deductible applies to losses.

## SECTION II—LIABILITY COVERAGES

In a homeowners policy, Section II defines the liability coverages payable to someone other than the insured. These coverages are known as Coverage E: Personal Liability Limit and Coverage F: Medical Payments to Others. Section II coverages are the same in all forms. These coverages are substantially the same as those provided in the Personal Liability supplement to the dwelling program.

**Coverage E: Personal Liability**   The insurer agrees to pay on the insured's behalf all sums up to the limit of liability that the insured becomes legally obligated to pay as damages because of bodily injury or property damage. The insurer also agrees to defend the insured in a lawsuit, even if the suit is fraudulent. The insurer may investigate and settle any claim it deems appropriate. The minimum limit is $100,000, but it can be increased. The cost of defense is in addition to the limit of liability.

**Coverage F: Medical Payments to Others**   The insurer agrees to pay all reasonable medical expenses (normally $1,000 per person) incurred within three years from the date of an accident to or for each person who sustains bodily injury to which the insurance applies, when such person is:

- on the insured premises with the insured's permission; or

- off the insured premises, if such bodily injury

  - is caused by the insured's activities or by a residence employee in the course of his employment by the insured,

  - is caused by an animal owned by or in the care of any insured, or

  - is caused by any residence employee and arises out of an act in the course of employment by the insured.

Coverage does not apply to the insured or regular residents of the insured's household. Coverage is paid without regard to fault or negligence. Therefore, it is a type of no fault coverage.

## SECTION II—ADDITIONAL COVERAGES

Coverage may also extend to property damage suffered by others, legal expenses, and first aid expenses for other parties to an accident.

- *Damage to property of others*—physical damage to property of others up to $1,000 per occurrence. This applies (1) even if the insured is not legally liable or (2) the property is in the insured's care, custody, or control.

- *Claim expenses*—no limit on legal and other costs the insurer incurs. The insurer pays only a maximum of $50 per day reimbursement to the insured for loss of earnings while assisting in claims settlement.

- *First aid expenses*—no limit for first aid expenses incurred at the time of an accident for persons other than the insured.

## SECTION II—EXCLUSIONS

With respect to Coverage E and F, the policy excludes coverage for bodily injury or property damage arising out of:

■ ownership, maintenance, use, loading, or unloading of motorized vehicles and aircraft; and

■ such use or operation of all motor vehicles or other motorized land conveyances, including trailers, owned or operated by or rented or loaned to the insured.

However, this exclusion does not apply to the following:

■ motorized golf cart when used to play golf on a golf course; or

■ vehicle used for service of an insured's residence or designed for assisting the handicapped or is in storage on an insured location.

Coverage also does not apply the ownership, operation, maintenance, use, loading, unloading, or entrustment of an excluded watercraft. Excluded watercraft include:

■ boats owned by the insured with inboard or inboard-outboard motors or rented by the insured with inboard or inboard-outboard motors exceeding 50 HP;

■ sailboats 26 feet in length or longer; and

■ boats with outboard motors exceeding 25 HP.

This confusing exclusion is meant to eliminate coverage for many types of watercraft, and yet there are many types covered by operation. The following types of powerplants and vessels *are* covered:

| Type of Engine/Vessel | Specifications | Relationship to Insured |
|---|---|---|
| Inboard or Inboard-Outboard Motor | ≤ 50 HP <br> ≥ 50 HP | Rented or Borrowed <br> Borrowed |
| Outboard Motor | ≤ 25 HP <br> ≥ 25 HP | Owned, Rented, or Borrowed <br> Rented, Borrowed, or Newly Acquired |
| Sailboat | ≤ 26 Long <br> ≥ 26 Long | Owned, Rented, or Borrowed <br> Borrowed |
| Any Type | In storage | Owned, Rented, or Borrowed |

In other words, the policy does not cover owned inboards, but coverage applies to small owned outboards, short owned sailboats, and anything while stored.

**Section II—Exclusions for Coverage E**  With respect to Coverage E liability only, the policy excludes:

■ contractual liability under any oral or written contract or agreement; (However, the exclusion is modified so that the policy covers written contracts that relate to the ownership, maintenance, or use of an insured location or where the insured assumes the liability of others before an occurrence);

■ loss assessments charged against the insured as a member of an association, a corporation, or a community of property owners;

■ bodily injury subject to workers' compensation law or a similar law;

**TAKE NOTE**

The additional residence rented to others endorsement eliminates the need to add the personal liability supplement to a dwelling policy issued to cover the residential structure the insured owns and rents to others.

■ property damage to property the insured owns, occupies, rents or to property in the insured's care, custody, or control; however, the exclusion is again modified so that the policy covers property damage caused by fire, smoke, or explosion, even if occupied by or in the care, custody, or control of the insured (known as *fire legal liability*);

■ loss from nuclear hazards; and

■ bodily injury to the insured.

**Section II—Exclusions for Coverage F**  With respect only to Coverage F, Medical Payments, there is no coverage for bodily injury to any:

■ person subject to a workers' compensation law or similar law;

■ insured;

■ person other than a residence employee residing on the insured premises (such as a boarder); or

■ residence employee if bodily injury occurs off the insured's location and does not arise out of or in the course of the residence employee's employment by the insured.

## CONDITIONS TO SECTION II

With respect to Coverage E and F, the policy includes the following conditions to any claim for bodily injury or property damage.

■ The limit of liability applies per occurrence and does not increase regardless of the number of persons the policy insures.

■ An insured's duties after a loss include giving notice of claims and forwarding any suits or demands.

■ The insured must cooperate in the defense and settlement of any claim.

## ENDORSEMENTS TO SECTION II

Endorsements available under Section II apply to the following:

■ *Personal injury.* This endorsement changes the definition of bodily injury to include false arrest, detention, or imprisonment, malicious prosecution, libel, slander, or defamation of character, invasion of privacy, wrongful eviction, and wrongful entry.

■ *Business pursuits.* This endorsement extends coverage under Section II to any of the insured's business pursuits listed in the endorsement. The endorsement does not apply, however, to businesses the insured owns or controls, to professional liability, or to injuries to fellow employees.

---

**TAKE NOTE**

The mobile homeowners form covers damage from earthquakes. The mobile homeowners form differs from the homeowners policy in some respects, while following it in others.

---

■ *Additional residence rented to others.* This endorsement extends liability and medical payments coverage to a one-family to four-family residence the insured owns and rents to others. The locations must be listed in the endorsement.

## ENDORSEMENTS TO SECTION I AND SECTION II

Some endorsements to the homeowners policy affect both Section I and Section II. Some of the more common endorsements include the following:

■ *Permitted incidental occupancies—residence premises.* This endorsement deletes or modifies the exclusions pertaining to a business under both the policy's property and liability sections. The business must be described in the endorsement and conducted by the insured on the residence premises. The endorsement eliminates the exclusion for other structures used in whole or in part for business, deletes the $2,500 limitation for business property under Coverage C, and eliminates the exclusion for business pursuits under the policy's liability section.

■ *Home day care coverage.* This coverage deletes the exclusion under Coverage B for business use, eliminates the $2,500 restriction on business property under Coverage C, and extends the coverage under Section II to apply to day care operations. The endorsement also changes the limit for Coverage E liability from an occurrence limit to an annual aggregate.

# MOBILE HOME INSURANCE

Mobile homeowners insurance forms are very similar to those presented in the homeowners policy section. Because of this similarity, the description of coverages presented here will be brief. Coverage for a mobile home may be provided by endorsement to a homeowners policy (HO-2 or HO-3).

## COVERAGE

The mobile homeowners form may be written on an open perils basis, and the coverage on the building (the mobile home) is settled on the basis of replacement cost. Additional items of property attached to the mobile home are covered on an ACV basis.

### Distinctions in Coverage
■ Mobile home coverage Section A applies to the building (mobile home), attached structures, utility tanks, and permanently installed items, such as appliances, dressers and cabinets, floor coverings, and similar property if installed on a permanent basis.

■ Mobile home coverage Section B for other structures is similar to the homeowners form.

- Mobile home coverage Section C for personal property generally is written with a limit equal to 40% of Coverage A rather than the 50% specified for homeowners coverage.

- Mobile home coverage Section D, loss of use, is 20% of Coverage A.

- Removal coverage is expanded to provide up to $500 for reasonable expenses incurred in moving the mobile home when threatened by a covered peril.

- The ordinance or law additional coverage (to cover increased costs of repair or reconstruction due to zoning laws or building ordinances that require upgrades after a loss) does not apply to mobile home policies.

## SUMMARY

Homeowners insurance is sold in one of several pre-packaged policies. Homeowners insurance may be used to insure 1–4 unit residential structures that are occupied by the owner of the residence. The homeowners policy protects the dwelling, other structures on the property, and personal property against a variety of perils. The policy will assist homeowners with expenses they incur when their home is uninhabitable after a covered loss and provides owners protection against liability claims.

Property and liability coverage is divided between two sections; letter codes A–F further divide the coverages provided by the policy. The policies define limitations and exclusions that apply. Homeowner policies may be endorsed to provide coverage for losses not otherwise handled by the standard policy.

# UNIT QUIZ

1. Which of the following is NOT automatically included in homeowners coverage?

   A. Personal property
   B. Personal liability
   C. Additional living expense
   D. Personal injury

2. Which homeowners form provides open perils coverage for the dwelling and broad perils coverage for its contents?

   A. HO-1
   B. HO-2
   C. HO-3
   D. HO-8

3. Homeowners policy Coverage A applies to which of the following?

   A. Other structures
   B. The dwelling
   C. Loss of use
   D. Personal property

4. If a dog chews up the insured's fur coat, which of the following homeowners policies provides coverage?

   A. HO-2
   B. HO-3
   C. HO-5
   D. None of the above

5. Homeowners policies contain special limits on each of the following items of property EXCEPT

   A. theft of money, securities, and valuable papers
   B. theft of jewelry, watches, and furs
   C. fire damage to guns and firearms
   D. theft of silverware or goldware

6. Under homeowners policies, what percentage of Coverage A applies to personal property?

   A. 40
   B. 50
   C. 70
   D. 75

7. All of the following are eligible for a homeowners policy EXCEPT

   A. an owner of a mobile home
   B. an owner of a two-family dwelling
   C. an owner of a condominium
   D. an owner of a dwelling under construction

8. Under the homeowners program, which of the following is included as an insured?

   A. Spouse of the named insured who lives in an apartment several blocks away
   B. A 19-year-old exchange student who resides temporarily with the insured
   C. Child of the insured who lives in an apartment on the other side of town
   D. 35-year-old invalid who is cared for by the named insured

9. If an insured's dog bites a neighbor on the neighbor's property, which of the following would pay for the neighbor's injury?

   A. Insured's homeowners policy under the liability section
   B. The neighbor's homeowners property
   C. Insured's homeowners policy under the property section
   D. Insured's homeowners policy under the dwelling section

10. Internal limitations on property covered under a homeowners policy include which of the following?

    A. Antiques and fine art
    B. Money, jewelry, and furs
    C. Furniture and clothes
    D. Appliances and equipment

11. Which of the following is a policy written to cover personal property only?

    A. HO-1
    B. HO-3
    C. HO-4
    D. HO-8

12. Bob has a homeowners policy with a $1,000 deductible. A small fire causes damage of $750. How much will the insurer pay?

    A.  $0
    B.  $250
    C.  $750
    D.  $1,000

13. Coverage A of the 2000 HO policy would provide coverage for all of the following EXCEPT

    A.  the dwelling
    B.  an attached garage
    C.  a backyard gazebo
    D.  an attached deck

14. Homeowners Coverage F covers reasonable medical expenses incurred within how many years of an accident?

    A.  1
    B.  5
    C.  3
    D.  2

15. Which of the following dwelling losses would not be covered by an HO-3?

    A.  A wild boar rampages through the insured premises causing damage to a patio door and several interior walls within the home
    B.  A hail storm damages roof shingles and siding
    C.  The insured premises is partially damaged by fire
    D.  A recently passed city ordinance requires the insured to update the plumbing inside the dwelling

16. Which of the following types of property would be covered by the homeowners policy?

    A.  A lawn tractor that is owned by the insured
    B.  A pet dog that is owned by the insured
    C.  A table saw that is owned by the insured and is being rented to another person
    D.  A television set that is owned by a tenant

1. **D.** Personal injury coverage can be added to the homeowners policy only by endorsement.

2. **C.** The HO-3 policy provides open perils coverage for the dwelling and broad perils coverage for its contents.

3. **B.** Coverage A of the Homeowners policy covers dwellings and attached structures.

4. **D.** Homeowners policies exclude damage to personal property by domestic animals.

5. **C.** The only limitation on firearms under the homeowners policy is a special limit of $2,500 for *theft* of guns and other items. No such limitation exists for fire losses.

6. **B.** Although not a contractual requirement, the homeowners policy includes a limit on Coverage C equal to 50% of the Coverage A limit, unless it has been increased by endorsement.

7. **A.** Eligibility for a Homeowners policy is limited to an owner-occupied one-family or two-family dwelling, the intended owner-occupant of a dwelling under construction, one co-owner occupant of a two-family dwelling, a person occupying and purchasing a home under a sales contract, and a person occupying a dwelling under a life estate.

8. **B.** Persons insured under homeowners policies include the named insured and a spouse if he/she resides in the household, resident relatives, and anyone younger than age 21 in the insured's care.

9. **A.** In this case, the liability section of a homeowners policy, Section II, will pay a neighbor if the insured becomes legally liable for the damages. Liability is extended to damage or injury caused by the insured's pets.

10. **B.** Coverage C has special limitations on personal property that limit the amount payable for a claim.

11. **C.** Because the insured in a rented building has no insurable interest in the structure, tenants' policies provide only coverage for personal property.

12. **A.** Because the amount of the loss ($750) is less than Bob's deductible ($1,000), the insurer will not pay for any of the fire damage. If, however, the damages were more than $1,000, Bob would pay the deductible and the insurer would pay the remaining amount.

13. **C.** A backyard gazebo would be considered an "other structure" and would be covered under Coverage B.

14. **C.** Homeowners Coverage F (medical payments) will pay medical and funeral expenses incurred within 3 years of the loss.

15. **D.** The HO-3 policy provides special form peril coverage for the dwelling (Coverage A). Special form excludes expenses related to building code or ordinance.

16. **A.** Vehicles used to maintain the premises are covered. Pets, property rented to others for a fee (business purpose), and property of renters are excluded from property coverage.

# 16

# Dwelling, Flood, and Farm Policies

## KEY CONCEPTS

- Dwelling policy compared to the homeowners policy
- Eligibility for the dwelling policy
- Dwelling policy forms
- Dwelling policy endorsements

Following multiple-line legislation, the homeowners policy began packaging coverages in a single contract to provide for most of a homeowner's, tenant's, or later, condominium unit owner's insurance needs.

These package policies were discussed in the previous unit. The dwelling fire policy available from Insurance Services Office (ISO) fills a significant need in the marketplace for owners of residential property who otherwise do not qualify for homeowners policies.

## OBJECTIVE

When you complete this unit, you should be able to:

- understand the purpose of the dwelling program and its special characteristics;
- identify the coverages provided under the basic, broad, and special dwelling forms;
- describe the endorsements available under the dwelling program and how they may be used to tailor coverage for an insured;
- explain how a location becomes eligible for national flood insurance;
- describe the coverage a flood policy provides and loss excluded by the policy;
- describe the property a farm policy does and does not cover; and
- explain the unique coverages the farm liability coverage form provides.

# DWELLING COVERAGE

When homeowners insurance is unavailable, an individual may wish to buy a dwelling policy, as in the following situations:

- a residential structure is owned by one person and rented to others (tenant-occupied);
- the dwelling involves certain risks that may not be acceptable to the insurer for homeowners coverage, such as age or value; and
- the dwelling is disclosed as a seasonal dwelling on the application.

The most common use of a dwelling form is to provide coverage for a single-family residential structure that the owner does not occupy but rents to others. Because this is the most common situation, the dwelling policy does not provide theft or liability coverage. The reason for these limitations is simple: If property is stolen from a rented dwelling, it does not belong to the insured, but to the tenant. Liability insurance usually is extended from the insured's homeowners policy using an endorsement. If there is a need to provide either theft or liability coverage under the dwelling program, both coverages are available as endorsements to the basic policy.

## ELIGIBLE PROPERTY

Properties eligible for dwelling coverage include:

- dwellings (except farm dwellings) that are:

    — designed for not more than four families or four apartments; or

    — occupied by not more than five roomers or boarders;

- mobile homes but only those on permanent foundations;

- private outbuildings used in connection with an insured property;
- household and personal property in the above risks; and
- vacant buildings.

## COVERAGE FORMS

**Dwelling Forms**   The dwelling fire (DF) program, first developed in the early 1970s, used the standard fire policy with the attachment of a separate dwelling form. In 1977, a new form was developed—the *dwelling policy* (DP)—a simplified or plain language policy. Unlike the DF program, the DP is a complete policy, not an attachment to the standard fire policy. Three versions of the DP form are available: DP-1 basic, DP-2 broad, and DP-3 special. The Basic and Broad forms of coverage are specified or named perils. DP-3, the Special form, is an open perils policy.

# THE 1989 ISO DWELLING POLICY

## COVERAGES PROVIDED

**Coverage A: Dwelling**   *Coverage A: Dwelling* applies to the dwelling building shown in the declarations, to attached structures, and to service-related equipment and outdoor equipment located on the premises. Coverage also is provided for materials and supplies located on or adjacent to the described location that are to be used in the construction, repair, or alteration of the dwelling or other structures.

**Coverage B: Other Structures**   *Coverage B: Other Structures* applies to real property located on the described location and separated from the dwelling by clear space. Structures that are attached to the dwelling only by a fence, utility line, or similar connection are considered other structures and should be included in Coverage B. Up to 10% of Coverage A is included automatically for other structures in all DP forms, so insureds with minimal exposures may not need to purchase it as a separate item of insurance.

**Coverage C: Personal Property**   *Coverage C: Personal Property* applies to personal property located at the described location that is usual to the occupancy of a dwelling. The property may be owned or used by the insured or family members. Rather than automatically establishing Coverage C limits as percentage of Coverage A, the policyholder selects (declares) the limits for Coverage C. This allows the owner of the rental property to decline coverage when no owned personal property is kept at the residence.

**Coverage D: Fair Rental Value**   Coverages D and E are indirect property coverages and apply only in the event there is a covered loss to other property items insured under the policy.

*Coverage D: Fair Rental Value* pays the fair rental value of the portion of the described location that is rented or held for rental to others at the time of the loss. Fair rental value refers to the market rental value less any expenses that would not continue in the event of a loss, such as utilities.

**Coverage E: Additional Living Expense** *Coverage E: Additional Living Expense* pays those expenses the insured incurs when the property cannot be used following a covered loss. Additional living expenses refers to the increased expenses that must be incurred for the occupants to maintain their normal lifestyles and standards of living. The dwelling must be owner-occupied for Coverage E limits to apply.

The additional coverages the dwelling policy provides, such as 10% for other structures, 10% for tenant's improvements and betterments, and 10% for fair rental value, are included as Additional Coverage under forms DP-2 and DP-3. Under the basic form DP-1, these amounts are included in the limits of liability and thus do not provide additional coverage.

## OTHER COVERAGES

Other extensions of coverage that do not increase the amount of insurance are:
- personal property located anywhere in the world (up to 10% of Coverage C);
- cost of reasonable and temporary repairs;
- property removed from an endangering peril (5 days in DP-1; 30 days in DP-2 and DP-3);
- $500 for fire department service charge

Both the broad and special forms provide additional amounts of insurance for lawns, trees, shrubs, and plants. Coverage is limited to 5% of Coverage A, subject to a sublimit of $500 applicable to any one tree, shrub, or plant.

## ENDORSEMENTS

As noted earlier, the dwelling program is designed for individuals who do not qualify for homeowners policies and, as such, is not intended to be as comprehensive in scope as the homeowners program. Therefore, some coverage must be purchased separately.

**Theft**  Coverage for theft of personal property may be added to any of the DP forms using an endorsement. Broad theft coverage is available only if the insured is an owner-occupant of the dwelling. Coverage is included for theft, including attempted theft, and for vandalism and malicious mischief as a result of a theft or an attempted theft.

**Personal Liability**  The personal liability supplement to the dwelling program is available for those instances when the owner cannot attach coverage to a homeowners policy. When included in the dwelling policy, coverage is essentially the same as Section II of a homeowners policy, discussed in the preceding unit.

# NATIONAL FLOOD INSURANCE

Historically, private insurers have considered floods an uninsurable peril. In 1968, Congress enacted the Housing and Urban Development Act, which included the National Flood Insurance Program. Since then, the program has undergone several major changes in how flood insurance is made available to the public. Beginning in 1983, flood insurance policies could be purchased from private insurers or from the federal government. Currently, more than 100 private insurance companies participate in the Write Your Own Flood Program. These companies issue policies, collect premiums, and handle claims. They are paid a servicing fee for performing these tasks.

However, the federal government fully backs (reinsures) the program, so no company is exposed to an underwriting loss for its participation in the national flood insurance program. The Federal Insurance Administration administers the program under the Federal Emergency Management Agency (FEMA).

## ELIGIBILITY

For land to qualify for national flood insurance, the community in which it is located must meet certain requirements. To participate in the National Flood Insurance Program (NFIP), a community must demonstrate that it is willing to enact land-use restrictions in special flood hazard areas identified by the federal government. These areas have been so-designated because flooding is expected to occur once every 100 years. In other words, a 1% or greater chance exists that the area will suffer a flood.

Two programs are available under the flood insurance program. The emergency program provides coverage, while a community determines the flood plain and develops ordinances to prohibit future building in an area subject to flooding. Then, after the community has accomplished these tasks, the regular program provides coverage. Rate maps prepared by the government distinguish between emergency and regular program areas. These maps are referred to as flood insurance rate maps, or FIRM.

## EMERGENCY PROGRAM

After a community (1) has agreed to but has not yet completed the process to adopt flood control measures, including zoning ordinances that prohibit new construction in the flood plain, and (2) has requested federal assistance and participation in the flood program, residents of the community can participate in the emergency program. The rates property owners pay are subsidized. The federal government also subsidizes the program if losses exceed premiums. Profits exceeding costs and service fees must be turned over to the federal government. The maximum coverage that may be purchased is shown in Figure 16.1.

**FIGURE 16.1   Emergency Program Limits**

|                              | Building   | Contents   |
|------------------------------|------------|------------|
| Single-family home           | $ 35,000   | $ 10,000   |
| Other residential structures | $100,000   | $100,000   |
| Nonresidential structures    | $100,000   | $100,000   |

## REGULAR PROGRAM

To qualify for the **regular program**, the community must have implemented the controls that it planned to adopt in the flood control program it submitted to become eligible for the emergency program. Limits are higher in the regular program than in the emergency program (see Figure 16.2).

**FIGURE 16.2   Regular Program Limits**

|  | Building | Contents |
|---|---|---|
| Single-family home | $250,000 | $100,000 |
| Other residential structures | $250,000 | $100,000 |
| Nonresidential structures | $500,000 | $500,000 |

## DEFINITION OF FLOOD

A flood is defined as a general and temporary condition of partial or complete inundation of normally dry land from:

- overflow of inland or tidal waters;
- unusual and rapid accumulation or run-off of surface waters from any source;
- mudslides and other abnormal flood-related erosions of shorelines; or
- the collapse or destabilization of land along the shore of a lake or another body of water resulting from erosion or the effect of waves or water currents exceeding normal, cyclical levels.

## PROPERTY EXCLUDED

All three flood forms contain lengthy lists of items that are not covered. In some cases, the exclusions pertain to property that typically is not covered by a property insurance policy, such as money, aircraft, and vehicles. In addition, no coverage is provided for:

- personal property in the open;
- contents, machinery, building equipment, finished walls, floors, ceilings, or other improvements in a basement with its floor below grade on all sides;
- fences, retaining walls, seawalls, swimming pools (indoor or outdoor), bulkheads, wharves, piers, bridges, or docks;
- land, lawns, trees, shrubs, plants, or growing crops;
- animals, livestock, birds, or fish;
- underground structures or equipment, including wells and septic systems;
- walks, driveways, or other surfaces outside a building's foundation walls; or
- containers such as gas and liquid tanks.

# FARM COVERAGE

The ISO farm coverages can be written as a farm combination policy that includes property and liability coverages, with a package discount on the property coverage. The farm coverage part also can be included in the CPP if it is combined with at least one other coverage part. When written for a family who lives on and works their own land, the farm coverage part ordinarily is issued as a separate farm combination policy.

## FARM PROPERTY COVERAGE FORM

**Coverage A—Dwellings Coverage**  A insures the policyholder's dwelling, structures attached to the dwelling, and materials and supplies on the premises intended for use in construction, alteration, or repair of the dwelling or attached structures.

**Coverage B—Other Private Structures Appurtenant to Dwelling**  Coverage B of the farm form insures other private structures used in connection with the dwelling. The form permits the insured to apply, as an additional amount of insurance, 10% of the Coverage A limit to structures used solely as private garages.

**Coverage C—Household Personal Property**  Coverage C in the farm form is similar in most respects to Coverage C in the homeowners policy. However, the farm Coverage C excludes farm personal property other than office fixtures, furniture, and equipment. Thus, coverage is provided for a farm office located in the home. The excluded farm personal property must be insured using a different form.

**Coverage D—Loss of Use**  Coverage D of the farm property form, like Coverage D of the homeowners policy, provides additional living expense for loss of use of living quarters in the residence premises, as well as the fair rental value of any portion of the dwelling or appurtenant structures covered under Coverage B that is rented to others. This coverage does not provide business interruption or extra expense coverage for farm operations.

## FARM PROPERTY—FARM PERSONAL PROPERTY COVERAGE FORM

**Coverage E—Scheduled Farm Personal Property**  Coverage E can be used to insure 18 classes of farm personal property on a scheduled basis. To be covered, the property must be itemized, and limits must be shown on the declarations. If the insured wants blanket coverage on farm personal property, it can be provided under Coverage F (see below).

Some of the types of property insured under Coverage E are grain, hay, farm products, farm machinery, equipment, and supplies, livestock and other animals, portable buildings and structures, and computers used as aids in farm management.

The policy definition of *farm business property* includes animals, equipment, supplies, and products of farming or ranching operations, including but not limited to feed, seed, fertilizer, livestock, poultry, grain, produce, and agricultural machinery, vehicles, and equipment. Several types of property are excluded from this broad definition, such as household property, racehorses, crops, and automobiles. Most of the excluded property may be insured elsewhere in the farm policy.

**Coverage F—Contrasted with Coverage E** Coverage F is written with a single blanket limit, in contrast to a separate limit for each class of property or item scheduled under Coverage E. The blanket approach of Coverage F is less complicated and less likely to leave the insured inadequately protected.

## OTHER FARM STRUCTURES COVERAGE FORM

**Coverage G—Farm Buildings and Structures** Coverage G's principle purpose is to insure farm buildings and structures other than dwellings for a single blanket limit shown in the declarations. In addition, other items can be covered for separate limits:

- barns, granaries, cribs, hog houses, and silos described individually;
- portable buildings and structures;
- all fences (other than field and pasture fences), corrals, pens, chutes, and feed racks;
- outdoor radio and television equipment, antennas, masts, and towers;
- tenants' improvements and betterments; and
- building materials and supplies for use in building, altering, or repairing farm buildings or structures kept on or adjacent to the insured location.

## FARM LIABILITY COVERAGE FORM (FL 00 20 09)

Like the ISO farm property coverage form, the ISO farm liability coverage form contains elements of both commercial liability and personal liability insurance. In format, the farm liability form resembles the commercial general liability coverage form with separate coverage sections for bodily injury and property damage liability, personal and advertising injury liability, and medical payments. However, many provisions of the commercial general liability coverage form are amended to match the personal liability coverage found in the homeowners policy or to address the specific liability exposures of farming operations.

**Mobile Agricultural Machinery and Equipment Coverage Form** The mobile agricultural machinery and equipment coverage form insures eligible equipment for special causes of loss subject to policy limitations and exclusions.

**Livestock Coverage Form** The livestock coverage form is a named peril form, insuring loss resulting in the death or destruction of livestock caused by the basic causes of loss (except vehicles). Livestock coverage may be extended to include death or destruction by accidental shooting, drowning, electrocution, attack by dogs or wild animals, loading or unloading accidents, and building collapse.

# SUMMARY

The Dwelling policy provides property insurance protection to properties ineligible for coverage under the Homeowner policies. Vacation homes and rental properties are typically insured through these policies. While the Dwelling policy has much in common with Homeowner contracts, liability and theft coverage must be provided separately.

The Farm policy provides comprehensive property and liability insurance to farm owners, addressing their personal and commercial insurance needs. The National Flood Insurance Program allows consumers to buy flood insurance through private insurance companies. Flood insurance provides some limited protection not offered by standard property and casualty contracts.

# UNIT QUIZ

1. Which of the following statements about flood insurance is CORRECT?

   A. It is available only through the government.
   B. It can be written on any property anywhere.
   C. It is written by private insurance companies.
   D. It is available only along rivers.

2. Which of the following is excluded from flood insurance?

   A. Overflow of inland waters
   B. Surface water run-off
   C. Mudslide
   D. Sewer backup

3. Which of the following statements describes flood insurance accurately?

   A. It provides federal assistance to communities.
   B. It involves federal coordination of all relief efforts.
   C. Private insurance companies collect premiums and fund losses.
   D. It provides subsidized premiums for residents of eligible communities.

4. What is the maximum limit on contents located in a residential structure under the regular program?

   A. $10,000
   B. $100,000
   C. $250,000
   D. $500,000

5. Which of the following describes the difference between Coverage E and Coverage F of the farm personal property coverage form?

   A. Coverage F is less expensive than Coverage E.
   B. Coverage E is scheduled, and Coverage F is blanket.
   C. Coverage E is special form, and Coverage F is named perils.
   D. Coverage F may be included only when Coverage E is written.

6. Coverage G—Farm Buildings and Structures is designed to cover which of the following?

   A. Structures attached to the farm dwelling
   B. Field and pasture fencing
   C. Private garages on the insured premises
   D. Barns and other farm structures

7. The farm liability form includes coverage for which of the following activities?

   A. All of the insured's business activities
   B. Only farm business activities
   C. Custom farming and all other activities
   D. The insured's farm business and nonbusiness activities

8. Which one of the following statements regarding Dwelling policies is TRUE?

   A. They do not provide special form cause of loss coverage.
   B. They do not automatically include theft coverage.
   C. They may only be written for owner-occupants.
   D. They are no longer used since the advent of homeowners coverage.

9. A dwelling policy is most often used to provide coverage

   A. better than that available under a homeowners policy
   B. for a home that is not eligible for a homeowners policy
   C. at a lower price than a homeowners policy
   D. when the insured cannot obtain full coverage on the dwelling

# ANSWERS AND RATIONALES TO UNIT QUIZ

1. **C.** Although the federal government still issues policies directly for flood insurance, private insurers also participate in the NFIP under the Write Your Own flood program. Flood coverage is available in any designated flood hazard area.

2. **D.** A flood policy specifically excludes backup through sewers unless certain conditions are met.

3. **D.** The federal flood program provides subsidized rates (the rates are not actuarially sound) for all residents of eligible communities.

4. **B.** Under the regular program, the maximum limit on contents of a residential structure is $100,000.

5. **B.** Coverage E provides coverage only for those categories of property listed in the form, while coverage F provides blanket coverage.

6. **D.** Coverage A insures structures attached to the farm dwelling. Field and pasture fencing is specifically excepted from the coverage provided under Coverage G. Private garages are insured under Coverage B.

7. **D.** The farm liability coverage form covers commercial liability [farm business] and personal liability [nonbusiness] (see page 268, Farm Liability Coverage)

8. **B.** Dwelling policies do not automatically include theft coverage since they are typically purchased by a non-occupant owner, and theft is only of concern to the tenant. The coverage may be added by endorsement if needed.

9. **B.** Homeowners forms are package policies that provide both property coverage and liability coverage, while dwelling forms provide only property coverage. The HO policy is usually used for an owner-occupant, while DP policies are usually written for owned property rented to others.

# 17

# Personal Automobile Insurance

## KEY CONCEPTS

- Compensation for auto accident victims
- Auto underwriting considerations
- No-fault law
- Policyholder duties and contract provisions
- Auto policy endorsements

Insurance for automobiles represents one of the largest segments of the property and casualty industry. By far, the most significant portion of automobile insurance premiums is generated by personal insurance policies. Although the premiums earned are large, so are the losses insurers must pay. Automobile accidents account for more than 50,000 deaths each year and millions of dollars in property damage. Many states have enacted laws making automobile insurance a legal necessity to operate a motor vehicle.

## OBJECTIVE

When you complete this unit, you should be able to:

- describe the various methods used to compensate auto accident victims;

- determine who is eligible to purchase a personal auto policy (PAP);

- list and describe the coverages the PAP provides;

- describe the PAP's limitations and exclusions; and

- identify major endorsements that can be used to tailor the PAP's coverage.

# COMPENSATION OF AUTO ACCIDENT VICTIMS

Under the current legal system, victims of automobile accidents are entitled to compensation from those who cause the accidents as a result of negligence. The many systems in place designed to provide that compensation vary by state. Some of the approaches used to compensate accident victims are:

- the tort system (civil litigation);

- financial responsibility laws;

- compulsory insurance laws;

- uninsured/underinsured motorists coverage; and

- no fault laws.

## TORT SYSTEM

Under the tort system, which is based on fault, anyone whose negligent operation of a motor vehicle results in injuries or damages to others may be held legally responsible for his actions. Damages usually are apportioned based on each party's degree of fault.

## FINANCIAL RESPONSIBILITY LAWS

Every state has a financial responsibility law that requires proof of financial responsibility when a person has been involved in an automobile accident, has been convicted of a serious offense, such as drunk driving, or has failed to pay a judgment from an earlier accident. Failure to provide proof of financial responsibility may result in loss of license, vehicle registration, or both.

## COMPULSORY INSURANCE LAWS

In an attempt to address the shortcomings in the financial responsibility laws, many states have enacted compulsory auto insurance laws. These laws require a person to demonstrate that liability insurance is in force before an accident, and usually are tied to vehicle registration, driver licensing, or some other event.

## UNINSURED/UNDERINSURED MOTORISTS COVERAGE

Recognizing that all other methods of eliminating the uninsured driver population were less than perfect, insurers began to include uninsured motorists coverage in all auto policies. This coverage is designed to reimburse the insureds for amounts due from negligent drivers who do not carry insurance. Initially, coverage was for bodily injury only but included general damages such as pain and suffering if the other driver was legally responsible for the accident. Coverage was later expanded to include underinsured drivers—that is, those who were insured, but carried limits of liability too low to cover the damages sustained by the injured party.

## NO-FAULT LAWS

Another way to compensate victims of automobile accidents is through no-fault automobile insurance. Under the no-fault system, the primary source of recovery for injuries sustained in an auto accident is the driver or passenger's own automobile policy. Unlike the tort system, no-fault laws require no determination of fault or negligence. In fact, a distinguishing feature of the no-fault system is that it limits or eliminates the right to sue the other party in tort for injuries or damages that result from an auto accident.

Many states have adopted no-fault laws in an attempt to reduce the amount of litigation arising out of motor vehicle accidents and thus the cost of auto insurance. To date, no state has adopted a pure no-fault statute. In every case, there remains a limited right to sue once a threshold has been reached. Some states impose a monetary threshold, such as $4,000 in Minnesota, and a claim below that amount is collected from the party's own insurer. In other states, the threshold is verbal, meaning the trigger for a tort action is something like serious bodily injury or loss of sight or a limb. Once the threshold has been reached, the person who has been injured or suffered property damage may initiate legal action against the negligent party.

# OVERVIEW OF THE PERSONAL AUTOMOBILE POLICY (PAP)

The personal auto policy (PAP) has, like other property and casualty products, gone through an evolutionary process designed to respond to changes in the law, driver and vehicle safety, and consumer demands. The discussion in this manual is limited to the policy developed by the Insurance Services Office (ISO), although it is important to understand that the predominant insurers of personal autos may use their own proprietary forms. Although no standard personal auto policy exists, the format, coverages, and policy terms are quite similar from carrier to carrier.

Note: The information in this unit is based on the 1998 version of the ISO Personal Auto Policy.

## POLICY FORMAT

The personal auto policy comprises four major parts relating to the coverages the policy provides:

- *Part A—Liability to Others Coverage.* This part covers bodily injury and property damage to others when the occurrence (accident or loss) is due to the insured's negligence.

- *Part B—Medical Payments Coverage.* This part covers necessary medical and funeral expenses for the insured, his family members, and others in the insured auto.

- *Part C—Uninsured/Underinsured Motorists Coverage.* UM/UIM covers the insured and others occupying the insured's auto when the occurrence is the fault of someone else who is not insured or does not have adequate insurance. These coverages normally are written together.

- *Part D—Coverage for Damage to the Insured's Auto.* This part covers auto losses resulting from collision, from other than collision (comprehensive) and consequential transportation expenses (in case of theft or other causes of loss.) Part D does not cover personal property in the auto; it insures only the auto and parts of the auto.

## MISCELLANEOUS POLICY AND UNDERWRITING CONSIDERATIONS

Many factors affect the premium calculated for the policy.

- *Inception of coverage.* The policy becomes effective at 12:01 am on the first day of coverage and expires at 12:01 am on the expiration date.

- *Premium determination.* In calculating the premiums for any insurance policy, the insurance company considers the amount of risk involved based on such factors as:

  — territory of garaging, such as the principal place (county, city, zip code) where the auto is garaged and where the car is kept (such as in a garage);

  — use of the auto, such as for pleasure, commuting to and from work, and business (in general, the more miles driven, the higher the risk and the higher the premium);

  — driver's age, sex, marital status, and driving records;

  — limits of insurance, because the higher the limits, the greater the premium; and

  — merit rating—companies may give discounts for insureds who have good driving records or students who earn good grades.

- *Limits of liability. Limits* are per person, per occurrence for both bodily injury and property damage.

## ELIGIBILITY

To be eligible for coverage under a PAP, an auto must be owned or leased by an individual or by a married couple who are residents of the same household. Autos owned jointly by other persons who are not related and residents of the same household may be insured with a special endorsement.

The types of automobiles eligible for coverage under the PAP include a:

- four-wheel, private passenger auto; or

- pickup or van, provided it does not exceed 10,000 pounds gross vehicle weight and is not used to deliver persons or property for a fee.

Further, a private passenger-type auto is deemed to be owned and eligible for coverage if:

■ it is leased under a written agreement; and

■ the lease is for a continuous period of at least six months.

## DEFINITIONS

The following terms appear in the personal auto policy.

The *named insured* is the individual named on the declarations page.

The *insured* is the person or organization described under the person insured section in each of the coverage parts (such as Liability to Others, Uninsured Motorist, and the like).

A *family member* (*relative*) is someone (1) related to the named insured or spouse by blood, marriage, or adoption and (2) who also resides in the named insured's household.

The *covered auto* (*owned automobile*) the 1998 PAP protects is any of the following:

■ automobile listed on the declarations page;

■ newly acquired automobile on the date the insured becomes the owner during the policy period;

— Both replacement autos and additional autos will be covered by this policy.

— A replacement vehicle will have the same coverage as the vehicle it replaces. The insurer must be notified within 14 days only if the insured wishes to add or continue coverage for Damage to the Insured's Auto.

— Additional vehicles will have the broadest coverage of any vehicle described on the declarations page, and a new vehicle must be reported within 14 days of acquisition.

— If the current policy does not provide physical damage coverage for any of the vehicles in the household, the newly acquired vehicle is extended physical damage coverage for four days with a $500 deductible

■ any trailer the insured owns (it does not have to be listed on the declarations page to have coverage for liability); or

■ temporary substitute auto for any other vehicle described in this definition.

A *temporary substitute automobile* is an auto or a trailer used, with the owner's permission, as a substitute vehicle for the insured's covered auto while the covered vehicle is out of normal service because of breakdown, repair, loss, or destruction.

A *nonowned automobile* is any auto or trailer (other than the covered auto) the insured uses occasionally, such as a rental car, or the incidental use of a friend's or neighbor's car. Consequently, that PAP covers insured persons while they operate a nonowned auto.

*Occupying* means in the auto, on the auto, or getting in, on, out of, or off the auto.

*Business* includes trade, profession, or occupation.

The following takes a closer look at the four parts of the PAP.

# THE 1998 ISO PERSONAL AUTOMOBILE POLICY

## PART A—LIABILITY COVERAGE

Coverage of the PAP states that the insurer pays, on behalf of the insured, damages for bodily injury (BI) or property damage (PD) for which any covered person becomes legally responsible because of an auto accident, including any prejudgment interest awarded against the insured.

The insurer settles or defends any claim as it deems appropriate, and the insurer pays in addition to the policy's limits of liability. However, the insurer's obligation to pay damages or defense costs ends when the limit of liability has been exhausted.

**Supplementary Payments** As with other liability policies, certain *supplementary payments* are made on behalf of an insured in addition to the limits of liability.

Supplementary payments include the following:

- expenses the insurer incurs in determining claims, including interest on judgments and other costs taxed against the insured;

- premiums for appeal bonds and bonds to redeem attachment in any suit the insurer defends;

- up to $250 for bail bonds, including related traffic law violations, required because of an accident (provided the policy covers the accident);

- interest accruing after a judgment is entered in any suit the insurer defends; and

- up to $200 a day for loss of earnings by the insured only because of attendance at hearings or trials and other reasonable expenses, if incurred at the insurer's request.

**Persons Insured** Part A insures the following persons:

- named insured for the ownership, maintenance, or use of any auto or trailer;

- any person who uses the covered auto with the named insured's permission; and

- any family member who resides in the named insured's household. This includes small children (whether or not licensed) and students who live away from home but still depend on the insured.

In addition, with respect to the covered auto, the PAP also covers any person or organization that becomes liable because of acts or omissions of a person using a covered auto. That is, insurance

> **TAKE NOTE**
>
> The general intent is to eliminate coverage for commercial vehicles used regularly in business. Business use of private passenger-type vehicles, however, is covered. Therefore, coverage extends to an insurance agent driving to visit a client.

extends to anyone who is *vicariously liable* because of the negligence of a person who uses the auto with the named insured's permission.

**EXAMPLE**   Eight-year-old Paul gets into his mother's car, starts it, and drives down the street, where he collides with another automobile. Coverage is extended to Paul, even though he is not a licensed driver. He is, however, a relative of the named insured residing in the named insured's household.

The number of insureds involved in a situation does not increase the limits of coverage. The policy's full limits of liability are available just once per occurrence, but the number of occurrences in a policy period is unlimited.

**Exclusions** The PAP's liability section does not provide coverage under the following circumstances

- *No permission.* The PAP provides no coverage for a person using a vehicle without reasonable belief that he is entitled to do so. The exception is a relative of the named insured who lives in the same household.

- *Livery.* The PAP provides no coverage if the insured is paid a fee for transporting people or property. Livery includes a taxi or a limousine service. However, if the insured accepts a small amount of money as part of a car pool (or similar situation), the insured is covered. This is considered to be a sharing of expenses rather than livery.

- *Intentional injury or damage.* Coverage is for accidental injury or damage only.

- *Employees.* The PAP does not cover an employee of any insured person who sustains bodily injury in the course of employment. This exclusion does not apply to a domestic employee unless workers' compensation benefits are required or available.

- *Automobile business.* The PAP does not cover an owned automobile while it is used by another person who is employed or otherwise engaged in the business of selling, repairing, servicing, storing, or parking automobiles.

**EXAMPLE**   If a service station employee has an accident while road testing a customer's car, the customer's PAP does not provide coverage for any liability. Neither is there coverage if an insured drives a nonowned auto in the auto business. (Automobile businesses must carry their own garage liability policies to cover their liability for the operation of customers' cars.)

■ *Business pursuits.* Maintenance or use (but not ownership) of any vehicle while employed or *otherwise* engaged in any business (trade, profession, or occupation) is excluded from coverage.

■ *War.* The PAP does not provide coverage for liability, damage, or destruction resulting from war, insurrection, or riots.

■ *Certain vehicles.* The insurer does not provide liability coverage for ownership, maintenance, or use of the following vehicles:

— a motorized vehicle of fewer than four wheels;

— a vehicle other than the covered auto owned by or furnished or available for regular use by the named insured, such as a company-furnished car for a salesperson; or

— vehicles designed primarily for use off public roads (e.g. golf carts, dune buggies).

■ *Automobiles used as a residence.*

■ *Farm machinery.*

■ *Physical damage caused by rust, wear and tear, freezing, tire damage, and road damage.*

■ *Sound reproduction equipment not permanently installed in the auto (e.g., unmounted speakers, citizen band radios)*

■ *No coverage for bailees.* If your vehicle is damaged while in possession of valet parking attendant, their policy is primary.

■ *Out-of-state coverage.* If the auto is used in another state (other than where it is principally garaged) where coverage limits required by a financial responsibility law are higher than the limits of the insured's PAP, the insurer interprets the policy to provide the higher limits required by the law. Similarly, if the insured is driving in another state where a compulsory insurance or similar law requires a nonresident using a vehicle in that state to maintain insurance, the PAP provides at least the required minimum amounts and types of coverage required by law.

■ *Other insurance.* If two or more policies cover one vehicle, each insurance company pays the portion that *its* policy limit bears to the total of all applicable limits (pro rata liability). However, for any vehicle the insured does not own (temporary substitute or other than the covered auto), the PAP pays that amount exceeding any other collectible insurance.

**EXAMPLE**         Loss of $100,000

|  | Company A | Company B | Total |
|---|---|---|---|
| Limits of liability | $100,000 | $200,000 | $300,000 |
| Total coverage | 33⅓% | 66⅔% | 100% |
| Amount of loss paid | $33,333 | $66,667 | $100,000 |

## PART B—MEDICAL PAYMENTS COVERAGE

The insurer pays reasonable expenses for necessary medical and funeral services incurred within three years from the date of an accident without regard to fault.

Covered persons in Part B include the insured and any family member while they occupy the insured vehicle or any nonowned auto. In addition, the insured and family members are covered if struck as pedestrians by an auto. Also covered are other persons while they occupy the insured auto.

**Exclusions**  The exclusions for Part A apply to Part B. In addition, Part B provides no coverage for bodily injury sustained while occupying any motorized vehicle with fewer than four wheels. Also not covered is bodily injury sustained while using the insured vehicle as a residence or premises.

**Other Insurance**  Any amounts payable under this coverage are reduced by amounts paid for medical expenses under Part A liability or Part C uninsured motorists. In other words, Part B medical payments coverage is excess to other coverages that might apply under the PAP.

When an insured occupies a non-owned vehicle, this policy is excess over any other auto medical insurance.

**Personal Injury Protection (PIP)**  *Personal injury protection* (PIP) is used in states (including Minnesota) that have adopted a form of no fault auto insurance. It provides first-party protection by covering the insured for bodily injury from any occurrence without regard to fault. This means that a person injured in an auto accident, whether as a driver, passenger, or pedestrian, receives protection under his own auto policy or that policy in effect on the vehicle he occupied.

A person involved in an accident looks to the insured motor vehicle for reimbursement for medical expenses, lost wages, and loss of service. Pain and suffering are not covered. Many states, including Minnesota, have a threshold whereby if a person is injured seriously, he can sue the negligent driver for damages.

## PART C—UNINSURED MOTORISTS (UM) AND UNDERINSURED MOTORISTS COVERAGE (UIM)

Part C of the PAP pays those bodily injury damages that a covered person is legally entitled to recover from the owner or operator of an uninsured motor vehicle. The intent is to provide coverage under this policy for what an injured person could have collected for bodily injury if the other person had been carrying insurance.

**EXAMPLE**  Patrick is injured in an auto accident. Jeremy is at fault in the accident. According to Minnesota no-fault law, Patrick's medical bills will be paid by his own auto policy (up to $20,000). If his bills exceed a designated threshold ($4,000 in Minnesota), Patrick may pursue a liability claim against Jeremy. If Jeremy has no liability insurance, or inadequate liability limits to cover Patrick's claim, Patrick would return to his own policy (Part C) for additional benefits.

**Limits of Insurance**  Some states require that if a person carries liability insurance, he must carry uninsured motorists coverage to some specified minimum limits—for instance, up to the limits of liability in Part A. To eliminate Uninsured Motorists coverage, the insured must sign a declination of coverage.

> **TAKE ✓ NOTE**
>
> While glass breakage is addressed under comprehensive coverage, if a collision causes the breakage, the insured may elect to have it included in the collision coverage to avoid paying two deductibles.

**Arbitration** If the insured and insurance company, under Uninsured Motorists coverage, do not agree on (1) whether the covered person is legally entitled to recover damages, or (2) the amount of damages, either party may make a written demand for arbitration.

**Underinsured Motorists** The coverage under underinsured motorists (UIM) is similar to but slightly different from uninsured motorists coverage. UIM coverage may be required by state statutes as part of the uninsured motorists coverage.

The limits under underinsured motorists coverage can be up to those of uninsured motorists coverage (if higher than the minimum required). Thus, if an insured is injured because of another driver's negligence, he can collect from the negligent party's insurer to the limits of liability the negligent driver has on his policy, then from his own insurer to the limits of liability under this endorsement.

## PART D—COVERAGE FOR DAMAGE TO YOUR AUTO

Part D provides two major types of coverage: other than collision (comprehensive) coverage and collision coverage. If these coverages are shown on the declarations page, the insurer pays for direct accidental loss to the covered auto and its equipment minus any deductible shown in the declarations.

**Other than Collision (Comprehensive)** Other than collision coverage protects against almost all accidental damage, with the exception of coverage provided under collision.

Coverage includes fire, theft, explosion, earthquake, windstorm, missiles, falling objects, hail, flood, vandalism and malicious mischief, riot and civil commotion, glass breakage, and collision with birds or animals (wild or domestic). Wear and tear, mechanical breakdown, and road damage to tires are not covered.

**Transportation Expenses** The policy pays for daily expenses up to $20, up to a total of $600, caused by loss of use of a covered auto due to collision or other than collision. The expense coverage is available after 48 hours for a theft loss and after 24 hours for any other eligible cause of loss. In either case, coverage ends when the covered auto is again available or a settlement has been paid.

**Collision** Collision coverage protects against damage done to the covered auto by (1) impact with another vehicle, (2) impact with an object, or (3) upset (rolling the car over).

**Deductibles/Loss of Use** Both comprehensive and collision coverage generally have a deductible of $100, $250, or more.

No loss of use coverage is provided with comprehensive or collision coverage. In other words, the policy contains no provision for a rental car or other transportation expenses unless the insured has comprehensive coverage and the car is stolen (in which case, limited coverage for transportation expenses is allowed, as previously noted). The insured might be able to recover for auto rental expenses from a negligent third party if the accident was that person's fault.

**Limits of Liability**   Under Part D of the PAP, recovery is on an actual cash value basis. The company pays the lesser of the:

- actual cash value (ACV) of the damaged or stolen property (based on either the ACV formula already discussed or by fair market value); or

- amount necessary to repair or replace the property with like kind and quality.

The insurer may pay for the loss in money or may repair or replace any damaged property. If a stolen vehicle is returned, the insurer pays for damage resulting from the theft.

**Exclusions**   Some of the Part D exclusions are the same as were discussed for Part A. In addition, Part D excludes damages from wear and tear, freezing, mechanical breakdown, and electrical breakdown unless these damages result from total theft of the auto. Also excluded is road damage to tires; damage to tires is covered if it results from fire, theft, vandalism and malicious mischief, or other coincident damage to the car.

Also excluded from coverage is special equipment, including loss to:

- equipment designed for reproducing sound, unless such equipment is permanently installed, including a citizen's band (CB) radio, mobile radio, telephone, or scanning monitor receiver (these must be permanently installed where the radio normally is);

- any custom furnishings or equipment in a pickup or van; and

- radar detection equipment.

Trailers are not covered automatically for Part D physical damage, as they are for Part A liability. If the insured desires physical damage coverage for a trailer, it must be added specifically as an endorsement to the policy.

**Other Insurance and Stacking**   If the insured carries more than one policy on the covered auto, each policy pays its proportionate share of the loss (pro rata distribution). Coverage on autos the insured does not own is excess over any other insurance. Many states have no-stacking rules that allow the insured to collect no more than the actual cash value of the damage to the auto.

This insurance does not benefit directly or indirectly any carrier or other bailee for hire. Thus, if a parking lot attendant damages an auto, the PAP pays the insured for damages but looks to the parking lot operator for recovery.

## DUTIES AFTER ACCIDENT OR LOSS

The insurer must be notified of how, when, and where an accident or a loss happens, including names and addresses of witnesses.

A person seeking recovery for damages must:

- cooperate with the insurer;

- submit to physical examinations and to examination under oath;

- authorize the insurer to obtain medical reports and other pertinent records; and

- submit a proof of loss when the insurer requires it.

Under uninsured motorists coverage, the insured must notify police promptly if a hit-and-run driver is involved.

Under damage to your auto coverage, the insured must:

- protect the auto and its equipment from further loss (the insurer pays reasonable expenses to do this);

- notify police promptly if the vehicle is stolen; and

- permit the insurer to inspect and appraise the damaged property before its repair or disposal.

## GENERAL PROVISIONS

**Policy Period and Territory** PAP coverage applies only to losses, accidents, or occurrences that take place during the policy period and within the United States, its territories and possessions, Puerto Rico, or Canada or while being transported between ports in any of those places.

**Right to Recover Payment (Subrogation)** The insurer has subrogation rights under all coverages of the PAP except under Coverage D against a person using a covered auto with a reasonable belief that he is entitled to do so.

**Changes** A written endorsement by the insurer that forms part of the policy is the only way to change the policy. Premiums are computed from the effective date of the change.

If the insurer changes its PAP form generally to provide more coverage, without additional premium, or if a statute requires a change in coverage, any PAP policy already issued automatically provides the additional coverage. (This is known as the *liberalization clause*.)

**Transfer of the Insured's Interest in the PAP (Assignment)** The PAP may not be assigned without the insurer's consent.

**Termination** The following conditions apply to the termination of a policy by the insured or the insurer.

*Cancellation during the policy period.* During the policy period, the insured can cancel the policy by returning it or giving advance written notice. If the insurer cancels the policy, it must provide 10 days' written notice when the cancellation is made:

- for nonpayment of premium; or

- during the first 60 days of a *new* policy for almost any underwriting reason.

The insurer must give 30 days' written notice when (1) the policy has been in effect for 60 days, or (2) it is a renewal or continuation policy and cancellation occurs because:

- the driver's license of the insured, someone who lives with the insured, or someone who normally drives the insured's auto is revoked or suspended during the policy period or since the last anniversary of the effective date; or

- the policy was obtained through material misrepresentation.

**Nonrenewal** If the insurer decides not to renew the insured's policy, it notifies the insured at least 60 days before the end of the policy period.

# ENDORSEMENTS TO THE PERSONAL AUTO POLICY

### MISCELLANEOUS-TYPE VEHICLE ENDORSEMENT

This endorsement allows the PAP to cover motorcycles, motorhomes, all-terrain vehicles (ATVs), dune buggies, and other types of vehicles that otherwise are excluded by the policy.

### EXTENDED NONOWNED COVERAGE FOR NAMED INDIVIDUALS

This endorsement provides coverage by effectively eliminating several PAP exclusions or limitations. First, it allows coverage for a nonowned vehicle furnished or available for the insured's regular use. This may be the company-furnished car. Second, the endorsement provides excess auto liability for business use of a commercial-type vehicle that the named insured does not own, such as one an employer owns. Third, the endorsement could be used to provide excess liability coverage for public or livery use of a nonowned auto, such as a taxicab. Finally, this endorsement also covers suits by co-workers arising out of automobile accidents in the course of employment.

### TOWING AND LABOR COSTS

When added to the PAP, this endorsement provides a selected amount of insurance ($25, $50, or $75) for the cost of towing or roadside service. When a car is disabled, such coverage pays for labor at the site of the disablement (such as jump starts and tire changes) and for towing charges.

Coverage also applies to the insured's use of a nonowned automobile.

# SUMMARY

In addition to providing property and liability protection, the Personal Auto Policy provides medical benefits to parties injured in an auto accident. The first-party medical benefits provided through the policy make the auto policy unique from other types of property and casualty contracts. Auto policy underwriting considers many factors, and eligibility for the policy is limited to vehicles intended for personal (not business) use.

As with other property and casualty contracts, the Personal Auto Policy excludes certain losses, and the policy may be endorsed to provide additional protection.

# UNIT QUIZ

1. An insured, while operating his automobile, negligently struck a light pole, damaging the pole and interrupting electrical power to a grocery store, which caused perishable food to spoil. The insured's property damage liability coverage pays for each of the following losses EXCEPT

   A. damage to the store
   B. damage to the light pole
   C. damage to the spoiled food
   D. damage to the automobile

2. Mr. Adams has an automobile policy with bodily injury limits of $15,000/$30,000, property damage limits of $10,000, and a $100 deductible for collision. He negligently runs into Ms. Smith's car. Ms. Smith is awarded $30,000 for her injuries and $6,000 for the damage to her car. Mr. Adams's car is damaged to the extent of $750. The total payment made under Mr. Adams's policy is

   A. $21,650
   B. $21,750
   C. $36,650
   D. $36,750

3. When an insured is driving a non-owned automobile on which there is other valid insurance, coverage under the insured's policy is what type of insurance?

   A. Invalid
   B. Excess
   C. Primary
   D. Contributory

4. Which of the following judgments would be paid under the bodily injury coverage for a PAP?

   A. Claim against the insured, the owner of a small manufacturing plant, by an employee injured in a car the insured drove
   B. Claim by a woman pedestrian injured by the insured while driving to work
   C. Claim by a driver of the insured's vehicle for injuries when using the vehicle without permission
   D. Claim by another driver injured while the insured used the vehicle as an airport taxi

5. Collision insurance covers which of the following perils?

   A. All damage to an auto struck by the insured, if the insured is legally liable
   B. Upset of the auto without a deductible applying
   C. Direct loss to the auto caused by collision with another object
   D. Collision of the covered vehicle with a large animal

6. An auto policy would provide coverage if an insured were driving his auto in all of the following places EXCEPT

   A. Alberta, Canada
   B. Paducah, Kentucky
   C. Mexico City, Mexico
   D. Honolulu, Hawaii

7. If an insured hits a garbage can while parallel parking, which part of an auto policy would cover the damage to the car?

   A. Medical payments
   B. Collision
   C. Comprehensive
   D. Liability

8. Automobile comprehensive coverage insures all of the following perils EXCEPT

   A. collision
   B. glass breakage
   C. fire
   D. theft

9. Which of the following persons would NOT be considered an insured under a Personal Auto Policy?

   A. The named insured's 10-year-old child who is permitted to start the car in the driveway
   B. The named insured's child while away at college
   C. The named insured's spouse who resides in the household
   D. The named insured's employee while working for the insured

10. Collision or upset insurance covers which of the following?

    A. All damage to an auto struck by an insured, providing the insured is legally liable
    B. Direct loss to an auto caused by collision with another object or by upset of an auto, subject to the deductible amount stated in the policy
    C. The pain and suffering of the policyholder when an accident occurs
    D. Damage to an auto caused by fire, theft, or collision with another object

11. Darren is insured under a personal auto policy with a split limit of 100/300/50. While driving a friend's car, Darren injures a pedestrian. If Darren's friend carries a personal auto policy with a combined single limit of $300,000, how much liability coverage will be available to cover injuries to the pedestrian?

    A. $100,000
    B. $300,000
    C. $400,000
    D. $600,000

12. What is the primary purpose of uninsured and underinsured motorists coverage?

    A. To cover the insured's injuries when the at-fault driver does not carry liability insurance
    B. To protect uninsured drivers against liability claims by the insured
    C. To cover the injuries of uninsured drivers who are involved in an accident with the insured
    D. To prevent subrogation against uninsured drivers

# ANSWERS AND RATIONALES TO UNIT QUIZ

1. **D.** Property damage liability insurance covers direct damage as well as loss of use of property that is caused by the insured's negligence. Damage to property the insured owns is not covered.

2. **A.** The amount of coverage for Ms. Smith's injuries is limited to $15,000. The damage to Ms. Smith's car, $6,000, is covered in full. The damage to Mr. Adams's vehicle is covered minus the $100 deductible. Thus, the total payment is $21,650.

3. **B.** The PAP states that the policy is primary as to any owned autos and excess when the insured uses a non-owned auto.

4. **B.** Injuries to employees are specifically excluded. Neither is coverage provided for use of a covered auto as a public or livery conveyance or use of a vehicle without permission (relatives in the insured's household excepted.)

5. **C.** Coverage for collision in an auto policy is designed to cover damage to the insured's auto that results from collision with another object or upset, e.g., rolling the car over by taking a corner too fast. Collision pays, whether the insured is at fault or not. A deductible applies to collision losses. Hitting a large animal is considered a comprehensive loss under an auto policy.

6. **C.** An auto policy would provide coverage while driving in the United States of America, its territories or possessions, Puerto Rico, or Canada. Because Mexico is usually not part of this coverage territory, accidents or losses occurring in Mexico generally will not be covered.

7. **B.** Collision covers upset or impact with another vehicle or object, including a garbage can. Exceptions would include being struck by a falling object or missile or striking an animal.

8. **A.** The physical damage portion of a PAP has two sections: Collision and Comprehensive (also known as Other Than Collision). Comprehensive coverage provides for fire, theft, vandalism, being struck by a falling object or a missile, and hitting or being hit by an animal.

9. **D.** Under a PAP, an insured includes the named insured, relatives of the named insured who reside in the named insured's household (by blood, marriage, or adoption, including a ward or foster child), and those using the vehicle with the reasonable belief they are entitled to do so. However, there is no coverage provided under a PAP for bodily injury sustained by an insured's employee. It is important to note that the policy does not exclude a nonlicensed relative of the named insured residing in the home. Coverage would be extended to the 10-year-old child. A person away at college is generally considered a resident of the household, as long as such person has not established an independent residence.

10. **B.** Direct loss to an auto due to upset or collision with another object is subject to Collision coverage. Choice A would be covered under the liability section of the insured's auto policy for property damage to others. Choice C would be covered by the negligent driver's liability insurance or by the insured's uninsured motorists coverage. Choice D would be covered under comprehensive coverage, also known as Other Than Collision coverage.

11. **C.** Liability coverage is provided first from the vehicle being driven (friend's policy); excess coverage may be drawn from Darren's policy. In this example, the two policies provide a combined benefit of $400,000.

12. **A.** The primary purpose of Coverage C (UM/UIM) is to provide coverage for an injured insured if the negligent driver does not have any (or enough) liability coverage.

# 18

# Commercial Property Insurance

## KEY CONCEPTS

- Commercial versus personal lines insurance
- The Package Policy concept
- Commercial property insurance
- Inland marine insurance
- Boiler and machinery insurance

In Units 15, 16, and 17 of this manual, we studied personal property and casualty products—those used by private consumers to help manage the risks they face in everyday life. The homeowners, dwelling, and personal auto policies routinely excluded coverage for losses relating to business activities. The property and casualty industry has developed an entire line of commercial insurance products for use by businesses and business owners. This unit presents a general overview of commercial property insurance and common property insurance policy provisions, and includes a review of the Commercial Package Policy (CPP).

## OBJECTIVE

When you complete this unit, you should be able to:

■  describe the property covered in and excluded from the building and personal property (BPP) coverage form, additional coverages, and coverage extensions;

■  describe the coverages the business income coverage form provides;

■  describe the coverages the extra expense coverage form provides;

■  explain the various endorsements available under commercial property insurance;

■  discuss the ways buildings, in the course of construction, may be insured using commercial property insurance forms; and

■  discuss the need for inland marine insurance and describe the policies that fall into that insurance category.

# COMMERCIAL PACKAGE POLICIES

The most common way to provide property insurance for a larger business or organization is with a commercial package policy (CPP). This policy may include coverage for liability, automobiles, crime, and other major lines of insurance. A common declarations page is combined with separate insuring agreements for each type of coverage. This approach allows the insured to select the coverage needed and tailor it to the needs of the insured's business. A business owner can select from among the following types of coverage:

■  commercial property;

■  inland marine;

■  boiler and machinery;

■  commercial general liability;

■  crime; and

■  commercial auto.

Note: Farm coverage may be purchased as a part of the CPP but is often purchased on a monoline basis.

Once the policyholder has selected the individual coverages they require, the individual components are assembled together into a single package. To simplify the discussion of the CPP, this unit will examine the property coverages in detail. This includes commercial property, inland marine, and boiler and machinery coverage. In Unit 19, we will explore the casualty coverages of the CPP, which includes general liability, crime insurance, and commercial auto.

# COMMERCIAL PROPERTY INSURANCE

Large businesses that own buildings, personal property, and manage inventory need property insurance. Commercial property insurance is the first of three coverages we'll examine in this unit. The property package includes Buildings and Personal Property (BPP) coverage, Business Income and Extra Expense coverage, and Builder's Risk coverage.

## BUILDINGS AND PERSONAL PROPERTY COVERAGE FORM

As its name implies, the buildings and personal property (BPP) coverage form provides insurance protection for buildings and business personal property. The form describes:

- what property will and will not be covered;
- additional coverages provided;
- any coverage extensions;
- the limits of insurance;
- the deductible; and
- specific conditions.

The form provides coverage for three major types of property:

- buildings and structures described in the declarations, including machinery and fixtures;
- business personal property at or within 100 feet of the insured location; and
- property of others in the insured's care, custody, or control, on or within 100 feet of the insured location.

## COVERED PROPERTY

Covered property includes the building, business personal property, and personal property of others. Each building and location must be identified specifically.

Coverage for buildings described in the declarations includes:

- completed additions;
- fixtures, including outdoor fixtures such as light poles;
- permanently installed machinery and equipment, such as a hoist or crane; and
- personal property the insured owns that is used to maintain or service the building or structure or its premises, including:
  - fire extinguishing equipment;

— outdoor furniture;

— floor coverings; and

— appliances used for refrigerating, ventilating, cooking, washing dishes, or laundering.

If they are not covered elsewhere, the form also includes coverage for additions under construction, alterations, and repairs to the building or structure and materials, equipment, supplies, and temporary structures on or within 100 feet of the described premises that are being used to make additions, alterations, or repairs to the building or structure.

Business personal property located in or on the building described in the declarations, or in the open (or in a vehicle) within 100 feet of the described premises, includes such items as:

■ furniture and fixtures, such as desks and filing cabinets;

■ machinery and equipment;

■ stock, which includes merchandise for sale (such as the clothes and furniture for sale in a department store), raw materials, and in-process or finished goods, plus supplies used in their packaging or shipping; and

■ all other personal property the insured owns and uses in his business.

Personal effects and property of others coverage that applies to business personal property can be extended to apply to personal effects owned by the insured or the insured's officers, partners, or employees (such as a fire at an office that destroys some employees' coats). This coverage can also be applied to personal property of others in the insured's care, custody, or control, such as customers' computers in a store for repair.

The limit is $2,500 at each described premises. The insurer pays the property owner, not the insured business owner. Because the dollar amount of coverage is limited, this is appropriate when the exposure is relatively small. For larger dollar values, coverage should be provided through a bailee's floater (discussed later).

**Coverage Extensions** The following coverage extensions apply if a coinsurance percentage of 80% or more is shown on the declarations page. Amounts arising from the following items are in addition to the limits of insurance shown on the declarations page. The coinsurance requirement does not apply.

**Newly Acquired or Constructed Property.** Coverage can be applied to new buildings while being constructed on the premises described on the declarations page and to buildings that the insured acquires at locations other than the described premises.

The limit for buildings is 25% of the amount for those shown on the declarations page but not more than $250,000 at each building.

Coverage can be applied to business personal property at any location that the insured acquires, with a limit of 10% of that shown on the declarations page for business personal property. This 10% limit cannot exceed $100,000 at each building where such personal property may be located.

**Valuable Papers and Records—Cost of Research.** Coverage that applies to business personal property can be extended to apply to the insured's cost to research, replace, or restore the information on lost or damaged valuable papers and records. This coverage includes information on electronic or magnetic media for which duplicates do not exist. The limit of coverage under this extension is $2,500 at each described premises.

**Property Off Premises.** Coverage may be extended to apply to covered property other than stock that is temporarily at a location the insured does not own, lease, or operate, for instance, office furniture taken to a shop for repair. This extension applies only if loss or damage is caused by a peril that would have been covered had it happened on the insured's premises. The extension does not apply to covered property in or on a vehicle, in the care, custody, or control of the insured's salespeople, or at any fair or exhibition. The limit under this extension is $10,000.

**Outdoor Property.** Coverage may be extended to apply to the insured's outdoor fences, radio and television antennas, signs (other than signs attached to buildings), trees, shrubs, and plants, including debris removal expense. Coverage applies when the loss is caused by or results from any of the following:

- fire;
- lightning;
- explosion;
- riot or civil commotion; or
- aircraft.

The limit under this extension is $1,000 but not more than $250 for any one tree, shrub, or plant.

**Additional Coverages**  Additional coverages are available for the following activities.

**Debris Removal.** Following a covered loss, the insurer pays for the expenses to remove the debris of covered property caused by or resulting from a covered cause of loss. The cost of debris removal is subject to a limit of 25% of the amount of the loss plus the extension for uncovered debris removal costs.

EXAMPLE    If a direct loss of $100,000 occurs and the policy extension is $1,000, the most that the insurer will pay for debris removal is $25,000 (25% of $100,000) plus $1,000, for a total of $26,000.

**Preservation of Property.** If it is necessary to move covered property from the described premises to preserve it from loss or damage by a covered cause of loss, the insurer pays for any direct physical loss or damage to that property occurring:

- while the property is being moved or while temporarily stored at another location; and
- only if the loss or damage occurs within 30 days after the property is first moved.

**Fire Department Service Charge.** When the fire department is called to save or protect covered property from a covered cause of loss, the insurer pays up to $1,000 for fire department service charges.

**Pollutant Clean-Up and Removal.** If a covered loss results in the discharge, dispersal, seepage, migration, release, or escape of pollutants, the cost to clean up those pollutants is covered up to a maximum of $10,000.

**Property Not Covered** Some property that is not covered includes:

- accounts, bills, currency, deeds, evidences of debt, money, notes, or securities;

- animals, unless owned by others and boarded by the insured, or owned by the insured and considered stock, such as animals in a pet store;

- automobiles held for sale;

- bridges, roadways, walks, patios, or other paved surfaces;

- personal property while airborne or waterborne;

- pilings, piers, wharves, or docks;

- property covered under any other policy in which it is described more specifically, except for the excess of the amount due (whether or not one can collect on it) from that other insurance;

- the cost to research, replace, or restore the information on valuable papers and records, including those that exist on electronic or magnetic media, except as provided in the coverage extensions;

- vehicles or self-propelled machines, including aircraft and watercraft, that are: licensed for use on public roads or operated principally away from the described premises; and

- the following property while outside of buildings: fences, radio, or television antennas (including their lead-in wiring, masts, or towers), signs (other than signs attached to buildings), trees, shrubs, or plants. Some coverage is provided under the coverage extensions.

## BUSINESS INCOME COVERAGE FORM

Business income coverage is an important part of the insurance program for nearly all businesses. Business income coverage is disability insurance for the business. When the business cannot earn income due to a covered loss, business income coverage replaces the lost earnings.

Loss of business income is an *indirect* or a *consequential* loss. This type of coverage also is called *time element coverage* because it pays for loss of income that occurs over a period of time, as opposed to a direct loss that happens at a specific time. The amount of the loss is calculated based on the firm's past financial performance, estimated into the future.

Business income coverage includes expenses to avoid or minimize the suspension of business and to continue business operations:

- at the described premises;

- at replacement premises; and

- at temporary locations.

Such expenses as relocation expenses and costs to equip and operate the replacement or temporary locations are covered. Also covered are expenses to minimize the suspension of business if the insured cannot continue business operations.

## COVERAGE

During the *restoration period*, the insurer pays for the actual loss of business income the insured sustains due to the necessary suspension of operations.

The restoration period begins on the date the direct physical loss or damage occurred at the described premises and ends on the date when the property at the described premises should be repaired, rebuilt, or replaced with reasonable speed and similar quality. The policy's expiration date does not cut short the period of restoration.

Business income includes the following:

■ net income (net profit or loss before income taxes) that would have been earned or incurred; plus

■ continuing normal operation expenses, including payroll.

## EXTRA EXPENSE COVERAGE FORM

With the extra expense coverage form, the insurer pays for any necessary extra expenses the business incurs during a period of interruption that follows a direct physical loss to property by a covered cause of loss. The expenses must be of a type that would not have been incurred had the loss not taken place. This is also a time element coverage, because the loss is continuous in nature.

This type of coverage is purchased by a business that must continue to operate if a loss occurs, despite the costs of keeping the business running. Such a business is one that will lose customers to competitors if it does not remain open and one that is the only businesses of its kind in the area.

---

**EXAMPLE**   Businesses that probably would buy extra expense coverage to enable them to continue operations despite a loss are a hospital, an electric company, and a dry cleaner. A hospital may be the only medical facility in the area. An electric company could be the only source of such power for an entire city. Even a dry cleaner could benefit from this coverage in that it would remain open and serve customers who otherwise would go to a competitor.

**Alterations and New Buildings**   The insurer pays for the actual loss of business income that the insured sustains due to direct physical loss or damage at the described premises. The loss or damage must be caused by or result from a covered cause of loss to:

■ new buildings or structures, whether complete or under construction;

■ alterations or additions to existing buildings or structures; and

■ machinery, equipment, and supplies.

If such direct physical loss or damage delays the start of business operations, the period of restoration begins on the date operations would have begun if the direct physical loss or damage had not occurred.

**Extended Business Income** This additional coverage provides insurance while a business is starting back up after a loss. When resuming operations after a major loss, the business probably will not receive as much income as it would have received had no loss occurred.

This coverage helps make up the difference between what the business could have earned and what it actually did earn. The insurer pays for the actual loss of business income the insured incurs during the period that begins on the date the property actually is repaired, rebuilt, or replaced and operations are resumed, and ends either in 30 days or when the business has achieved the level of income it would have had no loss occurred.

## Loss Conditions for Business Income Coverage

**Loss Determination.** The amount of business income loss is determined based on:

- the business's net income before the direct physical loss or damage occurred;

- the business's likely net income if no loss or damage occurred;

- the operating expenses, including payroll expenses, necessary to resume operations with the same quality of service that existed just before the direct physical loss or damage occurred; and

- other relevant sources of information, including:

  — the insured's financial records and accounting procedures;

  — bills, invoices, and other vouchers; and

  — deeds, liens, or contracts.

**Coinsurance** Business income coverage may be written with or without a coinsurance requirement. A contract with coinsurance often requires the insured to purchase coverage limits equal to 50% of their annual business income. If that requirement is met, they may be paid for business income losses up to stated policy limits, without any restrictions on what they can be paid in any given month. This approach may serve a seasonal business well—one that experiences significant fluctuations in their business income over the course of a year. As with any coinsurance requirements, failure to meet the requirement translates into a lower claim payment according to the coinsurance formula discussed in Unit 14.

If the insured purchases business income coverage without coinsurance, they select coverage limits and a monthly limit of indemnity. Through this approach, the insured could receive their entire policy limit, but their monthly recovery is capped.

---

 EXAMPLE    Diane's annual business income is $300,000, averaging $25,000 each month. She purchases business income coverage with no coinsurance requirement, selecting limits of $100,000 with a monthly limit of indemnity equal to 25%. If Diane's business is closed due to a covered peril, she could receive up to $25,000 each month (25% of her $100,000 limit) but no more than $100,000 (her policy limits) in total business income payments.

## BUILDER'S RISK COVERAGE FORM

Builder's Risk Insurance is a property policy designed to provide coverage for property while under construction. It covers the contractor's interest in materials at the job site before they are installed, materials in transit intended for the job, and the value of property being constructed until it is completed and accepted by the owner. The policy may be written to cover the whole structure for new construction or rehabilitation projects. It can also be used to cover specific projects such as a new room addition, a deck, or a remodeled kitchen.

## BUILDER'S RISK COVERAGE FORM

The insurer pays the insured for direct physical loss of or damage to covered property caused by or resulting from a covered cause of loss. The property must be at the premises described in the declarations.

**Covered Property** Covered property includes buildings under construction, as described in the declarations. Basic, broad, and special form peril coverage is available.

**Covered Cause of Loss** Covered losses are defined in the attached cause of loss form, as shown on the declarations page.

**Loss Payment** The loss payment condition provides that the insurer must do one of the following:

- pay the value of lost or damaged property;
- pay the cost of repairing or replacing lost or damaged property;
- take all or any part of the property at an agreed on or appraised value; or
- repair, rebuild, or replace the property with other property of like kind and quality.

**Coverage Termination** Coverage ceases at the earliest of the following:

- the policy expires or is canceled;
- the purchaser accepts the property;
- the insured's interest in the property ceases;
- the insured abandons the construction;
- 90 days have passed since construction is completed; or
- building occupancy occurs in whole or in part, or the building is put to its intended use.

Coverage includes the foundation, fixtures, machinery, and equipment used to service the building, as well as temporary structures if they are not insured elsewhere.

## ENDORSEMENTS TO COMMERCIAL PROPERTY FORMS

Many endorsements can be added to the commercial property portion of the Commercial Property Policy (CPP) to customize coverage for an insured. Some of the more important endorsements follow.

### PEAK SEASON

If an insured has inventory that tends to increase in value at certain predictable times of the year, it may wish to purchase a peak season endorsement. This coverage automatically increases the limit for business personal property to a preselected amount during the time period listed on the endorsement. This is particularly important to retailers that stock up during holiday seasons.

### BUILDING ORDINANCE COVERAGE

When a building suffers damage, three types of consequential losses may occur: the undamaged portion of the building may have to be torn down due to local building codes; there is a cost to demolish the undamaged structure; and there is additional cost to rebuild due to the passage of stricter building laws. These losses are excluded under the BPP form unless the building ordinance coverage endorsement has been attached to the policy. When provided, coverage applies to loss to the undamaged portion of the building, including demolition costs, and to the increased cost of construction necessary to meet current building laws.

### VALUE REPORTING FORM

For a policyholder who owns property that fluctuates constantly in value, the value reporting form allows it to select an amount of insurance that represents the maximum amount of exposure the insured has during the policy year, but pays based only on the actual amount of exposure. A report of values is sent to the company on a regular basis, and at the end of the policy term the average is computed and the final premium determined.

# INLAND MARINE INSURANCE

Inland marine insurance evolved out of ocean marine and was created to insure shipments carried by railroads, trucks, and aircraft. Marine insurance is not limited, however, to ocean-going or even transportation risks. Modern marine insurance policies cover any type of property that is being transported, has the potential to be transported, or is designed to move property or information from place to place, such as bridges, tunnels, computers, and broadcast antennas.

One of the earliest forms of insurance coverages was ocean marine, which covered ships and their cargo on the ocean. This contract covered physical damage as well as liability and tended to be very broad in coverage, what generally is referred to as *open perils*. Inland marine insurance developed out of ocean marine insurance to cover property being shipped by land or inland waterways. (Contrast this to fire insurance, which covers property at a specific location.) Because of this concept, the term *floater* is used and applies only to inland marine insurance. For purposes of this text, floaters may be interpreted to mean inland marine insurance policies.

**Nationwide Marine Definition** In 1976, a *Nationwide Marine Definition* was developed that makes no distinction between ocean marine and inland marine, grouping marine insurances together as marine, inland marine, and transportation policies. The principal effect of this definition is to explain inland marine insurance because the definition of ocean marine coverages generally is understood. Inland marine insurance usually is based on transit exposures, but it includes many situations where transit exposure is either negligible or absent.

Inland marine contracts usually are divided into several categories:

- domestic goods in transit;
- property held by bailees;
- mobile equipment;
- property of certain dealers;
- commercial and personal property floaters;
- means of transportation and communication; and
- difference in conditions policies.

The ISO has developed 13 filed forms for inland marine coverages that are designed to be included in the Commercial Package Policy (CPP):

- accounts receivable;
- camera and musical instrument dealers;
- commercial articles;
- commercial fine arts;
- equipment dealers;
- film coverage;
- floor plan merchandise;
- jeweler's block;
- mail coverage;
- physician's and surgeon's equipment;
- signs;
- theatrical property; and
- valuable papers and records.

## DOMESTIC GOODS IN TRANSIT

Usually, at least three parties are involved with respect to domestic goods in transit. Because of this, some uncertainty may exist as to who must bear a loss: the shipper (the one sending the goods), the consignee (the one to whom the goods are being sent), or the people actually involved in handling or moving the goods.

**Transit Insurance**   Transit insurance covers the owners of domestic goods in transit. Often, these policies offer very broad coverage for loss or damage to the property, with many of the policies written on an open perils basis. The coverage may be on an annual basis, or for specific cargo during a specific trip, or it may apply only to parcel post or registered mail. Some specific forms include a motor truck cargo-owner's goods on owner's trucks for a firm that transports its own cargo and a transportation floater for a firm that ships goods via a trucking company, a railroad, or an airline.

**Cargo Liability Insurance**   Cargo liability policies cover the carriers of domestic goods in transit. These policies usually provide coverage on a named perils basis and provide coverage only if the insured carrier is liable for loss or damage to the property. One form that could be used is the *motor truck cargo liability broad form*. However, the term *broad form* has a different meaning here than it does in general property coverage. In marine insurance, the term generally means open perils. This form insures against the direct loss of or damage to property of others that the carrier transports (care, custody, or control), but only if the insured carrier is liable for that loss or damage.

## BAILEE'S CUSTOMERS INSURANCE

Some businesses, known as *bailees*, have a large amount of customer property in their custody. A *bailee* is someone who has care, custody, or control of another's property. Bailees have custody of others' property for a fee and therefore have a higher degree of responsibility to care for that property while it is in their custody. The customers expect their property to be returned intact or to be paid for any loss or damage to the property, regardless of whether the business was at fault.

Businesses such as laundries, dry cleaners, warehouses, parking garages, and storage facilities find it advantageous to provide insurance for the benefit of their customers, even if the bailees are not legally liable. The bailee's policy also covers their own legal liability for damage to customers' property when they are negligent. The policy provides coverage under both circumstances, so this type of policy is called a *dual interest policy*.

---

EXAMPLE

When Bob drives downtown to run errands, he enters a large parking garage with a gated entrance, parks his car, and takes the keys with him. He then goes to a dry cleaner to leave some shirts for laundering. When Bob transfers temporary possession and control of the shirts to the dry cleaner, he creates a bailment. For a while, he cannot possess or use the shirts, and the dry cleaner assumes responsibility for their care. When he completes his errands, he returns to the parking garage. There he pays the cashier and drives his car out of the lot. No bailment was created with respect to the car because, by retaining the keys, Bob did not transfer temporary possession or control of the car to the garage. He did not intend to transfer possession or control of it to the garage and could drive it away at any time (after paying the parking fee). The garage also did not accept responsibility for his car.

Bailee's customers policies are purchased by laundries, dry cleaners, and other businesses that have customers' property in their care, custody, or control. The policies usually are written on a named perils basis. The insurance covers loss of customer goods regardless of legal liability on the part of the bailee. These policies usually permit a bailee, such as a dry cleaner, to settle small losses without submitting each small claim to the insurer individually. Such losses are limited, often to $500 per occurrence.

## CONTRACTOR'S EQUIPMENT FLOATERS

Contractors involved in constructing buildings and highways, for instance, may own equipment valued in the hundreds of thousands of dollars, ranging from small hand tools to large pieces of machinery. A contractor can negotiate with an insurer to cover specifically identified equipment as listed in the policy (this method usually is used for large and expensive equipment), equipment at a specific location only, or property on a blanket basis (this method is generally used for small, less expensive hand tools). The contractor also may obtain a combination of specified and blanket coverage.

## JEWELER'S BLOCK POLICY

Property covered under the jeweler's block policy is described in general terms but includes property customarily found in a jewelry store or in the jewelry department of a department store. Because jewelers often have custody of customers' property for repair, the jeweler's block policy includes coverage similar to the bailee's customers coverage discussed earlier. This policy excludes property worn by the insured, corporate officers, members of the firm, employees, family members, or relatives. The policy also excludes jewelry worn by a model or another jewelry dealer.

# BOILER AND MACHINERY INSURANCE

Boiler and machinery insurance is highly specialized. It usually covers unique hazards that generally are excluded from other forms of commercial property insurance. The classification can be a bit misleading because, in this day, boiler and machinery insurance can include steam boilers as well as pressure containers, refrigeration systems and units, engines, turbines, generators, and electric motors. The types of property insured are *equipment whose operation involves force, pressure, or energy as a significant factor.*

## COVERED CAUSES OF LOSS: ACCIDENT DEFINED

Insured losses are accidents to covered objects. The covered objects are those described in the object definition form(s) attached to the policy and identified in the declarations. Objects must be in use or connected and ready for use at the location specified for them.

As defined in the policy, an accident is a sudden and accidental breakdown of the object or a part of the object. At the time the breakdown occurs, it must manifest itself by physical damage to the object that necessitates repair or replacement. If a turbine is covered, for instance, an accident would be a sudden and accidental tearing asunder—that is, an accidental breaking of the turbine or electric generator that is part of the object. If an initial accident causes other accidents, they all are considered a single accident. In Unit 14, we previewed the Basic, Broad, and Special peril forms used in property insurance contracts. While explosions are a covered peril under Broad form, explosion is specifically excluded in commercial contracts. Boiler and Machinery contracts are required to provide businesses protection against such losses.

## EQUIPMENT BREAKDOWN COVERAGE FORM

Covers financial losses that stem from accidents to equipment.

- Direct property loss—the cost to repair or replace damaged equipment
- Costs for temporary replacement equipment
- Other expenses incurred to limit the loss or speed the restoration process
- The loss value of spoiled products or materials
- Business recovery expenses

Periodic inspection is an integral part of boiler and machinery policies. The insurance company will inspect the insured object(s). If an object is found to be in ill-repair or a dangerous condition, the insurer will suspend insurance immediately. Advance notice of suspension is not required. However, the insurer will mail written notice of the suspension to the insured.

# SUMMARY

Commercial insurance is used by business owners to help them manage the property and liability risks they face. The Commercial Package Policy, built to meet the needs of large businesses, is assembled from several separate policy components. In this unit, we studied the property coverages available in the Commercial Package Policy. This includes property, inland marine, and boiler and machinery insurance.

The property coverage form protects buildings and personal property used in the business. In addition, the coverage form provides business income and extra expense coverage to compensate businesses for lost revenue during a period of restoration. Builder's risk coverage may also be used by businesses who wish to insure new buildings under construction.

Because commercial property insurance coverage ends beyond 100 feet of the business premises, businesses need inland marine insurance to insure property in transit. The Nationwide Marine Definition has expanded the kinds of risks insured through inland marine contracts. Boiler and machinery insurance is a highly specialized line of insurance products used to insure boilers, machinery, and related equipment against sudden and accidental breakdown, failure, and explosion.

# U N I T   Q U I Z

1. Which of the following losses involving water damage is covered under the building and personal property coverage form with basic causes of loss?

   A. Merchandise in a retail store catches fire and sets off an automatic sprinkler system, resulting in damage to property.
   B. Water from a sewer backs up through a building's drains, causing severe water damage.
   C. A dam breaks, causing flood damage to a building and its contents.
   D. A window is left open, and rain causes extensive damage to the building's contents.

2. The form of coverage for business risks that is most similar to additional living expense for homeowners is

   A. extended period of indemnity
   B. business income
   C. extra expense
   D. loss of rents

3. A business income coverage form provides insurance for

   A. cancellation of a lease
   B. additional living expenses
   C. lost profits
   D. noncontinuing expenses

4. A property policy's coverage can extend to each of the following EXCEPT

   A. money and securities
   B. office equipment
   C. production machinery
   D. merchandise

5. When does a builder's risk policy terminate?

   A. When the building is occupied
   B. 90 days after completion
   C. When the purchaser accepts the property
   D. At the earliest of the above times

6. The Building and Personal Property Coverage Form covers all of the following property EXCEPT

   A. completed additions to the insured building
   B. indoor and outdoor fixtures of the insured building
   C. machinery and equipment
   D. money, notes, and securities

7. Which of the following insurance products covers mechanical breakdown of an air compressor?

   A. General property form
   B. BOP-general liability form
   C. Boiler and Machinery coverage
   D. Comprehensive General Liability

8. Which of the following statements about the boiler and machinery policy is CORRECT?

   A. It provides coverage for fire damage to the insured's building caused by a boiler explosion.
   B. It encourages loss control by providing for suspension of coverage on dangerous or defective objects.
   C. Both A and B
   D. Neither A nor B

# ANSWERS AND RATIONALES TO UNIT QUIZ

1. **A.** Water damage coverage is not provided for backup of sewers or drains except by endorsement. Flood damage is included only on separate policies. For water damage to be covered, there first must be exterior damage to the building. Discharge of a sprinkler system was caused proximately by fire, a covered peril, in the situation described in answer A.

2. **C.** Extra expense coverage insures the extraordinary expenses an insured incurs following a loss to maintain a business. This coverage is most similar to the additional living expense coverage designed to maintain a family's standard of living.

3. **C.** Business income coverage does not apply to losses due to lease cancellation or to expenses that do not continue following a loss. Additional living expense is a homeowners coverage.

4. **A.** Money and securities are specifically excluded personal property under a commercial property policy. Coverage for such items typically is secured using a crime insurance policy.

5. **D.** A builder's risk form provides coverage that terminates at the earliest of the policy expiration or cancellation date, when the owners accept the property, when the insured's interest ceases, when the insured abandons the construction, 90 days after construction is completed, or when the building is occupied in whole or in part or put to its intended use.

6. **D.** The Building and Personal Property Coverage Form covers additions to the insured building as well as its fixtures. Machinery and equipment are also covered. However, accounts, bills, currency deeds, evidences of debt, money, notes, and securities are not covered.

7. **C.** The Boiler and Machinery Coverage Form is designed to provide coverage for an accident, defined as a sudden and accidental breakdown of an object. There are four definitions of object in this form, including pressure and refrigeration objects, mechanical objects, electrical objects, and turbine objects. An air compressor would qualify as an object.

8. **C.** Coverage under a boiler policy may be suspended any time an inspection reveals an unsafe or hazardous condition of an insured object. This should serve to encourage good loss control on the part of the insured. Unlike other property and liability forms, the boiler form automatically covers damage to property in the insured's care, custody, or control.

# Commercial Casualty Insurance

## KEY CONCEPTS

- General liability insurance needs
- Occurrence and claims-made forms
- Liability limitations and exclusions
- Commercial crime insurance
- Commercial auto insurance

**TAKE NOTE**

Business owners can be legally liable for four losses: bodily injury, property damage, personal injury, and advertising injury.

**TAKE NOTE**

The four main business exposures are premises, operations, products, and completed operations.

# GENERAL LIABILITY

### GENERAL LIABILITY INSURANCE

*General liability insurance* is written to cover four major risk exposures:

- premises and operations;
- products and completed operations;
- vicarious; and
- contractual.

For each type of risk, coverage may be written for:

- events that occur within the policy period (*occurrence form*); or
- events for which a claim must be reported during the policy period (*claims-made form*).

### PREMISES AND OPERATIONS EXPOSURE

**Ownership and Maintenance of Premises**  The owner or tenant of a building can be held liable if a member of the public (third party) is injured or the third party's property is damaged as a result of a condition of, or arising out of the use of, the premises. It is easy to see how such conditions as a loose stair tread and a wet floor could cause a person to fall and be injured or cause the person's property to be damaged.

---

EXAMPLE    A customer dropping off a watch for cleaning trips on a loose carpet and drops the watch. She may suffer bodily injuries as well as damage to the watch.

---

**Conduct of Business Operations**  Liability also arises in the course of a business's daily operations. A firm may be liable if a member of the public is injured or his property is damaged either (1) on the premises where the business is conducted or (2) away from the premises by an activity of the owner or an employee.

---

EXAMPLE    A stock clerk, while stocking shelves in a grocery store, drops a box on a customer, causing bodily injury to the customer. An insurance agent, while calling on a client, puts his briefcase on the client's dining room table, causing property damage when the table is scratched. In both examples, some business activity takes place (operations) that causes the injury or damage.

## PRODUCTS AND COMPLETED OPERATIONS LIABILITY

**Products Liability**  A manufacturer or distributor of a faulty product that injures someone or damages someone's property may be held legally liable. Depending on the circumstances of the case, the person injured may seek recovery based on the legal doctrine of negligence, breach of warranty, or strict liability:

■ *Negligence.* Negligence may arise because of poor product manufacture or design or improper warning about dangerous qualities.

---

EXAMPLE    A machine's safety device is removable. If a person, after taking off the safety device, is injured, the manufacturer may be negligent for designing a safety device that is removable.

---

■ *Breach of warranty.* A product is sold with an implied warranty that it is fit for its intended purpose. If it causes injury during its use or consumption, the implied warranty was breached and liability can result.

■ *Strict liability.* Under the doctrine of strict liability, the person injured must prove the following:
  — the manufacturer or supplier knew or should have known that the product was defective when it left the manufacturer's or supplier's custody or control;
  — the defective condition made the product unreasonably dangerous; or
  — the defective product was the proximate cause of the injury.

**Completed Operations Liability**  Completed operations liability exposure arises when a business (such as a contractor) completes operations away from the premises it owns, rents or controls. When work off premises is completed or abandoned and someone is injured or his property is damaged, this is a completed operations exposure.

---

EXAMPLE    A contractor completes a building and turns it over to the retail merchant who owns the building and will conduct business in it. After the building is transferred and occupied, the roof leaks, causing damage to inventory. This is a completed operations liability exposure, and the contractor is liable. By contrast, if someone is hurt or his property damaged while the contractor is in the process of building the structure, it is a business operations exposure, described previously.

---

## VICARIOUS OR CONTINGENT LIABILITY

The general rule is that the principal that engages an independent contractor is not liable for the independent contractor's *torts* (civil wrongs). Some exceptions to this general rule exist, and the liability of the *agent* (contractor or subcontractor) is imposed on the *principal* (person, firm, or entity that engaged the contractor or subcontractor) in some circumstances. In other words, the principal is *vicariously liable* for the agent's actions. For example, the principal may be liable when he is negligent in:

■ selecting a contractor;

■ giving instructions; or

■ failing to stop any unnecessarily dangerous practices that come to his attention.

In addition, an employer who engages an independent contractor to do work that is inherently dangerous to others is subject to liability caused by the independent contractor's negligence. Examples of such inherently dangerous work are blasting and excavating in or near a public highway.

Vicarious liability also may be called *contingent liability*.

## CONTRACTUAL LIABILITY

A business may assume liability for negligent acts of another through a written or an oral contract. When such a contract exists, the business has taken upon itself another's liability.

---

**EXAMPLE**    In a construction contract, the landowner may want the general contractor to sign a hold harmless agreement. By signing such an agreement, the general contractor assumes (holds harmless) the landowner's liability during the construction period.

---

### COMMERCIAL GENERAL LIABILITY COVERAGE

The CGL policy covers four major exposures, including medical payments, in three coverage sections:

- Section A—for bodily injury and property damage resulting from the premises, operations, products, and completed operations (Among other coverages, it includes blanket contractual liability, fire legal liability, host liquor liability, nonowned watercraft liability, and limited worldwide products liability);
- Section B—for personal and advertising injury, including protection for such offenses as defamation (libel, slander), false arrest, and advertising liability; and
- Section C—for medical expenses resulting from accidental bodily injury on or away from the premises.

### OCCURRENCE FORM

The commercial general liability policy can be written on an occurrence or a claims-made form. Policies providing coverage on an occurrence basis pay if an insured is legally liable for injuries or damage that occurred during a policy period, even if a claim is submitted after the policy has expired. When an injury or damage is immediately obvious, this type of coverage poses no problem for the insurance company.

Some types of injuries or damages, however, are latent and not discovered until many years after a policy has expired. For a disease that takes a long period of time to develop symptoms, the problem is further complicated by the fact that it may be difficult to determine when the injury in fact occurred. Possibilities include:

- when the person was first exposed to a hazardous condition (the exposure theory);
- while the disease was developing; and
- when the disease first manifested itself (the manifestation theory).

As we have stated, with the occurrence policy, coverage applies if the damage occurred, started, or was discovered when the policy was in force—even if the policy has since expired. This raises an important issue. A business may have had several liability policies over the years. In this case, the problem is determining when the event occurred in order to know which policy applies. Obviously, if many insurers are involved, each may have its own opinion of when the event occurred and whether that insurer's policy was effective at the time of the event.

## CLAIMS-MADE FORM

To avoid such surprises, the insurance industry developed a claims-made form. The claim must be made during the policy period; the injury or damage must have occurred after the policy's retroactive date but before the policy expires.

A claims-made policy sets two important dates in addition to the policy's inception date:

- The first is the retroactive date, which can be:
    — the same as the policy's inception date;
    — a specified earlier date; or
    — no retroactive date.
- The retroactive date also can restrict coverage to:
    — all events after the retro-date;
    — events at a specific location; or
    — a specific event.

The retroactive date is designed to accept a claim that occurred before the contract's inception date but that has not yet been investigated by any insurer.

**EXAMPLE**    An applicant takes out a policy on January 1, 2005, with insurer A for the period 1/1/05 through 1/1/06. The policy has a retroactive date of 9/1/04. If a claim is made during 2005 for an injury that occurred on or after 9/1/04, insurer A is responsible for the claim if no other investigation of the claim has occurred and the insured is legally liable. If the injury occurred before 9/1/04, the retroactive date, insurer A is not responsible.

The second date is the *extended reporting period*, which is important in the claims-made form for claims first reported after the policy expired for bodily injury or property damage that occurred before termination of the policy expired but after its retroactive date. In effect, it extends the time, after policy expiration, during which a claim can be made so that possible coverage gaps almost always are eliminated.

Two types of extended reporting period exist. The basic extended reporting period (basic tail) is included in the CGL policy form. It covers claims made up to five years after the end of the policy period as long as an occurrence is reported to the insurer no later than 60 days after the end of the policy period. The bodily injury or property damage must have occurred before the end of the policy period and after the retroactive date. Typically, no charge is imposed for the basic tail.

> **TAKE NOTE**
>
> An extended reporting period, also called a tail, is a common provision in a claims-made policy. It does not extend the period of time in which occurrences may take place, merely the time frame for reporting those claims to the insurance company.

The insured also may purchase, by endorsement, a *supplemental extended reporting period* (*supplemental tail*). The insured must request to purchase the supplemental tail in writing within 60 days after policy expiration. When added to the policy, the supplemental tail contains its own aggregate limit equal to the expired policy's aggregate. Coverage under the supplemental tail begins when the coverage provided by the basic tail runs out. The reporting period under the supplemental tail has no time limit. Therefore, it is sometimes referred to as the *forever tail*. The premium for the tail is determined at the time the endorsement is requested. Generally, it may not exceed 200% of the original annual premium for liability coverage. The premium is fully earned, and the endorsement cannot be canceled.

**EXAMPLE**   An applicant takes out a policy on January 1, 2001 with insurer A for the period 1/1/01 through 1/1/02. The policy has a supplemental extended reporting period. If a claim occurs on 4/14/01, but is not discovered nor reported until 6/30/03, the policy issued by insurer A provides coverage.

# COMMERCIAL GENERAL LIABILITY POLICY

The CGL policy has five sections: Coverages, Who Is an Insured, Limits of Insurance, Conditions, and Definitions. A description of each section follows.

## SECTION I—COVERAGE

The CGL provides three coverages:

- bodily injury and property damage;
- personal and advertising injury liability; and
- medical payments.

**Coverage A: Bodily Injury and Property Damage**   The insurance company pays those sums that the insured becomes legally obligated to pay as damages because of bodily injury or property damage. The bodily injury or property damage must be caused by a covered occurrence and must take place within the *coverage territory* during the policy period. *Coverage territory*, the geographical limits to which the coverage extends, is defined in the policy.

Property damage includes physical damage to tangible property, including loss of use of that property. It also includes loss of use of the tangible property that is not physically damaged.

If property damage to a neighboring building makes access to an insured's property impossible, the neighbor's policy pays even though the insured's structure incurs no physical damage.

The insurance company has the right and duty to defend any suit seeking bodily injury or property damage even if such suit is groundless. This right extends to arbitration proceedings. The insurer pays for defense costs in addition to the limit of liability, but only until the limit of liability is used up.

**Exclusions**   Coverage A of the CGL policy has several exclusions:

*Expected or intended liability.* The CGL policy provides no coverage for bodily injury or property damage that is expected or intended from the standpoint of the insured. However, bodily injury resulting from using reasonable force to protect persons or property is therefore covered.

*Contractual liability.* The CGL policy does not cover damages the insured is obligated to pay because he assumes liability under a contract. Exceptions to this exclusion are for tort liability assumed under an insured contract (such as a hold harmless agreement) or a situation in which the insured would be liable even without a contract. The following are insured contracts, either oral or written, for which coverage *would* apply:

- municipal indemnity agreements;
- easement agreements:
  - easement or license agreements in connection with vehicle or pedestrian private railroad crossings at grade; or
  - other easement agreements;
- elevator maintenance agreements;
- leases of premises;
- railroad sidetrack agreements; and
- any part of any other contract pertaining to the insured's business under which the insured assumes the tort liability of another. (Tort liability means liability imposed by law in the absence of any contract or agreement. It includes liability for negligence or assault.)

The insured contracts under a CGL policy can be remembered using the mnemonic acronym LEASE:

**L**  Lease of premises;

**E**  Easement;

**A**  Agreement to indemnify a municipality;

**S**  Sidetrack agreement; and

**E**  Elevator maintenance agreement.

*Liquor liability.* The CGL policy does not cover liability incurred because the insured is in the business of manufacturing, distributing, selling, or serving liquor. However, *host liquor liability* is part of the liability policy. A casual host who simply serves alcohol is provided with liquor liability coverage under the policy.

*Workers' compensation.* There is no coverage under the policy for benefits payable under workers' compensation, disability benefits, or unemployment compensation laws.

*Employer's liability.* The CGL policy excludes coverage for bodily injury to the insured's employees for injuries arising out of or in the course of employment by the insured. As a result, this exclusion prohibits claims by spouses or families and so-called third-party-over actions. (A third-party-over action occurs when an employee sues a manufacturer for injuries caused by a product of that manufacturer, such as a machine, and the manufacturer subsequently sues the employer for negligence in operating or maintaining the machine.) These types of claims are covered under a workers' compensation or employer's liability policy.

*Pollution.* The policy does not cover cleanup costs or bodily injury and property damage arising out of the actual or alleged discharge, disposal, or escape of pollutants.

*Auto, aircraft, or watercraft.* Liability arising out of the ownership, maintenance, operation, entrustment, loading, unloading, or use of any automobile, aircraft, or watercraft is not covered in the CGL policy. The intent of this exclusion is to rule out legal liability other policies cover.

*Mobile equipment.* The policy provides no coverage for mobile equipment while it is being transported by an auto owned or operated by or rented or loaned to an insured, or while it is being used in an organized racing, speed, or demolition contest.

*War.* Liability arising out of war, insurrection, or rebellion is excluded even if it arises from liability assumed under a contract.

*Care, custody, or control.* The CGL policy excludes coverage for damage to property owned by, rented by, or otherwise in the care, custody, or control of the insured. An insured should have property insurance to cover such property.

*Property damage to the insured's work.* This provision excludes coverage for the cost of replacing, repairing, or otherwise redoing the insured's or the insured's employees' faulty work, including loss of use of the named insured's work. This exclusion does not apply if a subcontractor performed the work.

**EXAMPLE**
A TV repairperson comes to a house and fixes the TV on the premises. After that person leaves, however, the TV starts a fire, which ultimately burns down the house. The CGL policy covers the damage to the house, but not the TV. Similarly, suppose a contractor builds a roof over a pedestrian walkway, and three months after the work is completed, the roof collapses. The CGL policy does not pay for rebuilding the roof; however, if a person was injured when the roof fell, that loss is covered.

*Product recall (the sistership exclusion).* The policy excludes damage for loss or cost to the insured for recalling or replacing products or for redoing completed operations. Also excluded is loss of use of a product due to a known or suspected defect. A very limited number of insurers provide product recall coverage.

**Fire Legal Liability**  For a tenant to have coverage in case he causes a fire to rented property, the fire must be unintentional and the tenant must be the negligent party. The CGL policy excludes coverage for damage caused by a tenant's negligence when such damage affects areas of the property within the tenant's control. The tenant must purchase a fire legal liability insurance policy for that coverage.

**Coverage B: Personal and Advertising Injury Liability Coverage**  The insurance company pays those monetary sums that the insured becomes legally obligated to pay as damages because of:

- personal injury arising out of the conduct of the insured's business, excluding advertising, publishing, broadcasting, and telecasting by the insured; or
- advertising injury in the course of advertising the insured's goods, products, or services to which the insurance applies.

The company has the right and duty to defend any suit seeking damages up to the policy limits. The company may investigate and settle any claim at its discretion.

*Personal injury* means injury other than bodily injury arising out of any of the following:
- false arrest, detention, or imprisonment;
- malicious prosecution;
- wrongful entry into or eviction of a person from a room, dwelling, or premises that the person occupies;
- oral or written publication of material that slanders (spoken material) or libels (written material) a person or an organization or that disparages a person's or an organization's goods, products, or services; and
- oral or written publication of material that violates a person's right of privacy.

*Advertising injury* means injury arising out of oral or written publication of material that:
- slanders or libels a person or an organization;
- violates a person's or an organization's ideas or style of doing business;
- misappropriates a person's or an organization's ideas or style of doing business; or
- infringes on a person's or an organization's copyright, title, or slogan.

**Exclusions**  The following exclusions apply to Section B coverage:
- injury arising out of the willful violation of laws;
- liability assumed under contract;
- publication of material known to be false;
- failure of goods, products, or services;
- incorrect description of price of goods, products, or services; and
- offense committed by an insured in the business of advertising, broadcasting, publishing, or telecasting.

**Coverage C: Medical Payments Coverage**  The insurer pays up to the limit stated in the declarations for reasonable medical expenses incurred by any person who requires medical services because of an accident arising out of business operations. The policy pays medical expenses without regard to liability or negligence, but only if the person or event was one the insurer would insure under general liability coverage. This does not cover medical expenses arising out of automobile accidents.

In this coverage part, the insurance company pays reasonable expenses for bodily injury to a third party caused by an accident:

- on the premises that the insured owns or rents;
- on ways next to the premises the insured owns or rents; or
- because of the insured's business operation.

These medical expenses are paid *regardless of fault.*

**Exclusions**  Section C offers no coverage for:

- bodily injury to any insured;
- bodily injury to any employee of the insured (covered by workers' compensation);
- bodily injury to a tenant of the insured;
- injuries incurred while a person takes part in athletics; and
- damages sustained in accidents excluded under coverage A.

**Supplementary Payments for Coverages A and B**  The insurance company pays certain costs independent of the policy's liability limits. These costs include:

- all expenses the insurance company incurs (including defense costs, expenses for investigating the claim, costs taxed against the insured, and interest on judgments);
- up to $250 for bail bonds and release of attachment bonds (the insurance company provides the money, but the insured or an attorney must apply for the bonds); and
- reasonable expenses the insured incurs when the insurance company requests the insured's assistance in investigating or defending any claim or suit (including up to $250 per day for time away from work).

## SECTION II—WHO IS AN INSURED

If the business is a sole proprietorship, the insured is the designated person and spouse, but only for business acts. If the business is a partnership or a joint venture, the partners or coventurers and their spouses are the insureds—but, again, only for business acts.

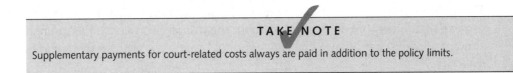

If the business is a corporation, the executive officers and directors are the insureds only for their business acts. The stockholders are also insureds, but only in relation to their possible liability as stockholders.

Employees other than executive officers also are insured for liability for acts they commit within the scope of their employment. An employee is not an insured for causing bodily or personal injury to a fellow employee because such injury covered is under workers' compensation.

An employee is not covered for bodily or personal injury that arises when the employee provides or fails to provide professional health care services. Individuals who provide health care services must carry their own medical malpractice coverage.

## SECTION III—LIMITS OF INSURANCE

The CGL policy sets six limits of insurance:

- general aggregate limit (sum of all medical damages under coverage C plus the damages under coverages A and B; excludes injury and damages included in the products and completed operations hazard);
- products and completed operations aggregate limit;
- personal and advertising injury limit;
- each occurrence limit (maximum under one limit);
- fire damage limit (maximum payable for property damage to rented premises for a single fire); and
- medical expense limit (maximum payable because of bodily injury to *one* person).

## SECTION IV—CONDITIONS

This section of the CGL policy deals with a number of issues, from bankruptcy to legal actions.

**Bankruptcy**  Bankruptcy or insolvency of the insured or of the insured's estate does not relieve the insurer of any obligation.

**Duties in the Event of Occurrence, Claim, or Suit**  In the event of an occurrence, a claim, or a suit, the insured's duties include:

- notifying promptly the insurer of an occurrence that may result in a claim (including how, when, and where the occurrence took place and the names and addresses of any injured persons and witnesses);
- providing prompt written notice of a claim or suit;
- providing immediate notice to the insurer of receipt of demands, notices, summons, or other legal papers the insured receives in connection with a claim or suit; and
- cooperating and assisting in the investigation of a claim.

Except at his own cost, no insured voluntarily makes a payment, assumes any obligation, or incurs any expense, other than for first aid, without the insurer's consent. If the insured does so, the policy is not void, but the insurance company is not obligated to cover this particular occurrence.

**Legal Action Against the Insurer** The insured must comply fully with all terms of the policy before taking legal action against the insurer. A party may sue the insurer to recover damages against an insured in the form of a settlement or judgment. Such a settlement or judgment can amount to no more than the policy limits.

**Other Insurance** Generally, the CGL policy is the primary policy. In some situations, however, it is the excess policy. If two policies exist, each with a provision making it primary, the method of sharing will be contribution by equal shares; if any other insurance does not permit contribution by equal shares, contribution will be by limits (pro rata to the total amount available).

**Premium Audit** The premium paid is an advance premium as a deposit premium only. At the end of the policy period, or during periods stated in the contract, the insurer audits the insured's basis of premium (sales, payroll, etc.) and computes the earned premium for that period.

**Separation of Insureds** Except with respect to the limits of insurance, the CGL policy applies separately to each insured against whom a claim is made or a suit is brought. In other words, the limit of insurance is paid only once per occurrence regardless of the number of claimants or the number of persons insured. For other costs, such as defense costs, each insured is separate.

**Transfer of Rights of Recovery Against Others to the Insurer** If the insured has rights to recover from a third party all or part of any payment the insurer has made, those rights are transferred to the insurer. The insured must do nothing to impair those rights. At the insurer's request, the insured must bring suit or transfer those rights to the insurer. This transfer of rights is known as *subrogation*.

## SECTION V—DEFINITIONS

Other key definitions that arise in CGL policies are explained below.

- *Bodily injury* means bodily injury, sickness, or disease a person sustains, including death resulting from any of these at any time.
- *Coverage territory* includes:
  - the United States (including its territories and possessions), Puerto Rico, and Canada;
  - international waters or airspace; or
  - all parts of the world if: the injury or damage arises out of goods or products the insured makes or sells in the territory described above, or the activities of a person whose home is in the territory described above, but who is away for a short time on the insured's business.

*Employee* includes a leased worker, but not a temporary worker.

*Occurrence* means an accident, including continuous or repeated exposure to substantially the same general harmful conditions.

*Property damage* means physical damage to tangible property, including all resulting loss of use of the property. All such loss is considered to occur at the time of the physical damage that caused it. Property damage also means loss of use of tangible property that is not physically damaged.

# CRIME INSURANCE

Insurance for losses due to crime has become more important than ever for businesses and other types of organizations. As the nation's crime rate continues to rise and the seriousness of those crimes escalates and extends to all aspects of modern life, the need to include crime insurance in a comprehensive risk management program increases. Crime losses can impact a business from one of two sources: crimes committed by employees and crimes committed by others.

## DEFINITIONS

*Custodian* means the insured and any partner or employee while that person has care and custody of insured property inside the premises. This term does not include a janitor or watchperson.

*Messenger* means the insured and any partner or employee who has care and custody of insured property outside the premises.

*Burglary* is the forcible entry into or exit out of an insured's premises with the intent to carry off property belonging to the insured. Visible signs of forcible entry or exit must be present. The forcible entry may be made by tools, explosives, electricity, chemicals, or physical damage to the premises.

*Robbery* is the forcible removal of an insured's property by:
- use or threat of the use of violence; or
- means of injuring or murdering a messenger or custodian.

*Theft* is any act of stealing. This broad term covers robbery and burglary, as well as larceny. Theft includes the stealing of property, but evidence of a holdup, forcible entry or exit, or physical violence is not necessary.

# COMMERCIAL CRIME COVERAGE FORM (LOSS SUSTAINED FORM)

The **Commercial Crime Coverage Form** consolidates earlier crime forms into a more streamlined approach to coverage. This form also includes 20 new and revised definitions that expand the scope of the earlier crime insurance forms.

## INSURING AGREEMENTS

This form contains seven insuring agreements. The insured may choose all or any of them, depending on the need for coverage. (The applicable exclusions are noted.)

- Employee Theft
- Forgery or Alteration
- Inside the Premises—Theft of Money and Securities
- Inside the Premises—Robbery and Safe Burglary of Other Property
- Outside the Premises
- Computer Fraud
- Money Orders and Counterfeit Paper Currency

**Insuring Agreement A.1: Employee Theft** The insured pays for losses concerning money, securities, and other property stolen by an employee who acts alone or with other persons.

**Exclusions** Losses caused by employees who were covered under a policy that had been canceled and not reinstated.

- Inventory shortages
- Losses resulting from trading
- Losses resulting from fraudulent warehouse receipts or related documents

**Insuring Agreement A.2: Forgery or Alteration** The insurer pays for losses due to forgery or alterations of checks, draft, promissory notes, or other promises to pay money. These instruments are covered if they are drawn by the insured or someone acting as the insured's agent.

If the insured is sued for refusing to pay a forged check, draft, promissory note, or other promise to pay money, the insurer may agree to cover the insured's legal costs of defense. This coverage is in addition to coverage limits.

**Insuring Agreement A.3: Inside the Premises—Theft of Money and Securities**
The insurer pays for losses resulting from the theft, disappearance, or destruction of money or securities inside the insured's premises.

If the premises or its exterior are damaged during the theft or attempted theft of money and securities, the insurer will cover the cost of repair or replacement. The insurer will also pay for loss or damage done to a locked safe, vault, cash register, cash box, or drawer inside the premises during a theft or attempted theft.

**Exclusions**

- Losses caused by accounting or arithmetical errors
- Losses resulting from the exchange or purchase of property
- Loss caused by fire, unless the loss involves money and securities or damage to a safe or vault
- Property lost from a money-operated device, unless a continuous recording instrument records the amount of money deposited in it
- Loss or damage to motor vehicles, trailers, semi-trailers, or equipment and attachments
- Property lost or damaged when transferred out of the premises or banking premises due to unauthorized instructions, threat of physical harm, or threat of property damage (although loss will be covered by Insuring Agreement A.5 if the property was money, securities, or other

property in a messenger's care while the insured had no knowledge of the threat when the transfer began or had knowledge of a threat, but the loss didn't result from the threat)

■ Losses due to vandalism of the premises; safe; vault; cash register, box, or drawer; or other property

■ Loss resulting from the insured's—or any authorized person's—voluntary transferring title or possession of property due to another's dishonesty.

### Insuring Agreement A.4: Inside the Premises—Robbery or Safe Burglary of Other Property

The insurer will pay for loss or damage to property other than money or securities that are within the premises, when such loss or damage results from the actual or attempted robbery of a custodian. It will also pay when the loss or damage occurs inside the premises due to an actual or attempted burglary of a safe.

If the premises or its exterior are damaged during the robbery of a custodian, the burglary of a safe, or the attempt to commit either, the insurer will cover the cost of repair or replacement to the premises. The insurer will also pay for loss or damage done to a locked safe or vault inside the premises during an actual or attempted robbery of a custodian or burglary of a safe.

**Exclusions**  These are the same as those for Insuring Agreement A.3.

### Insuring Agreement A.5: Outside the Premises

The insurer will pay for loss of money and securities from theft, disappearance, or destruction while outside the premises and in the custody of a messenger or an armored motor vehicle. Payment is also made for money and securities lost due to an actual or attempted robbery of the messenger or armored motor vehicle.

**Exclusions**  These are the same as those for Insuring Agreement A.3.

### Insuring Agreement A.6: Computer Fraud

The insurer will pay for loss or damage to money, securities, and other property that results from the use of a computer to fraudulently transfer them out of the premises, bank, or other safe depository to a person or place beyond the premises, bank, or safe depository.

**Exclusions**  Losses resulting from the exchange or purchase of property

■ Losses resulting from fraudulent directions to pay or transfer funds

■ Inventory shortages

■ Loss resulting from the insured's—or any authorized person's—voluntary transferring title possession of property due to another's dishonesty

### Insuring Agreement A.7: Funds Transfer Fraud

The insurer will pay for loss of funds resulting from a fraudulent instruction directing a financial institution to transfer, pay, or deliver funds from the insured's transfer account.

### Insuring Agreement A.8: Money Orders and Counterfeit Paper Currency

The insurer pays for the loss if the insured, during the course of business and in good faith, accepts money orders that are not paid or counterfeit money.

**Exclusion** Loss resulting from the use of a computer to fraudulently transfer money, securities, and other property.

## GENERAL EXCLUSIONS

The following exclusions are in addition to the usual exclusions of the general crime coverage form as noted above. Unless specifically covered by an Insuring Agreement, there is no coverage for losses resulting from:

■ theft or other dishonest act committed by the insured, partners, or members;

■ theft or other dishonest act committed by the insured's employees, managers, directors, trustees, or authorized representatives, unless covered by Insuring Agreement A.1;

■ property that is seized or destroyed by order of government;

■ lost income, payment of damages for legal liability, and payment of expenses incurred in determining the existence or amount of the loss resulting from a covered act or occurrence;

■ legal expenses, unless covered by Insuring Agreement A.2;

■ nuclear reaction, radiation, contamination, or related incident; or

■ war, warlike action, insurrection, revolution, or related incident.

# COMMERCIAL AUTOMOBILE INSURANCE

## BUSINESS AUTO POLICY

Automobiles owned or operated by individuals, unincorporated associations, joint ventures, governmental entities, partnerships or corporations, or autos that are not eligible for personal automobile policies because of auto type, can be insured under a commercial package policy by using a business auto coverage form. The coverages available under the business auto policy (BAP) are very similar to those presented under the personal auto policy. Because of this similarity, the description of coverages presented here will be brief. Coverages that are part of the BAP include only liability and physical damage coverage. Medical payments coverage, uninsured motorists coverage, underinsured motorists coverage, or personal injury protection must be added to the basic policy by endorsement. Business auto coverage can be included as part of a commercial package policy (CPP) or written as a monoline policy.

The business auto policy is divided into five major sections:

■ Section I—Covered autos;

■ Section II—Liability coverage;

■ Section III—Physical damage coverage;

■ Section IV—Business auto conditions; and

■ Section V—Definitions.

Two additional coverages, medical payments and uninsured motorists, must be added by endorsement.

**Section I—Covered Autos**   The BAP uses a system of nine covered auto symbols to denote the vehicles to which each of the policy's coverages applies:

- Symbol 1—Any auto;
- Symbol 2—Owned autos only;
- Symbol 3—Owned private passenger autos;
- Symbol 4—Owned autos other than private passenger autos;
- Symbol 5—Owned autos subject to no-fault benefits;
- Symbol 6—Owned autos subject to compulsory uninsured motorists law;
- Symbol 7—Specifically described autos only;
- Symbol 8—Hired autos (leased, hired, rented, or borrowed); and
- Symbol 9—Nonowned autos (owned by employees or partners of the insured).

Coverage can be customized to meet an insured's needs by selecting the appropriate symbols. Symbol 1 affords the broadest coverage, because it applies literally to any auto, owned, nonowned, or hired. However, it can be used only for liability coverage. Symbol 7 provides the most restrictive coverage because it applies only to autos listed in the policy and no others. Symbols 3 and 4 differentiate between private passenger autos and commercial vehicles. Symbols 5 and 6 are used only in states that have no-fault laws or laws that require inclusion of uninsured motorists coverage. Symbol 8 applies to autos the insured leases, hires, rents, or borrows, but not to autos the insured's employees own. Symbol 9 includes all autos the insured does not own, lease, hire, or borrow used in connection with the business, including those vehicles owned by employees or members of their households.

**Section II—Liability Coverage**   Section II coverage provides for: bodily injury or property damage resulting from ownership, maintenance, or use of a covered auto; and expenses to defend, investigate, and settle claims.

**Section III—Physical Damage Coverage**

**Comprehensive coverage.**   Comprehensive coverage pays for loss to a covered auto or its equipment for any cause, except collision and overturn (or upset). Glass breakage, hitting a bird or an animal, falling objects, and missiles are covered under comprehensive if the policy provides that coverage.

**Collision and overturn.**   A covered auto or its equipment is insured against damage from collision with another object or from overturn. Towing coverage is available only for private passenger autos.

Various deductibles are available for each of the physical damage coverages.

**Section IV—Business Auto Conditions** Section IV states the conditions applicable to the policy in addition to the common conditions. This coverage form contains five loss conditions and eight general conditions. Some of the BAP's important policy conditions include the requirement that the insured file a police report in the event of a theft, submit to an appraisal process if a claim is disputed, and cooperate with the insurer in defending any claim. The BAP provides primary insurance for owned automobiles, as well as excess over any other applicable insurance for nonowned autos. This is where the phrase "the insurance follows the car" originates, because the policy on the vehicle pays first and the driver's policy provides excess protection. This section uses the term first-named insured to clarify who must pay premiums and receive notices when many insureds are listed.

**Section V—Definitions** Some of the important definitions contained in the business auto policy follow.

- An accident includes a continuous or repeated exposure to the same conditions, resulting in bodily injury or property damage.

- Auto means a land motor vehicle, trailer, or semi-trailer designed for travel on public roads, but the term does not include mobile equipment. For liability insurance, the term includes mobile equipment only while a covered auto is carrying or towing it.

- Bodily injury means bodily injury, sickness, or disease any person sustains and includes death resulting from any of these.

- Property damage means damage to or loss of use of tangible property.

# THE GARAGE POLICY

Companies in the business of selling, servicing, storing, or parking autos have unique insurance needs. To meet the special needs of garages, the Insurance Services Office (ISO) developed a special Garage Program and the Garage Coverage Form (CA 00 05 10). The garage policy combines a business auto policy (BAP), a commercial general liability policy (CGL), and garage-keepers insurance, a special type of bailee coverage, into a single policy.

# SUMMARY

The Commercial Package Policy offers several casualty coverages including general liability, commercial crime, and commercial auto insurance. In this unit, we examined each of these casualty coverages in detail. As we saw in the previous unit, any one of these coverages may be included as a part of the larger package policy, depending upon the needs of the commercial client.

Commercial General Liability (CGL) coverage provides protection against a broad range of liability risk exposures. This includes premises, operations, completed operations, and personal injury claims. While commercial crime coverage protects businesses against burglary, robbery, and related losses, commercial auto insurance is used by businesses that own, operate, sell, and service vehicles.

# UNIT QUIZ

1. Each of the following is a duty of the insured in the event of an occurrence, a claim, or a suit EXCEPT

    A. promptly notifying the insurer of an occurrence that may result in a claim
    B. at his own expense, making any reasonable settlement with the injured party
    C. forwarding any legal papers, including suits, to the insurance company
    D. cooperating with the insurer in the defense of a claim

2. Which of the following is NOT a supplementary payment the CGL policy provides?

    A. Cost of bonds
    B. Interest on judgments
    C. Costs of investigation and defense
    D. Medical payments

3. For an event to qualify as an occurrence under a liability policy, which of the following statements must be TRUE?

    A. It must have been expected by the claimant.
    B. It must not have been expected or intended from the insured's standpoint.
    C. It must be unexpected and unintended from the claimant's standpoint.
    D. It must have occurred while the insured was not present.

4. A laundromat might purchase a CGL policy to protect against which of the following situations?

    A. Employees leaving to continue the same business elsewhere, resulting in a loss of customers
    B. Loss of revenues if the electricity goes off as a result of the utility's negligence
    C. Burning of a person in a restroom from hot water
    D. Damage to property from ruptured water pipes

5. Which of the following is included under the commercial general liability policy as premises and operations coverage?

    A. Guest slips on carpet in the insured's apartment building
    B. Insured is injured while repairing the roof
    C. Customer becomes ill after eating at the insured's restaurant
    D. Roof begins to leak after the insured installs new shingles

6. The commercial general liability policy covers which of the following accidents?

    A. Injury to a customer that is never reported to the company
    B. Injury caused by an employee to a customer while acting within the scope of employment
    C. Injury to an employee of the insured while acting within the scope of employment
    D. Injury caused by an employee while on vacation

7. A commercial general liability policy covers the policyholder for contractual liability arising from all of the following EXCEPT

    A. easement agreement
    B. railroad sidetrack agreement
    C. elevator maintenance agreement
    D. escrow agreement

8. Why are Symbols 8 and 9 unnecessary when providing coverage using Symbol 1 under the business auto policy?

    A. They are not available when Symbol 1 is used.
    B. Symbol 1 includes coverage for these vehicles as any auto.
    C. Symbols 1, 8, and 9 provide the same coverage.
    D. They are incompatible.

9. For which of the following reasons might some commercial insureds NOT wish to include medical payments and uninsured motorists coverage in their business auto policies?

    A. They are unconcerned about injuries to the passengers in their vehicles.
    B. Because some employees only drive certain vehicles, they are covered by workers' compensation.
    C. They do not feel a social responsibility to the passengers in commercial vehicles.
    D. They are covered for injuries to passengers under the bodily injury portions of their coverage.

10. Which of the following is a definition of theft?

    A. Loss of property
    B. Any act of stealing
    C. Wrongful taking of property, leaving visible signs of forcible entry
    D. Mysterious disappearance

11. Which is NOT covered under Commercial General Liability insurance?

    A. An employee who is injured on an escalator in the store
    B. A shopper who accidentally walks through a plate glass window in the store
    C. A shopper who trips on a bucket left by a janitor
    D. A patron who is injured after choking on food in a restaurant

12. The Commercial General Liability (CGL) policy includes all of the following types of limits EXCEPT

    A. aggregate
    B. personal injury
    C. occurrence
    D. combined

13. Loss that occurs when someone is mugged taking a deposit to the bank is considered which of the following?

    A. Theft
    B. Burglary
    C. Robbery
    D. Larceny

# ANSWERS AND RATIONALES TO UNIT QUIZ

1. **B.** The insurance contract precludes the insured from settling with third parties without the insurer's permission.

2. **D.** Medical payments, a separate coverage under the CGL policy, are not included in supplementary payments.

3. **B.** The first exclusion under the CGL policy eliminates coverage for insured's bodily injury or property damage that is expected or intended from the insured's standpoint.

4. **C.** The CGL policy covers bodily injury and property damage as well as personal and advertising injury. It does not extend coverage for consequential losses or for losses to property.

5. **A.** Premises and operations coverage applies to occurrences that take place on property the insured owns, rents, or controls or that arise from current activities. Coverage does not apply to the insured.

6. **B.** The CGL policy requires prompt notice of claims. Coverage does not apply to injuries to employees on or off the job.

7. **D.** Insured contracts under the CGL policy include leases, easements, agreements to indemnify municipalities, sidetrack agreements, and elevator maintenance agreements only.

8. **B.** Symbol 1 applies to any auto and therefore covers autos that the insured owns or non-owned autos that employees borrow, lease, rent, use, or own.

9. **B.** When the only occupants of an insured's vehicles are employees, workers' compensation is their sole remedy for injuries suffered in automobile accidents. Therefore, the insured may not wish to provide medical payments or uninsured motorists coverage for commercial vehicles.

10. **B.** Theft is a broad term meaning the taking of property belonging to someone else or any act of stealing, whether by robbery, burglary, or larceny.

11. **A.** The situations described in choices B, C, and D are the reasons a business owner would buy liability insurance. The purpose of CGL insurance is to protect a business against claims arising out of premises, the business it conducts, products it makes or sells, or operations in progress or completed. Workers' compensation coverage is available for injuries to employees.

12. **D.** CGL policies have a personal injury limit, a per occurrence limit, and an annual aggregate limit.

13. **C.** Robbery is the forcible removal of an insured's property by use or threat of the use of violence; or means of injuring or murdering a messenger or custodian.

# Businessowners Policy

## KEY CONCEPTS

- Prepackaged nature of the BOP
- Eligibility
- Property, liability, and optional coverages
- Endorsements to the businessowners policy

More than 30 years ago, insurance agents and policyholders sought a better method to deal with the exposures of small businessowners. Personal lines policies were being offered as a package or bundle of needed coverages, but commercial policies were still modular, needing to be built section by section. In addition, the rating system was cumbersome and time consuming. All of this required a level of sophistication and technical knowledge that was lacking among policyholders and some newer agents, who were likely to specialize in small business accounts. Originally, an insurance company developed the businessowners policy (BOP), but the ISO soon came up with its own version.

Today, major insurance companies generally offer their own BOP-type policies, with names specific to those companies, but most pattern their forms after the ISO policy. The discussion that follows is based on the ISO policy. Although no company uses the form without modification, it remains a good way to study individual company forms that follow similar formats.

## OBJECTIVE

When you complete this unit, you should be able to:

■ identify the businessowners policy's purpose and unique characteristics;

■ determine the types of businesses eligible for coverage under the BOP;

■ describe the property the BOP does and does not cover;

■ explain the additional property coverages the BOP provides;

■ discuss the BOP's extensions of property coverage;

■ describe the optional coverages;

■ discuss the BOP liability coverages; and

■ identify endorsements available through the BOP.

# PURPOSE AND CHARACTERISTICS

The businessowners policy is a package policy providing most of the property (both direct and indirect), crime, and liability coverages small and medium-sized businesses require. The property coverages are similar to the building and personal property coverage form and the business income coverage discussed in unit 18. However, the BOP automatically includes many of the coverages available only by endorsement in the CPP program.

## ELIGIBILITY

The BOP was designed for businesses that represent relatively low hazards and more innocuous exposures. Therefore, eligibility is restricted to apartment buildings, offices, eligible wholesalers, mercantile risks, and service or processing occupancies. Additional restrictions limit the size of the business that qualifies for coverage. For instance, sales are limited to $3 million, and the maximum floor area for mercantile, service, office, or wholesale risks is 25,000 square feet. Four new categories were included recently for eligibility under the BOP: contractors, restaurants (simple food preparation facilities only), convenience stores with gasoline pumps, laundries, and dry cleaners. The BOP does not cover businesses related to autos, bars, and banks.

## POLICY OUTLINE

The 2000 ISO BOP is a self-contained contract that includes the following parts:

- Businessowners declarations;
- Section I—Special Form Property Coverage;
- Section II—Businessowners Liability Coverage;
- Section III—Common Policy Conditions; and
- endorsements as required.

Many of the BOP's basic policy provisions are the same as the provisions discussed in unit 18 for commercial property insurance. This unit will note the differences.

## BUSINESSOWNERS POLICY DECLARATIONS

One of the BOP's unique features is that common coverages are included in the form, rather than being attached to it as policy endorsements. Coverage applies, however, only if it has been activated by a check mark in the declarations. Listing the optional coverages on the declarations page alerts policyholders to important coverages that are available but which they have not purchased.

## SECTION I—PROPERTY COVERAGE

The 2002 ISO BOP provides Special Form Property Coverage for the following:

**Building(s)**  The BOP covers the replacement cost of the buildings at the premises described in the declarations, including completed additions, fixtures, permanently installed machinery and equipment, personal property of a landlord in rented units, and personal property used to service or maintain the premises. If the buildings are not covered by other insurance, BOP coverage also includes additions under construction, building alterations and repairs and materials, supplies, equipment, and temporary structures on or within 100 feet of the premises being used to make alterations, repairs, or additions to buildings or structures.

**Business Personal Property**  The BOP policy covers replacement cost of the business personal property the insured owns and uses for business purposes at the premises described in the declarations and within 100 feet while in a vehicle or out in the open. Coverage also extends to the tenant's improvements and betterments, meaning the insured's use of or interest in fixtures, alterations, installations, or additions comprising a part of the building the insured occupies but does not own.

**Additional Coverages**  The BOP includes many additional coverages.

**Debris Removal**  The BOP covers the cost of removing debris of covered property that results from an insured loss. The most the insurer pays is 25% of the amount of the direct loss, plus the extension for uncovered debris removal. However, if the debris removal expense exceeds this amount, or if the combined amount of the direct loss and the debris removal expense exceeds the policy limit, the company pays up to an additional $10,000.

**Preservation of Property/Removal** When covered property is moved from the premises to protect it from damage by a covered cause of loss, coverage applies for 30 days while that property is being moved or is located at a temporary location.

**Fire Department Service Charge** The policy pays up to $1,000 for the cost of fire service to protect covered property.

**Business Income** One of the singular features of the BOP policy is the automatic inclusion of indirect loss coverage as an additional coverage. If business operations are suspended due to a covered loss, the policy pays for loss of business income during the period of time the property is being restored. Coverage applies for up to 12 months following a loss and is paid on the basis of the actual loss the insured sustains, in addition to any limits indicated in the declarations. Payroll expenses are covered for 60 days, allowing the business owner to compensate employees during a period of restoration.

**Extra Expense** Another important automatic feature of the BOP is the inclusion of extra expense coverage. Both the business income and extra expense coverage the BOP provides are similar to the CPP program's separate coverage forms.

**Pollutant Clean-Up and Removal** The company pays the cost to extract pollutants from land or water at the described premises if the release or discharge was caused by a covered loss during the policy period. The most that the policy pays is $10,000 in any 12-month period.

**Civil Authority** Business income and extra expense is extended to include loss caused by action of a civil authority that prevents access to the insured premises when there has been a direct loss to property other than at the described premises, such as an adjacent location. The cause of the loss at that location must be covered as if it had occurred at the insured location.

**Money Orders and Counterfeit Paper Currency** The policy pays up to $1,000 for loss due to acceptance of counterfeit currency or dishonored money orders.

**Forgery or Alteration** Loss due to forgery or alteration of an insured's check, draft, promissory note, or similar item is covered up to $2,500.

**Increased Cost of Construction** When buildings are insured under the policy, the company pays up to $10,000 for the additional loss caused by the increased costs the insured incurs in complying with an ordinance or a law that regulates the construction or repair of buildings or with a zoning or land use law.

## COVERAGE EXTENSIONS

Both BOPs provide six extensions of coverage in addition to the limits of liability shown in the policies.

**Personal Property at Newly Acquired Premises** A limit of up to $100,000 applies to personal property located at any premises the insured acquires during the policy period. Coverage ends after 30 days or when the values are reported to the company, whichever is earlier.

**Personal Property Off Premises**  A $5,000 limit applies to personal property other than money and securities, valuable papers, and records, or accounts receivable located off the insured premises. This includes personal property while in transit and at temporary locations the insured does not own, lease, or rent.

**Outdoor Property**  Insurance can be extended to apply to damage to outdoor fences, radio and television antennas (including satellite dishes), signs (other than those attached to buildings), trees, shrubs, and plants caused by the perils of fire, lightning, explosion, aircraft, riot, or civil commotion. The total amount of coverage is $2,500 under this extension, but a limitation of $500 applies to any one tree, shrub, or plant.

**Personal Effects**  The insured may extend coverage up to $2,500 for loss of personal effects, including those that officers, partners, or employees own. Coverage does not apply to loss due to theft or to loss of tools or equipment used in the insured's business.

**Valuable Papers and Records**  Loss or damage to valuable papers and records on the insured premises is limited to $10,000. A separate limit of $5,000 applies to loss off premises. Coverage is provided for the cost of researching, replacing, or restoring lost information, including information stored on electronic or magnetic media for which no duplicates exist.

**Accounts Receivable**  Loss or damage to accounts receivable records that causes accounts to become uncollectible is covered up to $10,000 on premises and $5,000 off premises.

**Property Exclusions**  The 2002 businessowners policy provides Special peril form coverage. Special form policies cover all perils except those specifically listed as an exclusion.

- power outage off premises;
- inherent defects/intentional acts;
- maintenance—mechanical/electrical breakdown;
- building code/ordinance;
- war/nuclear;
- flood and ground water;
- wear and tear, rust and mold;
- earth movement;
- smog;
- birds, insects, rodents, and domestic animals;
- steam boiler explosion;
- aircraft, automobiles, motor trucks, and other vehicles subject to motor vehicle registration;
- bullion, money, and securities;
- land, water, growing crops, and lawns; or
- watercraft (including motors, equipment, and accessories).

## OPTIONAL COVERAGES

**Employee Dishonesty** When designated in the declarations, the BOP covers loss of money or other business personal property caused by the dishonest or fraudulent acts of the named insured's employees. Claims are paid once an employee either admits to the act or is convicted. Coverage is for an amount not exceeding the limit of liability shown in the declarations and subject to the conditions that apply generally to crime insurance, as discussed in Unit 19.

**Outdoor Signs** While signs attached to the insured structure are covered to a limit of $1,000, outdoor signs are not covered at all. When designated in the declarations, coverage is provided for loss to all exterior signs that are the insured's property or the property of others in the insured's care, custody, or control. The property must be on the premises described in the declarations, and coverage is for direct physical loss. Although broad, coverage for exterior signs excludes wear and tear, corrosion or rust, latent defect, or mechanical breakdown.

**Mechanical Breakdown** When mechanical breakdown is designated in the declarations, the BOP covers loss from an accident to an object (as defined in the policy) that the insured owns, leases, or operates. Additional information about this type of coverage was presented in Unit 18, Boiler and Machinery Insurance.

**Money and Securities** Coverage applies to money and securities while at the described premises or at a bank or savings institution, in a custodian's control, and while in transit between such places. Coverage for theft, destruction, or disappearance typically is provided at a limit of $10,000.

## DEDUCTIBLE

A standard deductible of $500 applies to loss in any one occurrence. The deductible may be increased and a premium credit given. The deductible provision does not apply to losses under business income, extra expense, civil authority, and fire department service charge coverages. A 72-hour time deductible under business income and civil authority coverages applies, however.

## LIMITS OF INSURANCE

While the commercial property policy required the insured to satisfy an 80% coinsurance requirement, the businessowners policy has no such requirement. The policy will pay the applicable limits for any covered property loss. The BOP also provides an automatic seasonal increase in policy limits for business personal property. The seasonal increase of 25% automatically available through the businessowners policy was only available through endorsement on the Commerical Property policy.

## SECTION II—BUSINESS LIABILITY COVERAGE

**Business Liability** The insurer pays on the insured's behalf all sums that the insured becomes legally obligated to pay as damages because of bodily injury, property damage, personal injury, or advertising injury caused by an occurrence to which the insurance applies. Liability coverage is structured as an occurrence form contract. Liability claims are handled by the insurer who provided coverage when the loss occurred.

> **TAKE NOTE**
>
> The BOP may cover losses of money or other business personal property caused by the dishonest or fraudulent acts of the insured's employees.

**Exclusions**  The businessowners liability policy contains many of the same exclusions and limitations included in the CGL policy discussed in unit 19. The BOP excludes the following liabilities:

- expected or intended injury;
- liquor liability;
- workers' compensation;
- employer's liability;
- pollution;
- aircraft, auto, or watercraft;
- mobile equipment;
- war;
- professional services;
- damage to the insured's product;
- damage to the insured's work;
- recall of products, work, or impaired property; and
- personal or advertising injury (subject to coverage limitations).

Additional exclusions apply to the medical expense coverage under the policy. Coverage does not apply to a(n):

- insured;
- person hired to do work for or on behalf of an insured or an insured's tenant;
- person injured on that part of the insured's premises he normally occupies;
- person eligible to receive workers' compensation or other similar benefits; or
- person injured while taking part in athletics.

## BOP ENDORSEMENTS

A number of endorsements are available to customize the BOP according to a policyholder's needs. Some of the more common endorsements follow:

**Additional insured endorsements**  Several endorsements cover additional entities under the insured's policy.

**Limitation of coverage to designated premises or projects** Sometimes an insurer will not provide coverage on a comprehensive basis and requires a policy modification to make coverage applicable to only certain locations or activities.

**Hired and nonowned auto liability** If coverage is not provided on a business auto policy (usually because the insured has no owned automobile exposures), the coverage for employee use of automobiles in the insured's business and the insured's use of borrowed or rented autos may be provided in the BOP.

**Spoilage coverage** This endorsement provides direct damage coverage for spoilage of perishable stock, such as food products.

**Ordinance or law** This endorsement extends building coverage under the standard or special form to include loss to the undamaged portion of the building or structure.

**Utility services—direct damage** This endorsement provides coverage due to interruption of water, communication, and power services if the loss occurs off premises.

**Earthquake** Coverage is extended under either the standard or special form to apply to loss due to earthquake.

**Professional liability endorsements** A variety of endorsements is available for selected professional liability exposures, such as barbers, beauticians, funeral directors, opticians, printers, and veterinarians.

**Off-Premises Utility Services** Covers direct damage losses to insured property caused by an interruption of utility services that occurs away from the insured's premises. The services included are water, power, and communication.

# SUMMARY

The Businessowners policy is a pre-packaged contract providing the insurance protection needed by most small to medium sized businesses. Eligibility for the BOP is based largely upon square footage and business revenue; some small businesses are ineligible for a BOP due to the nature of their products or services they provide.

The Businessowners policy provides property, liability, business income, and crime coverage in a single contract. A variety of optional coverages and endorsements may be added to meet the specific needs of the policyholder.

# UNIT QUIZ

1. Which of the following statements about the BOP's business income coverage is CORRECT?

   A. It pays the net income that the insured would have received had no loss occurred.
   B. It guarantees a profit for the insured in the event of a loss.
   C. It pays only continuing expenses.
   D. It pays whether or not a direct loss has occurred.

2. Coverage A (Buildings) of the businessowners policy covers all of the following EXCEPT

   A. installed machinery
   B. maintenance equipment
   C. office furniture
   D. outdoor fixtures

3. Which of the following is eligible for a businessowners policy?

   A. Farmer
   B. Retail store
   C. Auto dealer
   D. Industrial repair service

4. The BOP automatically includes each of the following coverages EXCEPT

   A. property
   B. products and completed operations
   C. liability
   D. boiler and machinery

5. Which of the following statements about the Businessowners policy (BOP) is NOT correct?

   A. It is used by small and medium businesses.
   B. It excludes contractors, restaurants, certain convenience stores, and laundries from eligibility.
   C. It provides coverage for buildings and business personal property.
   D. Debris removal up to $10,000 is automatically covered.

6. The 2002 Businessowners Policy will provide $10,000 of property coverage for

   A. water damage to a vacant property
   B. theft of electronics
   C. increased restoration costs required by building code
   D. personal property temporarily off premises

7. The liability insurance provided by a business owners policy is written as a(n)

   A. endorsement to the policy
   B. occurrence version policy
   C. supplement to other sources of liability insurance
   D. claims-made policy

8. Which of the following losses would be covered by the hired and non-owned auto liability endorsement to the businessowners policy?

   A. The insured is sued when an employee causes an accident while driving a rented vehicle on a business trip.
   B. The insured is sued when an employee causes an accident while driving a vehicle that is owned by the insured.
   C. An employee files a claim for damage to her personal vehicle damaged in a two-car loss.
   D. An employee files a claim for damage to her personal vehicle vandalized while parked at work.

# ANSWERS AND RATIONALES TO UNIT QUIZ

1. **A.** The BOP's business income coverage pays actual business income loss and necessary expenses to resume operations. This includes reduction in gross earnings and loss of rents less noncontinuing expenses.

2. **C.** Installed machinery, equipment used to maintain the premises and outdoor fixtures all are included under the BOP definition of *building*.

3. **B.** Businessowners policies were designed for insureds who present relatively low hazards and more innocuous exposures. A retail store, as such an exposure, is eligible for the BOP subject to restrictions on sales and square footage.

4. **D.** Boiler and machinery coverage (mechanical breakdown), an optional coverage under the BOP, must be selected by the insured.

5. **B.** A Businessowners policy provides coverage for certain small and medium businesses such as contractors, restaurants, and convenience stores with gas pumps and laundries. Coverage is provided for buildings and the business personal property.

6. **C.** The BOP provides $10,000 of coverage for increased costs of construction, valuable papers, and accounts receivable. The BOP provides $5,000 property off-premises.

7. **B.** Liability coverage on the BOP is written as an occurrence form contract.

8. **A.** The hired and non-owned auto liability endorsement provides liability protection for businesses whose employees use personal autos for business or rental autos while on business trips. It provides liability protection only, and is not designed for businesses who own or operate their own autos.

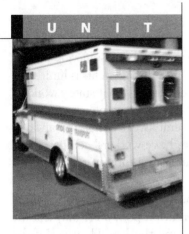

# 21

# Workers' Compensation

## KEY CONCEPTS

- The history and purpose of workers' compensation insurance
- Laws and legislation governing workers' compensation
- Workers' compensation benefits
- Policy provisions and premium calculation

Workers' compensation is a system of benefits mandated by law for most workers who suffer job-related injuries or diseases. These benefits are paid regardless of fault, and the amount of benefits is limited by law. Almost every employee hired and injured in a particular state is covered by that state's workers' compensation laws. A workers' compensation insurance policy is one means an employer can use to meet the requirements of workers' compensation laws. However, the employer's obligation and the limits of compensation differ in each state. Finally, a number of states have workers' compensation laws that allow workers' compensation insurance to be purchased from a state-run insurer only.

Workers' compensation is an exclusive remedy insurance program. This means that an injured employee can seek remedy for his loss only from the workers' compensation policy. He may not file suit against the employer, even if the employer was negligent in causing the loss. However, if the employer fails to carry workers' compensation, the employee may seek restitution through the courts, and the employer has no insurance protection.

## OBJECTIVE

When you complete this unit, you should be able to:

- identify the common-law requirements and defenses for employers with regard to their employees;

- explain the historical development of workers' compensation laws;

- describe the different methods used to provide workers' compensation coverage for an employer;

- describe the benefits provided under a workers' compensation statute;

- describe the major coverage parts of the workers' compensation and employers' liability policy; and

- identify federal statutes designed to protect employees engaged in certain categories of employment.

# WORKERS' COMPENSATION

## COMMON LAW ORIGINS

Before the enactment of state workers' compensation laws in the early twentieth century, common-law doctrines (legal precedents set through judicial rulings or court decisions as opposed to laws passed by a legislature) prevailed in the relationship between employer and employee.

**Common Law**   Under common law, an employer had obligations to:

- provide a reasonably safe place to work;

- provide reasonably safe tools;

- provide reasonably sane and sober fellow employees;

- set up safety rules and enforce them; and

- warn every worker of any dangers inherent in the work that the worker could not be expected to know about.

**Employer Defenses Against Liability**  Before workers' compensation laws, if an employee was injured on the job, the only recourse that employee had was to file a lawsuit against the employer charging that its negligence caused the injury. The employer, however, used several defenses against liability, which made it very difficult for the employee to win the lawsuit and recover from the employer for the work-related injury (or disease).

## STATUTORY WORKERS' COMPENSATION LAWS

Wisconsin passed the first state constitutionally acceptable law in 1911. Workers' compensation laws, now found in all states and territories, provide for the compensation of employees who have sustained injuries, illness, or death arising out of and occurring in the course of their employment. The laws also make workers' compensation the exclusive remedy when an employee is injured. In other words, the employee cannot sue the employer for injuries. The amount of compensation is fixed by law.

The intent of workers' compensation laws is to provide a just and fair means of compensating employees who are injured on the job. Their purpose is to eliminate the expense and delay that accompany a lawsuit. Instead, when an employee suffers a work-related injury or disease, benefits are determined by law. In most cases, no dispute occurs between the employer and employee.

The compensation, which takes the form of a specified monetary benefit, is paid without any consideration of fault or negligence on the part of either the employer or employee. In exchange for this right of compensation, the employee gives up the right to sue the employer for perhaps a larger (or possibly a smaller) but uncertain benefit.

## WORKERS' COMPENSATION COVERAGE

Workers' compensation provides an employee with insurance for accidental injuries, occupational disease, or death. In general, the law provides benefits to an employee, whether or not the employee or employer was negligent, as a type of no fault insurance.

**Coverage Territory**  Benefits are provided if the injury, disease, or death arises out of and in the course of employment. Where coverage applies depends on where the employee works.

- If an employee has a fixed place of employment, benefits will be provided for injury, disease, or death while at that location.

- If an employee has no fixed location, such as a salesperson, the employee may be covered from the time he leaves home until he returns.

- Benefits may be available to an employee while he is not working if the activity is construed as promoting the employer's goodwill and interest.

The courts have distinguished work-related injury or illness and recreational injury or illness.

EXAMPLE  Thomas is employed by a construction company. While working on a new building, he falls from a ladder and breaks his leg. Because this injury occurred while Thomas was performing his job, the company's workers' compensation carrier covers the medical bills and any lost wages that arise from this incident. Two years later, Thomas is playing in a volleyball game at his employer's annual picnic. He breaks his leg again while diving for the ball. This time, the injury arose outside the course of his employment; therefore, the carrier does not cover the loss. In addition, the scope of employment is very important.

---

**EXAMPLE**

Cindy is a clerk in a florist shop. Her duties include delivering floral arrangements in the shop's van. On her return trip after making a delivery, Cindy stops for lunch. She slips on a puddle of water in the restaurant and injures her back. This incident is covered by her employer's workers' compensation carrier because it occurred within the scope of her employment: eating lunch would be a usual activity of her work day. A year later, Cindy completes a delivery and drives to her dry cleaner to pick up her laundry. She slips on a wet sidewalk and breaks her leg. This incident occurred beyond the scope of her employment: She was running a personal errand that was of no benefit to her employer. Therefore, the carrier does not cover her loss.

---

Finally, workers' compensation is primary over other available insurance coverage.

**Liability** Under workers' compensation laws, an employer is assured that its liability is limited to the benefits specified in the state law, provided the company has complied with the provisions of the law. However, the employer may be liable if the injury or disease does not fall under the workers' compensation laws.

The employee cannot sue a negligent fellow employee or the employer, but an employee can collect under workers' compensation, then sue a negligent third party, such as the manufacturer of a machine that caused the employee's injury. If the employee collects from the negligent third party, the employer or the insurer is entitled to reimbursement for any benefits it paid to the injured worker.

**Types of Workers' Compensation Laws** Although workers' compensation laws vary from state to state, they fall into one of two categories: compulsory or elective.

■ *Compulsory laws.* In states with compulsory laws, every employer must provide the benefits and amounts stipulated in the laws or face penalties for noncompliance. These penalties include:

— paying the benefits;

— paying stipulated fines and penalties; or

— having officials close down the business as a public nuisance.

■ *Elective laws.* Only Texas has elective workers' compensation laws. In Texas, an employer can decide whether to provide workers' compensation benefits. If an employer does not provide the benefits and an employee is injured, the employee can sue. In such a case, the employer cannot use the common-law defense of contributory negligence, fellow servant rule, or assumption of risk. Due to the restrictions on defense, most employers voluntarily provide some form of coverage for their employees.

The federal government has also played a part in protecting workers not covered by state workers' compensation laws. For instance, it enacted the Federal Longshoremen's and Harbor Workers' Compensation Act (LHWCA) to cover injuries sustained by certain maritime employees such as longshoremen and harbor workers. The Federal Employees' Compensation Act provides benefits to injured civilians who are employed by the federal government. Because the federal government administers these systems and provides the benefits, no private insurers are involved.

**Methods of Insuring** Two basic methods of providing insurance comply with a state's workers' compensation laws: monopolistic and competitive. In a monopolistic state, insurance must be purchased from a state-run insurer. The five monopolistic states are North Dakota, Ohio, Washington, West Virginia, and Wyoming. Nevada, formerly a monopolistic method state, became a competitive method state on July 1, 1999.

A state that uses the competitive workers' compensation method can provide coverage through:

- an insurance policy from a private carrier;

- a state-administered fund (as a competitor to private carriers);

- an assigned risk or rejected risk plan; or

- self-insurance, though the employer must be able to demonstrate:

  — a financial ability to cover the losses;

  — a formal program to fund and handle the benefits; and

  — procedures to handle loss.

**Self-Insurance** Self-insurance is simply the retention of risk. An employer that is self-insured sets aside funds to meet projected losses and absorbs the difference between the actual and calculated probable losses.

In general, a company may not self-insure unless it has proven to the state that it has the financial resources and processes necessary to cover the types of losses to which it is subject. If it cannot demonstrate this ability, the state will require it to obtain insurance through an insurer.

**Assigned Risk Plans** An *assigned risk* or *rejected risk plan* is a risk-pooling arrangement for employers that cannot obtain workers' compensation insurance through private insurers or for those that simply prefer to purchase the insurance through this arrangement. Because workers' compensation is required by law, it is important that there be an insurer of last resort so that employers can comply with the law even if private carriers are unwilling to insure them.

**Covered Employment** The laws dictating which employees are covered by workers' compensation law vary widely from state to state. In some states, nearly every employee must be covered. In other states, the law exempts employers that have small numbers of employees, such as three or less. Other possible exceptions are corporate officers who are the sole shareholders, domestic employees who work a limited number of hours, volunteers, and agricultural workers. When benefits are not required by law, an employer still may provide them on a voluntary or an elective basis.

**Benefits** Benefits provided under workers' compensation as mandated by law include the following:

- *Medical expenses.* Coverage is provided for doctor, hospital, surgical, and similar expenses necessary to cure or relieve the effects of an injury or a disease.

- *Rehabilitation benefits.* Rehabilitation benefits are provided for vocational training, transportation, and other necessary expenses.

- *Indemnity for loss of income.* Loss of income benefits are available after a three-day to seven-day waiting period, but generally retroactive benefits are available to cover the waiting period if a disability extends beyond a certain period of time. Indemnity benefits are based on a percentage of an employee's salary up to some dollar limit per week for:

  — Temporary Partial Disability (TPD);

  — Permanent Partial Disability (PPD);

  — Temporary Total Disability (TTD); or

  — Permanent Total Disability (PTD).

A *temporary partial disability* usually results in a restriction of duties, but does not cause a great deal of lost time because the injury is relatively minor. Compensation is limited to the difference between pre-loss wages and post-loss wages for the recovery period.

*Permanent partial disabilities* include loss of a limb, sight, or hearing. Although these injuries do not result in an inability to work, they never go away. Therefore, in addition to any lost wages, the law allows a scheduled benefit based on the extent of the injury. Loss of a finger on the right hand of a right-handed person, for example, results in a payment higher than loss of a finger on the left hand.

*Temporary total disability* is the inability to work at all for a short period of time. Lost wages are paid in this case.

*Permanent total disability* is a severe injury or disease that means the employee never can work again in that particular employment. This employee is compensated for the estimated loss of wages for his anticipated working years.

The type of benefits awarded depends on the injury sustained:

- *Scheduled dollar awards.* Scheduled awards are provided for permanent injuries, dismemberment, or permanent total disability.

- *Death benefits.* Death benefits include burial expense and survivors' benefits. These benefits usually are a weekly sum based on a percentage of the employee's salary.

**Occupational Diseases**  Coverage for occupational diseases is limited to those that arise out of and in the course of employment.

EXAMPLE | Catching a cold from a coworker is not considered an occupational disease because it is not peculiar to the employment. Exposure to harmful chemicals on the job that results in cancer, however, would be compensable as an occupational disease.

Benefits received under workers' compensation usually are exempt from income taxes.

**Second Injury Fund** All states have second injury funds to encourage employers to hire disabled employees. The purpose of the second injury fund is to provide a source of funds for persons who have been injured and otherwise might be unemployable. After an employee has been injured, subsequent employers may be reluctant to hire that person. The employers are concerned about having to pay increased workers' compensation premiums or increased costs because of a second injury, perhaps resulting in total disability. To ease this reluctance, the fund pays some of the costs for a second injury.

EXAMPLE | An employee who loses sight in one eye in a work-related accident with one employer may be hired by a second employer. If a similar accident causes loss of sight in the remaining eye, the second injury results in a permanent total injury, despite the fact that the injury itself was only partial.

# WORKERS' COMPENSATION AND EMPLOYERS' LIABILITY POLICY

The Workers' Compensation and Employers' Liability Policy is designed to cover:

■ payments required by a state's workers' compensation law; and

■ the liability risk for occupationally incurred injuries and diseases.

The policy is designed to accommodate the varied state workers' compensation laws. Physically, the policy consists of an information page, a standard provisions form, and necessary endorsements. The policy's coverage is split into three parts.

## PART I—WORKERS' COMPENSATION

This part covers an employer's legal obligations under workers' compensation law. The policy adapts to the laws of the state as listed on the declarations page or information page. This coverage is considered the exclusive or sole remedy for recovery by an employee for injuries and diseases arising out of and in the course of his employment.

## PART II—EMPLOYERS' LIABILITY

This part covers an employer's legal liability, determined by negligence, for injury to an employee in a situation not covered under workers' compensation or an action taken by a third party. Liability under this part might arise from:

■ accidents or diseases not compensable under workers' compensation and for which the employee may sue the employer. Sometimes this arises out of a legal doctrine called *dual capacity*. In some states, the law recognizes that at times an employer stands in a two-fold capacity:one as an employer and another as a building owner, landlord, or manufacturer. In those states, the employee may retain the right to sue the employer in tort;

> **TAKE NOTE**
>
> Because workers' compensation benefits are considered the sole remedy for employees, the coverage provided by Part II applies only to claims brought against employers by third parties or by employees who are not subject to the workers' compensation laws. This may be due to an exemption under the law, such as the one for small employers, agricultural workers, or domestic employees. Coverage also applies to dual capacity claims.

- loss of consortium—that is, the legal right of the injured employee's spouse to sue the employer for loss of the employee's companionship; and

- a third-party-over case, which involves an employee who sues a third party, (e.g., the manufacturer of a machine that the employee was using when the injury occurred). In the third-party-over case, the manufacturer (third party) in turn may sue the employer because the manufacturer believes the employer was negligent, perhaps in maintaining or using the machine, in supervising the employee's activities, or in training the employee.

## PART III—INSURANCE IN OTHER STATES

This part provides insurance to cover benefits to an employee if an obligation for workers' compensation arises in a state other than the state(s) where the employer normally does business. Such states may be identified on the declarations page, or coverage may be indicated as blanket on the declarations page. Coverage does not apply in states the insured had operations in when the policy commenced unless they are listed on the policy.

# OTHER PROVISIONS: DUTIES OF INSURED EMPLOYER IN CASE OF LOSS

The insured's duties in the event of a loss include:

- providing medical services as required by workers' compensation law;

- providing information to the insurer about the injury;

- notifying the insurer promptly of all notices, demands, and legal papers; and

- cooperating with the insurer in the investigation, settlement, or defense of a claim.

## PREMIUM

The premium is based on the amount of payroll multiplied by the rates for various occupational classifications shown in the insurer's rate manual. Another basis is estimated exposures, subject to final audit at the end of the policy term. For a larger business, however, the premium audit may take place once a month. Premium factors include the classification of the business, its size, and its workers' compensation claim experience. The rates also vary greatly by employment classification.

**EXAMPLE**   Clerical office workers may carry a rate of $1 for every $100 of payroll, while roofers may have a rate of $30 per $100. The total premium for workers' compensation is the rate applied to the estimated payroll for each classification, less any applicable premium discounts or credits.

In addition, larger employers have an experience modification applied to their premiums. If their loss experience is better than the average in their classifications, the experience modification is a credit. If it is worse than average, it is a debit and increases the overall premium.

## CONDITIONS

The insurance company has the right to inspect the insured's premises, but is not obligated to do so. *Transfer of Insured's Rights and Duties and Assignment*, applies to workers' compensation.

## CANCELLATION

The insured can cancel workers' compensation insurance with written notice to the insurer. The insurer can cancel it with 10 days' written notice to the insured. Once again, some states have placed time restrictions on such cancellations, nonrenewals, or increases in premium. State laws determine whether additional restrictions apply.

## EXCLUSIONS

The following exclusions apply to workers' compensation:

- serious and willful misconduct by the insured;

- employment of a person hired in violation of the law;

- failure to comply with a health or safety regulation; and

- discharge or discrimination against an employee in violation of workers' compensation laws.

## FEDERAL WORKERS' COMPENSATION LAWS

Persons in certain employments are not covered by the provisions of any state workers' compensation law. Instead, they receive their benefits under federal law.

**Federal Employers' Liability Act**   Congress passed the Federal Employers' Liability Act (FELA) in 1908 to protect employees of interstate railroads. This occurred before the passage of state workers' compensation laws. The act provides broader protection to railroad employees than that available under state laws. Injured workers retain the right to sue their employers for negligence, and the employers cannot use certain common-law defenses. This law stands because railroad employees and their labor unions have not been willing to accept statutory workers' compensation benefits in lieu of the more favorable provisions of the federal act.

**United States Longshore and Harbor Workers' Compensation Act**   Employees engaged in maritime activities, including loading, unloading, building, or repairing vessels, are covered by this federal statute. The benefits provided to injured workers are significantly better than those available under state law. When an employer has exposures under the act, an endorsement ay be added to the workers' compensation policy to comply with the federal law. Coverage also is available under a separate policy.

# SUMMARY

Workers' compensation insurance is purchased by employers; the policies are designed to provide benefits to injured workers and protect employers from potentially larger, more costly lawsuits their injured employees might otherwise pursue. Today, employers across the country are required by law to purchase workers' compensation insurance. The policies provide statutory benefits for injuries and wage loss arising from a work-related injury or illness.

# UNIT QUIZ

1. Which of the following does workers' compensation coverage provide?

   A. Health insurance
   B. Unemployment compensation
   C. No fault insurance
   D. Auto insurance

2. What is the primary purpose of workers' compensation coverage?

   A. To provide compensation to employees for injuries arising out of and in the course of their employment
   B. To provide benefits to employees temporarily laid off
   C. To provide accident insurance for employees both on and off the job
   D. To improve employees' working conditions

3. Which of the following statements regarding workers' compensation coverage is CORRECT?

   A. Workers' compensation laws prescribe the nature and amount of benefits to be paid for injuries or death.
   B. In addition to receiving the benefits payable under workers' compensation, an employee has the right to sue his employer.
   C. An injured employee must sue his employer for damages.
   D. Workers' compensation laws are intended to prevent unsafe workplaces.

4. An injured employee receives payment under workers' compensation insurance from the

   A. employer
   B. insurer
   C. Division of Workers' Compensation
   D. State Department of Employment

5. Which of the following statements about workers' compensation insurance is CORRECT?

   A. All benefits are unlimited.
   B. Benefits are payable up to the policy limit.
   C. Benefits are payable as required by statute.
   D. An employee may select the benefit he desires.

6. In a state with a compulsory workers' compensation law, all of the following statements are correct if any employer fails to carry workers' compensation insurance EXCEPT

   A. the employer still may have to pay benefits
   B. the employer may have to pay a fine
   C. workers' compensation officials may close the business down
   D. the employer need not worry because no law imposes any penalties for failure to secure coverage

7. Workers' compensation pays under which of the following circumstances?

   A. Only when an employer is negligent
   B. Only when another employee is negligent
   C. Without regard to fault
   D. Only when an employee is at fault

8. Workers' compensation disability applies under which of the following circumstances?

   A. When an employee cannot work because he was injured on the job
   B. Only when an employee is totally disabled
   C. Only when an employee is partially disabled
   D. Only when an employer is at fault

9. All of the following losses are covered by workers' compensation EXCEPT

   A. death
   B. unemployment
   C. temporary total disability
   D. partial disability

10. Which of the following individuals is likely to have a valid workers' compensation claim?
    A. A retired employee injured while visiting his old workplace
    B. An employee who suffers a diabetic coma from failure to take prescribed medicine
    C. Sole proprietor injured in an auto accident while driving to a friend's house
    D. An employee injured while performing an operation in a manufacturing facility

11. Workers' compensation benefits that are only available through a state fund are considered
    A. elective
    B. compulsory
    C. monopolistic
    D. competitive

# ANSWERS AND RATIONALES TO UNIT QUIZ

1. **C.** Workers' compensation coverage pays for injuries to workers without regard to fault on the employer's part.

2. **A.** Workers' compensation coverage pays for injuries to workers resulting from accidental injuries, occupational disease or death.

3. **A.** Workers' compensation statutes specify the type of benefits and the dollar amounts to be paid.

4. **B.** The workers' compensation insurer makes required payments on behalf of the employer.

5. **C.** A workers' compensation policy sets no specific limit for benefits. The policy simply states that it pays statutory limits.

6. **D.** Although they vary by state, the penalties for failure to comply with the law in a compulsory state include fines, imprisonment, closing the business, and allowance for the employee to file suit against the employer.

7. **C.** Workers' compensation is not a fault-based system. It pays for occupational disease and injuries without regard to fault on the part of employer or employee.

8. **A.** Workers' compensation disability benefits apply in cases of both partial and total disability.

9. **B.** Workers' compensation benefits include medical, disability (temporary partial, temporary total, permanent partial, permanent total), rehabilitation, and death benefits.

10. **D.** Work-related injuries to someone actively employed would be covered by workers' compensation.

11. **C.** Monopolistic workers' compensation laws allow benefits be made available exclusively through a fund managed by the state.

# Other Commercial Contracts

## KEY CONCEPTS

- Professional liability
- Umbrella policies
- Surety bonds
- Ocean Marine insurance

A *professional* is a person who possesses the special knowledge and skills necessary to render a service. The knowledge and skills come from that person's education and experience in a particular branch of science or learning. Professionals include physicians, attorneys, engineers, insurance agents and brokers, accountants, and architects, among others. Such professionals must attain and maintain a minimum standard of special knowledge and ability and must exercise reasonable care in performing their services. A person who fails in this regard can be held liable to a client if the client is injured or damaged by such failure. Professional liability insurance protects professionals against claims for damages arising out of their providing, or failing to provide, services.

## OBJECTIVE

When you complete this unit, you should be able to:

- identify the exposures to loss individuals in various professions face;

- describe the basic provisions professional liability policies contain;

- discuss the major types of professional liability policies, including their insuring agreements and exclusions;

- explain the professional liability exposures of insurance agents and brokers;

- discuss the reasons for umbrella policies for individuals, businesses, and other organizations;

- explain the common features umbrella policies contain;

- identify the parties to a surety bond;

- distinguish between surety bonds and insurance;

- describe the major types of surety bonds and their purposes;

- describe the coverage an ocean marine insurance policy provides; and

- give details of the coverage an ocean marine cargo policy provides.

# MEDICAL MALPRACTICE

Medical malpractice insurance is a form of protection for various medical-related institutions and medical professionals where the exposure is bodily injury to a client. The injury may involve rendering a service or failing to render a service. These policies are issued to the following professionals:

- hospitals;

- physicians, surgeons, and dentists;

- nurses;

- opticians;

- optometrists;

- chiropractors;

- veterinarians; and

- pharmacists.

Medical malpractice policies usually are written on a claims-made basis rather than on an occurrence form.

# LEGAL MALPRACTICE

Legal malpractice insurance protects attorneys and law firms that perform legal services for clients. It also protects them from claims by third parties who were the intended beneficiaries of the legal services, but not the actual clients.

The injury in a legal malpractice claim involves the loss or compromise of a client's legal right due to the attorney's or law firm's negligence in performing—or failing to perform—its professional duties. It also may involve a monetary loss.

# ERRORS AND OMISSIONS (E&O)

Errors and omissions (E&O) insurance relates to other types of professionals, such as architects, engineers, insurance agents, and accountants. In fact, the list of professionals who may obtain insurance in the nonmedical and nonlegal professional liability lines is almost limitless. Unlike medical malpractice policies, errors and omissions policies generally exclude bodily injury and damage to tangible property because the professions E&O policies cover usually generate claims for financial damages. However, the nature of a profession ultimately determines the nature of malpractice claims, and the insuring agreement of the professional liability policy reflects that fact.

EXAMPLE

> The form covering architects and engineers covers claims for bodily injury and property damage because errors or omissions in the design of buildings or products often lead to bodily injury or property damage.

As with medical and legal malpractice insurance, E&O coverage is for rendering or failing to render a service. Errors and omission policies generally are written on a claims-made form rather than an occurrence form.

## E&O COVERAGE FOR INSURANCE AGENTS AND BROKERS

Two sources of professional liability claims against insurance agents and brokers exist. The first is insurance companies an agent represents. If the agent exceeds his authority and causes an insurance company to suffer a loss by paying a claim that should not have been covered, the insurer sues the agent to recover the loss. The second source of E&O claims against insurance agents and brokers is their clients. Some of the common causes of claims are failure to secure insurance coverage, failure to renew, and failure to advise of the need for coverage.

**EXAMPLE**   A customer calls to add a vehicle to her automobile policy. If the agent fails to do so, a claim that occurs might not be covered. In this case, the client would have a cause of action against the agent or the E&O insurer for the amount of the uncovered loss. If, on the other hand, the agent adds the vehicle to the insured's policy, but it violates an agreement the agent has with the insurance company, the claim would be paid, but the company would have a cause of action against the agent for reimbursement of the loss.

The major causes of errors and omissions losses for insurance agents and brokers follow:

## Claims Made by Clients

- Failure to place coverage promptly;
- Failure to place requested coverage;
- Failure to increase or update coverage;
- Failure to recommend needed coverage;
- Failure to explain coverage limitations;
- Clerical error or misunderstanding;
- Verbal extension of nonexistent coverage;
- Inadvertent cancellation or failure to renew;
- Failure to advise of cancellation, nonrenewal, or material restrictions; and
- Failure to place coverage with a solvent insurer.

## Claims Made by Insurers

- Failure to follow underwriting guidelines or exceeding authority;
- Failure to exercise reasonable diligence in discharging insurer's duties;
- Failure to act in the insurer's best interest;
- Failure to revise coverage upon request;
- Failure to cancel coverage upon request; and
- Failure to disclose material information.

Errors and omissions coverage for insurance agents and brokers is important for firms of all sizes. Such policies protect agencies from the variety of E&O claims listed above. Usually, a deductible applies under a policy to encourage the agent to engage in some form of loss control that will reduce or eliminate E&O claims. Loss control activities, which can have a significant positive impact in reducing errors and omissions losses for agents and brokers, include documentation of policies and procedures, audits to ensure adherence to standards, and use of checklists to reduce the possibility of overlooking important steps in an insurance transaction.

## DIRECTORS' AND OFFICERS' LIABILITY

Corporations are owned by stockholders and operated by boards of directors. The management of a corporation includes the board of directors, executive officers, and high-ranking employees. Corporate officers and directors may be sued for breach of corporate duties.

## LIQUOR LIABILITY/DRAM SHOP LIABILITY

Many states have special laws called *dram shop acts* that provide a right of action against a seller of alcoholic beverages if the purchaser injures a third party. The laws vary greatly in detail, with some applying only in situations where liquor is sold to a minor or an intoxicated person. In other states, the law recognizes a separate and independent cause of action on the part of the victims' dependents. Even if a state does not have a statute that pertains to the disbursement of alcoholic beverages, liability may be imposed under common law.

# UMBRELLA LIABILITY POLICIES

An *umbrella policy* is a catastrophic liability contract that provides high limits of coverage, usually with broader coverage than underlying policies, for insureds subject to liability claims of excess proportions. In many cases, professional or business insureds are primary targets for large settlements and are especially interested in this type of extra insurance protection.

Umbrella policies are designed to provide coverage either above the limits of the underlying insurance or above the self-insured retention (SIR) amount (the amount of loss the insured is willing to absorb without insurance protection).

Umbrella policies were developed to provide business firms and individuals with broader than primary coverage. In general, umbrella policies provide limits of insurance exceeding underlying coverage. However, umbrella policies can drop down to provide coverage for claims the underlying policies do not cover.

EXAMPLE   Perils such as slander and libel typically are excluded under primary liability policies but may be covered under umbrella policies.

## PERSONAL UMBRELLAS

*Personal umbrella policies* are designed to protect individuals against catastrophic lawsuits or judgments. Most companies provide coverage ranging from $1 million to $10 million, typically including liability exposures associated with the ownership of private homes, boats, autos, and sport and recreational vehicles.

Personal umbrella policies offer insurance exceeding any basic underlying policies that may apply. They are not substitutes for primary personal liability insurance. Personal umbrellas are intended to be used for losses that exceed primary limits and to cover those losses not covered by primary insurance because they just can't happen—yet they sometimes do.

Under a maintenance of underlying insurance condition, the insured must carry certain basic amounts of liability on the underlying homeowners, auto, and watercraft policies. The underlying policies are listed on the declarations page of the personal umbrella policy. If the required amounts are not maintained, the umbrella policy acts as though the underlying coverage remains in force. The insurer pays only that amount it would have been required to pay if the underlying limit had been kept in force.

Losses covered by the umbrella policy, but not the underlying insurance, are subject to a self-insured retention or deductible (usually $1,000). For instance, underlying liability policies typically exclude claims for slander, libel. and defamation of character. However, coverage is provided under the umbrella policies.

**EXAMPLE**    Bob has a homeowners policy with liability limits of $100,000 and a personal umbrella policy for $1 million with an SIR of $1,000. Bob's pet pit bull severely mauls a neighbor's child, and the court awards the neighbor $250,000. In this case, Bob's homeowners policy will pay $100,000 and the umbrella will pay $150,000. The SIR does not apply because there was underlying coverage.

Now suppose that Bob's homeowners policy has lapsed and the court awards damages of $250,000. If there is no underlying coverage, Bob would be personally liable for $100,000 of the loss plus the $1,000 SIR. The umbrella policy would pay the remaining $149,000. Bob cannot look to his umbrella liability insurer to pay the entire loss because it is liable only to the extent it would have been if Bob had complied with the maintenance of insurance provision.

Finally, suppose that the same insurance exists, but this time a judgment is made against Bob for $250,000 in damages because of slander. Because his homeowners insurance does not cover defamation, whether it is in force at the time of the slander is not an issue. However, the personal umbrella does provide coverage for slander and will pay $249,000; Bob must pay only the $1,000 SIR.

# SURETY BONDS

Surety bonds guarantee that specific obligations will be fulfilled. An obligation may involve meeting a contractual commitment, paying a debt, or performing certain duties. Typically, a bond is written for a certain amount and, if the party whose obligation is bonded fails to meet it, the bond amount is paid to the person or organization that required it, up to the full amount of the bond. A surety bond serves as a guarantee of performance. Once a surety bond is issued, it cannot be canceled and does not expire until the contract has been performed.

## PARTIES TO A SURETY AGREEMENT

There are three parties to a surety agreement.

**Principal**  Also known as the *obligor*, the principal is the responsible party who has agreed to perform a service, such as a contractor.

---

**TAKE NOTE**

A surety bond serves as a guarantee of performance. Once a surety bond is issued, it cannot be canceled and does not expire until the contract has been performed.

---

**Obligee**  The obligee is the insured—that is, the party who benefits from the bond. In construction, the obligee is the project owner.

**Surety**  This is the guarantor or insurance company that guarantees that the obligor will fulfill all undertakings, covenants, terms, conditions, and agreements of a contract. In construction, the surety guarantees that the obligor will complete the project and pay for all labor and materials.

**Differences Between Bonds and Insurance**  Most surety bonds are issued by insurance companies, although some companies specialize in bonds. Suretyship and insurance share some characteristics, such as indemnity, risk transfer, and contract law, but in many respects they are quite different.

A major contrast between insurance and surety is that the surety agreement involves three parties, whereas insurance has only two contracting parties. (The third party in a liability situation is not a party to the contract.) In addition, insurance contemplates that losses will occur, and the price of the insurance reflects that anticipation. Surety, on the other hand, if properly underwritten, involves no losses. Thus, the price of a surety bond is merely an administrative fee and does not have sufficient premium to pay losses.

Another major difference is that unlike insurance, the surety may pursue subrogation against its insured. If a default occurs under a surety bond, the surety may (and probably will) institute legal action against the person or firm bonded to recoup any losses. This is in stark contrast to a first-party insurance policy designed to pay claims.

**Underwriting**  The surety, in determining whether to issue a bond for a principal, bases its decision on the principal's

- ability to perform the prescribed work (technical ability);
- financial strength or ability to complete the project (financial ability); and
- character and reputation (in some cases, the principal's spouse also is investigated).

In surety bonds, the underwriting criteria often are called the three Cs:

- Capacity;
- Collateral; and
- Character.

## TYPES OF BONDS

The many types of surety bonds available generally can be classified as contract bonds, judicial or court bonds, and miscellaneous bonds.

**Contract Bonds**  Contract bonds are issued to guarantee performance of the terms and provisions of written contracts. The principals on these instruments are usually construction contractors, although the work of other types of firms may be bonded. Government entities typically require contract bonds for construction of roads, bridges, and other infrastructure items. For building construction, the obligee is usually a private firm or an individual, as opposed to a public entity. Some of the more common contract bonds are described below.

**Bid Bonds.** Sometimes contracts are awarded to the firms that enter the lowest bids. This is almost always true with government contracts. A bid bond guarantees two things: first, that the firm will enter into a contract if chosen, and second, that it will secure a performance bond for the work.

**Performance Bonds.** A performance bond guarantees to the owner (obligee) that the contractor (principal) will complete the contract as drawn. If the contractor fails to do so, the surety may hire another contractor to complete the work. In this case, the surety pays those expenses. If the original contractor fails to complete the work on time, the surety pays any losses that result from the delay in completion.

**Judicial Bonds**  These bonds are used in court proceedings guaranteeing that individuals or organizations will fulfill their statutory obligations.

**Bail Bonds.** Most people are familiar with bail bonds, the most common form of litigation bond. When someone is arrested, he may be held in jail awaiting trial unless a bail bond has been furnished to the court. When issued, a bail bond guarantees that the person will appear in court at the designated time and place. The court (federal, state, or municipal) is the obligee. If the person fails to appear, the bond amount is paid to the court as penalty. Bail bonds usually require collateral to protect the sureties. Generally, the issuance of bail bonds is left to firms that specialize in them.

**Court Bonds.** The other major type of litigation bond is a court bond. Courts cannot afford to operate on the assumption that those who initiate legal action can pay court costs. This is particularly true when a party loses a suit. Plaintiffs often are required to furnish court bonds to pursue legal action. A court bond guarantees that the plaintiff will pay court costs and damages to the defendant if the plaintiff loses the case. If the losing party appeals the case, an **appeal bond** guarantees that the judgment will be paid if affirmed and that any court costs for the appeal also will be paid.

**License/Permit Bonds**  Many local, state, and federal laws require that a bond be furnished before someone can obtain a license or permit. A wide variety of **license and permit bonds** exist, but they can be classified into two broad categories. The first is bonds designed to guarantee that laws and regulations of particular business activities are carried out. Such bonds cover funeral directors, private detectives, real estate brokers, and insurance brokers. The second category is bonds that guarantee that certain taxes are paid, such as for the sale of gasoline, liquor, and tobacco products.

# COMMERCIAL OCEAN MARINE INSURANCE

Despite technological advances in marine transportation, ocean disasters remain an ever-present hazard for those engaged in foreign trade. Four major classes of ocean marine insurance provide coverage against four types of losses.

- *Hull insurance:*
  - protects a vessel's owner against loss to the ship itself;
  - is written on an open perils basis; and
  - contains a special provision called the *running down clause* that provides a form of property damage liability coverage for collision damage to other ships.

- *Cargo insurance:*
  - is written separately from the insurance on the ship;
  - protects the cargo's owner from financial losses that result from the cargo's destruction or loss; and
  - offers a commercial ocean marine policy that covers jettison, which is the throwing of cargo overboard to save the vessel and its crew.

- *Freight insurance:*
  - is a special form of business income insurance; and
  - specifies that in the event the vessel is lost or destroyed, this coverage indemnifies the shipowner for the loss of any income that would have been earned upon completion of the voyage.

- *Protection and indemnity (P&I) insurance:*
  - is liability insurance that protects the shipowner from the consequences of his agents' negligent acts; and
  - provides workers' compensation insurance for the vessel's crew members.

The policies remain largely unchanged since the early days at Lloyd's coffeehouse, and the contract language has been tested in the courts.

# SUMMARY

There are many property and casualty contracts that may be purchased in addition to the more common contracts already discussed. Professional liability insurance is used by persons whose work requires special knowledge and skills. Those working in such trades have a duty to exercise care in performing their services and need such insurance to handle liability claims arising from the errors and mistakes they make. Umbrella policies can provide high liability limits to protect businesses and individuals from potentially catastrophic liability claims that would exhaust the protection provided by their underlying liability contracts. Insurance companies sell surety bonds to back a contractual promise between contracting parties. Ocean marine insurance is used to insure ocean-going vessels and their cargo.

# UNIT QUIZ

1. The primary cause of insurance agents' errors and omissions losses is failure to
   A. explain coverage limitations
   B. recommend needed coverage
   C. provide coverage
   D. advise of cancellation

2. All of the following are examples of the types of exclusions found in professional liability insurance policies EXCEPT
   A. uninsurable exposures
   B. contractual liability
   C. compensatory damages
   D. exposures covered under other policies

3. The reason to purchase an umbrella liability policy is to
   A. provide higher limits of liability
   B. expand coverage beyond primary policies
   C. provide coverage when primary limits are exhausted
   D. accomplish all of the above

4. An umbrella policy provision that requires the insured to participate in a portion of a loss not covered by primary insurance is a
   A. coinsurance clause
   B. participation clause
   C. deductible
   D. self-insured retention

5. An insured purchases a $1 million umbrella policy with a $1,000 self-insured retention (SIR) and agrees to maintain $100,000/$300,000/$100,000 as the underlying limits. Following a serious automobile accident, the insured is sued and injuries are awarded to the claimant in the amount of $200,000. What amount will the umbrella pay if it turns out the insured carried only $50,000/$100,000/$50,000 auto liability limits?
   A. $50,000
   B. $99,000
   C. $100,000
   D. The insurer will pay nothing because the insured violated the maintenance of the policy's underlying provision.

6. The face amount of a bond is called the
   A. face value
   B. limit of liability
   C. penalty
   D. stated amount

7. A bail bond is an example of which of the following types of bonds?
   A. Contract
   B. Performance
   C. Judicial
   D. Fiduciary

8. A performance bond guarantees that a contractor will
   A. enter into a contract if awarded
   B. complete the work described in the contract
   C. make payments to subcontractors
   D. pay a lender all amounts owed as a result of the contract

9. The four major classes of marine insurance include all of the following EXCEPT
   A. cargo insurance
   B. hull insurance
   C. liability insurance
   D. freight insurance

10. Which of the following losses would not be covered by professional liability insurance?
    A. An agent failed to renew a policy a customer wished to renew.
    B. An agent failed to update coverage as requested.
    C. An agent failed to recommend needed coverage.
    D. An agent embezzles money from a client.

11. The relationship between principal/surety is comparable to
    A. insured/insurer
    B. beneficiary/insured
    C. insurer/insured
    D. insurer/beneficiary

# ANSWERS AND RATIONALES TO UNIT QUIZ

1. **C.** Failure to place coverage promptly or to place requested coverage is the number one cause of E&O claims against agents by their clients.

2. **C.** Compensatory damages are given to claimants to offset the impact of such things as pain and suffering. Professional liability policies pay damages including both compensatory and special damages.

3. **D.** Umbrella policies provide higher limits on primary coverages, broaden the coverage the underlying policies offer, and drop down to provide primary insurance in some cases.

4. **D.** A self-insured retention is used in an umbrella policy when the umbrella does not exclude coverage but no underlying or primary insurance exists.

5. **C.** When the insured does not maintain underlying limits as stated in the umbrella policy, the umbrella carrier pays as though those limits were in effect. Therefore, it does not affect the amount of coverage under the umbrella; it merely means the insured must make up the difference between what was required and what actually is provided.

6. **C.** The face amount of a bond is called the *penalty* because it is that amount the surety must pay in the event of default.

7. **C.** Judicial or court bonds are a common type of surety arrangement. A bail bond guarantees that a person will appear in court at the time and place designated.

8. **B.** A performance bond, a type of contract bond, guarantees that a contractor will carry out the work specified in the contract.

9. **C.** Ocean marine insurance includes coverage for vessels (hull and machinery), cargo, protection and indemnity, and freight.

10. **D.** E&O policies will not cover fraudulent, criminal, or dishonest acts.

11. **A.** In a surety contract, the relationship between the principal and surety is comparable to the relationship between insured and insurer.

# Glossary

## A

**Absolute Assignment** The giving of all control and rights to a third party.

**Accident** An unintended and unforeseen event.

**Accident and Sickness** *See* Health Insurance.

**Accidental Death Insurance** A form of insurance that provides a benefit if the insured dies as a result of an accident.

**Accidental Means** A policy that pays for bodily injuries only if those injuries occur because the mishap itself was accidental. For example, an individual who was injured when jumping off a roof would be excluded. One who fell off the roof would be covered.

**Actual Cash Value** The sum of money required to pay for damages or loss, computed on the basis of replacement value less its depreciation. Today's replacement cost less physical depreciation.

**Actuary** A person who calculates rates, reserves, etc. for an insurance company.

**Adjuster** An individual who determines the amount of a loss.

**Admitted Company** An insurance company authorized and licensed to do business in a given state.

**Adverse Selection** Those with higher risk situations attempt to purchase insurance more often than those with average or below average risks.

**Agent** An individual, partnership, or corporation appointed by an insurance company to solicit, negotiate, or countersign insurance contracts on its behalf.

**All Risk** Insurance against loss or damage to property arising from any cause, except such as may be specifically excluded. May be called "Open Peril."

**Annuity** A contract that pays out for a stated period or life. This plan is designed to liquidate funds.

**Appraisal** An evaluation of property made for determining its insurable value or the amount of loss sustained.

**Appraisal Clause** The arbitration procedure in the policy used only for disputes involving the amount of the loss.

**Arbitration** A method of solving disputes between parties to a contract.

**Assigned Risk Plan** A plan that provides insurance protection for risks that underwriters do not care to insure. This plan is handled through the state, and the risks are assigned to companies.

**Assignment** The transfer of the legal rights under a contract from one person to another.

**Automatic Premium Loan** An optional feature of a life policy that allows the insurance company to borrow money from the cash value of the policy to pay any premium not paid by the end of the grace period.

## B

**Bailee** A person or business having temporary possession of property committed in trust from the owner.

**Beneficiary** A person(s) or organization that receives the benefits of a life insurance policy income tax-free.

**Binder** An agreement to provide insurance coverage.

**Blanket Insurance** A contract that covers all of a class of persons not individually identified.

**Blue Cross/Blue Shield** A service plan that provides health care coverages. Blue Cross plans were started by hospitals and Blue Shield plans by doctors. These are non-profit associations.

**Bond** A contract stating that one party will answer for the acts or failures to act of a second party who has agreed to perform in some manner for a third party.

**Broker** An individual, partnership, or corporation that represents a client, not the insurance company.

**Builders Risk Insurance** Insurance against loss to building or structures in the course of construction.

**Burglary** Taking of property of another through the forcible entry or exit of the premises.

**Business Income Coverage Form (Business Interruption Insurance)** An indirect form of property insurance that provides coverage for expenses and loss of profits which occur as a result of a direct loss.

## C

**Capital Sum** The maximum amount of benefit in one sum to be paid out in the event of accidental dismemberment.

**Cash (Surrender) Value** An amount of cash increasing annually that can be borrowed by an insured or withdrawn after a stated period of time (two or three years). Cash value is only found in permanent life insurance. *See* Nonforfeiture Options/Values.

**Certificate of Authority** A license issued to an admitted insurance company.

**Certificate of Participation** A certificate that an individual member receives under a group life and/or health policy that states the coverages in general.

**Coinsurance** A feature in major medical health insurance contracts where the insured participates on a percentage basis in all claims in excess of a deductible.

**Coinsurance Clause** A requirement that causes the insured to purchase insurance to value or to participate in a loss (become a coinsurer).

**Collateral Assignment** To assign all or part of a life insurance policy as security for a loan.

**Commercial Building and Personal Property Form (General Property Form)** An insurance policy that provides coverage for business buildings and business personal property (contents).

**Commercial General Liability Policy (CGL)** A policy that provides basic liability protection for business organizations.

**Commercial Package Policy** A policy that provides property and liability insurance under a single contract.

**Comparative Negligence** Two or more parties contribute unequally to a loss.

**Competitive State Fund** A program operated by a state that competes with private insurers to provide workers' compensation insurance coverage.

**Concealment** Deliberate failure of an applicant for insurance to reveal a material fact to the insurer.

**Concurrent Insurance** Two or more policies that provide identical coverage on the same risk.

**Conditional Receipt/Binding Receipt** A receipt that is given to a life or health insurance applicant only if the initial premium accompanies the application. It states that the policy shall be in force the date of the receipt (whether the policy has yet been issued or not), provided the insurance company would have issued the coverage using the company's standard sources of underwriting information.

**Conditionally Renewable** A health insurance policy that allows the insured to renew the policy until a stated age (such as 65). However, the insurance company may decline renewal only under conditions stated in the policy.

**Consideration** Anything of value or promise of value.

**Contingent Beneficiary** A person(s) or organization that receives the benefits of a life policy if the primary beneficiary predeceases the insured.

**Contractual Liability** Liability assumed under any contract or agreement.

**Contributory Negligence** Two or more parties contribute to a loss.

**Conversion** To change from one type of policy to another without evidence of insurability.

**Convertible** To change from a temporary plan (term) to a permanent plan (whole life/endowment) without evidence of insurability.

**Countersignature** The signatures of licensed representatives that are necessary to validate a policy.

**Credit Insurance** An insurance policy that pays a benefit to a financial institution (creditor) in the event that the person borrowing the money (debtor) should become disabled or die. Often funded with decreasing term policies.

**Crime Insurance** A type of casualty insurance that includes coverages including the perils of burglary, robbery, and theft.

## D

**Declarations** A section of an insurance contract that sets forth information that includes the insured, what is covered in the contract, and the property covered, as well as rates and premiums, limits, deductibles, coinsurance percentages, etc.

**Decreasing Term** A form of temporary (term) life insurance that provides a death benefit that reduces throughout the term of the policy until it finally reaches zero at the end of the term.

**Deductible** The first given number of dollars or percentages of expenses that the insured must pay in the event of a covered loss.

**Direct Loss** When a peril causes physical damage to the insured property.

**Direct Writer** A company selling direct to the public.

**Disability Income Insurance** A health insurance policy that provides payments to replace income when an insured is unable to work as a result of an accident or sickness.

**Dismemberment** Loss of a limb or part of a limb (also includes loss of sight).

**Dividend** The portion of the premium that is returned to the policyholder of a participating (PAR) insurance policy when losses and expenses are less than anticipated.

**Dividend Additions (Paid-Up Additions)** When dividends are used to purchase additional paid-up life insurance.

## E

**Elimination Period (Waiting Period)** A period of time between the beginning of a disability and the date benefits begin.

**Endorsement** An attachment to an insurance policy that modifies coverage.

**Estoppel** Legal doctrine that prevents a person from denying the truth of a previous representation of fact, especially when such representation has been relied on by the one to whom the statement was made.

**Exclusions** This is a limitation or restriction of coverages.

**Experience Rating** An increase or decrease in rates based on the past loss history of the insured.

## F

**Face Amount** The death benefit stated on the first page of the policy.

**Facility of Payment** A clause that permits the insurance company to pay the proceeds (usually under $1,000) to a relative or person who appears entitled to such payment.

**Fair Access to Insurance Requirements (FAIR) Plans** A program established within a state to provide insurance for property owners in designated urban areas.

**Fidelity Bond** A bond obtained by the employer to protect against the economic loss of dishonest acts of employees.

**Floater Policy** Provides coverage for those goods for which it is difficult to establish specific location.

**Fraternal Life Insurance Company** An organization that provides insurance protection for a member of an affiliated lodge or organization.

## G

**Garage Keepers Legal Liability Policy** Coverage of losses for which the insured is legally liable, caused by fire and explosion, theft, riot and vandalism, collision, and upset to automobiles in his care, custody, and control.

**Garage Liability** Policy liability protection for the owner of a garage operation. Necessary due to the special hazards that exist there.

**General Agent** An individual, partnership, or corporation that has a contract to represent an insurer in a specific territory.

**Grace Period** A period of time after the premium due date during which the policy remains in force.

**Guaranteed Insurability** An option that allows the insured to buy additional amounts of insurance at future time intervals without evidence of insurability.

**Guaranteed Renewable Health Policy** A policy that the insured has the right to continue in force and the company cannot deny renewal. However, premiums may be adjusted by the insurance company.

## H

**Hazard** A condition that increases the frequency or severity of a loss or the chance that it will occur.

**Health Insurance** An insurance contract that pays a benefit for losses that occur because of sickness or bodily injury.

**Health Maintenance Organization (HMO)** An organization that provides health care. Each member pays a premium for which they receive medical care if needed.

**Hold Harmless Agreement** An agreement under which the insured agrees to assume the liability of another party during a period of time in which a specific activity is taking place.

**Homogeneous Units** Units that are similar in size, value, and use.

**Hospital Expense Policy** A policy that covers daily hospital room and board charges and also covers miscellaneous expenses such as lab work, x-rays, etc. Generally, this policy limits the total number of days covered and/or the total amount of benefit it will pay out, such as $3,000 total in expenses.

**Host Liquor Liability** Liability imposed on the insured as a result of giving or serving alcoholic beverages at social functions incidental to the insured's business.

## I

**Incontestability Clause** A clause that states coverage cannot be denied for misstatement, concealment, or fraud in the application for life insurance after the policy has been in force for a stated period of time (usually 2 years).

**Indemnity** (Principle) Restore the insured to their pre-loss financial condition (no better - no less).

**Independent Agent** An individual or firm who represents one or more insurance companies and operates as an independent business.

**Independent Producer** An individual or firm who represents one or more insurance companies and operates as an independent business.

**Indirect Loss** (Time element loss) A loss of income and/or profits that occurs as a consequence of the direct loss to a property by an insured peril.

**Industrial Insurance** An insurance policy where the premium was collected at the door by an agent on a weekly or monthly basis. These policies were usually in small amounts or low benefits.

**Inflation Guard Endorsement** An endorsement that automatically increases coverage of property insurance by a specific percentage each month (quarter) to help meet rising construction costs.

**Inland Marine Insurance** Various types of insurance that cover property while in transit to various locations.

**Insurable Interest** A requirement that states that an individual or organization will suffer a financial loss. In life and health insurance, it must exist at the time of application. In property and casualty insurance, it must exist at the time of loss.

**Insurance** A device where many members or a group accumulate funds to pay the losses of a few members. It is a transfer of risk.

**Insurance Clause** The clause in all insurance policies that states in a brief description the contract's intent.

**Insurance Services Office (ISO)** A rating, inspection, and policy drafting organization formed in 1971 by combining six existing national rating bureaus.

**Insurance Solicitor** An individual who directs clients to a producer or broker and receives some commission or fee for doing so. Solicitors may not bind or sign policies.

**Insured** The individual or organization for whom insurance protection is being provided.

**Insurer** An insurance company.

**Insuring Agreement** A statement found in an insurance policy that states the perils and the promise to pay covered by the insurance contract.

**Irrevocable Beneficiary** A beneficiary that cannot be changed without the beneficiary's permission.

# J

**Joint Life Policy** A policy that pays the face amount when the first of two or more die.

**Juvenile Insurance** Insurance policy that is written on a child (usually under age 15 or any age established by the state).

# K

**Key Employee Insurance** Insurance that a business firm has to provide coverage for the loss of a key employee by death or disability.

# L

**Law of Large Numbers** A mathematical rule stating that as the number of exposures increase, the more nearly the actual results may be predicted.

**Legal Liability** A term used by the insurance industry to refer to damages that an insured causes to another party through negligence under Tort Law. Damages may include bodily injury or property damage.

**Legal Reserve Company** An insurance company that maintains the minimum reserves required. Not required of assessment insurance companies.

**Level Premiums Insurance** An insurance policy where the premium remains level throughout the life of the policy term.

**Liberalization Clause** A clause that automatically extends to an insured any advantageous change that is made in a policy form during the term of the policy if no additional premium is charged.

**Licensee** An individual or organization that has met the requirements to qualify for a license and has been granted that license.

**Limits** The maximum amount the insurance company agrees to pay.

**Limits of Coverage** The amount beyond which the insurance company will not pay.

**Livery Vehicle** A vehicle that is used for hire (e.g., taxi, bus).

**Loading** A dollar amount added to the pure cost of insurance to cover the operating expenses of the insurance company.

**Loss** An unintentional decline in or disappearance of value.

**Loss of Income Insurance** See Disability Income Insurance.

# M

**Major Medical Insurance** A health insurance policy that provides high lifetime limits (catastrophic coverage) and generally has a high deductible. Losses are paid on a participating basis (coinsurance - 80% by the insurer, 20% by insured).

**Master Policy** The policy issued to the employer (or other entity) under a group life or health insurance plan.

**Maturity Date** The date when a life insurance policy pays the face amount, either because of death or endowment.

**Medicaid** A medical assistance program for the needy that is administered by the state and subsidized by the federal government.

**Medical Expense Insurance** A health policy that provides benefits for medical and hospital expenses (also called hospital-surgical expense).

**Medical Information Bureau (MIB)** A bureau formed by insurance companies for the purpose of exchanging information about the physical condition of prior applicants.

**Medicare** Health benefits that are provided under a federal program as part of the Social Security program.

**Monoline Policy** Any insurance coverage written as a single line policy

**Mortgagee (the Lender)** An individual or financial institution that holds a mortgage (pledge of security in property for payment of a debt).

**Mortgagor (the Debtor)** The purchaser or owner who conveys real property as security for a loan.

**Multi-Line Insurance** A combination of several coverages from the traditional lines of property and casualty insurance into a single contract (e.g. homeowners, automobile, or special multiple peril).

**Multiple Benefits** In Basic Hospital-Surgical Expense insurance, surgical and miscellaneous coverage may be stated as a multiple of the daily benefit.

**Mysterious Disappearance** When personal property is missing and there is no explanation for its disappearance.

# N

**Named Insured** An individual, partnership, or corporation who is specifically named as the insured in the declaration section of an insurance contract.

**National Association of Insurance Commissioners (NAIC)** An organization whose membership is made up of the heads of the insurance departments of various states.

**Negligence** A tort; a civil wrong; it includes the failure to act as a reasonable and prudent person would have done in similar circumstances. See Tort.

**Noncancelable ("Noncan")** A health insurance plan that is guaranteed to be renewed to a stated age. The premiums are also guaranteed to that stated age.

**Nonforfeiture Options/Values** The values in a life policy that the policyowner does not forfeit even if he ceases to pay the premiums. The cash value in the policy will be used in one of three ways: (1) cash value returned to policyowner; (2) cash value buys extended term insurance; (3) cash value buys a reduced paid-up life insurance policy.

**Nonparticipating ("Nonpar")** Insurance that doesn't pay dividends.

# O

**Obligee** An individual or organization that has entered into an agreement with an obligor and expects performance.

**Obligor** A party that is to perform under an agreement with an obligee.

**Occurrence** A situation that exists over a period of time.

**Old Age, Survivors, and Disability Insurance (OASDI)** A program that provided old age benefits to a group of eligible retired persons. This program began with the passage of the Social Security Act of 1935.

**Optionally Renewable** A health policy where the insurer reserves the right to terminate coverage at any premium due date or anniversary.

**Ordinary Life** All life policies not classified as industrial or group.

**Other Insurance Clause** A provision found in nearly every insurance policy stating what is to be done in case any other contract of protection covers the same property or hazard.

**Owners' and Contractors' Protective Liability** Coverage that provides protection for owner if he is held liable even though the negligent act was that of an independent contractor.

# P

**Paid-Up Additions** An additional amount of life insurance that is added to current policy and paid for by policy dividends. This is a paid-up policy.

**Paid-Up Policy** A life insurance policy on which all premiums have been paid but that has not yet matured.

**Pair or Set Clause** A clause that states that if one of a pair or a set is lost or damaged, the insurance company will pay a proportional amount that the lost articles bears to the total value of the set.

**Participating** An insurance policy that pays dividends.

**Payor Clause** A clause that states the premium on a child's policy will be waived in the event that the parent paying the premium becomes disabled or dies prior to the child reaching age of majority.

**Peril** A condition that can cause loss (e.g., fire, hurricane, etc.).

**Personal Article Floater** A type of insurance that provides coverage for personal property that is at a non-permanent location (used for such items as art, jewelry, etc.).

**Policy** A formal, written contract containing a declarations section, an insuring agreement, and conditions and exclusions.

**Policy Loan** A loan that is made from the cash values of a life insurance policy.

**Preexisting Condition** A condition of health or physical condition that existed prior to the date the policy was issued.

**Premium** The monetary consideration that the policyholder pays to the insurer for a contract of insurance.

**Pre-Paid Hospital Service Plan** A plan where members pay a flat fee to an organization (Health Maintenance Organization, HMO) in exchange for comprehensive health care services.

**Principal Sum** The amount payable in the event of accidental death.

**Probationary Period** A period of time between the effective date of a health insurance policy and the date coverage begins.

**Producer** Anyone working in the sale of insurance products. Includes agents, solicitors, and brokers.

**Products and Completed Operations Liability** Coverage that provides protection if the insured causes injuries or property damage to another by a product or a completed operation of the insured. Operations include materials, parts, buildings, or equipment.

**Pro-Rata Cancellation** When a policy is canceled, there is no penalty charged against the premiums to be returned.

**Pro-Rata Liability Clause** A clause that states that, if there is more than one policy covering a loss, payment will be shared based on each insurer's coverage to the total amount of insurance.

**Proximate Cause** The first cause in a continuous unbroken chain of events that causes injury or property damage.

**Pure Risk** An uncertainty against financial loss.

# R

**Rebating** Refunding part of the commission, premium, services, or anything of value to the purchaser as an inducement to buy insurance coverage.

**Reduced Paid-Up Insurance** A nonforfeiture option that uses the cash value in an existing policy to buy a single premium policy with a much lower benefit than the original policy.

**Reinstatement** To put a lapsed policy back in force.

**Renewable Term** A term life insurance policy that may be renewed by the policyholder without evidence of insurability.

**Replacement Cost Insurance** A policy or endorsement that states that property will be replaced without any deduction for depreciation.

**Representations** Statements made by an applicant for insurance that are true to the best of his knowledge.

**Risk** Uncertainty concerning the occurrence of a loss.

**Robbery** A face-to-face criminal confrontation where a threat is present.

# S

**Salvage** The right of the insurance company to take title to damaged property after payment of loss.

**Schedule of Benefits**  A list of benefits that specifies what is being covered and the dollar amount of coverage. Accidental Death and Dismemberment, Dental, and Surgical benefits of Major Medical policies may use a schedule of benefits.

**Self-Insurance**  A program set up by an individual or organization in which funds are set aside to pay losses that could possibly occur.

**Service Insurer**  *See* Pre-Paid Hospital Service Plan.

**Settlement Options**  These are options available to the policyowner or beneficiary of a life insurance policy following the death of the insured (e.g., fixed amount, fixed period, interest option, etc.).

**Short Rate Cancellation**  When a policy is canceled, there is a penalty (usually 5% - 10% charged against the premium to be returned).

**State Fund/State Competitive Fund**  An insurance program established by the state to provide insurance coverages for workers' compensation. This program competes with the private insurers and is funded by taxes and premiums.

**Subrogation**  The right of an insurance company to recover funds paid to the insured for damages caused by an at-fault third party.

**Surety**  The party that guarantees that the principal/obligor will fulfill their obligation or damages will be paid. *See* Obligee; Obligor.

## T

**Term Life Insurance**  A life insurance policy issued for a term of years; after that period of time the policy expires without value.

**Tertiary Beneficiary**  The beneficiary to receive the proceeds or benefits if the primary and secondary beneficiaries do not survive to draw them.

**Time Limit on Certain Defenses**  A uniform mandatory provision that specifies after two years, no statements (except fraudulent ones) made in the application shall be used to void coverage in a health insurance policy.

**Tort**  An intentional or unintentional wrong that involves a violation of another's natural right. This includes injury to another person or property.

**Tort-Feasor**  The party that commits a tort.

**Twisting**  A misrepresentation made by an agent/producer to induce a policyholder to switch insurers.

## U

**Underwriter**  A person (or organization) that determines if a risk is to be accepted by the insurance company he is representing.

**Unearned Premium**  That portion of an advance premium that has not yet been used for coverage written. Thus in the case of an annual premium, at the end of the first month, 11 months of premium would still be unearned.

**Unilateral Contract**  A contract in which an act is exchanged for a promise.

## V

**Vacancy or Unoccupancy Clause**  A clause that suspends coverage if the building or structure is completely empty or there are no people occupying the building for a continuous stated period of time (e.g., 60 days, etc.).

**Valued Policy Law**  A requirement that states that the face value of the policy is to be paid in the event of a total loss to a structure.

**Variable Annuity**  An annuity contract in which the benefit paid out varies, usually in relation to the security market.

## W

**Warranty**  Statement of fact or a promise made by the insured that is part of the insurance contract and that must be true if the insurer is to be liable under the contract.

**Workers' Compensation and Employer's Liability Act**  A state law that provides that an employer is liable for death or injury to employees that occurs in the course of their employment.